W9-ABE-073

THE POLITICAL EVOLUTION OF THE MEXICAN PEOPLE

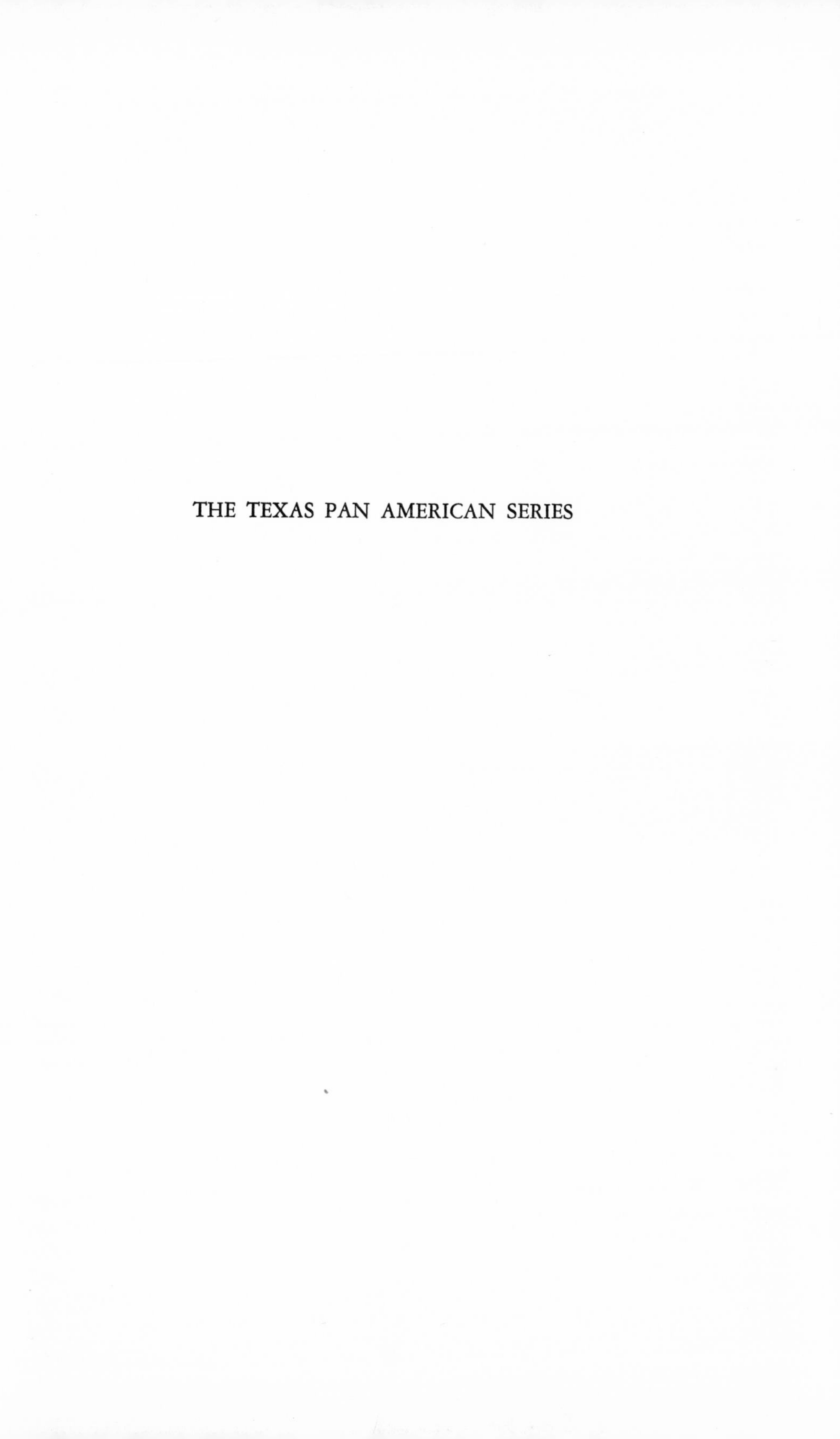

THE TEXAS PAN AMERICAN SERIES

The Political Evolution of the Mexican People

BY JUSTO SIERRA

With notes and a new Introduction by

EDMUNDO O'GORMAN

Prologue by ALFONSO REYES

TRANSLATED BY CHARLES RAMSDELL

UNIVERSITY OF TEXAS PRESS, AUSTIN & LONDON

The Texas Pan American Series is published with the assistance of a revolving publication fund established by the Pan American Sulphur Company and other friends of Latin America in Texas. Publication of this book was also assisted by a grant from the Rockefeller Foundation through the Latin American translation program of the Association of American University Presses.

Standard Book Number 292–78382–5
Library of Congress Catalogue Card Number 69–63009

Printed by The University of Texas Printing Division, Austin
Bound by Universal Bookbindery, Inc., San Antonio

PUBLISHER'S NOTE

This translation of Justo Sierra's *The Political Evolution of the Mexican People* is based on Edmundo O'Gorman's 1948 Spanish edition, published by the National University of Mexico as Volume XII of *Obras completas de Maestro Justo Sierra.* A new Introduction by Professor O'Gorman and Alfonso Reyes' Prologue to an earlier edition (Mexico City: La Casa de España en México, 1940) have been added.

Notes by Edmundo O'Gorman occasionally have been inserted into the text in brackets, and those referring to supplementary reading in Spanish have been deleted except where information on English translations could be substituted. All of the notes by Sierra have been retained.

INTRODUCTION

Aims

The object of this Introduction is to trace a perspective that will help the reader to understand better the meaning of this book. But the meaning of any work—particularly of a historical study—is obviously not something detached from the personal circumstances of the writer, nor is it alien to the intellectual trends and notions of his time. On the contrary, the meaning of a work consists, precisely, in the manner in which its author responds to those trends and notions and in the way it reflects his personal circumstances. If, therefore, our aim is to try to grasp the meaning or significance of Justo Sierra's *The Political Evolution of the Mexican People,* written and published at the beginning of this century, we must endeavor to place the book in its proper historical context, or, in other words, to show where and how it fits into the rather complex intellectual process of Mexican historiography. But in order to do this accurately, we must first try to understand the general situation from which that process derives, and then we must show the stages of its development up to the moment when the work we are concerned with made its appearance.

The Problem

For quite obvious and objective reasons, the Mexican past appears as made up of three easily distinguishable and clearly defined periods.

1. First we have the autochthonous or indigenous period, which springing from the twilight of an uncertain and remote antiquity, came to an end with the crushing victory of the conquering Castilian

hosts. The imprisonment of Cuauhtemoc, the very soul of resistance against the invader, marks dramatically the close of the first period.

2. Next we have the colonial period, which for three centuries followed its slow, but only in appearance monotonous course. We may place the end of it in 1810, when Hidalgo rose in arms against viceregal rule, or else, and perhaps more exactly, in 1821, when Agustín de Iturbide won political independence for the country.

3. The third period, finally, corresponds to Mexico's existence as a nation, strictly speaking.

In view of this heterogeneous pattern, it should not be hard to see that the Mexican historian's central problem has been how to comprehend his past as being all of one piece, without failing to recognize the uniqueness of the two earlier periods. The great problem, in other words, was how to conceive of Mexico's historical development as a unified whole, yet accounting for its plural objective reality. And, as we shall see, the book by Justo Sierra owes its importance precisely to its attainment of this difficult aim. But let us not anticipate; let us rather consider, first, the peculiar form that this problem took, in order to show thereafter how it was solved.

In all truth, it would be misleading, however, to say that the question of attaining a unified concept of Mexican history was foremost in the minds of the pioneer Mexican historians who wrote in the aftermath of their country's independence. While this was undoubtedly the central question, for the time being it was latent and not clearly visible due to the urgency of solving another problem—one that did indeed demand the immediate attention of these men. They all, and with good reason, felt under compulsion to explain what indeed seemed to be the tremendous historic failure of independence. Let us look closely at the situation.

The price Mexico had to pay for its independence, in lives and in economic ruin, was staggering. But independence had finally been won, and considering the hopes for the future those losses seemed justified. One of the mainsprings of revolution, perhaps the principal one, had been the desire to emulate the great neighboring republic on the north, which had become an international power overnight.

Throughout the struggle, whether fighting under the banners of the Insurgents or under those of Iturbide's Army of the Triple Guarantee, the Mexicans never lost sight of the example set by those northern colonies and their immense success in having united under a federative form of government. Why, then, should not New Spain expect to enjoy the same good fortune? Why, then, should not Mexico come to occupy, within the same short term of years, a place in the sun as eminent, if not more prominent, as the one achieved by its Anglo-Saxon neighbors? On every side, in manifestos, in proclamations, in speeches, one may still hear the echo of that hope, of that promise. But from the moment that a monarchy was adopted as the first form of government it began to be plain—and when this failed it was still plainer—that that dream of grandeur which had inspired the struggle against Spain was fading. There was more than a hint of magic-making in the adoption of a federal formula, next, in 1824. Indeed, this system of government, so alien to the inhabitants and to their traditions, was imposed on the country like a sort of miraculous balm, warranted to cure all its troubles and to bring progress and happiness. The first federal republic, it is true, managed to survive eleven years; not, however, eleven years of progress and peace, but years of turmoil and personal greed, for this was a training period for the politicians learning to play the fascinating game of how to climb the steps that led to the presidential chair. Attempt after attempt was made, in appallingly rapid succession, to set up new forms of government, all invariably accompanied by riots, barracks revolts, and revolutions which portrayed the dismal picture of the nation's first decades of existence. But let us not forget—and we would be ungrateful if we did not remember—that, along with ambition, betrayal, and crime, there were present always self-abnegation, patriotism, and good faith. And yet the upshot was that independence, far from fulfilling its dazzling promise, appeared to have brought only economic ruin, political disorder, administrative chaos, and a general weakening of the social ties and fibers. There is no need to dwell on this somber picture: the reader will find it fully described in the book he holds in his hands.

Enough has been said here, no doubt, to make it clear that the main problem confronting the pioneer Mexican historian was how to account for a disaster that was totally unexpected. It was a problem born of disillusionment, of seeing hopes that had seemed certain to bear fruit come to nothing.

Such was the starting-point of Mexican historiographical thought. We must not lose sight of it if we want to understand the progress of its development.

First Phase of the Process

When the men of that day beheld the catastrophic situation into which the country had plunged after winning its independence, and asked themselves in anguish what could have caused the disaster, they found ready-made, so to speak, two explanations, different in their contents, yet both stemming from roots of the same stock. There was the explanation that we may call providentialistic, and the explanation that we may class as idealistic.

According to the first, the course of history is directed and ruled by a divine will. Thus, if the annals of a given people exhibited a picture of anarchy and desolation, such as did those of the Mexican nation in its early years, it followed that the divine arbiter of history had ruled against that people. Could not that be the way to account for the Mexican disaster? Did not the events of Mexico's independent history plainly show God's displeasure? And, lastly, could it not be that independence had been condemned by God as a rebellious act against his wishes, and could not the calamities that plagued the inhabitants of New Spain thus be accounted for?

The second explanation, that which we classed as idealistic, was of a less archaic stamp, but equally transcendental. According to it the march of history, though surely not directed by the supposed will of a just God, was nevertheless ruled by the purpose of a metaphysical entity vaguely designated as Nature, an entity even more threatening, since it excluded the possibility of appeal to pardon through repentance. The intentions harbored by this entity could be discerned, not in the punishing of a rebellious people, but in a parcel of invariable characteristics, which clearly showed that people to be congenitally inferior, and hence incapable of governing themselves and of shaping their own destinies. Was not this, then, the reason for the national disaster? Did not the Mexican people, when they shook off Spanish tutelage, give plain proof of their native inferiority, since their political incompetence was so obvious?

Here, then, to choose from, were the two theses that offered an explanation to the Mexican historical problem. However and quite apart from the fact that both were of foreign origin, and dated from a distant past, it is clear that neither one could gain the acceptance of a nation who would thereby damn itself in the eyes of God, or else in the eyes of Humanity. Both solutions, of course, had to be rejected. But since it was out of the question to assume that the national catastrophe could be attributed to a supposed divine wrath, or to a supposed natural inferiority, to whom, then, could it be attributed? Who was to be held responsible?

In thus stating the problem we have shown the enormous importance of the two metahistorical theses that we have just expounded. For, while it is true that they were rejected, it is no less true that they left their mark by inducing historians to pose the national problem as a question of guilt, and thereby to fall into the facile, misleading, and pernicious mistake of seeking someone on whom to cast the blame.

Second Phase of the Process

Mexican historians, in their rejection of the idea of divine wrath and that of congenital inferiority, were, for obvious reasons, unanimous. But now, when we find them setting out on the search for a culprit on whom to blame the disaster, we see them sharply divided into two fields, which correspond to the two great ideological tendencies that have dominated Mexican history until fairly recent times. I refer to the conservative tendency—traditionalist, Catholic, and monarchical—and to its liberal opposite—modern, atheist, and republican. Let us examine the solutions offered by each in its turn.

According to the spokesmen for the first group, the country owed its chaotic condition, clearly, to a single nefarious fact, to wit: the influence of modern ideology on Mexican public life, which amounted to a deadly attack on the Latin and Catholic traditions that constituted the very foundation of the national structure. But who was to blame for this? No doubt about it: a small group of wicked Mexicans who had let itself be seduced by that ideology, the so-called liberals. The real responsibility, however, was farther to be sought, for they could not have done so much harm by themselves. The liberals were actually nothing more than instruments of a machination against the country—a machination conceived, guided, and fomented by the United States, that great malignant power which, with sinister ends, was sowing internal strife and preventing Mexico from advancing along the path of peace and progress.

The spokesmen for the second group showed the exact reverse of the medal. If Mexico, they said, has not attained the glorious destiny that awaits it, and finds itself torn by poverty and civil war, it is because the old ideology inherited from the Colony is still being imposed on every order of public life. The small number of reactionary Mexicans who try to hold on to their former privileges by resorting to the arms of ignorance and superstition are the ones directly to blame. But in this case, as in the preceding one, the real blame was allowed to gravitate beyond that group. The culprit, here, was not the United States, which, while viewed with some suspicion, continued to be admired, but the Spanish monarchy, bent on recovering its dominion, and the Roman Catholic Church, whose top hierarchy within the national territory was believed to be a nucleus of treason.

It is important to note that this second phase of the process shares with the preceding one the same attempt to explain our national history by resorting to a force or a power outside of its own sphere. Progress has been made, however, because that force or power is no longer infinite and transcendental (God or Nature), but finite and historical, as embodied in the United States, or the Spanish monarchy and the Papacy, as the case may be. It cannot be said, therefore, that the second phase is, like the first, of a metahistorical nature, and here we see a forward step. We must not fail to observe, however, that a relative aspect of that nature may be said to remain in the new solutions proposed by liberals and conservatives both, for while it is true that the culprits held responsible are located now within the bounds of history, it is still true that they represent forces placed beyond the bounds of the national history. We may say, then, that if the first phase is meta-historical, in an absolute sense, the second phase also is, but in a relative sense.

It is easy to perceive, at this juncture, that the next step must consist in accepting the responsibility instead of trying to unload its weight on alien shoulders. But, in order to show how so decisive a step was taken, we must point out, first, a most important consequence that was implied in both of the theses under discussion.

Each of them, indeed, contains a peculiar assumption as to the being of the Mexican people. The first thesis, traditional-conservative, assumes the protagonist of national history to be the same as that of colonial history. According to this view, the Mexican nation still is the New Spain, which, on arriving at maturity, demanded political independence, but did not thereby lose its historic identity. Thus, we can easily understand why the liberal modern ideas of the Anglo-Saxon world appeared to be an attack directed at the very heart of the national being. The second thesis, the modern-liberal one, assumes, on the other hand, the true protagonist of the national history to be the same one as that of pre-Hispanic Mexican history. According to this thesis, the colonial period is purely negative, something to be treated, actually, as nonexistent. The Mexican nation is not, therefore, identified with New Spain, as in the preceding case, but with the ancient indigenous empire, which, it is assumed, maintained its historic identity throughout three centures of unjust servitude. This explains perfectly why the traditional Catholic ideology of the Colony was considered as deserving the blame for the national disaster that followed on independence.

Keeping these things in mind, we see that the progress involved in the second phase was not made without cost. The price, indeed, was a split in the way in which the very being of the Mexican people was conceived, a schism and duality which found expression in bitter polemics and in a long series of violent acts.

Third Phase of the Process

The process of understanding the Mexican past, as we have seen, ran into a contradiction that seemed to be insoluble. Having started from the premise that the Mexican people was not to blame for the turmoil in its national life, the historians arrived at opposing concepts as to the very being of that people. It was therefore necessary to resolve this duality somehow. Let us see how this difficult goal was reached.

When an ideological process is paralyzed by internal contradiction, the cause must generally be sought in the original premise. Could it not be, then, that the error common to both the liberal and the conservative theses arose from the fact that both started from a false initial estimation concerning the events of the nation's history after independence? Here is the doubt that opened the door to a solution. Indeed, what is essential in the new development is the belief that the chaotic picture of the nation's independent life only appears as such when the attempt is made to explain it as the outcome of a blame, no matter whether the guilt is laid to the colonial tradition or to modern Anglo-Saxon ideology. The new historians will insist that these two tendencies must be understood as historical circumstances which, while they do enter into conflict, do not exclude each other mutually, like two enemies, but combine in a synthesis that will create a new situation. Considered in this light, the nation's independent history only reveals the painful process through which that synthesis is achieved, and therefore, despite appearances, it should be regarded as a spectacle of positive meaning, in which no question of guilt is involved, but only a problem of self-responsibility. One should not then see in that history a disaster caused by malignant foreign interference, but simply a historical process prompted by the supreme law of evolution.

Such, in few words, is the gist of the third phase of Mexican historiographical thought. It is distinguished from the preceding phase in that the explanation of the national past is placed within its own bounds, so that the fundamental notion that the Mexican people is in truth responsible for its own destiny finally appears. But, and this is the crucial question, just who is this people?

Up to this moment, as we have seen, the concept of the Mexican people's identity was hung on the horns of a dilemma: it was either a sort of mystical extension of New Spain, or it was the ancient pre-Hispanic empire, which somehow had remained mysteriously intact throughout the three colonial centuries. The new thesis obviously rejects both notions. According to this, the Mexican people is neither the one thing nor the other: the Mexican people is an entirely new entity on the stage of history and is neither the Spaniard of the colony, nor the Indian of Moctezuma's empire. The Mexicans, says Justo Sierra, are "the sons of the two peoples, of the two races," and this fact, he adds, "dominates our whole history; to this we owe our soul." They are, then, the result of a long process of racial and spiritual amalgamation which began in the Conquest and went on through the colony. It was this process that produced the mestizo, a name applied not only to a racial variety, but also to a type of man that has played a special role in history.

By understanding the Mexican people in this manner, it was possible not only to rise above the duality of the preceding phase, but to achieve a unified concept of the three distinctive periods in its history. In other words, the great historiographical problem set forth at the beginning of this essay was finally solved. Thanks, indeed, to the mestizo's promotion to the role of protagonist of the national drama, it was possible to regard the two earlier peirods as integrated parts of his past. The reason is obvious: The mestizo can claim the indigenous past as his own, as a peculiar and original form of historic life, notwithstanding that as a social and political structure it ceased to exist with the onslaught of the conquerors. But he can also claim the colonial past as his own, considered as a form of culture, admitting, however, that the viceregency is not an episode in the annals of Mexico, but belongs to the history of Spain.

This third phase, essentially based on the theory of evolution, implies, when compared with earlier phases, immense progress in the efforts of the Mexican to understand and to shoulder his past. Clearly, the process has not stopped at this point. I have tried to show, in other essays, that the progress made since then consists in overcoming the great fallacy implicit in the evolutionary thesis, which creates a gap between a people and their history, for it conceives of the latter as something that merely "happens to" the former, and not as something that is a constituent part of their being. But any further explanation of this new phase would exceed the limits of our present aims, since the preceding phase found its most finished expression in the work by Justo Sierra which the reader now holds in his hands. Such, therefore, is the significance of the book; such, therefore, its imperishable value as a turning point in Mexican historiographical thought.

Temixco, Mexico EDMUNDO O'GORMAN

CONTENTS

THE POLITICAL EVOLUTION OF THE MEXICAN PEOPLE

Foreword by Edmundo O'Gorman

(1948 Edition)

THE FAMOUS HISTORICAL ESSAY "The Political Evolution of the Mexican People" first appeared as two distinct parts of the book *México: Su evolución social* (Mexico City: J. Bellescá y Cía., 1900–1902), the greater part under the title *Historia política* (Tomo I, volumen 1, pp. 33–314) and the remainder under the title *La era actual* (Tomo II, pp. 415–434). The earlier chapters appeared again, it seems, in a book called *Historia política de México* (Madrid: Colleción Cervantes, 1917). The complete essay was published in a second edition by Casa de España en México (Mexico City, 1940), with the title *Evolución política del pueblo mexicano,* which is adopted here. The present edition is based on the second one, which has been collated with the first and corrected.

The principal source of information used by Sierra was *México a través de los siglos* (Ballescá y Cía. and Espasa y Cía., n.d.), as a comparison of the two works clearly reveals. It should not be supposed, however, that Sierra turned out a mere resumé, or that he consulted but a single authority. He expressly cites, among others, Orozco y Berra for colonial history and Molina Solís for Yucatán. But Sierra's work owes its originality and its lasting merit to his vigorous interpretation of Mexico's history in the light of his convictions, of his keen insight, even of his fears, with the result that *The Political Evolution of the Mexican People* exemplifies for us the most perceptive approach of its time, the dawn of our century, to the understanding of Mexico's past.

Prologue by Alfonso Reyes

(1940 Edition)

I

MEXICANS LOVE AND VENERATE the memory of Justo Sierra. His place is among the creators of the Hispano-American tradition: Bello, Sarmiento, Montalvo, Hostos, Martí, Rodó. For them, thinking and writing were ways of achieving social good, and beauty was a part of the people's education.

Men distinguished in action and in thought, they merit the eulogy of Menendes Pelayo:

> [They are] worthy to be compared to those patriarchs . . . who are presented to us in the classical myths as both poet and philosopher, who charm men with the spell of harmony in order to win them to culture and social life and at the same time raise the walls of cities and write on imperishable tablets the precepts of the sacred law.

Such were the patriarchs of America, bards and shepherds of their people, apostles preaching in the forests, priests of the alphabet. Imposing and serene, they advanced through the parched lands of the Americas like beneficent rivers. Thanks to them, we have not yet been reconquered by the desert or the thorny brush. There was nothing singular about them except their lofty spirit; they never took refuge in the morose eccentricities of the individualist. To the contrary, they became as one with the multitudes and acquired the people's hopes and aspirations. They seemed to cry out, like the second Faust: "I make room for millions of men!" Theirs is the voice of human warmth.

Like public fountains, they belong to everybody, and bountifully offer everybody all they have.

II

The last portrait of Justo Sierra, sent from Europe to the newspapers, shows him as he was: a white giant, monumental in his corpulence, with features that seemed carved in marble. His enormous kindliness made Jesús Urueta think of those elephants to whom parents in India confide the care of their children. He was the natural tutor of young men and the youngest among the old.

The ancients, if they had seen him counseling others, at times with just a glance or smile, would have compared him to Nestor, whose lips spoke wisdom and persuasion. His virtue was free of austere affectation, his authority unfrowning; for his fellow man he had love, understanding, and forgiveness; his faith in the triumph of right amounted to heroism. A certain good-natured mockery in his manner and a flair for epigram concealed his tenderness and made it less vulnerable.

His work as a writer graduated from poetry to prose, in which he attained full self-expression and won first place in our letters. From the rather narrow lyricism of his youth, his poetry expanded into the magniloquence that the humorist Riva Palacio found so censurable. His poetic style failed to keep pace with his spiritual growth. Justo Sierra could no longer sing in verse: he choked on Plethora. Carried away by human sympathy and spiritual enthusiasm, he let his verse grow lengthy and turgid, till it finally became prose. But he never lost the emotional intensity of his poetry, nor the fresh and robust receptivity to beauty.

Next it was history that absorbed him, and he threw himself into the passions and struggles of all mankind, sharing their joys and woes with such pathos and power that the reader is reminded of these moving words of Aeneas: "Here virtue will have praise; sorrow, tears; disaster, compassion."

A literary critic on occasion, his legacy is slim and includes but one piece of lasting merit: the Preface to the poems of Gutiérrez Nájera, where his explanation of the French influence on the Mexican lyric and his defense of modernism flaunt a superb disregard for shibboleths of the schools of poetry and for academic criticism. There is no contemporary essay on this poet to equal it, and so far as I know there has been none since. The style alone of that Preface has an exuberance not seen before among us: lively images, resilient phrases, a playful grace in the digressions that brings a smile. If there is more to be said about Nájera, I doubt that it will be said better.

Later, his style gained in force and sobriety. He renounced wayward humor, sought the clause of gold, sculptured sentences. He now had a style such as Walter Pater sought after, one to captivate the reader who is weary of reading. Even his official speeches display all the philosophical and literary notions of his time. He was the first in Mexico to cite D'Annunzio and Nietzsche.

III

In the historical work introduced by these words, the style, without losing dignity, at times shows signs of haste. The author falls into repetitions crowded close together, piles up incidental phrases, sometimes burdens the reader's retentive power by deferring the subject to the end of an interminable period.

In this book, he seems haunted by a vague presentiment, which drives him to set down as rapidly as possible the meaning of an epoch whose twilight he must have had some forebodings of. But if there are moments of hurried writing, we may be sure that his thinking was always thoroughly deliberate. There is an emotion that gives the book an indefinable pathetic rhythm.

No doubt Sierra was distracted by the demands of his labors as secretary of public instruction. His name would be honored, even if he had never written a line, for his mighty achievement in disseminating primary schools, scattering them all over the country. Successor to Gabino Barrera, who created the system of lay education when the triumph of Benito Juárez gave the Republic its definitive organization, Justo Sierra spread himself on his schools as if he hoped by fissioning into a thousand fragments to communicate through these with future generations. Toward the end of his days he crowned his work by bringing the separate liberal arts colleges of the University of Mexico together in academic harmony and rounding out the curriculum of modern humanities with unfailing foresight. It would appear that the educator sensed the rising discontent among the young and went to meet them halfway.

The official Positivism, attenuated by routine, was withering in the fresh new breezes. The generation of the Centenary of Independence [1910] entered upon life with a feeling of despair. But then we met Justo Sierra, who came to us offering—as one of us, Pedro Henríquez Ureña, has said—"the purest and newest truth." And the master himself said to us:

> The vague figure of a supplicant has been hovering about our official temples of learning for a long time: Philosophy, beautiful and once respected. Ever since that remote dawn when the mysterious portals of the oriental sanctuaries were first opened, she has served human thought as guide, for he at times is blind. With him she reposed on the steps of the Parthenon; in the tumult of barbarian invasion she nearly lost him, only to find him again at the doors of the University of Paris, the alma mater of thinking humanity in the middle ages. This tragic figure is the guide of Oedipus, who sees through the eyes of his daughter all that is worth seeing in this world: what is infinite, what is eternal.

Thus, the Secretary of Public Instruction himself assumed command of youth's crusade in search of philosophy, acting as counselor and alleviating the resentment that had begun to take hold on us. The Revolution thundered—through no fault of his. He sustained, between the old and the new regime, the continuity of the spirit, which to him was the thing worth saving at all costs, despite the general collapse and the onrush of change.

He was no longer at the University when I arrived, but I have experienced elsewhere that subdued fire animating his oral discourse and even vividly present in his books.

I have said that the historian in him was an outgrowth of the poet. He remained a poet, but one enthralled by the spectacle of human vigor displayed through the ages. He was romantic by temperament and training, for him the French Revolution was still the key to modern times, the supreme climax of history. This was the chapter he was always ready to comment on, the lesson he always had prepared. Whereby his prejudices as a political educator stand revealed. In that Revolution, he believed, there converged the teachings of the centuries, handed down from one epoch to another as the password for liberty.

The pupil who let himself be carried away by the visions which Sierra conjured up before his eyes, who followed the paths opened up for him by the glowing narrative, felt attracted by the same magnetism as those remote peoples—and seemed to see as in a panorama the men streaming like ants from north to south, and the sails skimming along the African coast, later turning toward the unknown sea. The master was steeped in geographic mysticism, in the fascination of the *terra incognita,* in the eagerness of those who sought the man made of ice in the arctic and the man made of charcoal near the equator, dreamed of by the nations of antiquity; he conveyed the longing of sea-going folk in the days of the discoveries, the longing to find the diamond mountains, the gold-and-marble houses, the islands made each of a single precious pearl, scintillating jewels of the ocean. The adventurers seeking the spice routes greeted with equal excitement the cries of gulls, announcing land, or the dazzling Southern Cross, whose shining seemed an augury. History was built amid the clangor of a gigantic epic; the earth was fertilized with the ashes of saints and heroes; peoples were born and sank from sight, bathed in their vigorous blood. Thus his narrative was enriched with the evocative and interpretive gifts of a stupendous poet who, the better to express himself, had abandoned rhyme and meter.

Justo Sierra excelled at both evocation and interpretation, the poetry and the understanding of history. He received the raw fact with open mind, but soon found the stimulus that motivated it, somewhere between the emotional and the strictly economic, with the religious and the political in between. History is not tragedy alone; he was not satisfied to treat the spectators to a salubrious catharsis of pity and terror.

History is the knowledge and the explanation of the conduct of great human masses. Justo Sierra brought to it a staggering fund of information and an astonishing gift for synthesis in the compendious strokes of his style. He resolves in an instant, with almost dizzying clarity, some points in Mexican history which, before him and since, have given rise to long-drawn-out arguments and disquisitions. The condensity of his work and the fresh winds that blow through it remind us of the lofty constructions of Tocqueville.

Sierra's eminent success with synthesis would have been impossible without his well-muscled esthetic faculties, for historical synthesis is the greatest challenge to literary technique. In Sierra's writing a single word takes the place of the digressive paragraph. The varied shades of certainty—Renan's constant torture—establish scientific honesty. The gift of artistry communicates by suggestion what would otherwise require a long roundabout explanation.

Within the modest limitations of a textbook, Justo Sierra's *Historia General* ["Universal History"] accumulates the potency of twenty atmospheres. Its only fault: it is over the heads of the youngsters for whom it was designed. Indeed, the reader is constrained to pause in order to distinguish all the colors that are here combined in the prism. And as good prose transports us with its music, I remember how, in my day, the boys of the preparatory school, to save themselves the trouble of analysis, no doubt, fell back on memory and learned those wingèd paragraphs by heart. Perhaps the *Historia General* needs the presence of Justo Sierra, for teaching purposes, as the University that he founded—since then turned over to such questionable aims—needs his direction.

Unless it is a mere inventory of bare facts, the historical essay, whether consciously or not, reveals the historian's point of view and the intellectual language of his epoch—a viewpoint and a language that bring into the historical picture the very moment of writing. All true history, says Croce, is contemporaneous, quite apart from the fact that it lets us live again, in our time, humanity's past. But, within the bounds of this psychological imperative, there should be room for the equanimity and the balance that, without concealing the author's philosophical tendencies, can give the work the permanent values of objectivity and truth; problems should be posed in such a way that the reader is free to draw his own conclusions. Especially when the historian is dealing with the essential movements in the evolution of a people, as Justo Sierra does in his reconstruction of Mexican history.

Justo Sierra remains, above all, Mexico's great historian. "He has left us," said Jesús Urueta, "his venerable fragments of Mexican history, replete with learning, art, and love, among which a small book for children is outstanding; if it is a thing of enchantment for them, for the old it is a jewel."

This judgment would be impeccable if the word "fragments" did not imply that he had left his major work unfinished, and if the very shape of the sentence did not appear to give a certain summary for children preference over *The Political Evolution of the Mexican People.*

IV

True enough, this summary is a book of rare quality, standing alone in its genre. Like all triumphs of simplicity, it gives proof of a lofty spirit. But nothing can compare to the majestic *Political Evolution of the Mexican People.* This work, now published separately for the first time [second edition, 1946], has hitherto been practically inaccessible as part of a collection of historical monographs on our national life written by various specialists, under Justo Sierra's general direction, and published with the title *México: su evolución social* ["The Social Evolution of Mexico"] between the years of 1900 and 1902, in three huge volumes profusely illustrated to please the taste of that period, which was far different from that of our day.

México: su evolución social, put together in the evening of the Porfirio Díaz regime, was intended to present the progress of the country from its origins to what was considered to be its apogee. But the pages by Justo Sierra, as we have said, reveal a sense of pressure: the patrimony of our history must be completed in time, before the surprise overtakes us.

Not counting works of investigation, some of them exceedingly brilliant, or historical essays of a special character and purpose, not designed as popular synthesis, *The Political Evolution* occupies a place all to itself in Mexican historiography, in spite of the lapse of time since it was written.

In comparison, the other works of its kind are unimpressive. They may add a few decades to its story of more than four centuries, but they cannot replace it. Some of these works appear, beside Sierra's, to be personal divagations on historical themes or violent attempts to adjust our realities to a predetermined theory. Many who derive from Sierra exaggerate to the point of paradox what in him was merely a rapid turn of expression. The Revolutionary uproar that came later, focusing attention on immediate problems, invited polemics and propaganda and was liable to distort perspective.

Justo Sierra's history is no blind apology: he never mitigates errors but, on the contrary, draws attention to them, being the first to apply the scalpel in some cases. But his vigorous interpretation and the generosity that pervades it makes the history, in a sense, a justification of the Mexican people.

Whosoever does not know this history does not know us, and whosoever does know it will hardly deny us his sympathy.

Devoid of malice or of any appeal to base prejudice, frank to tell the truth when necessary, it is a long essay in understanding, with the accompaniment of a chorus of facts. The explanation of the past is always gentle, even in censure; the passions and sorrows of men are never derided; none of that morbid delight in condemning a people is apparent, even for an instant; all criticism is constructive, and the road is left open to hope.

The Political Evolution spans our history from remote origins to the author's epoch, on the eve of the Mexican Revolution. The origins are treated prudently, and with a holy horror of the futile parallels with other cultures which were the bane of our archeology till then. Pre-Cortesian history, it is well to remember, had barely taken its first wobbly steps in Sierra's day; what is now known for sure is all of recent finding. The reader, taking this into account, should admire the early chapters as a somewhat premature endeavor to impose logical order on a mass of haphazard information, with the understanding that many of those generalizations will fail to stand up in the light of later investigation. Mexican archeology has been made over entirely since then, but the time has not yet come, unfortunately, to attempt another synthesis like Sierra's. At any rate, his appreciation of the ancient civilizations, from both the human and the political point of view—which is what matters in a work of this kind—remains valid; so does his dynamic vision of the ebb and flow of peoples, intermingling and influencing one another; so does his clear perception of the decadence in some respects, and of the debility in others, of the so-called Aztec empire.

Justo Sierra never succumbs to the simple-minded vagary of those who claim our indigenous ancestors to be the only direct forefathers of our modern Mexican nationality. While he gives the Indian race its due as an ethnic factor, he bows to the courage and determination that deserved and won the victory. And he demonstrates the mysterious solidarity of human groups throughout the centuries who, confronted by the same challenge of nature, make the same response: draining lakes and swamps, working the soil, building cities.

The tragic panorama of the Conquest, moving through his pages with the precipitation of an earthquake, is packed with lightning and massacre; amidst the toppling ruins stratagems are enacted, barricades are raised. There follows the fecund slumber of the colonial era, pregnant with a nation, while contrary bloods circulate, restlessly seeking peace.

But none of the earlier parts, for all their merits, is the equal of the one dealing with modern times, with the real Mexico, in which this historian fulfills his mission as political educator and also achieves a sense of the present as the projection of the total sums of the past.

In applying the evolutionary notions fashionable at the time, or rather the notion of progress so dear to the nineteenth century—the historical metamorphosis of the physicists's theory of the conservation of energy (the accumulation of work is discernible at any instant)—which might have distorted the perspective of a lesser man, Sierra seems to say that the destiny of the past is to create a necessary future and that the moment of yesterday which is nearest to us is the one richest in lessons for today. As he approaches the period of Independence, the historian focuses his attention ever closer, as if trying to see clear to the bottom of things. The most recent episode carries the weightiest accumulated meaning; Justo Sierra prefers it to all others because he is an educator, and, for that reason, perhaps, he is the least biased, the best balanced of our historians.

He treats his own epoch with the respectful anxiety and the careful moral scruples of a man solemnly dedicated to truth who is performing a delicate vivisection.

Sierra's work is illumined by a supreme virtue: sincerity. His liberalism, his trust in democracy, his devotion to education, the emotional outbursts that would seem affectation in others but that here flow as if impelled by natural necessity, the rhetoric that would sound hollow in others but that here appears to be intimately welded to the very shape of the thought—all is sincere, the intention, the idea, the word. And so is his preoccupation with country, the patriotism that inspires him. He said, when he founded the University:

> Our hope is that students in this school will learn how to investigate and how to think by investigating and thinking, and that the results of their investigation and thought will not become crystallized within these walls, but will become, instead, dynamic ideas of permanent value that can be translated into teaching and into action. Only thus can ideas turn into forces. We should not like to see marble towers here, nor the contemplative life. Perhaps it is well that such things exist elsewhere . . . but not here. . . . We should not like to see adored, in the temple to be erected here, an Atheneas without eyes for humanity and without a heart for the people. . . . Let this be a place where Mexicans come to worship the science that makes their country strong.

When these words were written, the perversion of science to the service of bastard interests had not yet been invented; exhortations to patriotism had not yet been abused to the extent that they inspired distrust. These words must be accepted in all their purity, without suspicion of fraud. For the entire life of this great Mexican bears them out.

It may be thought that this history, stopping on the eve of the Revolution, would need to be revised in the light of that same Revolution. But no: it simply needs to be completed. It contains all the premises for the future, as witness the analysis of the social state of the Indian, of the mestizo, of the Creole. And the candor with which it is written proves that there is no need to twist or falsify facts in order to explain the present.

When Justo Sierra confronts the errors inherited from colonial days—the worst of all being those incorporated as defects in the Mexican character—he says:

Unfortunately, these congenital habits of the Mexican have become a thousand times more difficult to extirpate than the domination of Spain or of the privileged classes established by Spain. Only a sweeping change in the conditions of work and of thought in Mexico can ever bring about such a transformation.

Justo Sierra's political evolution marches on, and so does the inspiration of his work. Do not say he is dead: like that traveler through the Carpathians, he sleeps on his bridle. The gratitude of his people is his companion.

BOOK ONE

Aboriginal Civilizations and the Conquest

CHAPTER ONE

ABORIGINAL CIVILIZATIONS, I

First peoples. Maya and Quiché; the civilization of the South.

EVERY SORT OF CONJECTURE has been made as to the origin of the American Indian, but nothing is known for certain.[1] Was America in contact with the Atlantic shores of Europe and Africa by way of the long since submerged Atlantis?[2] In that case American man must have appeared in the Tertiary, for the Atlantis belongs to that period. And yet, man did not exist in the Tertiary. There was only his precursor, the creature from which we probably sprang, our zoological ancestor. No trace of him can be found in American paleontology, however. Did America communicate with Asia by means of the Bering Strait and its magnificent intercontinental bridge of islands? Did the population arrive by this route, or was it aboriginal in the full sense of the term—meaning that the American continent was a center of creation, as those who believe in the multiple origin of our species affirm? These, obviously, are questions that touch on the most baffling problem in the natural history of mankind. Like flickering torches, they reveal the darkness that envelops genesis but fail to illuminate anything. Nonetheless, beyond all doubt,

[1] Studies of indigenous cultures that have been completed since the date of Sierra's book have arrived at conclusions that modify substantially some of the author's observations in this synthesis.

[2] The Atlantis is no longer acceptable as an explanation for the arrival of man in America. Father Joseph de Acosta was the first to set this hypothesis definitely aside.

men have been in America since the Quaternary period, men who are ethnically close kin to the peoples of insular Asia. Let us assume, then, that a vast archipelago existed in the North Pacific before Asia and America took on their present configuration and that on it the progenitors of the people who eventually would inhabit some regions of eastern Asia and of North America made their appearance. Perhaps the Eskimos are the remnants of those proto-Americans, perhaps the Tierra-del-Fuegans at the far southern tip of South America. More than likely, various families from the Asiatic mainland became mixed with this first people. What is certain is that marked differences in anatomical structure and striking diversity of skull form among the very early Americans indicate the presence of families with separate origins.

In any case, the central plateau of Mexico has been inhabited ever since the Quaternary. Primitive man witnessed the tremendous conflagration that melted the Valley of Mexico into the shape it has today. His silent canoes furrowed the lake which reflected the flames—eternal, he no doubt thought them—of Ajusco's erupting crater. Were these early men the forebears of the sedentary peoples who learned to cultivate the soil and who were already settled in the Valley when the first waves of the Nahua migration got there and named it Anahuac? Or were they forebears of the Otomi, who organized considerable social entities and built such cities as Manhemi on the smiling banks of the Tula?

During Quaternary times, two phenomena of supreme importance determined the ethnic destiny, so to speak, of the American continent.

1. The final phase of the uplift of the Andes, a gigantic chain of volcanoes which had been rising for hundreds of centuries from the waters of the Pacific, gave America its present aspect, separating it from Asia.

2. In consequence of this transformation, there came a drop in North America's temperature, which had ranged between hot and temperate (as animal and vegetable remains found on the polar rim abundantly attest), and this change fostered the rapid increase of immigration. With the gradual cooling, American man began to move south. The fauna and flora underwent a change: hot-climate species migrated or vanished, or turned dwarf and, like the Siberian and the Eskimo, sur-

vived in a girdle of arctic ice. The tribes went south and spread over America in the long night before the dawn of history, halting in the valleys of the great rivers, in the lake regions teeming with fish, seeking a ready supply of food, climbing into the mountain fastnesses in search of game or security, always fleeing southward from the menace of other fierce nomads, treading on one another's heels. Some were able to sink roots into the soil, and these, resisting the assaults of the human torrent, became the founders of civilizations.

In the valleys of the Mississippi River, of the Missouri, of the Ohio, there lies hidden, perhaps, an impenetrable secret: the origin of Mexico's great civilizations.

In what is called Isthmic America, comprising the Mexican and Central American republics, there was remarkable diversity in language, as well as in culture. Most, if not all, of the languages belong to one of three main families: Maya, Nahuatl, and a third group, much vaguer and more diffuse, which may correspond to the aboriginal element. The immigrant tribes found peoples already settled everywhere. Some mixing with the newcomers, were absorbed by them; others, like the Otomi, remaining hostile and defiant, kept their ancient autonomy.

Among the civilizations of Isthmic America, two were outstanding. That of the Maya-Quiché, with its center in the Usumacinta basin, prevailed throughout a vast region comprising the present states of Yucatán, Campeche, Tabasco, and Chiapas, plus the Isthmus of Tehuantepec and Guatemala. That of the Nahua, with its center in the lake country of the Mexican plateau (Anahuac), expanded along the great southern valleys and penetrated the civilization of the South, modifying it profoundly. The civilization of the Mixteca and Zapoteca and that of the Tarascans of Michoacán are perhaps composite, rather than original, and there are plain indications that an early people, possibly the forebearers of today's Otomi, also attained a high degree of organization and founded large cities, one of them being Manhemi, on whose site the Tolteca were to build their capital.

Everyone knows that huge mounds dot the river basins which today are the principal arteries for the circulation of Anglo-American wealth and that these were raised by the inhabitants of those regions in prehistoric times. These mounds, built to serve as fortresses, sepulchers, or foundations of temples, show a variety of shapes. Shards of pottery and vestiges of good-sized towns, unearthed on them on near them, attest to the residence in a remote area of a numerous people well on the way toward civilization. This people has been baptized by the Anglo-American archeologists with the name Mound Builders. The peoples who, in Mexico for the most part, created the civilization of the South were also builders of mounds. Their temples, their palaces, their fortresses, in the watered valleys and on the arid Yucatán Peninsula, stood upon artificial hills. Can all these farflung peoples have been ethnically kin?[3]

The mounds in the northern regions which were given the shapes of animals, such as the mastodon, that disappeared in the Quaternary or shortly afterward; the pipes shaped like elephants, llamas, parrots, indications that the temperature now called tropical still lingered on at latitudes near the polar circle when the Mound Builders thickly populated the valleys of the Mississippi and its tributaries; the century-old forests which have successively overgrown the giant structures—these are evidence of the remote antiquity of this people's culture. They were a people who lived, it seems, under a theocratic or sacerdotal regime, which alone could have commandeered the staggering sum of human toil required for the building of the huge mounds which emboss the American continent.

Invasions by nomadic tribes fleeing the glacial cold and seeking warmth and game in the South forced the Mound Builders to multiply their defenses and then, reluctantly, to give ground and, little by little, yield their entire territory. At some time in that dim twilight before history the emigrating Mound Builders were strung out in scattered groups along the northern shores of the Gulf of Mexico from Tamaulipas to Florida. Some, no doubt, perished; others, reverting to a savage state, were dissolved in the nomadic flood; others, continuing their centuries-long exodus, followed the western coast of the Mexican Mediterranean southward. Still others, perhaps, navigators accustomed to crossing rivers and scouting shores in light barks provided with sails,

[3] In order to conserve the synthetic character of this work, we can only offer the evidence in support of our opinions, without going into further discussion, thus keeping them within strictly hypothetical bounds. (Author's note).

like the Yucatecs described by Columbus, dispersed themselves over the islands of the Antilles. Could they not then easily have sailed from Cuba to the western strands of the Caribbean Sea—to the Yucatán Peninsula? While it never will be possible to prove, it seems most likely that the speech of the Maya and that of the Antillian peoples belonged to the same linguistic family; there must have been communication between the islands and the Peninsula from earliest times.

Maya tradition has handed down the story of an early tribe of immigrants called the Chan, whose totem was the serpent.[4]

The Chan went inland on the Yucatán Peninsula, leaving the sea at their back—which should be sufficient indication as to whence they came. They no doubt subjected and enslaved the native population and imposed on it their language and religion. And the natives built for them the mounds and temples scattered over the Peninsula from Honduras to the Caribbean Sea and the Gulf of Mexico. This tribe [known to history as the Itzá] established flourishing towns everywhere in the region which they civilized and called Chaknovilán. These towns were watched over by superb buildings on the crests of artificial mounds: houses for the gods, for the priests and priestesses, for the chiefs; sepulchers, fortresses, observatories; ruins which, while slowly crumbling through our negligence, thrill us and baffle us with their mystery and grandeur. First Bakhalal, then Chichén Itzá, became the capital of this theocratic monarchy, organized by a person or a hieratic family known in tradition by the name of Itzamná. Is it too far-fetched to suppose that Na-Cham, later called Palenque, in the Usumacinta basin, was founded in this epoch of vague chronology (but which, according to the most careful studies, must have corresponded to the second or third century of our era) by a branch of the Chan tribe? What is certain is the close kinship between the Maya [of the Yucatán Peninsula] and the Quiché [of the Guatemala highlands], a kinship that is patent in their physical aspect, their manner of building and of living, their

[4] As we acquire a better understanding of the origins of religion, through the gradual accumulation and classification of data, we learn to appreciate increasingly the importance of totemism, a form of animal-worship, or zoolatry. We know that the worship of the grandfather, who was distinguished in the clan by the name or totem of an animal, evolved into the worship of the animal itself. The cult of the serpent was the one that had the greatest appeal for the peoples of America. (Author's note).

writing and their language. The differences between the two peoples are simply variations within a single culture.[5]

What is certain, besides, is that the early compilers of the traditions handed down by the Maya and by the Quiché attribute the same Antillian origin to both peoples and that Itzamná, the mighty priest who founded the civilization of the Maya, is the same as Votan, who founded that of the Quiché.[6] About the latter civilization we know little beyond its artifacts, edifices, and monuments—and the inscriptions on these are still undeciphered. About the Maya we know considerably more.[7]

Some of the great Maya and Quiché capitals had already been founded when a new tribe of immigrants appeared at a point on the Yucatán Peninsula (Champotón) within the present state of Campeche. Was this still another offshoot of the Mound Builders, who, in their grand exodus from the Mississippi Valley, had spread out gradually, in scattered groups, over the Gulf plain from Louisiana to Tabasco, some even climbing the eastern Sierra Madre to the plateau of Anahuac? There is a recollection of their arrival in Yucatán among the legends, where it is called the great migration of the Tutulxiu or Xiu. According to the chronographers, this took place in the fifth century.[8]

The Itzá, governed by their king-priests, formed a kind of federation around Itzamal, T-ho, and other centers, under the hegemony of Chichén Itzá. Then the Tutulxiu made a series of terrible attacks on Chichén and destroyed it, and its priests fled to the Gulf coast and established themselves in Champotón. Thence, some three centuries later, the Itzá, the holy men, returned to the Peninsula, where the

[5] In this brief resumé of the Maya culture I have followed the monograph of the learned Yucatecan Juan Francisco Molina Solís: *Descubrimiento y conquista de Yucatán* (Mérida: R. Caballero, 1896). (Author's note).

[6] The author refers to: Bernardo de Lizana, *Historia de Yucatán* (Mexico City: Museo Nacional de México, 1893 [original edition dated 1633]) and to Ezequiel Ordoñez, *El Sahcab de Yucatán* (Mexico City: Imprenta del gobierno, 1903).

[7] The most important recent work on the cultures of Yucatán is Sylvanus G. Morley, *The Ancient Maya* (Palo Alto, California: Stanford University Press; Oxford: University Press, 1946).

[8] The extremely scarce osseous remains of the Mound Builders show a pronounced brachycephaly—additional evidence in favor of their kinship with the Maya. (Author's note).

Tutulxiu, having built cities—the most important was Uxmal—were well entrenched and held sway. The conflict was stubborn and appears to have ended in a pact, in accordance with which the Itzá rebuilt their sacred city, Chichén, while under their auspices the federal city of Mayapán was founded as the capital of the combined Itzá and Xiu.

The era of Mayapán, the middle era of Maya culture, marked the beginning of close contact with Nahua culture, which had already infiltrated the Quiché. A prophet and lawgiver (or, more likely, a priestly family) planted on the banks of the Usumacinta the new cult of Gugumatz and, entering Yucatán by way of Champotón, raised altars in Mayapán to Kukulcán—the terms Gugumatz and Kukulcán being exact transcriptions of the Nahuatl name Quetzalcoatl.[9]

The sculptures of Palenque and those of Uxmal and Chichén reveal the immense transformation that was brought about in the myths and rites by priests who preached in the name of their divinity. Although the introduction of human sacrifice on a large scale is attributed to Kukulcán, his message called for peace and reform. Certain religious customs among the Maya, such as baptism and confession, seem to have had their origin in the teachings of the Nahua god's apostles. There was steady progress in knowledge of astronomy and in writing after the great Nahua's doctrine became widespread. This period may have coincided with the decline of the power of the Nahua-Tolteca in Anahuac (the ninth century).

And it came to pass, say the chronicles of Yucatán, that the lord of Chichén and the lord of Mayapán quarreled over a woman's heart and went to war. The latter appealed to the Aztecs (or Mexica) who had established military colonies in Tabasco and Xicalanco, and with the aid of these fierce warriors he overcame his enemies. Then the triumphant Cocom tribe oppressed the entire land of the Maya with

[9] The name Quetzalcoatl is generally read as a pure ideogram; it is in reality an ideophonogram. As an ideogram, it means "serpent with feathers of the quetzal bird"; as a semiphonetic sign it means "the twin birds" or "the twin quetzals." Read thus, it is a hieroglyph for Lucifer or Venus. The Nahua thought the morning and evening stars were twins, not knowing they were one and the same, and they called them *coate*, which was represented in writing by the sign of the serpent, *coatl.* The cult of Quetzalcoatl, then, is the cult of a double divinity, which the Romans knew as Hesperus and Vesperus. (Author's note).

terror, till the lords of Uxmal took the lead in a rebellion which, arousing all the peoples, drove out the Aztecs and destroyed Mayapán. Strangely enough, in the course of this fierce war the victorious Tutulxiu abandoned even Uxmal, their great city in the mountains; the moribund splendor of its regal ruins was left to solitude and mystery forever. The Maya empire eventually was broken up into any number of independent units, ruled by families who claimed descent from the legendary dynasties. And thus the Spanish conquistador found them, divided and in perennial bitter strife.

Among the Maya, who, despite the baffling riddle of their writing, have been extensively studied, and among the Quiché as well—in Chichén and Uxmal as in Palenque and Copán—we find all the characteristics of a complete culture, just as we find them in Egypt and Chaldea. Like those cultures, or even to a greater degree, perhaps, this one is an amazing phenomenon of spontaneity, of native invention growing out of its own self: the manifestation of a tremendous psychic force within a people. We find, in the civilization of the South, a religion, a cult, and dependent on them an art and a science, a morality, a social order, a government—all these on no rudimentary level but at an astonishingly high stage of development.

The religion of the Maya was based on a spiritism which, growing out of the primitive worship of cadavers, had evolved into ancestor worship. Ancestors were known by the names of animals, by their respective totems: hence the cult of zoolatry. The person possessing the ability to communicate with the soul of the dead became the witch doctor, the prophet, the astrologer who could read the destiny of each mortal in the stars. Finally, a priestly caste arose and organized the body of beliefs, transferring the notion of divinity, of superhuman powers, to natural objects or to the mighty atmospheric phenomena. Thus it came about, perhaps, that an invisible being was regarded as the essence of the divine element, a being whose symbol was the sun and who was the father of Itzamná, lawgiver and civilizer, who, being the son of the sun, came from the east. The solar divinity had created also four principal gods, chronometric symbols of the four cardinal points; under them came a swarm of deities. Not one palm's breadth of that mysterious land (the land of hidden waters), not one act of life but had its tutelary god, and many of these gods had their "shadows," which were evil or diabolical. Three famed sanctuaries on the Yucatán Peninsula were meccas of popular devotion: the sacred well of Chichén Itzá, the sanctuary of the sea-god at Cozumel, and one erected on the crest of a magnificent sepulchral pyramid in honor of a king of Itzamal, deified according to Maya custom. Later, the cults of the Nahua, especially that of Quetzalcoatl, became highly popular among the Maya and Quiché.

The cult of the Maya consisted of offerings and gory sacrifices—often human, a sign of the pervasive influence of the Nahua—of penitences, at times fearful, and of festivals in such amazing variety that the Maya-Quiché could be said to have lived in a perpetual round of festivals. They prepared for them by fasting, commenced them with endless dancing and song, and finished them off with the inevitable drunken orgies.

The need and the anxiety of these constantly migrating peoples for a dwelling place, a home, a temple, gave the priesthood among them immense importance. Without priests, there could have been no American civilizations. In Chichén as in Babylon, in Palenque and Tula as in Thebes, the priests observed the movements of the stars, in order to distribute their festivals through the year. They were chronologists who devised calendars and employed numbers, methods of counting which they applied to time. They created a system of phonetic writing: the Maya priesthood invented one of the three or four systems of true writing known to mankind. They traveled about and applied what they learned to the study of disease and of the effects of herbs on the organism. They compiled a history which was venerated as holy writ. In their cities, which were clusters of huts roofed with palm, they erected superb monuments, upon pyramids as a rule, which were designed as mansions for the priest-king or warrior-king, or for his wives, or for the gods. These monuments, dating from different periods, are remarkable in form and appearance. Their architecture is simple and rudimentary, being characterized, apart from the mound, by the corbel arch, which is the same in Palenque as in Chichén and Uxmal. But what makes the most profound impression on the observer is the contrast between the sobriety of the decoration within the buildings and the profuse exuberance of the outer ornamentation, especially in the friezes. These admirable monuments, encrusted with sculptures, monoliths, statues, bas-reliefs, and inscriptions, are the expression of a vigorous and exuberant civilization.

The lack of domestic animals for labor and burden-bearing was the deficiency that, more than any other, kept the American civilizations from attaining a higher level. If they had possessed these animals, perhaps cannibalism, even in its religious form as sacred communion, would have disappeared. But there was no pastoral age among the Americans. They went straight from hunting and fishing to agriculture. Their agriculture and industry required slaves, and these they had in abundance. But even the free men submitted to rigorous laws which imposed respect for religion, for the princes or caciques and their agents, for the family, for property, and for life (the Maya nonetheless were prone to suicide). Farming lands, as in all pre-Columbian America, were held in common, and the produce was distributed in shares.

As the son of god, or, frequently, as a god himself, the prince was lord of all; his patriarchal tyranny was undisputed. With organized armies obedient to his whim, he waged ceaseless war. If only the American Indians had known how to forge iron—they did use copper, though sparingly, and adorned themselves with silver and gold—perhaps the Spaniard would never have been able to conquer their more formidable empires. Their ingenious arms and consummate skill in warfare, both as individuals and in battalions, gave them, time and again, the opportunity to show their heroism, but never could give them the victory.

We delve no deeper into the culture of the isthmic regions south of the Mexican plateau; it has been described extensively elsewhere. Developed in accordance with the background of inheritance and environment by peoples under the domination of the Maya-Quiché, the civilization of the South was imposing in some of its aspects and fascinating in all.

CHAPTER TWO

ABORIGINAL CIVILIZATIONS, II

Aborigines on the plateau. Olmeca and Xicalanca. The Nahua: the Tolteca, their history and culture. The barbarian invasions: Chichimeca. Contact between Tolteca and Maya-Quiché. The heirs of Toltec culture: Alcohua; Aztecs. The intermediate civilization: Zapotec; Tarascans. The Mexica empire at the opening of the sixteenth century.

THE ABORIGINAL PEOPLE, to whom the Nahua immigrants gave the name of Otontlaca or Otomi, have occupied from time immemorial the basin of the Atoyac between the Zahuapan and the Mexcala, on the central plateau.

It is not possible to describe with accuracy the movements of any people in the twilight dawn of our history. If we study the chronicles, which at times relate contradictory traditions, perhaps because these were poorly understood, and examine what little can be deciphered from the monuments, and if we weed out the tangle of interpolations made by the friars in good faith to demonstrate a primitive divine revelation, we come up with extremely scant results, hardly more than conjectures about the origins of the civilization which unfolded with tragic majesty on the Mexican plateau.

The accounts that seem most reliable say that the Olmeca and Xicalanca, climbing to the plateau from the east, conquered giants and marked their progress with mounds or pyramids from the Pánuco basin to the high plateau, where they built the monuments at Cholula and Teotihuacan. These Olmeca, as the Nahua called them, in our opinion were Mound Builders, who had been dispersed along the Gulf coast; gradually climbing to the plateau, they founded a theocratic civilization in which a role analogous to that of Votan and Itzamná was played by Xelhua [Xehua, a mythological personage], builder of the huge mound at Cholula, which is only one third the height of the pyramid of Khufu but much wider at the base. Their kinsmen the Xicalanca, as the Nahua called them, made contact with the Quiché and influenced their culture, and even more profoundly affected the Maya culture of the Cocom tribe. What seems quite certain is that these early civilizers maintained their contact with the civilization of the South, as the little idols of Teotihuacan reveal by their dress and physical type.

Because of a climatic change, perhaps, or possibly because of the reckless felling of forests in the basins of the Gila, the Colorado, and the Rio Grande, the region of the United States now called the Southwest became in prehistoric times what it is today: an immense desert, "the land of thirst," of scant rains absorbed at once by a bottomless porous soil, of dry riverbeds, of bald mountains, rocks, and gorges. From this desolate region, once densely populated, as innumerable ruins and vast quantities of pottery show, the inhabitants [Cliff Dwellers] fled to the fluvial lands of the Mound Builders, or southward in a trek that swept all before it.

Among these emigrants came wild fierce tribes of Chichimeca and the Nahua. The latter, so their traditions say, were not nomads. They once lived in a pleasant, cultivated country, the ancient Tlapalan, and thence went south. The Nahua climbed to the plateau from the Pacific side, fought the aborigines (so successfully that one of the Nahua tribes, the Colhua, took possession of Manhemi, the Otomi capital), and collided with the representatives of the civilization of the South, whose pupils they were to become.

An elite Nahua tribe, sacerdotal rather than warlike, followed the general course of emigration, and, hugging the Pacific shoreline, reached the southern coast of present Michoacán. Heeding the voice of their gods, of their priests, they climbed to the central highlands, and after a long and arduous pilgrimage reached the banks of the Pánuco River. There they set up their sanctuary and, expanding, established close contact with the culture of the South in the Huasteca region, which had long before been colonized by the Maya and remained a northward outpost of the southern civilization. Then, climbing back up the Pánuco Valley, the Nahua tribe forced their kinsmen the Colhua to cede them the ancient Otomi capital and named it the "city of reeds," Tollan, or Tula, [1] as we call it. The people of Tollan were known from then on as "Toltecatl," and Toltec came to have the connotations of "artist," "scholar," "sage."

The chroniclers, both native and Spaniard, have so confused the history and the mystic symbolism of this people, who attained one of the most interesting of America's high cultures, that we can scarcely glean even a modicum of truth.

Their history seems to have passed through a period of expansion, when the Tolteca dominated, besides the fertile valley of the Tula, a good part of the valleys of Mexico and Puebla. They conquered the pyramidal sanctuaries of Teotihuacan and established their holy city there, dedicating the largest pyramids to the sun and the moon; they took over also the huge mound at Cholula, which they consecrated to the cult of the star Venus, or Quetzalcoatl.

The second period was one of consolidation, and during this time the culture of the Nahua reached its apogee. It appears that a cult morally superior to the cruel rites demanded by the moon-cult had arisen at "Little Tula" (Tulancingo). Heretofore, human sacrifice, a relic of primitive cannibalism of peoples, the consequence of famine, had been the supreme rite. This the apostles of Quetzalcoatl repudiated, we are told, and they became so renowned for their knowledge of astrology and of the arts and crafts and for their accurate predictions to farmers, since they studied the heavens, that they made converts even in the capital, Tollan. Until this time the warrior caste had reigned. One day, in a nationwide revolt, the high priest of Quetzalcoatl in Tulancingo took the throne. This happened, say the chronographers, at the beginning of the ninth or tenth century. The king-priest assumed the name of his divinity, and he is invested by legend and tradition with all the virtues of the Toltec

[1] Recent excavations at present Tula, in the state of Hidalgo, have definitively settled the argument as to the site of the ancient city.

civilization. He purified the cult, cleansed it of blood: only simple sacrifices were offered. It is probable that, in this golden age of theocracy, the priests of Tollan, of Teotihuacan, and of Cholula set down on monuments and in books of ideographs their stupendous conceptions as to the origin and hierarchy of the gods and the origin of the universe, of the earth, and of mankind. They told how man had come to inhabit the patch of planet with which they were familiar, and they set down the memories of early races, cults, and migrations, the episodes of their wanderings and their connections with other peoples. They related in colorful myths how new cults had replaced the old, how the ancient gods had died in Teotihuacan, and how the Nahua-Toltec star-gods had been born. [2]

Like other religions which, starting as worship of the dead, pass through ancestor worship to the cult of natural forces and, because of a tendency to unity that is part of man's intellectual structure, become the cult of a single spirit or god, and before that of a superior god, on whom all the others depend, the Nahua's religion had come to regard the sun, called in various ways and represented by different images, as the supreme divinity. All the priesthoods recognized it as such, and in some of its sanctuaries, certain chroniclers tell us, there was belief in the existence of a being whose symbol was the sun but who, because of his sublimity, could be neither represented nor adored. This was Tloque-Nahuaque, invisible being, creator who had never been created. He was the author of the first human couple.

Among the swarm of divinities whose symbolic history was woven together in an amazing fabric of legends and myths, unsurpassed by any of the earth's peoples, Tezcatlipoca (the moon) and Quetzalcoatl

[2] We must bear in mind that the systematic destruction of everything reminiscent of the ancient cult, carried out by the Spanish missionaries, and the silence on pain of death imposed on those few priests who survived the Conquest have deprived us of the documents indispensable to any study that could amount to much more than guesswork. The handfuls of original documents rescued from the burning temples—the religious literature of the ancient Nahua and Maya—cannot be read, but only interpreted, because they consist almost entirely of ideographs, which give us at best an approximate notion of their meaning. Moreover, the post-Cortesian chroniclers are generally vague or confused and contradict one another or use different terms for the same ideas. Hence, there are insuperable obstacles to the accurate understanding of the great American civilizations. (Author's note).

(or Venus) were the most outstanding divinities, after Tonatiuh, the sun. They were on a par with the principal divinity of each tribe. And, just as the pyramids of Teotihuacan and Cholula are the basic columns of the cult, the three stars are the vertex of the Nahua theogony. Privileged places in the Toltec pantheon were also held by Tlaloc, the god of waters, to whom the high places were consecrated, and by his wife, Chalchiutlicue, the fertile earth. Tlaloc's grand fetish was the volcano Popocatepetl; his wife's was the volcano Ixtacihuatl.

The Nahua cosmography and geogony were confused; the memory of great floods and meteors was linked to a singular belief in cosmic transformations. They believed, as science believed until well into the nineteenth century, that the different stages in the formation of the terrestial crust were marked by a series of total cataclysms. They called this series the five periods or ages, or, as the chronographers translate it, the five suns. The first sun was the age of water; the second, the age of winds; the third, that of fire, of volcanic eruptions; the fourth, that of the earth, a real Nahua Quaternary; and finally, there was the historic age, the present. To all these cataclysms, according to the codices, the human race had been a witness. May we not believe that the autochthonous race in Anahuac, which saw the Valley of Mexico converted into a huge lake, which undoubtedly saw Ajusco in eruption, which hunted the enormous pachyderms of the last geological age—the "giants"—would have communicated its traditions to the founders of the pyramidal sanctuaries of Teotihuacan and of Cholula? Would not the priesthood of these sanctuaries have transmitted those notions to the Tolteca—notions already diffused throughout the immense area of the civilization of the South?

After this geogony, in the succession of beliefs, came the revival of the totemic or zoolatrous cult in the sanctuaries of Anahuac, whose center was Teotihuacan, and the consecration of the pyramids to the sun and moon; from that instant they were Nahua.

But within the priestly caste of the Nahua we note the consequences of a schism, with the divinity of night and darkness and death and human sacrifice on one side and the twilight divinity, which dies and is born again eternally in the gigantic blaze of the sun, on the other —a struggle between Tezcatlipoca and Quetzalcoatl, between the moon and Venus. This schism, source of bloody strife, was caused, no doubt, by the proscription of cannibalistic rites and by calendar reform.

The Tolteca, extremely active traders and ingenious builders, were obviously able to count and had a primitive arithmetic consisting simply of the four rules, as is shown by their drawings, in which the position of signs indicates addition or multiplication. Like all primitive numeration, theirs is based on the count of fingers and toes: the sum of these, twenty, is the fundamental number in the Nahua and Maya-Quiché systems. By multiplying the products of twenty they could count to 160,000, giving each total a special and expressive name. We may be sure they knew how to increase the quantities to whatever degree their needs required.

They applied their numeral system admirably to the computation of time. They had a religious calendar for their numerous festivals: it is no exaggeration to say that the entire religious year was made up of festivals (not including the household festivals), each with its sacrifices, rites, and idols. This *tonalamatl* was a lunar calendar, like the first ones of all the people on earth; it was composed of thirteen months of twenty days each. The priesthood that used this calendar was that of Tezcatlipoca, the moon. Later, the period of visibility of the twin star Quetzalcoatl was made the basis of the religious calendar, and this reform probably brought on the conflict that hastened the decline of the Toltec monarchy. In this epoch also the 105¼ days of the civil year were added to the religious year, bringing it close to the astronomical one. This calendar, so like that of Julian, is one of the proofs adduced by the distinguished historian Orozco y Berra to support his theory of the European origin of the apostle-reformer Quetzalcoatl Topiltzin, the white and bearded priest dressed in sacerdotal robes bordered with crosses. [3]

The definitive correction to the calendar that was made in Aztec times brought it even closer to the astronomical year, say the experts, than the one now used in the Christian world.

[3] The opinion alluded to by the author can be found in Manuel Orozco y Berra, *Historia antigua y de la conquista de México* (Mexico City: Tip. Gonzalo A. Estevá, 1880), Tomo I, p. 102.

The count of time shows remarkable knowledge of astronomy. The Tolteca were aware of the apparent path of the sun between the tropics, and the solstices were the four ends of the Nahuillin cross. They had observed the movement of Venus and the moon; the culmination of the Pleiades played an important part in the renovation of fires after each maximum period of time, which was the 52-year cycle, or its double, 104 years, the *ahau-katun* of the Mayas. The two Bears, the polar star, the Milky Way, the Scorpion were stellar bodies familiar to the priests and were also gods, who carried on in the heavens the eternal drama being played on earth. Eclipses, comets, and meteors were eagerly and superstitiously studied, for the influence of the stars on men was so obvious that all the calendars may be described as astrological, just as among the historic peoples of the old world.

Linked to astrology were witchcraft and magic; linked to magic, knowledge of the effect on the organism of certain plant juices and other substances—the first glimmerings of therapy among those peoples.

The writing, to judge by the extremely few genuine specimens left behind by the Tolteca and their cultural heirs, can hardly be called that. It is the depiction of objects to express ideas, a pictography already stylized and abbreviated, an ideography. But some of the signs are undoubtedly phonograms, and this is a clear indication that, on the eve of Cortés' arrival, the transition from ideography to real writing was in progress.

The relics of Toltec art in Tula, Teotihuacan, Cholula, and elsewhere reveal the astonishing aptitudes of these particular Indians. Their simultaneous use of such materials as stone, lava, brick, and earth in construction made it possible for them to achieve whatever symbolic, esthetic, or practical forms their imaginations could devise. Temples, palaces, tombs, ballcourts—traces of all these remain, in the form of foundations, fragments of walls, columns, pillars, and inscriptions. From the sculptural decoration of their buildings—the bas-reliefs, altars, and statues—we can see what extraordinary gifts were developed by these spontaneous cultures. Monstrous masks portraying their gods and the charming little heads—ex-votos, probably—represent the extreme links of an artistic chain which, though it has not yet been studied, compels our admiration. The stuccos, colors, and frescoes, lavished on the interiors of palaces and tombs (including what has been destroyed and can only be guessed at), the ceramics, in a multiplicity of forms, painted and decorated with a wonderful exuberance of fancy, are like the tatters of an immense book which is going to pieces before our eyes—a book which tells us how they lived and felt and thought, those men eager to reveal some particle of their religion, of their history, of their soul, of their life in every work shaped by their hands.

We need only to contemplate the vast quantity of objects which, in fragments and in dust, are like a pavement covering Anahuac and the regions that nourished the civilization of the South in order to realize that the population around the great Toltec centers was dense, as it was in the Maya and Quiché lands, where scarcely an inch of earth, it seems, was left uncultivated. We need only to know the traditions, or the vestiges, of their crafts, their artifacts of cotton, of colored fabrics, of feathers, of silver and gold, the wonders that made the word Tolteca a synonym for "ingenious artist," if we want to envisage the social order of those peoples. The peasants, if they were serfs, cultivated the land for the lords and priests. Otherwise, they cultivated the land as collective owners, distributing the produce in shares, under the supervision of the chieftain, the cacique, reserving a part for the god and another for the lord. Craftsmen belonged to guilds, in which processes were secretly handed down from masters to apprentices. And in this social order habits of obedience, discipline, and conformity were manifest and constituted an unwritten code of morals and justice, a code powerfully sanctioned by faith and by fear of punishment in this world and in the other.

Such discipline is a sure sign of a ruling priesthood, as is also the magnitude of the works constructed for cities and fortresses and other monuments, nearly all built on huge mounds, under the divine pressure that a theocratic despotism could bring to bear on thousands of human beings who hardly had essential food and clothing, only the bare necessities, and these never varied. Prayers and sacrifices, moral precepts, and respect for matrimony, the family, and authority were the foundation of the Nahua's intimate life, according to the chroniclers who wrote—and embroidered—on the subject and according to the fragments of poems and of novelesque tales which can be gleaned from those adulterated records; none of this does more than confirm what the mere aspect and variety of objects allows us to infer.

This Toltec civilization still flourished, essentially the same, among the Aztecs and the Acolhua, its heirs, at the time of the Spanish Conquest; the civilization of the South left its mark all the way from Mitla to Chichén. And now, let us make plain our conviction that if Quetzalcoatl, the civilizer, had really been a European and had brought the Tolteca a faith—"God is good; man is sacred to man; woman represents on earth the divine function of nature"—if he had brought them writing, if he had taught them to use iron, the Tolteca would have maintained their supremacy on the plateau, and Cortés would have come up against an unconquerable people. The Conquest would not have been a frightful struggle, but a transaction, a pact, a supreme benefit, without oppression and without bloodshed.

There is no evidence to indicate that human sacrifice was not prevalent among the Tolteca and their kinsmen the Colhua, resident also in Tollan. The evidence tends to support the assertion of the chroniclers that the king-priest Topiltzin Quetzalcoatl suspended those rites. It seems that he dissolved the priesthood of Tezcatlipoca, and that these priests stirred up the populace, especially those Nahua and Meca tribes still in a savage state. Living scarcely organized, in caves or kraals, they practiced cannibalism because they believed the human victim would be transformed into a protecting divinity; thus, by eating him, they were manufacturing a god. With such allies, then, the disinherited priesthood and the Colhua tribe went to war against the reformer. The war lasted many years, and events, as the chronicles relate them, are extremely confused. Several times Quetzalcoatl was vanquished. He fled, he died, he came to life again—which seems to indicate that the cult of Venus triumphed several times over the fierce Tezcatlipoca. But the tribes spent their energies in these religious wars, and their members, abandoning the fields, which incessant invasions by nomads left desolate and fallow, began to immigrate to the southern valleys of the plateau, or, following the Gulf shores to the Isthmus, settled in Chiapas or Guatemala, Tabasco or Yucatán. A legend set down by the chronographers informs us that *octli*, or pulque, invented by the Mexica, who were already wandering through that region (*metl,* the maguey, is the root of the word "Mexica"), contributed no little to this decadence; and so it is today—the regional beverage of Anahuac is one of the causes that have kept our indigenous people from sharing in civilization.

The Toltec empire fell easily apart. Tollan was evidently no more than the nominal capital of a loose confederation of feudal baronies and of sanctuaries such as Teotihuacan and Cholula. The religious wars brought on invasion by nomadic tribes, which had pursued the Tolteca from one setlement to another, all the way to Anahuac.

The king-priest, say the chronicles, after fleeing his capital, established himself in Cholula and converted that little sacerdotal city into a perfectly organized metropolis, to which the adherents of the dethroned sovereign came flocking. Even the priesthood of Teotihuacan probably gathered there, and perhaps the abandonment of the holy city dates from this epoch. We still find the evidences of a strange procedure which consisted in walling over the sanctuaries and in burying the priestly mansions underneath small mounds. Perhaps this was done during the frightful war which the tribes that had triumphed in Tollan waged on Cholula and its royal guest.

And so it happened that the capital-in-exile at Cholula was looked on by Huemac, a king-priest himself and the incarnation of Tezcatlipoca in Tollan, as a challenge, a threat, and above all a sacrilege. He waged war on the flourishing city. The prophet fled to the Gulf, where he disappeared, turning into the star Venus, which the people of Cholula saw shining on the crystal peak of Orizaba (Citlaltepetl, "mountain of the star"), like a promise, like a hope. Many fled; others stayed and no doubt compromised with the sect of human sacrifice. There is reason to believe that human sacrifice, which had been considered until this time not only as an offering to the gods but as the creation of a new divinity (since this was within the power of the god to whom the offering was made), had been converted, through the influence of the priesthood of Quetzalcoatl, into a kind of communion with the very divinity to whom the sacrifice was offered and who took part in the sacred banquet together with his adorers and became identified with them. So this rite, hideous and repugnant like none other, became informed with the same aspiration as the communion of the early Christians in their eucharistic feasts. This, at any rate, was the meaning which sacrifice had for the Aztecs, according to the chroniclers, and when Quetzalcoatl himself, as a fugitive from Cholula, or any of the missionary colonies he sent among the Maya and Quiché failed in the effort to suppress cannibalistic rites, these were given the sacramental character that they later took on in Tenochtitlan.

We have spoken of the fecund contact of Lucifer's priesthood with the Maya and Quiché; if the inscriptions could speak, they would tell us plainly what the transformation consisted in, but at any rate the arts, religion, customs, and political organization seem to have entered on a new era from the day the Tolteca encamped on the banks of the Usumacinta and beside the well of the Itzá (Chichén Itzá) and the artificial lakes of Uxmal. Only the transformation brought about by the Spaniard was more radical than the one that took place in the tenth and eleventh centuries.

Huemac, the conqueror of Cholula, was soon forced to abandon his great Toltec capital, Tollan, and the empire went to pieces. Some individuals made themselves strong in such baronies of the Valley of Mexico as Chapultepec or Colhuacan, others became mixed with the Tlaxcalteca, still others went in search of their brothers in Tabasco and Guatemala. It was as if the Supreme Sower had tossed the seeds of civilization to all the winds of Mexico.

In the Southwest region of the United States, traces of cave dwellings abound among the rugged mountains and canyons. Those desolate lands, in former times, were watered and wooded. Woods, water, towns have disappeared, leaving a few nearly pulverized cities in the valleys of the Gila, the Colorado, and the upper Rio Grande and some habitations among almost inaccessible cliffs and canyons. Hunting and fishing were the occupation of those vanished Cliff Dwellers, and their preoccupation was defense against the nomads that came in torrents, wiping out or scattering every living thing that stood in the way of their rush to the south. These endless invasions by savages determine the whole course of pre-Cortesian history. We have seen the Mound Builders, fleeing from the nomads, peopling the shores of the Gulf and perhaps of the Caribbean; we have seen the aborigines of Anahuac and of isthmic and peninsular Mexico mixing with the newcomers, losing their personality, or retreating to the bleak mountains on the east and west; we have seen the tribes following the Pacific shoreline, treading on one another's heels, crossing the central tableland in different directions. Our early history, then, is all migration, all movement, one long series of ethnic waves, flowing from the heart of the United States to the Isthmus of Panama. The ruin of the Toltec empire was accomplished, no doubt, by the biggest and strongest of these waves. It is a strange story. After many years of wandering, the chieftains of the barbarous Chichimeca—or a succession of chieftains, all with the same name, Xolotl—on coming into contact with the well-ordered towns of the Tolteca, finally settled down and established a curious empire whose center was in the mountains, honeycombed with caverns, that rim the Valley of Mexico. There they exacted tribute from conquered peoples, and their palaces were grottoes, like the habitations of the Cliff Dwellers in the cradle of the Chichimeca tribes.

These cave-dwelling hunters, without idols, with no cult except simple sacrifices to the gods of sun and earth, came out of their caverns little by little, say the chroniclers, built huts, formed towns, and, after learning from the Tolteca how to raise corn, they put on clothes, adopted the refined language and the gods of the Nahua tribes, and, in short, became civilized. It is fascinating to read the claims with which, after the Spanish Conquest, each of the native lords of Anahuac tried to prove his rights to ownership of land by relating his background, for here we see how barbarians strove to assimilate an alien culture and become Tolteca. The intervention of the erudite priesthood of that great people in the education of the Chichimeca princes (legend of the priest Tecpoyotl); the influence of the Nahua in persuading the savages to take up farming (legend of the resurrection of corn); the advent of a foreign Nahua tribe, the Acolhua, who absorbed the Toltec culture and portions of the Chichimeca peoples, called their empire Acolhuacan, and established their capital, rebuilding the old Toltec town of Texcoco, on the edge of the salt lake—these are heroic or tragic or romantic chapters in that shadowy history. And then there was the epic resistance to civilization by a large part of the savages, the bloody battles, and the ultimate victory of the cultured groups, united in defense of their new homes, and the segregation of those recalcitrant to progress in the mountain fastnesses and their fusion with the aboriginal Otomies.

Among the loosely joined baronies of the Acolhua's feudal empire, not long after the struggle to save civilization, there emerged one city, on the opposite side of the lake, which was on the point of taking over and enslaving the whole empire: the domain of the Tecpaneca, Atzcapotzalco. Ruled by kings of terrific energy, it succeeded in conquering the entire Valley, and, had it not been for the presence of the Mexica and their alliance with the Acolhuas, Cortés would have found not an Aztec but a Tecpaneca empire in Anahuac.

If analogies and parallels could serve any purpose in history except a purely literary one we might be tempted, in describing these Mexican regions, to draw comparisons between them and the peoples described in the ancient history of the Old World. The oriental peoples could be compared to the Maya-Quiché; the Toltecs could be regarded as the Greeks of pre-Cortesian America, and the Aztecs or Mexica could be assigned, not without citing some curious coincidences, the role of the Romans.

Let us forego, however, these facile tricks of rhetoric and sum up the vital evolution of the Aztec tribe, who acquired through brute force the privilege of incarnating in history the spirit of earlier peoples whose moral and intellectual reach was far higher.

Some writers group together the Nahuatl-speaking peoples who lived in the Valley of Mexico at one time, or even outside of it, as "the seven Nahuatl tribes." This is inaccurate. The Tlaxcalteca, for example, are Chichimeca (or Teochichimeca), emigrants from the Valley who conquered a Toltec population, which named them and civilized them, making them Nahua. The truth is that various Nahua families making their way south, perhaps from the river valleys north of our frontier, followed the slopes of the Pacific coast to avoid the bands of nomads infesting the northern and central Mexican plateau and climbed to the high valleys of Anahuac along a more or less identical route. They left scattered groups strewn behind them on their path, and these, still speaking the language, are today like living signs that mark the ancient road of the Nahua. The last of the tribes to take part in this secular exodus, say the chronicles, was that of the Aztecs, who came from Aztlán, "the lake of the cranes," which, according to Chavero,[4] was situated on the Sinaloa coast. Descending the western shore in slow stages, they found themselves among the Tarascans, who had a different culture. The rites of human sacrifice were exactly the same among all the advanced peoples of Mexico—the Nahua, the Tarascans, and the Maya-Quiché—which clearly indicates a single origin, and that origin is Toltec. These peoples had passed from the cannibalism of starving tribes to religious anthropophagy, in which the slave or prisoner, when sacrificed and shared in communion (that is the proper word), united man and god. This was progress with respect to cannibalism pure and simple: those who adopted the bloody rite took part in the revolting banquet only in certain festivals, and at no other time.

The Aztecs became acquainted with these religious practices in Michoacán. There they adopted them, and there they gave to their principal god (spirit of the tribe's warrior ancestor) the name of Hummingbird (Huitzilopochtli), after the bird honored by the Tarascans, who had even given their onomatopaeic word for it to Tzintzuntzan, the capital of their kingdom, on the shores of Lake Pátzcuaro. When the Aztecs departed from the Tarascan land, their moral baggage, so to speak, consisted of a priestly caste and a parcel of religious rites and legends—the first form of history. A lake people, they had gone from Atzlán to Chapala to Pátzcuaro and Cuitzeo, and hence to the lakes in the Valley of Mexico. Around these the Aztecs roamed incessantly from the early tenth century until early in the fourteenth. Coming from a region that abounded in the agave or maguey (*metl*, in Nahuatl) they found the Valley also rich in this plant, to them divine, from which they derived the name of their primitive god. Settling down, they either invented or propagated the use of pulque, the fermented juice of the *metl*, which makes men happy because it makes them brave; from then on they were known by the name of Mexica. The Tolteca, unfortunately

[4] Alfredo Chavero, "Historia antigua y de la conquista," in Vicente Riva Palacio, *Mexico a través de los siglos* (Mexico City and Barcelona: Ballescá-Espasa, n. d.), Tomo I, p. 462.

for them, sampled and took a liking to the invention, which contributed no little, according to the legends, to their discord and final downfall.

The destruction of the Toltec empire, in which the Mexica no doubt participated, seemed to them an opportunity to take advantage of the general chaos and entrench themselves permanently on the lakeshore. They were not successful. A coalition of the Valley's kinglets hurled them from the formidable crag of Chapultepec, and then the Colhua enslaved them. Finally breaking free, thanks to their ferocity and the hatred that their savage rites inspired, they managed to build a stronghold in the middle of the lake itself. They settled on the two largest islands, raised miserable fishermen's huts of mud and reeds and a temple (*teocalli*) to their patron gods, and blindly obeyed the counsel of their oracle and guide, Tenoch. These wretched island villages were called Tlatelolco and (the larger) Tenochtitlan. The city founded by Tenoch, and ruled for a time by him and his descendants, at first paid tribute to the king of the Tecpaneca, at Atzcapotzalco, and sent soldiers to the wars incessantly waged by this bellicose lord.

The Mexica changed their form of government from a theocracy to a kind of elective monarchy and made an alliance with the Acolhuan kings, who had been despoiled of a good part of their territory by the Tecpanecan lord. This alliance was disastrous in the beginning, and some of the lords of Tenochtitlan died in captivity. But the Mexica did not give up: together with their allies, the Acolhua of Texcoco, they finally vanquished the Tecpaneca, killed their indomitable king, and reduced the state of Atzcapotzalco to vassalage. This was the beginning of the Aztec empire.

Our land is strewn with superb monuments whose builders are unknown to us, such as the ruined edifices at La Quemada, near Zacatecas, and those at Xochicalco. In the present states of Oaxaca and Michoacán two civilizations had their centers; each, no doubt, was a mixture of an aboriginal and a later culture: that of the Maya-Quiché was the later one in Oaxaca, that of the Nahua, the later in Michoacán.

The Tarascans of Michoacán built no monuments; their monument is their language. Entirely different from Nahuatl or the isthmic tongues, it was spoken over an area that includes parts of the present states of Querétaro and Guanajuato. The Tarascans had their capital on picturesque Lake Pátzcuaro. Their social organization (especially with regard to industry) was ingeniously devised; their political organization, though monarchic, was saturated with theocracy, like that of nearly all of the civilizations of Isthmic America. Their rites were bloody, their legends dramatic and fascinating. The Tarascans were so warlike, they invariably defeated the Mexica; nevertheless, they offered no resistance to the Spaniards. The fate of Tenochtitlan, their hereditary enemy, plunged them into a stupor that made them forget honor and country.

The Zapoteca in the mountains of Oaxaca did build a monumental culture. Much has been written about their ruins, the remnants of their highly ingenious fortifications, their crafts, the exquisite style of their work in gold and other metals, truly artistic in taste, and their magnificent edifices, now moribund—dead, rather, and in a state of decomposition.

Some think the Zapoteca and their kinsmen the Mixteca to be relatives of the Maya; others consider them to be proto-Nahua, of the first wave of immigration. The truth is, the Zapotec region was a melting pot for all the pre-Conquest cultures that were present on the Isthmus of Tehuantepec. The proof is to be found in the sacerdotal city of Mitla, the City of the Dead, in the vestiges of its marvelous architecture.

To sum up: two great spontaneous civilizations sprang up in our country, that of the Nahua and that of the Maya-Quiché, and there were others that likewise revealed a conscious evolution, a sustained effort, and, finally, a stupendous accumulation of faculties, which gradually atrophied over a period beginning before the Conquest and continuing afterward.

Once the yoke of the Tecpaneca was shaken off, the victors, who divided among themselves the spoils of the conquered kingdom, affirmed their alliance, and the empire of the Mexica entered upon its period of grandeur. Two giant figures stand out from this period: the first Moctezuma and Netzahualcoyotl, the former as a superior product of a race active and bellicose like none other, the latter as the last and ripest fruit of the Toltec culture. "The Aztec empire," as it has been called, not without some reason, never consolidated its gains, nor were these ever as extensive as the vast reach attained by its victories (from the Lerma and Pánuco rivers to Guatemala) might lead us to believe. For even in the very center of their domain the Aztecs always had to face irreconcilable enemies. And they had no means of conquest save terror and blood.

Moctezuma Ilhuicamina was the soul of the war for independence that destroyed the supremacy of Atzcapotzalco. He subjugated the peoples of the Valley, many of them fierce and wild, conquered the Huasteca of the Pánuco River basin, and raised the victorious standard of Huitzilopochtli on the sands of the Gulf from Tuxpan to Coatzacoalco. His armies carried frightfulness into the present states of Oaxaca, Guerrero, and Morelos, razing temples, burning towns, butchering the defenseless, taking hundreds of captives to serve as sacred victims for the endless death feasts of the tribe's ancient gods. In order to make his conquests secure, he scattered colonies over the subject countries; some of these are flourishing cities today.

God's vicar, and adored like a god, Ilhuicamina not only shines in history as a conqueror, but also as the supreme practitioner of human sacrifice. And if he is an imposing figure as a warrior, he is terrifying when, at the dedication of the temple to Huitzilopochtli, he stands on the summit of the great *teocalli,* towering above the awed multitudes, painted black, garbed in rich mantles and precious stones, crowned with eagle feathers, the steaming obsidian knife of the tragic Mexican rites in his upraised hand. His piety led him to build innumerable temples, to placate the irritable gods with human blood so that, gorged and happy, they would nevermore vent their wrath on a faithless people. The ancient Toltec gods became Aztec gods; they all had their temples, the awesome Quetzalcoatl, converted into a god of winds and prophecies, and the sanguinary Tezcatlipoca. And while the melancholy king of Texcoco was raising a lofty pyramid in honor of a god without a name, the Mexica were erecting a temple to all the gods, a remarkable example of syncretism; the only analogy is found among the ancient Romans.

The gods rained numberless calamities down on Tenochtitlan. What with floods and drouths and famines, following one on the other, year after year, the empire came near to dissolving, like a lump of clay, in the waters of the lake. The Aztec monarch attacked all these problems with terrific energy; assisted by the wise lord of Texcoco, he commenced the fearful struggle with the water and the mud that must be waged if the divine mandate was to be obeyed and the island of prickly pears transformed into a gigantic city which would eventually join its artificial soil to the solid earth. This struggle is still going on; the enterprise begun by the Tenocha, the inhabitants of Tenochtitlan, may be likened to an abyss, which can only be filled up by tossing into it the fortune and the health of countless generations.

But Tenochtitlan was reborn, again and again, from its disasters. It grew up around its temples and along its four cardinal causeways, which, converging on the bloodstained altar of its tribal goddess, separated between them the space that the city would wrest, little by little, from the lake. These works are proof of a powerful social order. At the bottom was a servile class so tightly wrapped in an infinite net of superstitious practices, it was virtually enslaved by the gods. The gods controlled the labor of these peoples—all the tribes that settled in Anahuac adopted the same social order—and also the fruits of their labor, their property, their lives (where we have written "gods," read "priests"). This was the foundation of the social state: communal ownership of land; monogamy, but with no prohibition of extraritual polygamy; the duty of mutual aid between father and son; extremely rigid moral notions, indicating a high degree of social organization; respect for old age; the inflexible subjection of women (which did not preclude a certain measure of respect); terrible punishment for unfaithful wives. The whole state was pervaded by a profound feeling of religious fear. Nothing could be more fearful than those gods and goddesses with terrifying faces, never satisfied with human flesh and blood, who awaited the traveler from earth to eternity on the bridge of death to torment him if he had disobeyed or to speed him on his way to the regions of the sun if he had died fulfilling the precepts of religion, or on the battlefield, or on the stone of ordinary sacrifice, or in the heroic sacrifice of gladiatorial combat.

Priests were trained in special schools, where the turnover was rapid because the demand for them was constant. They were eternally active, timing the festivals inscribed in the religious calendar, watching over the domestic feasts held in the *jacal* (the primitive Mexican hut, still in use today, a replica of which was always built in the main patio of each stone or adobe mansion and adorned with flowers at fiesta-time) and over those held in the palaces of princes, and directing the ceremonies that, with horrible sacrifices, took place in the temples and surrounding courtyards.

Religion and war—and war was inevitably a consequence of religion—these were the mainsprings of the empire of Moctezuma I. There was also a special school where young noblemen were trained for war. It was like the Athenian *ephebeum:* from it the flower of knighthood went to the battlefield; from it, at times, princes of the royal family ascended the throne. When the empire was organized on the basis of a triple alliance (between Tenochtitlan, Texcoco, and Tlacopan, now called Tacuba), the neighboring peoples realized it would be invincible; in order to maintain their independence, they agreed to a pact which is probably unique in human history: by common consent there would be wars at stated intervals between the triple alliance and the sovereignties of Tlaxcala, Huejotzingo, Atlixco, et cetera (which were oligarchies in the form of republics), for the sole purpose of securing captives to sacrifice. And since the Mexica, as their power and dominions increased, felt ever more oppressed by the dreadful obligation to feed the sun, as they put it, the other peoples adopted the same custom, which halted the progress of those civilizations toward the higher level that the Tolteca had begun to attain. The eagle upon the prickly pear of Tenoch could not fly: the air around the voracious idol Huitzilopochtli was too thick with blood and groans.

If it had not been for this, for the anguish aroused everywhere by the caracol war-trumpet of the Aztec lord, by the rumble of his golden drum, the native qualities of that extremely energetic tribe would have achieved untold results. The Aztec merchants scouted incessantly every land bordering the empire and were the harbingers of conquests and colonies. Trained systematically in their homes to be slaves of the gods, to walk the day long without rest, to carry a burden at all times (an indispensible practice in a country where, unfortunately, pack animals were unknown), to stay always sober, the Aztecs crisscrossed the high plateau, making offers of trade and barter, visiting the marketplaces. They observed everything and reported everything to Tenochtitlan and

Texcoco. They descended the gigantic stairsteps to the oceans and reconnoitered the coasts and rivers, where magnificent ruins astonished them. From Tabasco and Chiapas they went to Yucatán, where their countrymen had staunchly backed the Cocom's tyranny until Mayapán was destroyed; they went south to Guatemala. Thanks to an unvarying policy followed by all the Mexica kings, every time a merchant was hindered in the pursuit of his trade by some foreign lord, a protest was made effective by force of arms; and thus it came about that on orders from the first Moctezuma his imperial hosts reached the Gulf and the Valley of Oaxaca, and those of his successors triumphed as far as Guatemala.

After one of these expeditions, which like those of the Egyptians were veritable *razzias* for the purpose of bringing captives to Tenochtitlan and exacting tribute, the empire's borders would appear to shrink; the Aztecs never took the time to consolidate them.

A contemporary of Moctezuma who is made to appear as another David by the chroniclers, intent on finding in the traditions of the empires of Anahuac as many parallels as possible with the peoples of the Bible, was Netzahualcoyotl: warrior who founded a kingdom, sinner who bewailed his sons, sensualist who surrounded himself with beautiful women even in his old age, erotic and melancholy poet, restless, weary, yearning for truth like a dilettante of our day or of the decadent days of the Roman Empire. Two of the kings of Texcoco, Netzahualcoyotl-David and Netzahualpilli-Solomon, took a hand in all that concerned the life of Tenochtitlan, as if to prevent misunderstandings. They saved the city from floods, directed the construction of the aqueducts that brought fresh water to the great capital, and were members of the electoral college which, on the death of each Aztec king, chose his successor from among the princes of the royal family. They played the principal role at the coronation festivals, where they assumed the odious duty of performing the rite of human sacrifice and composed the official harangue of the new monarch. They accompanied him to war, if they were called upon, and then returned to their domain and shut themselves up in their seraglios surrounded by splendid gardens, of which there are still some delightful remnants.

They joined with their sages and soothsayers in the study of the heavens, to learn the secrets of destiny, and in the study of plants, to seek the elixir of youth. The aptitudes of these Texcocan princes, leading them to improve on the legacy of the Tolteca, could have placed them at the head of a cultural advance had this not been frustrated and rendered abortive by the fearful superstition of the Aztecs.

From time to time a new temple was erected; each new monarch had to have his own, like the Pharoahs, and to build it multitudes of slaves and captives worked for the chieftains without receiving any salary whatsoever. There was no machinery except that admirably articulated lever known as man. By amassing him in vast numbers and making him suffer, those colossal works so admired by the Spaniards were contrived, works which have left impressive ruins where they were made of stone. In the capital of Anahuac, however, where the buildings were mainly of clay (though some were faced with stone), they have almost entirely crumbled and melted into the mucky earth from which they were raised.

Moctezuma Ilhuicamina's sucessors followed in his footsteps and, as the imperial power expanded, carried on the policies of the cruel and heroic warrior. More and more territory came under tribute. Not that the Mexica were invincible: on occasion some of the empire's inveterate enemies, the Tarascans in particular, would inflict grievous punishment on them. But they stubbornly kept fighting or turned their attention elsewhere, and, in any event, the wars went on and on. War was the normal condition of the empire, and it had not emerged from that stage when it was destroyed. The city grew: houses, gardens, aqueducts, temples multiplied; great mansions of adobe, decorated in dazzling colors gaudily combined, the dwellings of nobles and kings, became ever more luxurious, contained ever richer collections of artifacts from the countries under tribute and frequently resounded to the noise of *teponaxtle* and *huehuetl*, which could be regarded as musical instruments only when they accompanied sad or voluptuous songs. Some echoes of these songs, in naive, amorous, and melancholy poetry, have come down to us.

The cult of the gods became a craze: the prestige of the man-eating deities became immensely inflated after a few of the human hecatombs at the temples happened to coincide with the end of a calamity; the sacrifices, turned into butcheries of entire captive populations, bathed the city and its people in blood; [5] the stench of blood was everywhere. It was high time this religious insanity came to an end; the cross or sword that would cut it short would be truly blessed.

The priests, as guardians of the astrological traditions bequeathed by the Tolteca, had sculptors to carve symbolic idols and calendar stones. Outstanding among these is the admirable disc called by Chavero "the Sun Stone," [6] which, in the space between the central mask, representing the sun and the twin star, and the star of Quetzalcoatl carved on the rim, comprises and sums up the chronometric and cosmological systems handed down by the Tolteca with such precision that it can rightly be declared unequalled among the works of isolated peoples, including the early Egyptians, Chaldeans, and Chinese.

It was a proud apogee: those who belittle it, against the evidence of the monuments and of the conquistadors themselves, compare that tradition with the present state of the aborigine and insist on picturing Tenochtitlan as a clutter of huts around a group of adobe houses at the foot of an earthen pyramid always red with gore. There was something of this, but there was a great deal more. We must remember that from those huts came the traders who prepared the way for the conquest of the plateau and of both sea coasts; from those adobe houses came the chieftains who carried the victorious ensigns of the Mexica as far as Guatemala; and on the summit of that bloodstained pyramid the Sun Stone glistened under its crimson varnish. It was a proud apogee for the Aztecs, this beginning of the sixteenth century. Netzahualpilli reigned wisely in Texcoco. The successors of Moctezuma Ilhuicamina, the young Mexica kings Axayacatl, Tizoc, and Ahuizotl, had conquered many tribes, sacrificing thousands on the central *teocalli,* which had been rebuilt time and again, each time

[5] Manuel Orozco y Berra estimates at twenty thousand the number of victims in a single day under the auspices of the emperor Ahuitzol. (Author's note). See *Historia antigua y de la conquista de México*, Tomo III, p. 395.

[6] On this important monolith see Alfonso Caso, *The Aztecs: People of the Sun,* trans. Lowell Dunham (Norman: University of Oklahoma Press, 1958).

on grander scale. Their successor was Moctezuma II, a royal priest and a favorite of Huitzilopochtli. The empire, paralyzed with hate and fear, obeyed him. The eternal enemies seemed to await the moment when the giant would fall, when they would dispute the prey amongst them. The wild Chichimeca, hidden in the fastnesses of the sierras or dashing in elusive bands over the northern plateau, from the Lerma and Pánuco rivers to the Rio Grande, the indomitable Tarascans, the ill-tamed tribes of the Huasteca mountains, and, above all, the well-organized and war-wise Tlaxcalteca, offering, in their superb defenses, refuge and protection to the empire's enemies—all seemed to sense that the hour of ruin was near: they readied themselves for the gruesome banquet.

As pope and emperor, Moctezuma had followed the policies of his forebears, but because he was more obsessed with his divine nature, his tyranny was more onerous. In his hands, trained to hold the obsidian knife of the sacrificer and the censer of copal, the military empire founded by the first Moctezuma became once again a theocracy. The people bowed their head still lower in servility. The nobles, formerly the monarch's proud comrade-in-arms, were turned into domestic servants who waited upon him and carried him about in the hammock of gold and brilliant colors that he used on trips for recreation or to the battlefield. A complicated ceremonial served to keep the young human god apart from ordinary mortals, and he ensconced himself in his palace, his seraglio, his priestly chapel, or exhibited himself in sumptuous barbaric splendor before the prostrate people. "I scarcely ever saw his face," said one Aztec noble to a Spanish missionary.

As a priest, he was one of the initiated: he knew that the god of the prophecies, Quetzalcoatl, had announced that he would return or would send his own people, white and bearded men, carrying crosses, who would come from the east. And the victories won in the "flower war" [to get victims for sacrifice] and those that marked the course of his conquests beyond the bounds of empire failed to calm the Aztec lord's anxiety. His subjects, too, had heard of these predictions. For some time the Spaniards had been in definite, if intermittent, contact with peoples under tribute to the empire. The news reached Tenochtitlan and Texcoco in the form of rumors, and the aged Netzahualpilli had compiled what were probably accurate reports on the ephemeral passing of the first Spanish expeditions along the Gulf coast. Hence, all cosmic phenomena and earthquakes and meteors were given the same interpretation: the light of the zodiac forecast ruin; the comet of 1515 forecast ruin; even the dead arose to forecast it. (After the Conquest the chroniclers described these presages in legendary style.) Moctezuma gave himself over to despair, at times, in the melancholy certitude that the auguries were true. At other times he ordered massacres of soothsayers or, more optimistically, waged bloody wars with Tlaxcala and other free states to bolster the prestige of his empire or plotted to consolidate it by absorbing the states of Texcoco and Tlacopan, his allies. But his pride was outrageous, the voracity of the gods grew ever more insatiable, and the hatred of those who paid tribute to the empire was more ominous than all the auguries.

CHAPTER THREE

THE CONQUEST

The precursors of Cortés. Hernán Cortés and the empire's tributaries. The Conquistador and Moctezuma. Cortés threatened by Spaniards and Aztecs; defeats the former and is defeated by the latter. The siege of Tenochtitlan; the Emperor Cuauhtemoc.

IN MEXICAN HISTORY, "the Conquest" is the title given to the period of Spanish conflict with the Aztec empire. But the Conquest lasted longer, and, what with the unfinished business of colonizing and pacifying, it can hardly be said to end with the sixteenth century. Nonetheless, the work of Cortés is basic: once that captain of adventure, without mandate or legal authority, had carried his daring enterprise to a triumphant conclusion, all that came after was merely the result of his achievement.

The fund of energy deposited in the Spanish character by centuries of battle and adventure could not be spent in agricultural or industrial labor, nor in any occupation where the rewards were meager. Such efforts left an enormous reserve unused, lacked the excitement of the unexpected, of the risk faced with the help of God and the sword, the incentive of a rich prize for the winner. Those predatory and boundlessly greedy but heroic men, who had lived in a continuous epic, who had become accustomed to miracles as an everyday occurrence, only to find themselves in a Spain which, after the conquest of Granada, had been placed in an iron frame of order and security by the firm hand of Ferdinand and Isabella, received the news of Columbus' discovery as if it were the guerdon of Providence for their services to the Cross, the supreme miracle which lighted the highroad of Spain's stupendous destiny, revealing a field of action where all desires could be satisfied: the greed for gold, the passion for adventure, the yearning for the unknown and the marvelous that gave their endless dreams fantastic shape. The typical Spaniard of the sixteenth century, who in Cervantes' analysis was separated into two elements, Don Quixote and Sancho Panza, was joined together again in most of these earthy and sublime adventurers. According to circumstances, each of these men could become a pirate or found a kingdom. Only the gold fever among the placer miners of California or the Klondike excitement in our time can compare with the state of mind that prevailed among the future conquerors of America.

The expedition of Francisco Hernández de Córdoba (1517) started as an armed foray for the purpose of trafficking in Indians among the islands and selling them as slaves in Fernandina (Cuba) or Española (Santo Domingo). It was suggested, no doubt, by one of the most intrepid seamen of the day, Antón de Alaminos, who had come to the Antilles as a youth with Columbus on his second voyage and had taken part in the expedition to Florida led by Ponce de León, in search of the fountain of youth, in 1512. Alaminos recalled the great Admiral's belief in the existence of rich and fertile lands among the regions bathed by the Gulf, so the expedition set out to look for them. It wound up on the Yucatán coast, on the bay called "The Bad Fight," where it was utterly shattered by resistance which, according to one writer, had been organized by a shipwrecked Spaniard who had offered his useful services to the natives in return for a pardon from the sacrificial knife.

Diego Velázquez, governor of Fernandina by grace of Emperor Charles V [Charles I, king of Spain], a man of great greed and enterprise, yet frank and open, was the soul of these explorations. All of Spain's efforts to take possession of Mexico, from the early sixteenth century to past the middle of the nineteenth, have been organized in Cuba, but only the effort led by Cortés was successful. After Hernández de Córdoba's expedition came that of Juan de Grijalva (1518), which Velázquez sent to discover lands and to trade—that is, to exchange gewgaws for gold, silver, and precious stones. Grijalva went back and forth along the southern Gulf shores, discovering the river in Tabasco that bears his name and the coasts of the present state of Vera Cruz, where the name of his patron saint, San Juan de Ulúa, is perpetuated, while a picturesque river bears the name of a member of the expedition, Alvarado. Grijalva's return with a little gold and tales of wonderful countries barely glimpsed fanned to white heat the imagination of the adventurers who had already enlisted with Hernán Cortés, the captain chosen by Velázquez to be the leader of a fresh and definitive effort. The new captain was greedy, like all his comrades, but more ambitious than any of them. When Velázquez became aware that his agent was a man capable of anything, when he sensed the steel hidden under the velvet of polite forms, under the persuasive glibness of a man who had spent his life until then in petty adventures, he wanted to deprive him of his command. Velázquez had the power to do this, but did not know how to go about it. The swiftness and boldness of his captain's decisions left him stunned. Proceeding like a pirate, Cortés snatched from the shores of the Greater Antilles whatever he needed for the success of a venture which he felt sure was bound to be gigantic, which for that very reason attracted him with magnetic force, and which little by little brought out a genius that unfolded along with the enterprise.

Don Hernán set out with no credentials other than his audacity and his faith, which were equal; he put the former at the service of the latter. For faith's sake he risked his life and his lifework. Guided by Alaminos, he navigated the courses that led to the "isle of Yucatán." There, at Cozumel, he planted the cross of Christ above the crosses in the Maya sanctuary and acquired an interpreter (one of the shipwrecked Spaniards). And in Tabasco, after a furious fight on the banks of the Grijalva, he acquired Doña Marina, the Indian woman who has been called a traitor by the retrospective adulators of the Aztecs but who was adored by the Aztecs themselves almost as a goddess, the Malintzin, "the Tongue," the Conquest's Voice.

On the hot, sandy, unhealthy shores opposite the island of San Juan de Ulúa, discovered by Grijalva, Cortés commenced his mighty work.

Soon there were repercussions: his explorations of the coast, anxiously observed by the natives, who exchanged warnings and signals galore in his sight, were reported to the emperor of the Mexica (or Culhuas, as the coastal tribes called them). Moctezuma, at first news of the Spaniards' presence in the Gulf, hastened to consult his gods and prophets. Grijalva's expedition had demonstrated the truth of the presages: Quetzalcoatl, keeping his promises, was coming to reclaim his kingdom. The Emperor tried to flee, but was dissuaded by his priests. When Grijalva disappeared, he took heart, plunging into diversions, into the joy of command, or tyrannizing, of asserting the divine ascendency that fear had uncrowned. Never before had imperial oppression weighed so heavily on his nobles, on the people, on allies and tributaries. Again the Spaniards appeared, and Moctezuma, again frightened, redoubled his ambassadors, his presents (terrible incentives to the intruders' greed), his offers, his supplications, his efforts to prevent Cortés from making the journey to Tenochtitlan. He sent wizards and soothsayers to conjure the cross-bearers away and to make them vanish, for they objected to the sacrificing of the human host on the holy altars. They were gods because they made lightning and thunder do their bidding, and toppled the local gods from bloodstained altars, and they were not annihilated. And still they wanted gold and gold and more gold. And they had caused, by their mere presence, an insurrection of all the maritime tributaries of the empire. The Emperor felt himself being dragged down into the abyss by his dead gods. He was vanquished by Quetzalcoatl; he was vanquished by Christ.

Cortés very quickly took charge of this situation. He knew the history and the circumstances of the Aztec empire, its resources and the Emperor's fears. He cultivated friendly relations with Moctezuma's enemies, managing to make close allies of them and, at the same time, to lull the prince's eternal suspicions. The expedition for barter and conquest was transformed into one for domination and conquest. Never in history, perhaps, has there been an achievement, starting with so little, to equal it.

His powers, illegal to begin with, had at any rate run out. Velázquez' henchmen, numerous among the handful of men that made up the army, grumbled, broke discipline, and plotted to haul the expedition back to Cuba. The men wavered. Cortés maneuvered. Deciding to colonize the land, he set up a municipality (the first Vera Cruz), and that simple and natural form of political life gave life to Cortés' legal personality. He became chief justice and captain general of the royal arms, and everything was to be submitted to the King of Spain for his approval. Astuteness, firmness, clemency—all these were employed by Cortés to control that group of men, each one of whom could see himself as captain. Cortés, with amazing self-confidence, destroyed the ships which the storms were about to destroy, salvaging the parts that could be used, if need be, to build other ships, moved the town to a better site, organized and fortified it. And now, having cut off communication with the Spanish world and having bound, with all the trappings of legality, the neighboring tributaries of Moctezuma in fealty to their new lord, King Charles, he set out to make the titanic ascent of the eastern sierra, on his way to visit Moctezuma.

We need not relate the fascinating details of this epic march. One episode of extreme importance concerns the alliance made with Tlaxcala, which, from hatred of Tenochtitlan, became the vassal of Spain. In spite of the immense superiority of the Spanish arms, which were most effective when the masses of Mexica warriors were thickest, if it had not been for the Tlaxcaltecan auxiliary, which surrounded the group of Spaniards with a dense human wall, these would have vanished in combat or on the altar of sacrifice.

When Cortés reached Tenochtitlan, he became aware of the monarch's incapacity for resistance, but aware also of the probable adamant resistance of the sullen and hostile populace that hemmed him in. He began to feel like a hostage in this immense city of the *teocallis* and lakes, and with astounding audacity decided to invert this desperate position: he made Moctezuma his prisoner. The Emperor-god would be his talisman and shield. For the Mexica, however, the divine image of the fatherland took the Emperor's place on his vacant throne.

If what reliable chroniclers tell us was fact and not hallucination, the Spaniards had been given lodgings in the midst of a treasure. Those who saw it marveled at such riches, and their greed swelled to formidable proportions. That collection of precious plumes, of multicolored mantles, of gems, of objects of silver and gold constituted the treasure of just one of the dead Aztec kings, Axayacatl; since his reign the conquests had expanded and the tributes doubled. With such temptation before their eyes, the Spaniards felt no qualms about the enterprise they had begun: all were resolved to see it through. The nobles guarded the captive Tecuhtli. The Spaniards, as a rule, treated him well, and he showered them with all sorts of favors; he even went so far as to solemnly declare himself a subject of the King of Spain. In only one particular he never gave ground: in what pertained to his religion. He listened to the preaching of Fray Bartolomé de Olmedo, listened to Cortés, who had his points as theologian and poet (and his bachelor's ribbon). But, with the mute stubbornness of the pusillanimous and the soft, he remained recalcitrant.

Cortés' attention was not confined to Tenochtitlan; he kept in touch with Tlaxcala and with the coast. Following his policy of striking every now and then a terrorizing blow, as he had done in Cempoala, as he did on his way to Mexico in Cholula, where he ordered and saw carried out a frightful massacre in cold blood, in Tenochtitlan he accused several lords, or *tlatoani*,[1] of hostile acts and had them burned to death in front of the palace barracks, in view of the assembled populace of the *calpulli*, the city's divisions and suburbs.

But Cortés was uneasy, sensing that the princes were preparing an uprising of the Mexica army, an admirable hierarchy, which awaited only the command of its chief, the *tlachocucatl* Cuitlahuac, who was momentarily a prisoner. Missionaries to the feudal lords, vassals of the empire, and to the tributaries crossed the country in all directions. At the weekly market held in Tlatelolco, rival island city recently conquered and annexed by Tenochtitlan, hate and menace glittered in the eyes of the multitude, which awaited only its sovereign's command to rush into battle. In these circumstances, Cortés visited the main *teocalli* and, with a daring no words can do justice to, dragged the man-eating idols from their sanctuary. Then desire for vengeance leaped in the hearts of the Aztecs, and the human sea beat ceaselessly about the *tecpan* in which the conquistadors were dividing up Axayacatl's treasure,

[1] The *tlatoani*, or "orators," made up the supreme council, with one member from each clan; it performed judicial and directive functions. See George Vaillant, *The Aztecs*. (2nd ed.; Garden City, New York: Doubleday and Co., 1962).

not without keen discontent and turbulence among the soldiers, who expected a much larger share. Cortés quieted them with promises.

It was high time: Spanish ships sent by Velázquez had arrived at Vera Cruz. The news was imparted to Cortés by Moctezuma, who urged him to abandon his enterprise if he did not care to die in it. Cortés, with a picked force of Spaniards, went to meet the envoy of Velázquez and maneuvered so cleverly that Pánfilo de Narváez, the envoy, lost his army and came near losing his life.

Cortés returned in triumph to Tenochtitlan. But the city, mad with fury, was besieging the Spanish barracks; the brainless Pedro de Alvarado, left in command by Cortés, had murdered a large part of the nobility during a religious festival, to get loot, and the populace of the *calpulli* had risen as one man. Cortés sought the good offices of the captive Emperor in vain: the Emperor was repudiated and wounded by one of the royal princes, young Cuauhtemoc. There was no alternative to flight. The soldiers loaded themselves with gold. Moctezuma was assassinated. Surrounded by Tlaxcaltecans, the conquistadors departed under cover of night; attacked by the Mexica on the causeway to Tlacopan (Tacuba), some were killed, some were drowned, and a number were sacrificed. The rest fled in the fearful gloom of *la noche triste*, the night of sorrow.

Huitzilopochtli had been avenged. In his restored temple, on new altars, blood flowed in his honor. All the Spanish prisoners were sacrificed. The new high priest, Cuauhtemoc, son of the bloodthirsty Ahuizotl, supervised the purification of the temples and no doubt was the one who crowned the brave Cuitlahuac, the real leader in the battle of *la noche triste*. The city was then cleansed of enemies; from the chief justice on down, all who had been friendly with the invaders were killed. The capital was put in a state of defense. Garrisons throughout the empire were reinforced, especially those in the zone through which Cortés was retreating on his way toward the sea. Ambassadors were sent to independent lords and vassals to set up a common alliance and a plan of defense. But the Mexica were fighting for a lost cause. Smallpox, introduced from the islands to Yucatán and thence carried to the coast of Vera Cruz by the soldiers of Narváez, spread with horrible swiftness, leaving the Spaniards almost unscathed and attacking the Indians with dreadful voracity. The flower of the Mexica army, its intrepid veterans, the Emperor Cuitlahuac himself, succumbed. The divine sickness, as they called it, believing it to be witchcraft, prepared Cortés' triumphal way.

Don Hernán kept his alliance with the Tlaxcaltecans firm (with cajolery and by giving them absolute license to loot the regions that had not yet submitted and permission to eat their prisoners). From Segura de la Frontera (Tepeaca), the second city founded by the Spaniards in this country, he directed forays over an immense radius, forays which resulted in the amassing of a tremendous booty, consisting especially of prisoners, who were delivered from being eaten by being enslaved. The opinion that prevailed was the one held by most Spaniards on the Antilles: there was little difference between an Indian and a beast, and those who were cannibals should be reduced to slavery and branded with a hot iron—this was done thousands and thousands of times. To add to his good fortune, Cortés was able to replace most of his losses. For Velázquez, in Cuba, kept sending ships to look for Narváez, and Francisco de Garay, in Santo Domingo, sent one expedition after another to take possession of the Pánuco basin, as indeed he was authorized to do; all these outfits turned up at Vera Cruz and fell into Don Hernán's hands. He made up his mind to capture Tenochtitlan by securing control of the lakes and had boats (the famous bergantines) made for this purpose in Texcoco. He sent a report to the King on what he had done, telling him what he was about to do, and asking that the new lands be given the name that the soldiers had been giving it ever since Grijalva's expedition: New Spain.

This man, whose military exploits and political activities had expanded to such a degree that he now assumed, before the hordes of vanquished Indians, the attitude of a sovereign and supreme judge, who looked on the Mexica as rebel subjects, since Moctezuma had pledged his kingdom in fealty to Charles V—this stupendous adventurer found an opponent worthy of him in the new emperor of the Aztecs, the high priest Cuauhtemoc, noblest epic figure in American history. Cortés himself, and, in profuse and fascinating detail, the inimitable Bernal Díaz,[2]

[2] Cortéz, in his "Third Letter" (see *Five Letters, 1519,* trans. J. Bayard Morris [New York: W. W. Morton, 1962]); Bernal Díaz del Castillo, *The Discovery and*

have described the siege of the Aztec capital: the gradual constriction of the Emperor's forces, disputing every inch, always attacking, returning each day to put up an ever more determined resistance in spite of the steadily increasing number of the Spaniards' allies, who decimated them, and in spite of the smallpox, which weakened them profoundly, picking off their chiefs. The Spaniards, burning and destroying the towns of the Aztecs and their vassals, always with an eye to booty, especially gold, and to prisoners that could be branded and enslaved, made themselves masters first of the Valley, and then, with their bergantines, of the lakes, and finally of the bridgeheads on the causeways. From that instant the days of Tenochtitlan were numbered.

Cortés has written the best eulogy on the defense of Tenochtitlan. "I saw," he says in one of his letters, "how rebellious the people of this city were, and that they had 'the greatest courage and determination to die that any generation of men ever had,' and I did not know how to go about delivering ourselves from so many dangers and vexations without destroying them entirely, together with their city, which was the most beautiful thing in the world."

Tenochtitlan was torn down as fast as it was occupied. Gaunt with disease, hunger, and exhaustion, the defenders wished only to die. In the last combats, they hardly had the strength to wield the macana, the national sword, and to hug their shields. The innumerable canals and ditches of the city were filled with dead bodies and debris. On came the besieging thousands, trampling the bodies and the ruins of houses and temples, leaping over the sculptured stones and the broken idols. Wild hordes from the Chichimeca lands and the region of Jalisco drawn by the stench of blood and death saw the fearsome agony of the eagle. The gods turned silent and died. Sure of defeat, those men and women, who went so far as to devour their children rather than see them slaves, fought to the last heartbeat, without hope. O people of Tenochtitlan! If history has paused in amazement to contemplate your valor, how can we do less, we who are sons of the land exalted by your patriotic agony? Because of it the country you died for deserved to rise again: the very hands of your conquerors prepared the way; from your blood and theirs,

---

Conqeust of Mexico, trans. with an Introduction and notes by A. P. Maudslay [1908] (New York: Farrar, Straus, and Cudahy, 1957).

both heroic, was born the nation that is proud to adopt for its own the name of your wandering tribe, that has engraved with profound filial piety on the ensign of its eternal liberty the eagle of your primitive oracles.

When Tlatelolco also had been bled and razed and Cuauhtemoc, soul and genius of the resistance, captured and enchained, the end had come. The foundations of conquest had been laid: all that followed was the result of Cortés' unparalleled achievement.

We Mexicans are the sons of two countries and two races. We were born of the Conquest; our roots are in the land where the aborigines lived and in the soil of Spain. This fact rules our whole history; to it we owe our soul.

BOOK TWO

The Colonial Period and Independence

CHAPTER ONE

FOUNDERS AND SETTLERS

Don Hernán Cortés; gold. The capital. Submission of Michoacán. Expeditions to the coasts and Isthmus; foundings. Cortés, governor and captain general: the Pánuco; Alvarado and Olid; the journey to Honduras. Nuño de Guzmán in the west. Yucatán, Campeche, Mérida, Valladolid, Puebla, and Morelia. The caciques as conquistadors. The last conquests; typical founding. First political division.

THE PURELY HEROIC PERIOD of the Conquest had come to an end. After mid-August of 1521 there were still countless expeditions and no dearth of high deeds: the daring Spanish heart found a vast field to triumph in. But in the midst of these epic ventures the exigencies of reconstruction and organization and pacification—which added up to Christianization—became more and more pressing. And we must admit that Cortés' great character, in this second stage of his work, in spite of lamentable faults and errors, manifests itself on the same high level as in the first.

Commenced as a private enterprise, for Cortés lost his titles through the very act of undertaking it, and carried out with no other mandate than the highly dubious one given him by a council he had created himself, the glorious acquisition of the Aztec empire had been a stupendous adventure. To transform this enterprise and make it permanent, purging it of everything that was irregular, legalizing it by making a donation to the Crown of Castile of something the Crown had never spent a penny on (that is, by renouncing powers that had been born of necessity)—to organize it, in short, was Cortés' next task. He was the genius who, after improvising a great work, turned it over to others for safekeeping, not without paternal anxiety, and yet with the religious faith of a loyal vassal.

There was no limit to the powers of the Conquistador when he towered above the ruins of Tenochtitlan. Cuauhtemoc, "the fallen eagle," lay at his feet, and with the heroic prince lay the whole federal empire of Anahuac. The allies, who had been the principal instruments of conquest, drunk on blood and gorged with booty, acclaimed La Malinche and retired to their mountains or their cities, so impressed with the prestige of the conquerors, it might be said of them that they had conquered themselves for all time. The undisciplined Spanish soldiers, relaxing from the nervous tension demanded by a war requiring the utmost in self-sacrifice, vigilance, and courage, disgruntled at not finding the mountains of gold and precious stones that their fantastic greed imagined as islands in a lake of Aztec blood, and egged on by partisans of Diego Velázquez, who were eager to blame their disappointment on Cortés' perfidy and fraud, passed from recriminations and attempted revolt to Bacchic song, from alarums to orgies. But it was all momentary: this man without legal authority could, like Caesar, with his mere presence and words regain ascendancy over his comrades in battle, who let him command and chastise them; even if the hand gripped the hilt of the sword, the rude head was bowed and trembling.

It can be said that, from one point of view, New Spain (a name spontaneous with the conquistadors, afterwards confirmed by the kings) was born independent. If Cortés had called upon all the predatory men in the Antilles, where veritable colonies of fugitives from the galleys and prisons had congregated in those days, and had offered them feudal domains in the immense territories that he had subjected, perhaps Spain would never have been able to establish its power in Isthmic America. On a later day Cortés' devoted friends, irked at the King's ingratitude and injustice, offered to forge a crown for him in Mexico and to defend it with their swords. Cortés indignantly rejected the offer. The monarchy was an element of the Spanish soul's religion after eight centuries of patriotic war in the shadow of the Cross and royal pennon.

Cortés later, against his will, gave in to the instances of one Juan de Alderete, who was the royal officer in his small army, and to the clamor of his soldiers—probably to quiet suspicions that he was in collusion with the captured chieftains and plotting to reserve fantastic treasures for himself—and consented to the torture which crippled Cuauhtemoc as a soldier but which placed beneath his charred feet a pedestal that raised him to heights of glory far surpassing his glory as a warrior. Martyrdom made the imperial hero a human hero.

Lust for gold, the moral sickness which kills all piety, all tenderness in the heart, at frequent intervals attacked those men of steel, who blindly believed that, as a reward for their eight centuries of battle, a grateful Providence had tossed them America for a prize. In search of gold they sailed in ships which were unsubstantial molecules, battered by boundless seas and endless storms, toward continents they had always dreamed of, under skies they had never dreamed of. Their energy increased with danger, was strengthened by obstacles, became gigantic in adversity. Only death could conquer them—but no, not even that: their religion of hope would take care of them and would bring them before the Supreme Judge, bathed in blood, but with their lips on the Cross of the sword and in their hearts faith in the sword and in the Cross.

From Cortés' camp among the spurs of lava from Ajusco, in Coyoacan, Spaniards and their Indian allies came down to rummage in the debris, disembowel the tombs, take the temples apart, and scour the ditches in Tenochtitlan and Tlatelolco. In the miasma of death that suffused the atmosphere of that boggy abattoir, they passed their days interrogating the cadavers and the ruins, torturing death to make it reveal the hiding place of treasures. And they got little or nothing. Still searching, they pounced upon the living wealth, which breathed and suffered, and took to making slaves of Indians and branding them on the cheek or the calf with a red-hot iron.

Cortés, about this time, seemed to develop a new personality, that of the paternal protector of the conquered. He took pains to modify the treatment of captives and hoped to reform it. Meanwhile, he resolved to build a center for his dominions of the day and for his conquests of tomorrow, and he chose the very city that had witnessed the glory of the Mexica and his own glory: from the ruins of Temixtitan, as he called it, he swiftly raised the capital of New Spain. He laid out a quadrilateral plot, comprising the nearly razed imperial palaces, bordered it with ditches which the lakes kept filled, divided it by a grand canal, provided it with potable water by repairing the Aztec aqueduct, set the foundation of the future church beneath the very altar of the man-eating gods, and within that area fortified at intervals and supported by an armada of bergantines, he placed his Spaniards. Outside it, he distributed the Mexica in groups, under the tutelage of their lords, who obeyed their powerless Emperor and his vicar, the *cihuacoatl.* Thus was born the City of Mexico, on a level with its encircling lake and below the level of other lakes nearby. It was born under sentence, as its mother Tenochtitlan had been, to battle without truce against the water, which would penetrate every pore in its foundations and impede healthy circulation in its veins. From the city of Cortés an American Spain would reach out toward the seas and toward the centuries.

In the camp at Coyoacan, where permanent buildings were beginning to be raised, the pictographic records of the tributes paid to Moctezuma were studied to see what places in the empire contributed gold in order to go there, no matter what the obstacles, just as Francisco Montaño had climbed into the smoking crater of Popocateptl in search of sulphur. Some soldiers made excursions, at their own risk and expense; one of them brought news of Michoacán, a gold-bearing country. The greedy eyes of Cortés' army were turned in that direction.

Relations were established between the court of Tzintzuntzan and the camp at Coyoacan. The king's envoys, bringing rich presents, aroused the cupidity of the Castilians. The Purépecha (the Spaniards called them the Tarascans) were the dominant people of the Michoacán empire, which reached from the bounds of the Aztec empire and Chichimeca territory to the beaches of Colima, and they were ruled by a king who was frightened by oracles and terrified by reports of Spanish power. A war party had tried to organize resistance, but the king, Tzintzitcha [properly, Tangaxoan II] had chosen to save his life and keep his throne as a vassal rather than fight for his honor and his country. He came with a grand retinue to see Cortés, pledged full fealty to the King of Castile, had himself baptized, and returned to his capital on the shores of Lake Pátzcuaro with the profoundly contemptuous name of Caltzontzin, which the Mexica had given the coward. A little later Cristóbal de Olid crossed the Michoacán empire on his way to Colima, visited the capital, and was entertained by the monarch. The star-worshipping Tarascans had accumulated treasures in their temples, although there were no idols in them, we are told. These rich temples—to the God-Sun, to mother nature, to the Southern Cross—were quietly being dismantled; the sepulchers (*yácatas*) were profaned, robbed of their treasures. Michoacán was divesting herself of her jewels in order to receive her new masters. The master was unspeakably cruel when he was a conquistador named Nuño Beltrán de Guzmán, but when he was the missionary bishop named Vasco de Quiroga he was a redeemer.

In a celebrated document which could be called, if the term did not have too many modern connotations, the first constituent charter of New Spain, written by the King in June of 1523, one paragraph reads:

> I am informed that on the coast below that country there is a strait allowing passage from the Northern Sea [the Gulf] to the Southern Sea [the Pacific], and since it is very important to our service to discover this, I charge and command you [Cortés] to undertake immediately to find out if said strait exists and to send persons to look for it and bring you a full and true account of what they find there, and that you thereupon write and send me a full account of what was found there, for as you can see this is a matter of great importance to my service.

Toward the south of that country, the King added, there was a sea which "contains great secrets and things that Our Lord God and these kingdoms would greatly profit by"; and he ordered the Conquistador to find out what truth there might be in all this. Ever since Nuñez de Balboa had taken possession of the Pacific for the kings of Castile in 1513, the principal object of most expeditions had been the discovery of a passage which should join the two seas. Indeed, it is strange that no such passage exists in a continent so extremely longitudinal as America. The Americans in the coming century should correct this defect of nature.[1] The expeditions to the Gulf, to the Isthmus, to South America, so richly rewarding to Spain with their chance discoveries and

[1] The Panama Canal was finished in 1915. The possibility of some such project had been discussed since the sixteenth century.

marvelous acquisitions, had for their original object the search for the strait.

Cortés kept the strait always in mind. Even before the fall of Tenochtitlan he had sent his explorers southward to the Isthmus. He would be the one, he felt sure, to discover the passage that would bring Spain closer to the lands of spices and gems and incense, to complete the voyage that Columbus had cut short and that Magellan was to complete by way of the southern ocean. The first expeditions ran into the indomitable Mixe in their mountains, with disastrous results. After the fall of the Aztec capital, one expedition after the other battled the mountain Indians, year after year; gold and silver abounded in that rugged country, it was said. Finally, as in all the regions where a monumental civilization had been attained, internal feuds and dissensions aided the Spaniards more than their own guns and horses, or the dogs that were used to devour Indians on the expeditions of the fierce and fearless Pedro de Alvarado. The Zapoteca made war against the Mixteca, and then surrendered to the Spaniards and became their allies; so, at last, did the warlike Mixe, obeying their kings, who were scared by the priests. In this period the Spaniards founded the town of Espíritu Santo (Coatzacoalco) on the far side of the Isthmus. In the valley of Huaxyacac (once a military colony of the Mexica) a town called at first Segura de la Frontera, like the second town founded by the Spaniards, after being abandoned was definitely settled in 1526 and given the name Antequera; today it is Oaxaca. The indefatigable Gonzalo de Sandoval, who founded cities on the Gulf (Medellín and Coatzacoalco), founded also, as conqueror and pacifier, the city of Colima, near the Pacific. Meanwhile, in Zacatula an intrepid band commenced to build ships which would attempt the voyage to India. In the Isthmus the pitiless Alvarado terrorized the caciques and, followed by his hungry greyhounds, converted the tears of the Indians into blood and gold, amassing an enormous booty, which aroused greed in his soldiers and a revolt that he suppressed with an iron hand. From Tabasco this cruelest of all those birds of prey returned to the City of Mexico.

Thus, before Cortés received the royal decree that gave him the title of governor and captain general, signed in October of 1522, he had accomplished the subjection of Moctezuma's whole empire.

Cortés did not lie idle in his camp at Coyoacan. He supervised the building of the City of Mexico, which made rapid progress thanks to the thousands of Indians (many of them slaves, their faces branded with the iron) who worked at it. The capital was built by them at the cost of their labor and often of their lives. Fray Toribio de Benavente considered the rebuilding of the City of Mexico as one of the great misfortunes (the seventh plague) that befell the Indian family.[2] Cortés could sense, almost perceive, through the rumors that came from Spain, the desperate struggle between his fame and his enemies, headed by Governor Velázquez and supported by the bishop Juan Rodríguez de Fonseca, who was prejudiced against any great enterprise in America. When the titles arrived he rejoiced. But he did not relax. A little earlier, on learning that Garay, governor of Jamaica, was once again attempting the conquest of the Pánuco basin, this time with ample supplies and commissions obtained from the King, and that the experienced Juan de Grijalva was leading the expedition, he marched swiftly to the Pánuco with an army of Aztec auxiliaries, who competed with the conquistadors in committing atrocities. After executing some caciques and branding hundreds of captives, he ordered his faithful Sandoval to found the town of Sancti Esteban del Puerto (now Pánuco). Garay, when he arrived, met with furious resistance from the Indians, which, on Cortés' orders, was brutally repressed by Sandoval, who burned several caciques alive. But Garay's comrades, defeated and dispersed by the Indians and about to starve, fell into Cortés' hands. The Governor himself had to ask for asylum; he was gently treated and allowed to die in peace.

Rid of this grave threat, Cortés turned his attention to a couple of ambitious projects he had been hatching for some time, both linked with the search for the passage between the oceans, in the existence of which he had absolute faith. He planned to conquer the part of Central America that was nearest to New Spain; he would thereby steal a march on the governor of the isthmic regions, Pedrarías Dávila, and win the glory of discovering the strait. One of these expeditions, under the command of Alvarado, would go by way of Oaxaca and the

[2] *History of the Indians of New Spain*, trans. Francis Borgia Steck (Washington: Academy of American Franciscan Studies, 1951), Part 1, Chapter 1.

Isthmus of Tehuantepec to Guatemala, which, according to the overtures of some caciques, was merely awaiting an opportunity to deliver itself to the Crown of Castile. The other expedition Cortés, unfortunately for both men, confided to Olid, who would go by sea, acquire men and provisions in Cuba, and head for the region of Honduras (Las Hibueras), of which wonderful tales were told and which he was to conquer and colonize at Cortés' own expense.

Alvarado was successful in his enterprise. But Olid was subverted by the bitter enemies of Cortés in Cuba, and, after landing in Las Hibueras and founding a town, he raised the standard of revolt, imitating his commander's rebellion against Velázquez. When Cortés learned of this, he sent an expedition against the rebel; battered by storms, it fell into Olid's hands. But Francisco de las Casas, head of the expedition sent by Cortés, and other conquistadors from Mexico got hold of Olid through treachery and cut his throat. Cortés, aware of only the first act of the tragedy, the capture of his envoy, proposed to take personal vengeance. He prepared a grand expedition, which he insisted on leading himself, despite the counsel of friends and the instances of the royal officers recently arrived from Spain to organize the fiscal administration of the colony. No one could dissuade him. With regal pomp, the chroniclers tell us, he set out from the City of Mexico, leaving the government in control of the treasurer and the accountant sent by the King and adding a lawyer to form a triumvirate, whose powers were so vague they were unlimited. Other royal officers set out with the Captain General but promptly returned to the City of Mexico. With him went the Emperor Cuauhtemoc, the *cihuacoatl,* and the lord of Tlacopan, among others. Cortés, foreseeing that the expedition might take a long time and yet not be successful, snatched from the center of his conquest every man who was capable of heading a strong rebellion. As far as the mouth of the Coatzacoalco River all went well, and the expedition conserved the regal aspect afforded by the pomp and retinue of the Conquistador. But from there on it was a bedraggled procession across rivers and mountains, through jungles and swamps and lakes known only to wandering savage tribes and wild beasts, into regions of lush vegetation where, at the cost of infinite privation and fatigue, it was necessary to constantly improvise the trail, the road, the bridge, the raft, in order to go forward, no one knew just where. And yet, Cortés always kept that forlorn crowd, weak with sickness and exhaustion, fairly compact within his iron hand. Had Olid still been alive he would probably have captured that disarmed, hungry, gaunt expedition on its arrival in Honduras, and Cortés would have wound up in Cuba, at the mercy of Velázquez' friends. On the way, doubtless fearing that the Emperor and his companions might escape and turn up in the City of Mexico, he invented the existence of a plot and had the Aztec prince and some of his comrades hanged. The stoic serenity of the young Emperor, who had let himself be baptized and had taken a Christian name, probably to save his people, faltered not at all, but showed his towering moral superiority over his conqueror. Cortés' conscience seems to have whispered something of the sort in his ear, according to Bernal Díaz, and the echo of his crime later found a loud voice in Charles V, who solemnly reproved the cruel and senseless deed. Cortés never allowed scruples to interfere with his ends. Like nearly all men great in war or government, he no doubt believed what Napoleon expressed with tragic cynicism, that those who accomplish great enterprises are above the moral law—as if moral laws could be anything else but the formulation of society's vital needs; as if they were not, therefore, laws of nature; as if the giants of history could emancipate themselves from the laws of nature when a microbe from the swamps of Babylon in Alexander's veins, or a grain of sand in Cromwell's urethra, is sufficient to finish them off!

When after months of terrible suffering the expedition finally reached Las Hibueras, there was no longer any point in it, for Olid was dead. Moreover, the riches of the region turned out to be a tall tale. The only results were the founding of a few insignificant towns, the ruin of Cortés' prestige, and, in the City of Mexico, the destruction of his power and fortune through the malfeasance of the royal officers. Sick and miserable, he arrived in Vera Cruz a year and a half after his departure from the City of Mexico; those of his companions who had not remained in Honduras or joined Alvarado in Guatemala returned in dejection with the Conquistador. From then on nothing turned out well for Cortés. The noose that hanged Cuauhtemoc projected its black shadow on the twilight of a life replete with triumphs and sorrows.

The Indian populace and the conquistadors received with endless ovations the man who had been given up for dead. He spent months trying to recover his wealth and position and to bring his despoilers to justice, and nothing turned out according to his wishes. Under investigation by the Court and required to appear in person, about two years after his return from Las Hibueras he was on his way to Europe when the government of New Spain, which he considered to be his work and almost his property, was taken over by an Audiencia, a tribunal of justice and administration, which was going to show itself more hostile and damaging to him than his worst enemies. At the head of this set of judges the King, with astonishingly bad judgment, placed the notorious Nuño Beltrán de Guzmán, who had been governing the province of Pánuco with the good results that might be expected from a visitation of the plague. His cruelties had forced the Indians to abandon their villages and take to the brush; those unable to flee were reduced to slavery and frequently were sent to the Islands in exchange for cattle, which soon teemed on the grassy plain between the mountains and the coast of Tamaulipas. Even the Spaniards were terror-stricken.

This was the man chosen to administer justice as president of the first Audiencia in the colony. In the City of Mexico he took a hand in, and promoted with enthusiasm, every kind of corruption. And when he learned that Cortés was coming back from Spain loaded with honors and realized that a new Audiencia would punish him for his crimes, he decided to wash his misdeeds in the glory of a conquistador, and succeeded only in washing them in blood. Nuño de Guzmán is the archetype of the primitive conquistador, who thought any means permissible in order to get gold, whose only motive was greed, and whose procedure with the subjected regions was exactly the same as with a city sacked and put to the sword. Whatever there was of audacity, courage, cleverness, even intelligence, in this man served only to bring out his dominant characteristic: greed. By his order the King of Michoacán, the famous Caltzontzin, was iniquitously murdered, after being tortured and robbed of his gold. Guzmán and his lieutenants,

Juan de Oñate and the royal officer Pedro Almíndez Chirinos, crossed in different directions the territory now shared by the states of Jalisco, Aguascalientes, Zacatecas, and Tepic, and it is hard to say which is most amazing: their ferocity in torturing caciques, in reducing to slavery and branding hundreds of captives, in allowing the Mexica and Tlaxcalteca allies to burn towns, or their iron will in overcoming perils and privations, in exploring that rugged terrain at the cost of incredible exertions. They came together at a point in Jalisco toward the end of 1530, and the next year the "tyrant Guzmán" (as a contemporary chronicler calls him) and his companions, "robbing God of His souls, the Emperor of his vassals, and the Church Militant of her sons," went down the slopes of the sierras toward the sea. It was then that the Conquistador named those parts "The New Castile of the Better Spain" (which was dropped for "Nueva Galicia") and founded Compostela. A government of sorts was organized in Tepic, and the expedition headed north, crossing swollen rivers, fighting terrific battles, and taking possession of the populous Acaponeta Valley, which was hideously laid waste. The news from the City of Mexico warning Guzmán of imminent disgrace, the exhaustion of the allies, who died by hundreds, the lack of burden-bearing Indians, even the mutiny of Spaniards—some were hanged, together with many caciques who protested—failed to dismay the leader, who advanced as far as Sinaloa, where he founded the city of Culiacan. Oñate had already founded a city which he changed from one site to another and named after his birthplace, Guadalajara. Nuño de Guzmán, in Compostela, which he vainly tried to build up into an important town, awaited events, determined to face up to them.

Towns built and towns destroyed; endless insurrections among the mountain Indians, who retreated to the fastnesses rather than be made slaves and see their women and children, even those at the breast, branded with the wicked iron; defiance by Guzmán of the Audiencia and of Cortés, even to the point of imprisoning their envoys; outrages committed by the soldiers (many of them moved on to that land of gold, Peru, for Nueva Galicia was good only for agriculture, and the Indians there were recalcitrant to slavery); and, finally, the abandonment of his conquests by the president of the first Audiencia and his imprisonment in the City of Mexico—these were the results of Guzmán's enterprise, which was indeed virtually fruitless, as it all had to be done over again. Dying poor and friendless in a Spanish prison, this man did not live to expiate his visitation of blood and fire on the western reaches of New Spain.

While conquest was being prepared rather than achieved in the west, in the extreme east an important enterprise was in the making. Don Francisco de Montejo, who had been Cortés' attorney in Spain, in partnership with another agent of the Conquistador, Alonso Dávila (or de Ávila), capitulated with the King for the conquest and settlement of the islands of Cozumel and Yucatán. The Court had learned something from experience, and the royal instructions were notably sound. The Conquistador would be rewarded with lands, a portion of the tributes, lucrative offices, honors, and titles; but each town founded must include one hundred Spaniards, not from the Antilles, but from Spain; only horses and cattle could be taken from the Islands. Immigration was encouraged by concessions of land and slaves (rebellious Indians or those bought from masters) and by exemptions from taxes. The Crown would reserve certain quantities of all metals; a part of all fines would be applied to public works; encomiendas would be established, with each encomendero responsible for the religious instruction of a certain number of Indians, in exchange for their personal services—this was the gist of the insructions regarding administration, which were typical of this kind of concession. But there were further instructions regarding the Faith and the conquered. The settlers must bring with them a certain number of religious, who would see to it that the Indians were neither mistreated nor robbed, nor made to build houses or do any work that harmed them in body or interests. Only in extreme cases should war be resorted to, and then only after a solemn warning. This provision was derived from the bull of Pope Alexander VI on the donation of America to the King of Spain and on the King's right to make war; whosoever resisted this donation (which the Pope had made of something that never was his) could be reduced to slavery, and his property confiscated. Most important is what concerns the kind treatment of Indians, who could not be required to work without due compensation, and the good moral example the Spaniards were supposed to set them.

With these capitulations and the things they called for—boats and men from Spain, animals and victuals from the Islands—Montejo and Dávila, accompanied by royal officers, landed at Cozumel in the fall of 1527 and a little later on the coast of what was for them the Island of Yucatán. They were weakened and decimated by sickness. Frequently they had to fight Indians; at other times welcomed and entertained by the caciques. The expedition was a failure, and in 1529 Dávila and his people abandoned the enterprise, withdrawing to Tabasco, where Montejo and his son, Don Francisco, had preceded them. They decided to attempt the conquest from the south. After terrible suffering, Dávila and his men reached Champotón, near Campeche; thence, by a fearfully long, hard march to the Lake of Chetumal, where Dávila tried to found a Royal Town (Villa-Real) but was defeated and nearly destroyed by the hostility of nature and the Indians; he retired by sea to Honduras.

The Montejos still made a mighty effort: in alliance with the Cocom tribe, they believed they had founded a permanent city amidst the marvelous ruins of Chichén Itzá. But no, they were besieged there, only by a miracle escaping with their lives, and retired to Campeche. After eight years of effort, the Peninsula was abandoned. The work of conquest was no farther along than it had been when the famous capitulations were signed.

The Maya were afflicted with terrible plagues (locusts and famine), with gory internecine wars, and with fears for the future, which the priests fomented with terrifying prophecies, attempting to conjure adverse destiny with bloody sacrifices. Such was the chapter of Maya history in the years when they were free of the Spanish presence. Meanwhile a group of Franciscan friars, who at Viceroy Antonio de Mendoza's request had set out from Mexico to evangelize unconquerable Yucatán, commenced their fruitful work at Champotón. But the holy and heroic work of the missionaries was frustrated by a party of Spanish bandits who, acknowledging no government, had established themselves nearby and traded in Indians and committed nameless crimes.

Now the former page of Hernán Cortés, Montejo the Younger, having become an experienced captain, begins to play the principal role, as heir of his father's projects. While governor of Tabasco, in 1537, he sent a band of conquistadors to Champotón, where after hard trials they were on the point of abandoning the enterprise once again. Meanwhile, the elder Montejo, involved in disputes with Alvarado in Honduras, signed his powers over to his son, Don Francisco, who went to the City of Mexico, obtained supplies, and in 1540 landed in Champotón. He took possession of Campeche, where he founded a town in 1541, invaded the Peninsula by land, and set up headquarters at T-ho, ancient seat of an Indian cacique. There he founded the city of Mérida. He sought and consolidated an alliance between the Spaniards and the Cocom tribe, and beat off a tremendous assault by hostile caciques on Mérida. Then his cousin Montejo made an excursion to the east and founded the town of Valladolid. From then on the Conquest continued without a halt. After the bloody repression of formidable rebellions came the establishment of encomiendas, the intervention of Franciscan friars in favor of the Indians' liberty, the separation of Yucatán from the judicial authority of Guatemala and from the ecclesiastical authority of Chiapas. Then came the persecution of the Montejos, accused of grave abuses in the distribution of lands, tyranny with the Indians, and mistreatment of priests. There must have been much exaggeration in the charges, for Indians, friars, and Spaniards bewailed bitterly the family's disgrace. The old man died at Court, poor and friendless; the son lived on in Yucatán, highly esteemed. They were the founding fathers of Yucatán.

Not all the towns founded by Spaniards in those early colonial days stood on the site of bloody conquest. Some were built for such practical purposes as stations on trade routes, places of refuge for Spaniards in case of insurrection, points of collection for the agricultural products of a zone. Thus, to protect the traffic between Vera Cruz and the City of Mexico, which passed through the almost exclusively Indian towns of Cholula and Tlaxcala, the government in the capital (the second Audiencia) ordered the erection of a new city, which was laid out with the help of Franciscan friars, and above all by Motolinia [Fray Toribio de Benavente]. By the end of September 1531[3] the town had been established, and until half a century ago the seal of the mystic spirit of its planners was conserved in the name Puebla de los Angeles. The friars were aided in the material phase of their work by thousands of Indians from the large neighboring towns. Fearing a rival, the City of Mexico's council put up strong opposition to the erection of Puebla. But the Audiencia persisted, bringing in Spanish families from Vera Cruz, where the deadly climate was decimating them, and in 1532 obtained the royal decree which made the new town a city.

Michoacán, where the industrial culture was so well organized before the Conquest, after the invasion by Nuño de Guzmán entered on a period of suspicion and hostility toward everything Spanish. The towns were deserted, the inhabitants took to the woods and there reverted to a state of savagery. The governing Audiencia, which had made several unsuccessful attempts to correct these conditions, finally decided to send to the wounded realm the noble and humane Vasco de Quiroga. Among the men who consecrated their souls and their lives with the utmost zeal to the gentle initiation of the Indians into Christian culture, this officer of the Audiencia deserves special mention.[4] Men like Bartolomé de las Casas, Juan de Zumárraga, and Vasco de Quiroga persuade history to become reconciled with the Christianization of the American Indian as carried out by Spain, even though its inevitable antecedent was conquest, with all its violence and horror.

Quiroga, in Michoacán, fixed his residence in the kingdom's ancient capital, Tzintzuntzan, "the City of Michoacán," as the royal decrees call it. There he convoked the representatives of the nation which had disintegrated in the flames that burned Caltzontzin. They came, full of suspicion, heard the missionary of peace, and returned, enchanted, to their homes. The very memory of their kings, their gods, and their glory faded in the hearts of the Tarascans with the love that they felt and feel today for the man who became their bishop and was always

[3] The first founding was on April 16, 1531; the second and definitive one on September 29 of the same year.

[4] In 1533 Quiroga went to Michoacán with the office of visitor; in 1537 he was made bishop of that diocese.

their father. He understood the needs and respected the traditions of the groups that made up the Tarascan family, and he applied to their economic organization a system of division of labor (very effective in those days), which gave each town a single trade. He also established hospitals that were veritable schools of the arts.[5] And he saw prosperity, with work and peace, return to all. In the midst of these flourishing towns, between the lakes of Pátzcuaro and Cuitzeo, the city of Valladolid was founded in 1541 or 1542; of secular origin, it was soon covered with the mantle of religion. Now Morelia, its name was changed in honor of its illustrious son, José María Morelos.

These were not the only types of foundation. In the sixteenth century, as before it, all the nomadic tribes of the north were known as "Chichimeca." Because of the depredations, ever more disturbing, that they made on the frontiers of the provinces controlled or subjected by the Spaniards, the government of New Spain decided to send Christianized Indians to pacify the savages in their rugged wilds. This was done. The expeditions set out from Acámbaro, previously founded on the boundary of Michoacán. The caciques, delighted with their role as conquistadors, showed off their Spanish arms and horses. There were curious fights without arms, and there was a miracle: Santiago [St. James] appeared during the battle and took the side of the Christian Indians, clearly demonstrating that, in the eyes of Heaven, an Indian was just as good as any European. And out of all this Querétaro was born. Some conquered Chichimeca gathered around a stone cross, which promptly turned miraculous, and this was the cradle of the future city. As we said before, if there is a single proven fact in our history, it is that the conquest of New Spain was accomplished for the kings of Castile by the Indians themselves, under the direction and with the help of the Spaniards. The supreme achievement of Hernán Cortés consists in his having marked out this course for an undertaking so colossal that any other approach would have failed. And nothing could be more to the point than the speech of the cacique Don Nicolás

[5] Two principal hospitals were founded by Quiroga: one near the City of Mexico (in the town of Santa Fe), the other in Michoacán; both were called Santa Fe. Quiroga drew up the *Ordenanzas* (Regulations) for these hospital-towns, Thomas More's *Utopia* being his source of inspiration.

de San Luis Montañés,[6] who was made captain general (in his words) "by the King my lord, His Majesty" for the conquest of the Grand Chichimeca, which later became Santiago de Querétaro. After his mission was accomplished, he said to all the assembled caciques under his command: "With the strength of our arms we won these lands, which His Majesty ordered us to conquer."

The work of conquest and pacification did not end with the sixteenth century, but did advance far enough so that the boundaries of New Spain were set. And they were indeed far-flung: from Honduras on the south to the vast indeterminate space between Texas and Florida on the north; and on the west not simply the shoreline, still unexplored along the Southern Sea, but, beyond the ocean itself, the Philippine Islands, which an expedition organized in Mexico had taken possession of in the name of Philip II. The great figure of Cortés is outstanding also in this maritime phase of conquest and exploration. He had no sooner taken Tenochtitlan than his agents began to build ships in Zacatula and Tehuantepec in order to explore the coast of New Spain in search of the famous strait, or cross the Southern Sea and find the Isle of Spices, or found in Cathay a colony like New Spain and place it at the feet of the Caesar, the Emperor Charles V. The expense of energy, patience, and daring by this man Cortés in his efforts to realize his dreams is beyond belief. Materials freighted from Vera Cruz to the coast of Michoacán and to the Isthmus, construction of ships regardless of cost, and trips to Acapulco, to Zacatula, to Manzanillo to supervise the departure of expeditions; failure of them all because of fires, shipwrecks, mutinies; loss of all or nearly all the ships, whose castaway crews Nuño de Guzmán used to imprison and maltreat—none of this dismayed the Captain General. The stories of friars and explorers coming from Florida or scouting from Mexico about the existence of vast kingdoms, marvelously rich, beyond the Sinaloas began to cause excitement. Cortés himself headed an expedition that reconnoitered the coasts of Sinaloa, Sonora, and Lower California, crossing the gulf that bears his name, and he returned to the City of Mexico when everyone

[6] Cacique of Jiltopec, descendant of Moctezuma. Under his command the conquest of Querétaro was begun in 1522.

thought he was dead. And still new projects buzzed in his brain, despite the dismal results of his latest voyage.[7]

The Viceroy Mendoza had to repair the shoddy work of Nuño de Guzmán. Nueva Galicia had not been pacified: uprisings were constant and general, the tribes defiant. Pedro de Alvarado, who, with the King's good will, had got himself a sort of feudal barony in Guatemala, passed through Jalisco on his way to launch his ships for the exploration of the Southern Sea, and, going to the aid of Governor Oñate, who was sorely beset by Indians, he lost his life in consequence of a fall in the mountain fastnesses.[8] It was the Viceroy who, by fighting and dealing, consummated the enterprise.[9] Soon Nueva Galicia, with its capital and its Audiencia, became the most distinguished member of the colonial family.

Meanwhile the legend of the kingdoms of Cibola and Quivira was exploded.[10] A strange thing! Those fabulous riches were really there, but some were concealed and others potential in the gold-bearing soil and in the astounding fertility of California. But the Viceroy and Cortés continued to order conquests. The Conquistador, believing his rights had been undermined, returned to Spain to seek redress for his grievances, and died there.

The century approached its end, and the work of pacifying the Indians neared completion. The search for minerals resulted in the founding of Zacatecas, originally a mine; thus the limits of Nueva Galicia were expanded. Next Durango was founded on the banks of the Guadiana, rounding out the province of Nueva Vizcaya, which had for an outpost the fort of Chihuahua. Then began the exploration and conquest of the New Kingdom of León—Nuevo León. The friars were

[7] The source used by Sierra for his account is Manual Orozco y Berra, *Apuntes para la historia de la geografía en México* (Mexico City: Imp. Francisco Díaz de León, 1881), pp. 8–11. The Gulf of California was formerly called the Gulf of Cortés.

[8] Pedro de Alvarado died in Guadalajara July 4, 1541.

[9] The war against the rebellious Indians of Nueva Galicia was decided on in the City of Mexico, May 31, 1541, and Mendoza left at the head of his forces to suppress the revolt on September 22.

[10] The reference is to the famous and fantastic story of his travels by Fray Marcos de Niza, 1539.

the real consolidators of this new acquisition; one of them founded Monterrey. The necessity for a defense against the nomadic tribes that crossed the northern plateau, back and forth, from one sierra to the other, made the establishment of fortresses imperative; this was the origin of Celaya, of San Miguel de Allende, and of San Luis Potosí—which received the last part of its name because it was believed to compare in mineral wealth with the famous zone in Peru. The task of pacifying the Chichimeca tribes—who called themselves by other names—could not be completed in this century and was passed on to the next. Everything was tried—combats, missions, forced reductions of Indians to congregations and towns, establishments of other Indians already Christianized, like the Tlaxcalteca—but with only limited or long delayed success. At the end of the century of conquest, the Spaniards had not yet been able to establish their supremacy in the north of Sinaloa or in Sonora and were in New Mexico only as marauders seeking the fabulous kingdom of Quivira.

Let us see how the Spaniards went about founding a town. First the colonizers chose a site, usually temporary, for a cluster of houses and a church did not make a town—a town was an institution and could be transplanted, as happened with Guadalajara (definitively located by the first viceroy) and as happened with Villa-Real, whose founding we describe briefly because, according to our most distinguished authority on colonial times [Manuel Orozco y Berra], it was typical.

Once the heroic resistance of the Chiapas Indians had been overcome—rather than surrender to the conquistadors, many leaped with their women and children from the bluff that was their last redoubt—Captain Mazariegos, a kind man, showed them a place, probably Chiapa, where they were to live in community and hear the preaching of the missionaries. And he chose nearby a temporary site for a Spanish town, which was to serve, like the Roman colonies, as a center of pacification, of colonization, and of vigilance for that region. In one respect only were the Spanish colonies different from the Roman: they were also centers of religious propaganda, something the Romans were never concerned with. On this site the Indians built temporary houses for the Spaniards, who then assembled in the house of the captain general and governor of the province. He announced to them his intention of here temporarily establishing a town, which he would call Villa-Real. He proceeded to name alcaldes and received their oaths to conduct themselves well in their office and to be faithful to God and to the King; he handed them their staves of office and named regidors, who in turn chose a jailer and town crier. Then a major-domo for the town, an attorney, and a sheriff were named; the visitor general and secretary, appointed by the Viceroy in the City of Mexico, were also given possession of their offices, and the government of the town was ready to function.

The conquistadors ceased to be soldiers the minute they became settlers: they were citizens and enjoyed all the rights of a member of the community. When the first meeting of the town council was held, the salaries of employes were set, the whipping post was placed in the plaza, and the gallows on the nearest hill. A register of settlers was started, which gave them the right to share in the distribution of Indians and of town lots; it also conferred the honors and privileges granted to first settlers and exempted them from the persecutions to which vagrants were liable. The town then was removed to a better site, streets were laid out and named, the church was built. Such was the origin of Villa-Real, which became San Cristóbal de las Casas, capital until recently of the state of Chiapas.

So far the Spanish design was to consolidate and strengthen New Spain. The main plan was sketched, but not finished. The whole system, without sufficient cohesion as yet, but on the way to achieving it, was divided officially thus: under one viceregency, the Audiencias of Mexico and of Nueva Galicia. The Audiencia of Mexico comprised all the territory along the shores of the Gulf and Pacific and the provinces of the central plateau in between. The Audiencia of Nueva Galicia comprised a large part of the present states of Jalisco, Zacatecas, Aguascalientes, and Durango. The province of Nueva Vizcaya was ruled directly by the viceroy. In truth, nothing was definite: it was a vague and changeable picture, within whose spacious frame a new nationality would take form and come to life.

CHAPTER TWO

THE PEACEMAKERS

The apostles; the first Franciscans; the propagation of Christianity. The defense of the Indians; Las Casas; Zumárraga; Fuenleal; Quiroga. The friars: churches and convents. Inquisition; the Jesuits.

N THE HEELS of the two priests who came to Mexico with the conquistadors and who, if they occasionally took the Indians' side, were either unable or unwilling to do much for them, there came the first Franciscans, a simple apostolic mission of two friars and a lay brother, who was called Pedro de Gante [Peter of Ghent].[1] These were the pioneers of the host that would evangelize New Spain.

The appalling doctrine, secretly or openly professed in the Antilles, that the Indian was not a rational being, or just barely one—a diabolical pretext, as certain friars declared, to palliate the insatiable rapacity of the slave dealers, which had wiped out the entire population of the West Indies—never entered the minds of these friars, not even as a vagrant wicked thought. In all fairness, neither did Cortés profess it. The Indian was a rational being, a younger brother waiting for redemption and worthy of it. With this motto blazoned on his banner, Gante set out to teach in Tlaxcala and in the City of Mexico, and his companions went about preaching as best they could, with the aid of

[1] Fray Juan de Tecto, Fray Juan de Ayora (or Aora), and Fray Pedro de Gante. They arrived at Vera Cruz August 30, 1523.

dramatic gestures, of infantile but expressive paintings, and of interpreters.

Later the twelve Franciscan friars of the "Custodia," as it was called, arrived with Martín de Valencia, the "custodian," as their leader: thirteen[2] friars in all, true apostles of faith, of humility, of poverty, of zeal, men in whom the angelic spirit of the founder had returned to the world. All the tenderness, all the gentleness of the religion of Francis of Assisi was required to show the contemporary world that some Spaniards were not hard or cruel. The friars of the Custodia were hard and cruel only to themselves.

The Indian, from the outset, was their adopted child. The principal business of the friars was the study of the Indian languages and the conversion of the peoples. They soon mastered the more important tongues and, with the aid of pictures which showed the climactic moments in the life of Christ, they began to travel about New Spain and the other American territories. Before the end of the sixteenth century, the whole pre-Columbian world, with the exception of nomadic tribes that could not be reduced to congregations, had been baptized. But was it then Christian?

The apostles destroyed temples by the hundreds, shattered or burned idols by the thousands, and any historical paintings or writings that represented, or seemed to represent, idolatry were annihilated; men so ardent, in the circumstances, could not have done otherwise. The flames consumed precious historical data on the life and thought of the aboriginal families. And the loss is not offset by what little the friars finally saved of these priceless documents, or by their investigations, or by the records they had the Indians make or made themselves. It is offset, however, by the sweeping initiation of the Indian race into Christianity, by the abolition of bloody superstitions, by having put this race firmly on the road that should lead them to solidarity with the civilized world. Just as history absolves the cruelty inflicted on the

[2] This is an error: they were twelve in all, counting Fray Martín de Valencia. The mission arrived in the City of Mexico June 17 or 18, 1525. For an excellent comprehensive view of the evangelizing work of the three orders, see Robert Richard, *La "conquête spirituelle" de Mexique* (Paris: Institut d'Ethnologie, 1933). English translation: *The Spiritual Conquest of Mexico*, trans. Leslie Byrd Simpson (Berkeley: University of California Press, 1966).

Aztecs by the Conquest, it also absolves the destruction of the Indian documents. For those men were apostles, not archeologists; they did what they felt was necessary; their loftiness of aim surpassed the value of any monuments, no matter how precious. The loss was irreparable, the gain immense.

In order to preserve the Indians, it was imperative to prove that they could become Christians; they had to be converted. But were they then Christians? They were indeed, from the conquistador's point of view, and that fact made his iron hand, always ready to chastise, hesitate and falter. The conquistador generally confused religion with cult, with ritual, with the veneration and protection of the saints, with a fetishism based on material images. His was a semi-idolatrous religion. The Indians never became Christians in the sense that Francis of Assisi was Christian because their psychological pattern did not permit them to master the regions of pure metaphysics—neither before nor after they had been educated in schools or universities, neither before nor after they had become mixed with the Spanish race, which, when it came to the creation of a transcendental philosophy, was equally inept. The Spanish universities produced some marvelous dialecticians. But did they produce even one philosopher, one man capable of encompassing existence with a single thought and explaining it with another, while demonstrating an irrefragable bond of dialectic unity between the two? The names of two or three individuals might be mentioned, but their importance as philosophers will always be debatable. No, the Christianity that was preached to the Indians was a plain tangible thing, and rightly so. Its basic tenets were: dependence on a Supreme Judge and Lord; a soul that survives the body and answers for its deeds before that Judge; rewards and punishments, these last being particularly fearful, as is suitable for races only recently delivered from the ethnic matrix, for races in their infancy; absolute equality before that Judge with their conquerors, their masters; reform of their customs, aiming especially at the eradication of polygamy, at the moral emancipation of women, and at the abhorrence of idols and bloody rituals. And because the Supreme Judge was very remote and very severe, consolation and refuge had to be found in the mediators, the advocates, in the Virgin Mary and the saints, who must be appealed to constantly so that they would plead the sinner's case before God. All the gifts, the offerings, the supplications were for them, and all the affection. The Indian's feeling toward God was tremendous fear; his love was all for Mary. The whole theology of the Indian race is summed up in the Indian woman who kneels before the altar of Mary of Guadalupe, her mother, an Indian like herself, and confides her troubles and hopes in a dialogue that, whether in Nahuatl or Otomi, has for its eternal response the sweet compassion in the Virgin's eyes. And because the friars were the ones who brought the power of the advocates and saints to this land, it was to them that the offerings and hearts of the people were given. Thus, the religious orders came to act as fathers for the entire family of the conquered. The Indian race repaid the Church for the immense boon received from it—for they knew and believed it had saved their lives—by delivering themselves totally into its hands. And because the cult of the saints could easily be fitted in with the rites of their idolatry, they merely transferred the rites to the cult—not all, but some of them—under the paternal eye of the friars, who, unable to change their mentality or tradition, substituted images for idols (they are homonymous) and built sanctuaries on the spots where the bloodthirsty gods had been placated. And little by little the Indians stuffed the holy grail of Christianity full of all the superstitions that they possessed already, plus the new ones that they learned, an admixture as sacrilegious as it was inevitable. The Indians, therefore, in spite of being Christians, have never ceased to be worshippers of idols, and their idolatry has deeply tainted the religion of Creoles and mestizos. What the great Christian missionaries accomplished in New Spain was the rescue of the conquered family, threatened with extermination, the suppression of bloody rites, and the kindling of hope in the hearts of serfs. This is not all that they accomplished, but it sufficed for the life of three centuries.

What remains for us to accomplish today is entirely a task of emancipation: the riddance of superstitions. This task (which is the duty of the Church also) is the responsibility of science, of the schools, of the teacher. If only our schoolmasters could be missionaries, just as the missionaries were schoolmasters!

Pedro de Gante and Martín de Valencia may be taken as examples of that era of fervor and boundless self-abnegation. Despite Gante's ignorance of the language, he taught the Indians, with incredible patience, everything he could, how to read, write, pray, sing. And he taught them to play certain musical instruments, probably in order to deliver his pupils from the dreadful *teponaxtle* (a kind of drum) and *chirimia* (the Indian flageolet), which must have contributed mightily to the chronic mood of ferocity that kept them always eager for their interminable wars. Martín de Valencia, the custodian, walked barefoot from coast to coast, preaching tirelessly through his interpreter, for he was never able to learn any of the native languages, but preaching, above all, with the sublime eloquence of his acts, with humility, with affection, with poverty and tears.

But along with these friars, or a little later, there appeared others who systematized, so to speak, the Christian apostolate and who had a clear understanding of their mission, not only as evangelists, but as redeemers of the Indian. There were many of them; they were legion; they preached not only in Mexico but also in Spain, not only to the Indians but to the conquistadors, not only to the despots of New Spain but to the monarchs of the Court. Among this admirable group four bishops stand out, four men who, with their faith and charity, put the final seals on the titles that gave the Church its unlimited power over the conquered people. They were Las Casas, Zumárraga, Fuenleal, and Quiroga. The first, Bartolomé de las Casas, is a giant figure in a century when all humanity seems to have grown a span. He was a man of one idea, and it was this: "The Indians have a right to be Christian, and consequently a right to be free. The Conquest, therefore, is the continuing violation of a right. It is the duty of a good Christian to undo the deeds of iniquity." On his arrival in the Antilles in the dawn of the sixteenth century, he had achieved an understanding of his calling as priest and at the same time of his calling as apostle. He had stood up for the Indians' right to liberty before the primates of the Spanish Church, before the Council of Indies, before the monarch, with such persistence, with such fervor and such utterly frank speech, that even today his bold humanitarianism astounds us. The disappearance of the conquered race in the West Indies, thanks to maltreatment by the conquistadors, had left indelible marks on his soul; he had been an eye-witness to this catastrophe. Las Casas never abandoned his task, never faltered in his blessed labor of charity. In his bishopric of Chiapas he converted and protected the Indians. At the Court he obtained the promulgation of the famous Nuevas Leyes (the "New Laws" of 1542), which at one stroke put bounds to the supposed "rights" of the conquistadors, changing them into plain duties. In the City of Mexico, where he transmitted his burning zeal to others, he inspired the declaration that the Conquest had been condoned by the Church solely to make Christians and not to make vassals or serfs or slaves. He was dauntless in his efforts, whether binding the monarch to entrust the acquisition of new lands to the evangelizing of the missionaries, persuading Viceroy Mendoza to organize formal efforts at peaceful conquest through the friars, or writing his vehement pamphlets and his invaluable history of the discoveries and conquests. The hatred of the conquistadors and even of certain friars (Motolinia)[3] pursued him always and acted as a stimulant. He was a great Christian, and we who descend from Indians and conquistadors have proved ourselves closer kin to the latter by denying monuments or homage to the Spanish Dominican. He exaggerated, no doubt, the native goodness of the Indians and the wickedness of their exploiters, as other documents attest. But men of this kind, who exaggerate and distort in good faith their picture of evil, are needed in times of crisis; thus the remedy, even if inadequate, is sooner forthcoming.

Juan de Zumárraga, the first bishop of Mexico, named protector of Indians, as Las Casas had been, was led by religious zeal, like fanatics of his age and of all ages, to attain his ends by inhumane means (destruction of idols and perhaps documents and the burning of a refractory Indian at the stake[4]); he nevertheless deserves a preeminent place among the defenders of the conquered race, among the peacemakers. His conduct was heroic when, meeting head-on the tyranny of the first Audiencia, a tribunal of monsters, he prevented them from carrying out a program of unbridled abuse of the Indians, a program

[3] Motolinia's "Letter to the Emperor," signed at Tlaxcala, January 2, 1555. See Toribio de Benavente (Motolinia), *History of the Indians of New Spain*, trans. Francis Borgia Steck (Washington: Academy of American Franciscan Studies, 1951).

[4] The reference is to Don Carlos Mendoza Ometochzin, cacique of Texcoco.

seemingly aimed at their extermination. The Bishop was proclaimed sole judge over the Indians by virtue of his office as protector, and this was the beginning of the struggle, which attained terrible proportions, between the civil and the ecclesiastical power. The Church defended justice and human rights, and history takes its side, usurpations and all. For history, even if it runs the risk of compromising its ideal role as scientific examiner and impartial coordinator of facts, cannot always avoid moral judgments. Zumárraga, when the tyranny was ended, devoted his energies wholly to uplifting the Indian soul. His idea was this: the proof that the Indian is a perfectly rational being is that he can mount the heights of pure reason. And he founded the college of Tlatelolco, a veritable normal school, where future professors and evangelists were trained and where theological and philosophical points were argued so brilliantly, the enemies of education for Indians were frightened as though by the Devil. He founded also a college for the instruction of Indian girls, which was not as successful. All these works were apostolic and wise: their purpose was to enlist the Indians in the service of the Church, for the conquest of souls, just as Cortés had enlisted them for the conquest of empires.

Sebastián Ramírez de Fuenleal, president of the second Audiencia [which began to govern in 1531], was the first officer since Cortés to place the whole authority of the government behind the promotion of the Indians' welfare and redemption, and in this he went farther than Cortés. He inaugurated the almost uninterrupted era of peace in which the Mexican nationality gradually took form.

Vasco de Quiroga was the chief companion and collaborator of Bishop Fuenleal. We have seen how he pacified the Tarascans with the strength of his goodness and mercy and how he organized the industry and resources of Michoacán, which later became his bishopric, with a curious distribution of labor (a different occupation for each town). There, and earlier in the City of Mexico, this holy man founded colleges and hospitals. The hospitals were ingenious experiments in Christian communism: episcopal trades schools, as we said before, built and governed for the purpose of alleviating the Indians' poverty. "Poverty," in the words of Quiroga himself, "such as is scarcely ever seen or heard of elsewhere, is the lot of the poor miserable orphan Indians, and is so dreadful they sell themselves, or let themselves be sold, and the orphans and youngsters are snatched away by adults and sold, and others wander about the marketplaces, watching for a chance to eat the leavings of pigs." In these establishments, the Indians' traditions of a communal life and a collective personality were combined, and civil life and cooperative work were fully entered on. Communism, as we well know, far from being the shape of the societies of the future, belongs to those of the past.

Such were the remarkable men who guided and directed the great work of pacification. They put limits on the power of rulers to do harm and reins on the rapacity of the lords created by the Conquest; they did their best to civilize and elevate the conquistadors. Civilization and peace were synonomous.

The work of the peacemakers, admirably seconded by the religious orders, began to deteriorate when the apostles themselves died. After the pioneers came the organizers, and after them the exploiters. So long as the friar's zeal was stimulated and his spirit of self-sacrifice stirred by the perils attending on the conversion of the wild tribes that surrounded the conquered territory like a belt of shifting sand, he turned missionary, and the halo of apostles and martyrs shone about his head. The generation of the Conquest, for the most part, had been converted en masse through the submission of its princes and caciques, rather than by evangelization: the whole Aztec empire, it has been said, was baptized along with the Emperor Cuauhtemoc. But after this generation came one, in mid-century, of Christian birth. Then the friars had only routine duties to perform, and their exploiting hands discarded many of the noble ideas put into practice by the Quirogas and the Zumárragas. The long moral slumber of the great Indian family began. It has stayed in one place, at the foot of the altar, and even in our day many of the peoples are there yet, with the same customs and the same superstitions. The locomotive will have to whistle in their ears for quite some time, the schools will have to breathe the truth into their souls for two or three generations, before they move.

The friars, after royal decrees had put the conquered race into their hands, quarreled among themselves for dominion over it: the Franciscan wrangled with the Dominican, who, arriving later, was in a hurry to catch up with his predecessors.[5] The Franciscans were always indignant at abuses on the part of authority; the Dominicans usually took authority's side. The former were liberal, as we would say now; the latter, in spite of the immense services they rendered the Indians at Court, were conservative. Then came the struggle between the friars and bishops who wanted to remove the religious of the orders from the parishes and replace them with priests. This seemed to the friars an usurpation: they had sowed and watered; now others came to reap. The entire country, meanwhile, was being dotted with churches, rarely artistic[6] but nearly always massive and costly. Costly? But they cost the friars nothing. The Indian, as pupil and beloved son of the friar, received from his fathers (the *padrecitos,* "little fathers," as he still calls the priests) the harsh punishment that fathers used with their sons in those times—frequent whippings. Moreover, he gradually acquired the habit of docile obedience that had been his attitude toward his Indian caciques and priests. This obedience made him in fact a serf, and he was employed as a serf in the tremendous task of building churches and convents, receiving neither salary nor maintenance. Archbishop Montúfar,[7] an intelligent and dispassionate man, pronounced judgment against the friars on this point, declaring that an intolerable burden had been saddled on the Indian with this forced labor and with the terribly paternal abuse inflicted by those who compelled their protégés to feed and house them.

Gradually, not without hitches, the Church brought normal order and regularity to its domination of society. Franciscans and Dominicans became adjusted to the routine enjoyment of their privileged situation, of their blessed comfort, in the era of peace resulting from the total conformity of the conquered race and of the new race that it was giving birth to. The secular clergy, educated in the universities, in the seminaries, had come to share a part of the friars' power toward the end of

[5] The Dominican mission arrived in the City of Mexico about July 2, 1526. The Augustinians did not arrive until May 22, 1533. The author, not without injustice, passes them over.

[6] In our day, to the contrary, the colonial religious monuments are the nation's most highly prized artistic treasures.

[7] Dr. Fr. Alonso de Montúfar, O. P., became archbishop of Mexico September 4, 1551, died March 7, 1572.

the century. The early wrangles as to the validity of the baptisms performed by the first missionaries by virtue of the apostolic faculty granted them by the Pope, baptisms consisting of scarcely more ceremony than aspersion and a brief formula, had now become only a memory. Matrimony, too, had ceased to be a subject for dispute, in spite of the controversy over it in the early years. All the caciques had lived in polygamy, their vassals giving them their daughters "as fruit," says a chronicler, in order that they might serve as wives and servants; therefore it had been very difficult to decide which woman should be elevated to the rank of Christian spouse. This difficulty came to an end with the bull of Paul III and especially with the new generation that succeeded that of the Conquest.[8]

The Mexican Church met together in convocations, the first being held under Cortés' auspices when New Spain was under his government and the most important being the councils[9] called by the second and third archbishops, which organized canonically the tutelage of the Indian family, who were condemned to remain perpetually in the status of minors.

By the time the Inquisition was started in Mexico—a tribunal that here even more than in Spain, perhaps, was the secret and fearful court of the ecclesiastical government, with its heresy trials, its tortures, and its awesomely solemn autos-de-fé—there was no longer any reason for discord between the Church and the native aristocracy. Only in the zone which had not yet entirely submitted to Spain did the rule of monogamy meet with resistance, even with fierce rebellion. The second and third generations after the Conquest adjusted their ancient customs to religious precepts as best they could.

By the middle of the sixteenth century, the Church was a tree that covered the entire country with its shade; within that shade the society of New Spain clung to the tree and grew.

Philip II was determined to found the Inquisition on a full scale in

[8] This problem produced an abundant polemic literature. The most famed treatise on the subject is *Speculum Conjugiorum,* by Fray Alonso de la Veracruz (Mexico City: Joannis Pauli Brissensis, 1556).

[9] First Council, 1555; Second, 1565; both were convoked and presided over by Archbishop Montúfar. The Third Council, 1584, was convoked and presided over by Don Pedro Moya de Contreras, third archbishop of Mexico.

his New Spain. It was to be an indispensable part of his political and religious scheme: the New World must live in isolation, and the object of the Inquisition was to maintain this policy at all costs. It was to have the same function in the intellectual and religious sphere that modern boards of health have in the field of hygiene: ideas were the microbes, the deadly germs to be exterminated. Let us try to conceive of a set of rulers who look upon intellectual epidemics as infinitely more to be feared than physical plagues—which was actually the case—and then we can understand the Inquisition. But not absolve it; the author of the Sermon on the Mount would never have absolved it. Here, as in Spain, the Inquisition staged grandiose autos-de-fé,[10] witnessed with fear or enthusiasm by rulers and serfs. Many were tortured; much property was confiscated; some were sent to the stake. Only the Indians, thanks to their status as minors, were beyond the reach of the dreaded tribunal.

Not until the last quarter of the century did the fathers of the Company of Jesus, long awaited in the colony, arrive in Mexico, having been sent, on the petition of a rich colonist, by Philip II, pursuant to an agreement with St. Francis of Borja, general of the Order.[11] They got their house and church at once; a cacique furnished three thousand Indians to do the work. The admirable group of pedagogues that came thus tardily to New Spain was destined to become quickly as rich as the other religious orders, to share with the others in their dominion over the Indians, and to enjoy almost exclusive control over the educated class of New Spain. This control was to have consequences that not even the Jesuits themselves could foresee.

[10] The first auto-de-fé was in 1574; the tenth and most famous took place on the Zócalo in the City of Mexico December 8, 1596. The last, not long before Hidalgo's cry of Independence, was held on December 4, 1803.

[11] The Company arrived at San Juan de Ulúa September 9, 1572.

CHAPTER THREE

SOCIAL ORGANIZATION

The Indians. The Creoles. The Spaniards. The Mexicans.

THE CONQUISTADORS, before the Spanish king's government could be organized in his recently acquired American dominions, had become the owners of the Indians. But in order to exploit their ownership they maintained intact the system that had existed prior to the Conquest: the native masses were distributed, under the rule of the emperor, among the grand lords and feudal barons, who, like their counterparts in the Indies, were called caciques by the Spaniards. Thus, Cuauhtemoc became the vicar of Hernán Cortés. The tyranny of the caciques was immutable, deeply rooted in tradition and custom. Women, property, everything else was theirs to dispose of, and they disposed of the life and liberty of their subjects as they saw fit. The necessity for solidarity and mutual protection—that is, for making war—modified this tyranny in the days before the Conquest. But in the aftermath, as the Spaniards gradually imposed peace, there remained only the brutal exploitation of the native masses by their lords, who earlier had often hurled them against the Spaniards in rebellion. Now cacique and Spaniard became partners in a pitiless despotism; one of the most profitable businesses of those days was the sale, contracted between the two, of Indians as slaves for the mines.

Cortés wanted to divide all the land and people of the Aztec empire among his fellow soldiers, according to the system he had seen put into effect in the Antilles. Gold and silver, supreme object of the conquistadors' greed, turned out to be scarce; the mines were just being discovered and could be made productive only by expending thousands of human lives in their tunnels. The real treasure was the Indian. So Cortés distributed Indians. The distributions or "deposits," as the Conquistador called them, did not make the Indian serfs or slaves of the person into whose charge they were "commended," who was thereupon known as the encomendero. They were free and paid their customary tribute to the cacique, who turned it over to the encomendero in a sum previously agreed upon (the maximum was two thousand pesos annually), the remainder going to the royal office. The encomendero's obligation was to see that the "commended ones" were converted and received religious instruction. The system of distribution was the only means of holding and working the land, as Cortés declared, and he was right. The friars would have accomplished nothing of any permanence in American regions if the sword had not carved a path for them. And the Conquest would have aborted if the conquistadors, who had no chance of getting pensions from the Spanish king, had been forced to set out again in search of new conquests and new adventures and new spoils or if they had remained in the country, in a state of revolt, exploiting the Indians without hindrance and engaging in a duel to the death with them. Cortés was right: the system of distribution was the only way to hold the land.

Opposed to the system, however, were two powerful interests: one religious and one political. The Church was concerned because of the eloquent and terrible example of the Antilles. There the system of distribution inaugurated by Columbus had effectively brought about the annihilation of the inhabitants: the brutal clash of an embryonic civilization of the stone age with one of the age of steel, the terrific abuse of the Indians' limited strength, had made an end of them. Was the same thing about to happen in New Spain? It could not happen because here were large sedentary masses with a higher culture. This was no embryonic society, but a perfectly organized hierarchy; while the rites were atrocious, the customs of the people were good: they were social, that is to say, moral. Therefore the people of Mexico did not become extinct. If they had been nomads, like those the English colonists found on the shores of the northern Atlantic, they would have been wiped out. But maltreatment can bring about much the same result, and the encomenderos, finding the Indian passive in character, used to slavery, and trained to do the work reserved for beasts of burden in Spain, took shocking advantage of them. This to the religious was sacrilege: the Pope's object in permitting the Catholic kings to proceed with the Conquest was the conversion of the Indians, but if the Indians were going to vanish, how could they be converted? Millions of souls would be lost to the Faith. The duty of the Church, in which the monarchs were bound to concur, was to save the race in order to save souls; this duty, and the great compassion of the apostles, determined its conduct.

The political interest—that is, the king's—was affected thus: hereditary ownership of the land and of its population, granted to the conquistador, amounted to a dismemberment, a diminution of the royal sovereignty and of the political law; it was feudalism. Never could the Castilian kings consent to this, since they had destroyed the semifeudalism of the nobility and towns of Spain. Therefore they purposed to do away with the encomienda first and then with the right to inherit the encomienda.

Besides the distributed Indians, who were ostensibly free—they were hardly so, in reality, despite the good intentions of the monarchs—there were personal servants, who could be sold by their owner and were actually serfs. And there were slaves, despite the fact that the great Queen Isabella, when Christian civilization dawned over the Americas, expressly forbade any enslavement of Indians.

Yes, the kings forbade slavery and forbade the system of distribution. But then they began to compromise and permitted the enslavement of prisoners of war, of rebels, of those sold by their fathers or by caciques. The slaves were sent to the mines, which were just beginning to be discovered, and there they died by the thousands, with the horrible brand on their cheek. Because of the clamor raised by the missionaries, a clamor heard the world over, conditions were improved through reiterated royal decrees and through the introduction of Negroes, who had to be isolated from the Indians, however, for they treated them worse than the Spaniards did. Then came the beasts of burden, above all the redeeming ass, to which the Indian gives the same harsh treatment that he himself has received. The useful animals of Europe that became acclimated (the horse, the ass, the ox, the sheep, the dog, the pig) and the cultivated plants such as sugar cane and the many fruits that soon flourished here (the apple, the peach, the orange—introduced by the admirable chronicler Bernal Díaz) changed the face of the countryside. Even if we consider this aspect alone, the contact with European civilization brought about a thorough transformation, a step forward in evolution, which definitely set the Americas on a new road; it meant progress, which is a phase of evolution.

Cortés, disobeying the royal orders, persisted in distributing Indians, to others as well as to himself. The King compromised with him, stipulating that the encomiendas were to be temporary and that the Indians were to be treated well. Then the ceaseless agitation of the apostles, the attitude of the Spanish Church, the pronouncements of the Pope, and the burning indignation of Las Casas produced the famous New Laws (*Nuevas Leyes*) as soon as the viceregal government was established. These laws again forbade ownership of encomiendas by civil or ecclesiastical officers, restricted them in other ways, and prohibited their conveyance or renewal. Slavery was almost completely suppressed. Again the King had to compromise. The uprising in Peru had taught a terrible lesson; the regime could not be abolished; the only solution was to modify it, and friars and viceroys directed their energies to this end.

New orders were issued with the object of forcing the Indians who had fled or otherwise put themselves beyond the reach of the government to gather in towns, in congregations, to settle down, in short, and become civilized. These decrees were scarcely effective and gave rise to many grave abuses. The measures adopted on advice of the religious orders, who regarded the Indians as their property, had the effect of isolating them from the Spaniards, to the extent of avoiding all contact between the races, even between encomenderos and their charges. But the results were disastrous. The Indians could become fully assimilated with the new culture only by undergoing change themselves—that is, by mingling their blood with that of the bringers of new thought—and the system of isolation put up barriers to thwart this intermingling.[1]

The ardor of the apostles soon gave way to the monotonous routine of the friars of the second and third generation after the Conquest. In peace and harmony with the caciques, the friars exploited the Indian. The caciques were still the masters of the rural population, though tribute and encomienda were things of the past. Superstition among the Indians had followed a new tangent, but remained essentially the same, sapping their minds. Those individuals or groups who entered the schools and universities founded by the Spaniards and absorbed the highest culture of their time inevitably became merged with the conquerors and their descendants. The great masses remained the slaves of superstitution and of drunkenness, which increased notably among the conquered after the Conquest. While lending this people, whose qualities of character predispose them to moral grandeur, a certain animal gayety that triumphs over circumstances, the addiction to alcohol has at the same time kept them in a spiritual atrophy that, fortunately, is not beyond remedy.

The contact with the conquistadors, the harshness of the encomenderos, and terrible epidemics which seemed to single out the native population reduced it during the sixteenth century, by several millions.

The Creoles—that is, the Spaniards born in America—quickly came to form a special element in the new society: from them the Mexican element sprang. But at first they were restive, unruly, fond of novelty, and they ruthlessly exploited the Indian. They became involved in a conspiracy—the so-called "plot of the sons of Cortés"—a stupidly bungled attempt to throw off the Spanish monarchs, who had ignored the Creoles' right to dominion over the peoples subjugated by their fathers. After this they gradually slumped into idleness, vices (gambling and luxury), and passive conformity to the status quo. Nonetheless, the Creole never gave up his conviction that the American countries belonged by right of conquest (which was considered superior, in those days, to any other right) to but one class of Spaniard, to the Creole. Like his father, the conquistador, the Creole was loyal to his

[1] A royal decree dated August 23, 1538, in Valladolid, required Indians to live in isolation from Europeans.

king and therefore obeyed him, loyal also to the king's representative, the viceroy, whom he respected and revered. But, as an aristocrat, a noble: with famous ancestors and a family tree, he despised the recently arrived Spaniard either as an upstart usurping positions that rightfully should belong to the Creole according to early decrees of the kings or as a churl without breeding, that is, without the good manners, the suave amiability of the subject race, the honied courtesy in social intercourse which the Indian's speech and immutable poise had taught the Creole—manners influenced also, perhaps, by the climate, so soft, warm, and caressing. The Spaniard also lacked the education that the Creole, if lawyer or priest, had acquired in the colleges, which the trader or miner or workman coming from Spain hardly ever took the trouble to attend.

The newcomer eventually became a Creole through his descendants —and often became a noble by purchasing his title from the needy Spanish treasury. He acquired the Creole's same secret resentments, the same vices, the same attachment to the land (considered just as Spanish as Old Spain). The Spaniard who came for business reasons only and then departed, sinking no roots, left nothing behind but contempt and deep hostility. Often he strove to get rich, with success. A different kind of Spaniard was the ecclesiastic; in many cases a man of lofty character, of large theological learning, he made friends with the Creole and cultivated in him feelings of social responsibility, of friendliness toward the Church, which received from him countless gifts—for schools, for the university, for charitable works, for donations to the king.

One of the first viceroys ordered that the illegitimate sons of Spanish-Indian parentage be gathered up and given proper education. This was the first attempt to bring together the mestizos, the new family born of the two races, the real Mexicans. The Marqués de Mancera (twenty-fifth viceroy),[2] in the following century, describes them as already constituting a sizeable part of the population and eulogizes them. They increased but slowly, it appears, because of the systematic isolation of the two races. Here we have the Mexican nationality, which would form a nation, growing out of the nucleus of mestizos, as the viceroys called them—of Mexicans, as we prefer to call them.

[2] Antonio Sebastián de Toledo, Marqués de Mancera, took office in 1664.

CHAPTER FOUR

POLITICAL ORGANIZATION

The government of Cortés and of his lieutenants. The first Audiencia. The second Audiencia.

NEW SPAIN was born independent. Cortés exercised nearly absolute power, limited only by his circumstances and his self-interest, his need to establish regular and permanent contact with the motherland. When this contact had been established, and the King had sanctioned his work and legalized his titles, he went on arrogating to himself whatever powers happened to suit his purposes; he was, in truth, supreme lord of the land. The first legislative orders, as we might call them, that reached him from Castile (those forbidding the distribution of Indians) were for him a dead letter; he did not obey them. Unfortunately, his spirit of adventure traversed and shattered all his political plans; he had remarkable aptitude for government, but could not leave off being a conquistador. Thus, he had only just overcome, but had not yet pacified, the bellicose empire of the Aztecs; he had barely laid out and sketchily organized the nucleus (Tenochtitlan) from which his program of pacification and administration was to branch—and Cortés did have practical ideas, as his letters show—when he set out on his expedition to the shores of the Caribbean Sea, in search of new empires of fabulous wealth.

He left his lieutenants in the City of Mexico: two of the four royal officers that the Court had sent and a friend of his, a lawyer, made up the governing triumvirate, which was supposed to work in perfect harmony with one Rodrigo de Paz, attorney for Cortés' interests. At the first report of disturbances, Cortés sent back the two royal officers who had left with him, giving them full powers to meet any emergency. This brutal and greedy pair decided to make themselves masters of the field; they were the tax collector, Gonzalo de Salazar, and the inspector of taxes, Chirinos. The two who had remained in the City of Mexico were the treasurer Alonso de Estrada, bastard, it was said, of Ferdinand the Catholic, and the accountant Rodrigo de Albornoz.

The arrival of Salazar and his companion set off a train of turbulence in the city—barely laid out, barely swept of debris, its Indian barrios or sectors only just organized (with tiny churches and rude unfinished houses for the *ayuntamiento,* or town council, for the friars of the Custodia of Fray Martín de Valencia, for Cortés' servants, who occupied the best one)—a turbulence that came near totally wrecking the work of consolidating the Conquest.

Each of the parties struggling for power attempted to make the *ayuntamiento* the instrument of lawless ambitions; each claimed the authority of Cortés as the excuse for crimes and malfeasance. But after he disappeared in the direction of Honduras, news of his death was bruited about, his obsequies were solemnly performed, the wives of the soldiers who had left with him were permitted to marry again. And because Cortés' attorney, Rodrigo de Paz, refused to allow Salazar and Chirinos (who, shunting the others aside, set up a ruthless dictatorship) to seize the Conquistador's property, which they hotly coveted, believing it to be fabulous, they attacked him in Cortés' own house, taking it by assault, and imprisoned him. Even as Cortés had treated Cuauhtemoc, so did these Spaniards treat the representative of Cortés, torturing him to make him reveal the whereabouts of secret treasures. They forced him to climb, mutilated and bleeding, the steps to the scaffold.

With Paz out of the way, the tax collector and his accomplice began to redistribute the Indians that Cortés had already distributed. They had no rule of conduct but spoliation and despotism, and all the energy of the angelic Franciscan custodian and his friars was needed to prevent the frightful extermination of the Indians or a general uprising.

Then news came of Cortés; an envoy arrived from him. His friends, conspiring under the roof of the Franciscan convent, stirred the town to revolt, overthrew the tyrants, and displayed them in cages on the Zócalo. The royal officers who had been dispossessed by Salazar recovered their authority, and the plots, the executions, the violence went on and on until Cortés returned to a tumultuous ovation, being hailed as a savior.

The Court, astounded at the reports from the new colony, called Cortés to Spain and turned the government over to a tribunal similar to the one which had governed Hispaniola under the regency of Bishop Fuenleal. It was the logical thing to do. But there were so many conflicts to settle, such as those arising over the distribution of Indians and of encomiendas, so many rights to define, so urgent a need to render justice to the conquered—for the kings persisted in considering them as vassals and not as serfs—that only a panel of upright judges, vested with full authority to wield public power, could have carried out that program.

Unfortunately, men of egregious violence and rapacity were appointed to the tribunal, which was presided over by the savage Nuño de Guzmán and counseled by the infamous Salazar and Chirinos; the result was an appalling series of wrongs and persecutions. As Martín de Valencia had done before, Bishop Zumárraga now interposed himself between the despots and their victims, not with patience and humility, but zealously laying about with the Church's weapons—excommunion and the interdict; he even exhorted the people to revolt. For the cup of iniquity had flowed over. By good fortune, Cortés returned from Spain heaped with honors and determined to place his towering prestige wholly at the service of the second tribunal, sent out from Spain under the presidency of the renowned Fuenleal; and the newly-titled Marqués del Valle de Oaxaca did just that. The government of the second Audiencia moderated the fervor of the friars, curbed Cortés' abuse of his powers, and repaired the damage inflicted during the recent dark years on the oppressed Indians, in whose behalf the Fuenleals, the Quirogas, the Zumárragas, each with bowed head, circled by a saintly nimbus, implored compassion.

The first viceroy arrived in 1535. In Spain the Council of Indies, which was functioning by then,[1] had become convinced that, in order to enforce the judgments of the Audiencia and to modify both the rights that the conquistadors believed they held in the land they had won and the pretensions of the Church, which had arrogated to itself the exclusive guardianship over the Indian family, what was required was the presence in the colony of the monarch himself, incarnate in a viceroy; therefore the sound and admirable Don Antonio de Mendoza came to New Spain.

We have expatiated to the point of upsetting somewhat the planned proportions of this work in an effort to characterize the elements, one as important as another, which will go to make up the new organism; but we doubt if our analysis can be complete unless we show the part that each element played in history. We now recapitulate, in a few lines, much as one steps backward to get a better view of a picture that is rather diffuse and disharmonic in design.

The center is the group of conquistadors, formed by men of insuperable strength of character, who put their lasting seal on their accomplishment. They were conquerors and wished to be lords of a vast empire, to rule over a large family of peoples, to replace a culture inferior on many counts with a better one; thus, they forced the long slow road of Indian evolution to take a new way, they produced a revolution. But the result of this revolution was an overlordship, not a colony. The conquistadors disdained to exploit personally the wealth of the conquered country—it was not in their nature; they had not fought to that end; they were fighters, not exploiters. The exploitation had to be done through members of the conquered race itself.

With ostensibly different objectives, the conquistadors and the peacemakers, the redeemers, disputed the exploitation of the conquered. Compromise between these two elements resulted in the more or less legal and slowly ameliorated servitude of the Indian, his submission to the tutelage of the Church, supervised by the civil authority, and his conformity with his status as a minor, which alleviated his burdens but kept him bound forever to the status quo. The Indian family was the first property in America to be brought by the Church under mortmain.

[1] The Council of Indies was established in August of 1524. Its first orders were issued 1542–1543.

This condition, at first, was beneficial to the Indians, but it became, through the very fact of persisting, an evil aggravated with each new generation.

The population of Spaniards was concentrated in the City of Mexico, where it was constantly being renewed with bureaucratic personnel. Small groups, scattered along the southern shores of the Gulf, sought a place intermediate between the gold of their dreams and the sea—that is, between commerce and the mines, the two faces of their obsession to get rich off the land. There were no mines in those parts, only agricultural wealth, which they did not know how to exploit; they strewed its potential seeds (exotic plants and animals) carelessly on the soil. But the great commercial highway from the center to the Gulf, from Mexico City to Vera Cruz, was indeed populated fast, and so, above all, were the mining towns in the hinterland. These settlements of the ruling race produced, as they grew, Creoles and mestizos. Around these foci of exploitation, as around the cellular nuclei of organic protoplasm, a new world was taking shape. Its active life was ruled by the sword of the conqueror, soon rusty, but still feared; its moral life was dominated by the Cross on that sword.

CHAPTER FIVE

SOCIAL GROWTH (SIXTEENTH AND SEVENTEENTH CENTURIES)

Paternal despotism of the House of Austria. The organizers: Mendoza, the Velascos. Progress of conquest and pacification; compromises and solutions; political experiments; Audiencias and visitors. The work of conciliation in the seventeenth century: territorial expansion; foundings. The Marqués de Mancera; Fray Payo Enríquez. Church and State; conflicts. Social growth: public wealth; education. Toward a superior State.

THE VICEROY was the king. His business was to hold the land—that is, to conserve the king's dominion, New Spain, at all costs. The way to conserve it was to pacify it; hence the close collaboration with the Church. In view of the privileges granted by the Pope to the Spanish king in America, it could be said that the Church in America was under the Spanish king: this was called the Royal Patronate. But the ascendancy that the Church had acquired in Spanish America, because it consolidated, through conversions, the work of the Conquest, made it actually a partner in the government. The viceroy maintained the authority of the king by exercising it; hence he battled against those who tried to undermine the king's power over his vassals in an attempt to make personal slaves or tributaries of them. The king wanted free men in America who would pay tribute to him directly, but the House of Austria lived out its historic term in Spain without ever being able to achieve this design. The king, in truth—since the whole new kingdom should be considered as his encomienda, administered by the viceroy—was duty-bound to set the example of a good encomendero, such as the Council of Indies intended to create by law: a father who would look out for the conversion of the Indians, who would not force them to work without pay, who would respect their liberty and assist them in misfortune. This is how most of the viceroys in the sixteenth and seventeenth centuries understood their mission. All had good intentions, and many carried them out. Some, superior politicians with an admirable grasp of the needs of the society they ruled, found suitable ways to satisfy those needs.

The first viceroy, the two Velascos, and Don Martín Enríquez[1] were highly effective in their immense labor of definitively reorganizing this society, which had already been organized once, centuries before. The conquistadors or encomenderos had tried to disorganize it in order to make it feudal, to their advantage, while the Church at the same time was trying to reorganize it, not as a civil society but as a theocracy.

The task that confronted the viceroys was a staggering one; some could not cope with it, but tried to do their duty while feathering their nest. But there were others, to be sure, and we have named them, who won great personal prestige, owing to their thorough probity, their severity with dishonest Spaniards, their paternal attitude toward the conquered race, their dignified relations with the Church. In short, they were men of character, and this, in political life, amounts almost to genius. As good politicians, they proceeded by means of compromises,[2] which they put into effect by acts of authority.

Mendoza was invested with ecclesiastical authority also, for he had the power to punish bad priests. A good part of his labor, since the leading conquistadors still lived and all of them spent their time hatching new enterprises, consisted in supplanting erratic adventurers like Cortés and Alvarado with the royal authority which he represented, for he was determined to expand the king's dominions by normal and

[1] Antonio de Mendoza became viceroy in 1535; the first Luis de Velasco in 1550; Martín Enríquez de Almanza in 1568; the second Luis de Velasco in 1590 and again in 1607.

[2] This idea of politics as the art of compromise is a favorite one with Sierra.

direct action. To consummate the work of the Conquest and stretch the limits of the colony as far as possible in all directions, to bring the Southern Sea (the Pacific) under the viceroy's rule, to define the relations of the social classes in New Spain, to foment religious missions as nuclei for new province—this was the Viceroy's program; it was inherited by his successors.

His conquests in the west, which he directed in person, owed less to his arms than to the staff of friars that accompanied him. His explorations to the north in search of mythical kingdoms had for result, after a time, some puny settlements beyond the Rio Grande. In the Pacific, the acquisition of the Philippines was his achievement. In the country itself there was progress, thanks in part to the New Laws, which alleviated the Indian's lot to some extent. In short, the colony was well on the way to being organized by the end of the first viceroy's regime. The two Velascos and Enríquez, working in harmony with the Church, carried on the task. The plan to suppress the encomiendas was modified; no drastic measures were taken, but kings, viceroys, and friars managed to introduce more kindness and justice between encomenderos and their tributaries. It was time, however, that changed the nature of the encomiendas; even though they were generally renewed, they no longer entailed local political power but mere ownership of the land, to which, indeed, the Indian was as strictly bound—and is to this day, in many places—as the serf to the glebe. But slavery in the mines had to be done away with, above all. Mendoza tried to abolish it; the first Velasco did so, saying, "The freedom of the Indians is more important than all the mines in the world, and the royal rents are not of such a nature that would justify trampling on laws both human and divine." These words are worthy to be engraved on tablets of bronze at the foot of a statue.

Outstanding among the labors of the second viceroy are the founding of hospitals, the establishment of a university, which became the alma mater of Creole society and gave New Spain intellectual rank, tireless dedication to the improvement of the Indian's condition, and, finally, the subjection and pacification of the central zones of the plateau, an accomplishment whose steps were marked by the nuclei of future cities. Later viceroys carried his work on; in the transition from the sixteenth to the seventeenth century, the second Velasco made a signal contribution.

The City of Mexico, center of the viceroys' monumental labor of organization, attracted a good part of Spain's scant male population, which was steadily being further diminished by the Austrian dynasty's European wars. But the City was the center of everything. The capital was taking shape: in the shadow of grandiose edifices, religious for the most part, its blocks were aligned with regularity and with almost mathematical relation to the four cardinal points. [3] Ever so often the Lake of Texcoco, the collecting basin for the whole lake region of the Valley, would spread once again over the lands that Tenochtitlan and the City of Mexico had wrested from its waters, and the capital, notwithstanding the causeway dikes and canals, seemed on the verge of disappearing in a disaster. Velasco and nearly all the other viceroys of the first two centuries tried to save Cortés' daughter-city from shipwreck, moving it to higher levels or delivering it from a muddy death with the artificial and partial diversion of the Valley's waters; to this vexing problem the city fathers and the viceroys gave their best attention. And, as a result, a beginning was made on the plans and the long-drawn out excavation of the Huehuetoca drainage ditch, which cost so much gold and caused so many dramatic accidents.

This danger past, the viceroys returned to the struggle with the nomadic hordes of the central plateau, who were permanently pacified by the second Velasco; to the struggle with the privileged religious communities, which, as masters and fathers in Christ of the Indian family, defied all secular jurisdiction; to the struggle with the owners of "distributions" of Indians, which vacillating royal policy failed to regulate by any definite system of obligations and rights.

And this, the relations between conquerors and conquered, was the gravest matter the viceroys had to attend to. They intended that there should be no Indian slaves, only Negro slaves, that Indians should be freed from labor in the mines, that the freedom of the

[3] Cervantes de Salazar has left us a description of the early City of Mexico: *Life in the Imperial and Loyal City of Mexico in New Spain*, trans. Minnie Lee Barrett Sheperd (Austin: University of Texas Press, 1953).

distributed Indians should be maintained at all costs, that they should be paid a fair wage, that they should never, even with their own consent, be used as beasts of burden. In addition, the kings and viceroys insisted, with good reason but with disastrous results, that the Indians be forced to gather in congregations and in towns where they could be converted, supervised, and civilized and where it would be easy to collect their tribute. But this was impossible: they returned to their mountains, their homelands, their wild freedom or died of despondency or even committed suicide. It is a great pity that the effort failed. The towns that were founded for the purpose disappeared; a few, such as Irapuato and Silao, were resettled with Spaniards.

On top of these troubles, the Crown demanded ever larger tributes. The king needed money and more money in order to maintain his position in Europe, a position which was another colossal gamble. The mines gave him a portion, the Indians another portion, and even so there arrived in Spain only irregular remittances. For sending silver across the sea was another terrible gamble: pirates and hurricanes turned many a voyage into tragedy.

And then, attention had to be paid to the increasing demands of the sons of conquistadors, who were generally mestizos and who believed they had exclusive right to all colonial offices, especially those relating to Indians. The wise observations of the viceroys prompted the kings to decree that aptitude for the service should be the prime requisite for filling offices. By this decision social justice stood to gain, no doubt, but the conquistador's descendant, Creole or mestizo, felt he had been deprived of a right, and he always nursed a grudge.

The kings attached great importance to the Audiencias, even after the viceregency was established. They governed in the absence of a viceroy, ineptly as a rule. Thus, when the Audiencia of Mexico, on the death of the first Velasco [1564], took over the government and heard reports that the dissatisfaction of the conquistadors' sons had taken the form of defiance against the king's authority in New Spain and that the soul of this defiance was Hernán Cortés' own son, the Marqués Don Martín, natural leader of the Creole aristocracy, the reigning judges made so much out of what was probably a tissue of juvenile folly and worked so hard to make it appear a formidable plot for independence that they seemed lenient when they passed sentences of exile, death on the scaffold, irons, and torture as an example to terrify society and keep the country in subjection. But the Audiencia usually took the part of the encomenderos against the viceroys, which was natural, in view of their origin and interests. As Philip II required the viceroy to consult always with the Audiencia, it became aggressive and meddled in all the affairs of the new dominions. Nueva Galicia, which was nearly self-sufficient on account of its rich mines and large population, had its own Audiencia, which flaunted such notions of sovereignty and independence that it did not hesitate, on occasion, to oppose the viceroy head-on in defense of its privileges, even at the risk of civil war.

But the institution which, though modest enough originally, took on extraordinary importance in certain cases was the office of the visitor, who was a dictator in the whole strength of the word; viceroys and Audiencias bowed before him. He could punish or remove from office anyone from the viceroy on down, and he was empowered to assess the death penalty against those he adjudged guilty of failing in their duty. One visitor, Muñoz, [4] used these powers to bloody the capital of New Spain with torture and gallows, and, wishing to inspire for his master Philip II the same dreadful awe among the colonial Spaniards that the Duke of Alba was inspiring for him at the very moment in the Netherlands, he set up a reign of terror, with the object of stamping out the very last flicker of the spark of liberty which was alleged to have flared boldly through the plot conceived by the friends of Cortés' family. It took a fulminating order from the King to tear this tyrant from his prey. And it is well to reflect that, while the deeds of Muñoz were hideous, any emancipation of New Spain brought about by the encomenderos would have been worse, would have ended in disaster: either the enslavement and annihilation of the Indian or his return to empire. In either case the seed of Mexican nationality would have been crushed.

To be sure, not all the visitors were bad; there were some, like Pedro Moya de Contreras, whose severity was a force for good. This

[4] Alonso de Muñoz arrived in the City of Mexico in October, 1567.

priest, in the penultimate decade of the sixteenth century, held, one after another, the highest offices of New Spain. He was inquisitor general (and founder of the Holy Tribunal in Mexico), which means that the King placed the favorite instrument of royal politics in his hands, the one that ensured His Majesty's dominion over souls. Next he was archbishop, then visitor, then on the death of the Conde de la Coruña,[5] viceroy and captain general. Hard with those who committed abuses, severe with corrupt magistrates, terrible with royal officers (he had several hanged), he was kind and gentle with the Indians. His spirit moved the Third Council to interpose the menace of eternal damnation, a paralyzing threat in those days, between the Indian and his tenacious exploiters.

The machinery set in motion by Spanish rule to assimilate the sedentary peoples of America reached its highest peak of efficiency in the seventeenth century. But this was the very epoch in which Spain, through senseless waste of blood and wealth, ceased to be a power of the first rank—ceased to be a great naval power while continuing to be a great colonial power (a contradiction that eventually brought about the loss of its American empire). Since it never had been able to colonize thoroughly, owing to the scantiness of its own rural population, the result was a paralysis in the development of New Spain. Everything was consolidated, but then everything remained in a state of stagnant routine, in the status quo. The sixteenth century was a period of creation; the seventeenth, of conservation; the next, of disintegration. Beneath these surface phenomena, social growth made slow but continuous progress.

All the colonial boundaries were vague at the beginning of the seventeenth century. Between the oceans on either side and the well-organized provinces there were peoples still hardly subdued, which the viceroys and Audiencias strove, with only middling success, to civilize. On the north the viceroys, at times urged on vehemently by the Crown, did their best to expand the Spanish domain. The numerous Chichimeca tribes, pushed beyond the tropic parallels, took refuge in the sierras which form the two divergent arms embracing the Mexican plateau. The conquered territory was fenced off with a chain

[5] Don Lorenzo de Mendoza, Conde de la Coruña, became viceroy in 1580.

of forts or presidios; some of these eventually became important towns. The subjection and pacification of the tribes was never thoroughly accomplished, and conflict would break out again and again. The missionaries, especially the Jesuits, were the martyrs and apostles of this gigantic effort to close the immense northern frontier of New Spain on a line that ran from California to Florida. They often made peace without the aid of arms; at other times they were the cause of uprisings, with their insistence that the Indians do with a single wife or with their unremitting war on witch doctors and sorcerers, who were the promoters of idol worship and heathen superstitions. These uprisings occurred not only in the north and west but also to the south of Oaxaca and of Yucatán; they were always bloody and always put down, but never permanently. New provinces, such as California, New Mexico, Texas, and Nayarit, were being organized in the subdued regions. Other provinces were established near the center, and many cities were founded. One of them, Córdoba, owed its founding to the need to control the bands of Negroes that had become numerous in the Hot Country and would rise in arms to shake off the bonds of slavery. Even the capital was horrified by an attempted uprising which ended in massacre. But this belt of halfway conquered territories, frequently occupied, abandoned, and occupied again, maintained the security of Spanish rule within the huge area that it surrounded, like a bolster protecting the work of consolidation. The names or titles of various viceroys of the seventeenth century are preserved in towns of the present Mexican Republic: Guadalcázar, Córdoba, Cadereita, Salvatierra, Cerralvo, Monclova, and so on.

In the second half of the century two notable viceroys ruled New Spain: the Marqués de Mancera and Archbishop Enríquez de Rivera. [6] The colony was in a bad way when the Marqués took over the government; abuses seemed ineradicable, the prestige of authority languished, the churlish disdain of the Creoles for the native Spaniards increased, external dangers (pirates and corsairs) paralyzed commerce and communication with the motherland. The Court demanded more and

[6] Don Antonio Sebastían de Toledo, Marqués de Mancera, became viceroy in 1664. Don Fray Payo Enríquez de Rivera, archbishop of Mexico, became viceroy in 1673.

more pecuniary aid, which was spent in hopeless wars and senseless extravagance. This was the time when, with the military power of Spain nearly annihilated by the nascent European hegemony of Louis XIV and its maritime power utterly annihilated, a child, weak in body and mind, ascended the throne, a symbol of the hopeless decadence of the House of Austria. And the child's tutor, Mariana of Austria, was dominated first by the astute Jesuit Nithard and then by the raffish Andalusian Valenzuela, who died under proscription in Mexico, and her rights and wishes were continually trampled by the brutal and ambitious bastard of Philip IV, Don Juan of Austria. Spain, in truth, seemed about to die.

Mancera, who began to govern in the last years of Philip IV, brought to every problem the unflagging intelligence that only a superior man is capable of: he sent pecuniary aid to Florida, supplied Cuba periodically with foodstuffs, promoted new explorations in California, saw to it that the Philippines had good government, organized a fleet that could give assistance to the Spanish squadrons on their arrival and departure, and sent military aid to the forces fighting pirates in the Antilles. He gathered large donations to send to the Court (he was the first donor) and, with the same object, collected a huge reserve. This could only be done by augmenting the tributes; to make them less onerous he eliminated abuses and tried to enforce in all their pristine vigor the orders proclaiming the absolute liberty of the Indians. He opposed the unlimited expansion of the Negro trade, odious source of income for Spain. He restrained the malfeasance of alcaldes and other officials in the mining regions, whose thievery had sapped this source of wealth. He repaired and fortified the two ports by which commerce across New Spain entered and left. He attended to works of public utility, such as the partial drainage of the Valley, which went forward with open sluices. He finished the interior of the cathedral in the City of Mexico and became protector of the University, of authors and letters (his wife was the close friend of Sor Juana Inés de la Cruz, the outstanding poet of colonial times, as Ruiz de Alarcón was the only great dramatist). Mancera had visited the courts of Europe as a diplomat, and his ambition was to prove to the civilized world that Spanish rule in Mexico was not, as it was said to be, a badge of shame for Spain, that the Indian population had not diminished in the seventeenth century, that the Creoles were profoundly attached to Spain (though not to the Spaniards, or Gachupines, as they now began to be called), and that the new people, the mestizos, were well fitted to form a social group destined to grow in importance day by day.

Fray Payo Enríquez de Rivera, with kin among the nobility, was archbishop and viceroy; he continued and perfected the work of the Marqués de Mancera. The business of pacifying the north grew more and more difficult; the indomitable tribes in those parts would combine to attack the Spanish settlement with a fury as great as the heroism displayed by the settlers (as in the defense of Santa Fe, in New Mexico, which was abandoned, and El Paso del Norte founded). Uprisings were constant here, as well as in Chihuahua and Sonora. It seemed as if Spanish domination in those regions would always be precarious. The main labor of pacification, in truth, was done by the Jesuits, who let neither distances nor martyrdom dismay them. The Archbishop-Vicerory, in the extensive area that lived in peace while surrounded by pirates and insurrection, showed amazing energy in rooting out the practice of graft among officials in charge of the Treasury and in purging the administration of justice; he protected the Indians and was zealous in works of charity and public welfare.

We have picked out these two viceroys for examples, not because they did anything extraordinary, but because they characterize so well the best effort of the Spain of those days to maintain supremacy in America, defending itself against external enemies, keeping internal order, and making itself beloved by subject peoples and the new society. The defects of a state of things that was undermined at the foundations could not be corrected, but they could be alleviated and modified by men like these.

The kings of Spain who had the gift of foresight, like Charles I and Philip II, realized what a tremendous part the Church would have to play in the acquisition of the Americas for the Crown of Castile, and they had secured the Pope's authorization to rule the discovered countries, in return for the obligation to convert the natives. And when the kings called first on the religious orders and later on the whole ecclesiastical body to collaborate in the mighty task, they were careful to reserve expressly to themselves the government of the Church in America (except, of course, in matters of dogma or higher discipline) by means of a series of concessions made to the monarchy by the Pope. These, constituting the Royal Patronate, were as follows. The Church relinquished tithes (ancient canonical tax) in exchange for certain pecuniary obligations of the State to the Church and was required to obtain civil permission for the creation of bishoprics and parishes, for the building of churches, monasteries, and hospitals, and for friars or the clergy to enter the colonies. The State was given the authority to appoint bishops, who would take office before the Pope confirmed their election (as in the case of Zumárraga[7]), to bound dioceses, and to nominate all ecclesiastical officers (from bishop to sacristan). The State could also reprimand and punish the servants of the Church and overrule ecclesiastical tribunals. Finally, the king's consent (*placet*) was required before the Pope's orders could be put into effect, and the State was given the authority to resolve quarrels within the Church. These concessions made the king head of the Church in the Indies; he was, in fact, a sort of vice-Pope.

But the Church, in the shadow of these rights, while recognizing them, had acquired immense power of its own. If the Church was governed by the king, the Indies were governed by the Church. Notwithstanding the complaints of town councils, viceroys, and bishops, the growth of its spiritual power had kept pace, on the whole, with the growth of its mundane power. Convents multiplied at an astounding rate, and the clergy increased steadily in number; thus, a good part of the population were unable to serve the colony's urgent need —matrimony, the proliferation of families. All the religious communities, all the churches grew richer without cease; the secret of the Church's dominance in the Catholic Europe of yesteryear is the same as that of the Protestant Church's ascendancy in North America today: the amalgamation of spiritual power with the material power of wealth.

While this meant a practical compromise with the exigencies of

[7] Nominated for the Mitre in 1527; he held office from 1528 until his death in 1548.

the world, where the kingdom of Heaven does not hold sway but only the struggle for life, so similar, at times, to the kingdom of Hell, it is nevertheless true that a portion of this wealth was used to assist the poor and to encourage—alas!—beggary, mortal vice of peoples who grow up in the shadow of convents. Another goodly portion was used as a bank to meet the needs of private persons and of governments, who obtained loans on advantageous terms, at extremely reasonable rates of interest, from the Church's inexhaustible coffers. Thus, charity and education were provided for in the colony. But a huge accumulation of stagnant wealth, endlessly augmented, in the hands of a corporation created a problem with two aspects: (1) political, because if wealth is power, there can be no doubt that the Church held the power and that the State was willynilly subordinated to it; and (2) economic, because there was only the scantiest trickle of wealth in circulation around the huge, inert treasure in the hands of the Church, and without the circulation of wealth social growth is rachitic and unhealthy.

This unhealthy situation was perfectly understood by the men of those days. By the end of the colonial period the problem had been precisely defined; in order to put off its solution indefinitely the Church helped the colony to achieve independence. The struggle to resolve this problem in favor of the civil power is the key to the trend of our history in the nineteenth century. The Republic could not take the highroad of progress or join in the march of civilization until, in the third quarter of this century, a final solution had been reached.

The Church, though subject to the king, who in any case could not have repressed its expansion, took advantage of the immunities and privileges granted by the king to forge an arm for the defense of its position and dared oppose the authority of the viceroys head-on.

The Church adamantly opposed the Conde de Priego,[8] the first viceroy to govern New Spain in the reign of Philip IV. A priest being tried in a civil court alleged the violation of ecclesiastical immunity in his person; the archbishop intervened and was overruled by the Viceroy, who was seconded by the Audiencia. The prelate then excom-

[8] Don Diego Carrillo Mendoza, Marqués de Gélves, Conde de Priego, became viceroy in 1621.

municated the authorities, placed the city under interdict, and retired with the clergy. The Viceroy ordered his arrest. Tumult among the people, destruction of a part of the palace, flight of the Viceroy, and the triumphal return of the archbishop to the city. The Viceroy, lacking in moral character, did not return to [New?] Spain, even though he was held to be in the right. The archbishop was deposed, the authors of the tumult severely punished. But the investigator sent by the King to find out the facts came up with the following observations: the clergy was omnipotent; loyalty to Spain was contingent on loyalty to the Church; the common people abhorred Spanish domination; and they would accept it only in the form of the supreme rule of the Church. The Church was, therefore, the *instrumentum regni*. This situation could hardly be reversed.

While conflicts between civil and ecclesiastical authorities were frequent and not seldom deteriorated into serious disturbances, the clergy nevertheless acted as the moral army of the government every time the people broke out in riots caused by some calamity. This happened in the City of Mexico in the reign of the Conde de Galve,[9] when short crops, poverty, and hunger caused a terrible riot. The Indians, crying, "Long live the King and down with bad government"—the cry that Hidalgo's Indians echoed a century later—set fire to the palace and the houses of city officers and would have ended by destroying a good part of the city if the clergy and the friars had not intervened and calmed the multitude.[10]

But the Church itself was split, and not by heresies or by Judaism, which the irons and stakes of the Inquisition took good care of, but by the eternal controversy between the secular clergy and the religious orders, which reached a climax when the Jesuits were at the peak of their power. The people, and sometimes the Audiencias, sided with the friars. But the Court repeatedly ordered the viceroys to allow no friars in the colony without special license, to discipline those who

[9] Don Gaspar de la Cerda Sandoval, Conde de Galve, became viceroy in 1688.

[10] Irving Albert Leonard, *Don Carlos de Siguënza y Góngora: A Mexican Savant of the Seventeenth Century* (Berkeley: University of California Press, 1929), pp. 210–277: Sigüenza to Admiral Pez, recounting incidents of the corn riot in Mexico City, June 8, 1692.

relaxed their rules (a common occurrence by this time), and even to demolish churches and convents built without permission. The bishops were able to make very little headway against the friars; the viceroys practically none.

In the middle of the seventeenth century the episcopal throne of Puebla was occupied by Don Juan de Palafox. He had been conspicuous in the Court of Spain for his origin in the south of France, his gallant youth, and his political aptitude; in the universities for his great intellectual gifts; and in the Church for his integrity, strength of character, and Navarresque stubbornness. He came to Mexico as bishop of Puebla, as judge in the *residencia* of certain viceroys, and as visitor. When Portugal's war for independence broke out, the viceroy, the Duke of Escalona,[11] was suspected of Portuguese sympathies; moreover, his ostentation and his favoritism toward usurers and bribe-takers were the scandal of New Spain. The Court of Madrid, making the Visitor Palafox archbishop of Mexico and viceroy simultaneously, commissioned him to depose the Duke of Escalona and to carry out or attempt thoroughgoing reforms in the corrupt administration.[12] Relieved of these temporary duties, Palafox returned to Puebla where, intent on recovering his usurped rights and powers as bishop, he collided with the overreaching privileges of the Jesuits and commenced a struggle with them that came near ending in tragedy. The Jesuits preached against the Bishop, who counterattacked with suspensions and excommunications. A decision against the Bishop was pronounced by a panel of judges illegally appointed by the viceroy (the Conde de Salvatierra)[13] to settle the conflict. Whereupon there were ceremonies of interdict in the cathedral of Puebla (erected by Palafox with astounding speed), riots, flight of the Bishop, and, finally, a decision of the Royal Court in favor of the prelate, who was given a bishopric in Spain, leaving behind him in New Spain imperishable marks of his talent, integrity, and love of learning.[14] The Jesuits, nevertheless, continued to prosper.

[11] Don Diego López Pacheco, Duke of Escalona, became viceroy in 1640.

[12] Don Juan de Palafox y Mendoza became archbishop of Mexico in 1642.

[13] Don García Sarmiento de Sotomayor, Conde de Salvatierra, became viceroy in 1642.

[14] Palafox, in 1645, gave statutes and a constitution to the University. On his return to Spain, he was appointed bishop of Osma, June 23, 1653.

By the end of the seventeenth century, all the fruits of the lordly regime implanted in New Spain were plain to see. The Indian population was no longer decreasing; the Mexican one was increasing visibly; the Creole class (to which some mestizo families descended from conquistadors and the Indian nobility belonged) was increasing, though less rapidly. At the head of the society was a colonial nobility, of which there is scarcely a trace today, for the ancient titles that survive were purchased from the needy Court at Madrid by one-time farmers, tradesmen, and miners of humblest origin; very few were obtained through good services to the colonial fatherland, which would have made them worthy of respect.

Whenever the Creoles and mestizos were called to battle wild Indians, uprisings, pirates, or even the invaders of other Spanish possessions, (as happened in Jamaica and Santo Domingo), these sons of two fighting races took up arms with enthusiasm and fought with valor, once covering themselves with glory by defeating European forces (the French, in Santo Domingo). After these interludes, everyone would return to his quiet affairs. The Creole would show off his horses and ornaments of silver and gamble incessantly in the public fiestas, nearly all religious, and in the private ones; a very few took courses at the University. The mestizo imitated the Creole in the cities or looked after his small industries; many attended colleges, seminaries, or the University with the hope of reaching high positions in the Church (in the seventeenth century an archbishop and a Dominican superior general were Mexicans), which sometimes rejected him and sometimes admitted him only. As clergy, doctors, and lawyers, the second-class or poor Creole, the mestizo, and a very few Indians constituted the intellectual aristocracy of New Spain.

Land was endlessly distributed and redistributed. The Indian towns and communities owned, almost never individually, almost always in common, as before the Conquest, the lands that surrounded their habitations, lands which Spaniards and their descendants frequently tried to take away from them. The Indians defended their land with extreme obstinacy, and their lawsuits were interminable; they carried them to the Audiencias and even to the viceroy and gave shysters and pettifoggers many a field day. The King had ordered the land, which was his by right of conquest, to be divided up; some received their share as a gift or grace (the lands of the Indians belonged in this class), others through more or less fictitious sale, including the so-called vacant or "royal" lands. The entire expanse of New Spain could have been covered with the papers involved in the lawsuits brought on by this distribution of the land. The result, two centuries after the Conquest, was the amortization in the hands of the clergy and religious communities of more than half the landed property and the concentration of vast tracts in the hands of a few owners. These haciendas were cultivated only in part. Cereals, grains, constituted the principal crops, apart from regional plants like the maguey; some commercial plants, like the mulberry, were prohibited. On these lands the Indian labored, as he still does on many of them, for two reals a day (the classic rural wage), which was actually paid him in the form of seeds, rum, and pulque; the rest of his earnings went to the Church (offerings, candles, ex-votos). But was there anything left over for the worker? No: there were debts, contracted, in the main, for the above-mentioned offerings; family expenses for clothes and food—which could never go beyond corn, beans (very nitrogenous and nutritious), and a stimulant, chile (barnyard fowl and pork were eaten only on special occasions)—were insignificant. Debts mounted steadily, never could be paid. By this system, which did not violate the letter of the benevolent Laws of the Indies, the Indian was kept in a state of servitude. He was the servant of the property, passing with it from heir to heir, from seller to buyer. He was—and in many places he still is—the serf of the glebe, of the soil.

The hacienda produced mostly corn, or maize, the American grain that was responsible for the founding of civilizations in pre-Cortesian North America; because of it people settled down to farm. Unknown to Europe before the Discovery, it now, with each day that passes, contributes a larger proportion of the Old World's diet. The hacienda produced also beans, likewise of American origin, whose nutritive value complements that of corn; also wheat, which was imported by the Spaniards and was not within the rural Indians' reach. The adaptability of corn made it easy to grow in all the graduated climates between the sea and the high plateau. Thanks to corn and the abundance of grasses, the cattle, horses, and sheep which were brought in small numbers from

Spain multiplied fantastically, first in corrals and then at liberty, forming immense herds, which fled with the nomads to the north and helped the tribes to maintain their fierce independence. The savage on horseback escapes the action of civilization; it is civilization, as a rule, which succumbs to him, though later, perhaps, it subdues him by outsmarting him. The viceregal government had to set up special courts to deal with disputes over wild cattle, courts called "of the Mesta," like those in Spain; because of their privileges they made themselves odious.

Agriculture hardly produced enough to supply the country. This was as true in the high plateau as in the Hot Country, where sugar, tobacco, and cotton were produced, all on a small scale, by mestizos of African admixture and by Negroes (the pure Indian was little by little pushed out, except in the isthmic regions and their extension into Yucatán and on a good part of the Pacific coast). Thus, a series of crop failures in any region was followed, because of the poor distribution of the produce, the meagerness of it, and the lack of means of communication, by hunger and its funereal cortege of epidemics and riots all the way from Yucatán to Jalisco.

The principal source of economic energy in the colony was mining, especially after the discovery of the method of amalgamating silver and quicksilver. The Indian, used as a slave in the first mines but emancipated by the viceroy, who snatched him thus from death, for the anemia of the mines was killing him fast, gave way to the Negro and the mestizo, stronger and more active. The wealth acquired in mining was invested in agriculture (rich mine-owners became the lords of vast domains) and in commerce and religion; charity and education received some part. As the business was even more a gamble in those days than now, the Spanish adventurers after the Conquest and their descendants could devote themselves passionately to it. The mythical empires with rivers of gold dreamed of by the Spaniards of Cortés' time turned out to be hidden in the earth: they were subterranean, real infernal empires. The spirit of adventure, which consists in risking all and trusting one's hopes for happiness to luck, and not to normal toil, lived on in the hearts of the Neo-Spaniards, thanks to the mines.

Quicksilver, which could be got only from Spain, kept the colonial mining industry dependent on the motherland. It was sent at definite intervals in fleets, whose arrival was essential to the day-to-day life of the mines; its distribution, supervised by the viceroy or his agents, was an occasion for the grossest favoritism and venality.

Trade in metals, grains, and skins with Spain—trade between the American colonies was prohibited—and in Chinese artifacts with Asia constituted the external aspect of the movement of wealth (a movement whose end product was mere frills—that is, luxury, comforts, pleasures, well-being). As for internal commerce, without natural highways for communication and with the classic impediment of the *alcabala* tax, it scarcely existed.

The discovery and possession of the Philippines by Spain was the most important event in the commercial history of the sixteenth century, after the discovery of America. In the Philippines the Spaniards established the central relay station for the trade between industrial Asia and Europe, across America. In El Parián at Manila an emporium was opened for this trade; in Acapulco a second market; near the Gulf coast, the third. When the merchandise reached the City of Mexico a selection was made that enriched the country with fine porcelains and splendid silks, the decoration and luxury of Creole homes. When the Asiatic merchandise, accompanied by American products, reached the Gulf coast, it became the cargo of the fleet that had brought quicksilver for the mines and European manufactures to the Spaniards employed in offices or in food stores and was carried to Spain in those vessels.

This trade enriched some Spaniards in Europe and some in Mexico. It enriched—or, rather, fell into the bottomless pits of—the Royal Treasury. It did not enrich the Spanish people. Spanish industry, one of the world's most flourishing at the time of the Discovery, was abandoned by the soldiers who went to Italy, Germany, and Flanders, by the emigrant who went to America to make his fortune in the mines, by the enthusiast or loafer who sought refuge in the convents on either side of the ocean. Love of work tended to disappear, while overweening pride and insatiable greed prevailed. The industry of Western Europe filled the vacuum that Spain had left, and its manufactured articles, with only the payment of duty to the Royal Treasury, passed through the contracting office at Seville on their way to America.

But in the sixteenth century, when Spain's maritime power was on the decline, a formidable plot against Spanish commerce took form spontaneously and flourished for two centuries, sometimes with, sometimes without the connivance of royal governments. France, England, and Holland took active part in it; the seizure of Jamaica, in the Antilles, by the English and the conquest of the magnificent Portuguese colonies of Indonesia by the Dutch furnished bases for the colossal business of international pillage in the Pacific and, above all, in the Gulf. To describe how the corsairs installed and maintained establishments, even when Spain was at peace with France or England, from the Antilles to the island of Términos (now the Isle of Carmen), how they deposited the stolen merchandise, in periods of international peace, on desert islands where the Spanish merchants themselves procured supplies, would require a whole book, and so would the tragic story of the incessant attacks by pirates on most of the coastal towns, from Florida to Brazil. In New Spain there were frightful depredations on Campeche and Vera Cruz, which had to be guarded with impregnable fortresses.

Smuggling soon became almost a normal activity in the mercantile life of the colonies and was tolerated to the extent of allowing the boats used for contraband to enter the ports freely, under one pretext or another; the smugglers had their emporiums in the Antilles, where merchants could select their stock. Such was the result of the absolute monopoly that Spain, like all the European nations with colonies, imposed on its American possessions, without wielding the huge naval power required to sustain that monopoly. The consequence was increase in the Spanish population of America: it was preferable to live in the places where colonial wealth—the only wealth that Spain had—was produced than in the country where it was consumed, a country fast deteriorating, becoming a mere distributing center of colonial articles and metals for the rest of Europe.

Education was designed during the period of colonial consolidation to foment the intellectual growth of New Spain, but was not altogether successful. The kings and viceroys persisted in their highly intelligent and civilizing program of unification through a single language; schools were created for this purpose, and classes set up in the University, in the colleges of the religious communities, in the seminaries. No attempt was made, as in other countries, even in our day, to prohibit the use of the native languages, and efforts to make Spanish the national tongue were carried on by persuasion, by pointing out the practical necessity.[15] A great deal was achieved, but the long-term undertaking is still not accomplished, for our governments have almost entirely lost interest in it and the clergy pursue it without enthusiasm.

Students from all classes—Indians and Creoles, but mainly Mexicans—came to the colleges and to the University, which was under the protection of the State. This institution was extremely important, for it shaped the mind of the developing Mexican personality, and within that mind a soul was sparked. The higher education which was given to the Mexicans by professors from Spain or born in the colony, as most of them were, was eminently nonscientific, a grave defect and irremediable in that day, for it was one from which all civilized Europe suffered. This does not mean that the sciences were despised: mathematics and cosmography were cultivated, but physics (still in swaddling-clothes) was all conjecture. There were authors who wrote on scientific questions, such as Enrico Martínez (whose personal history, linked with the first drainage ditch of the Valley of Mexico, is so singular) and Sigüenza y Góngora.[16] The Jesuits produced men notable for their scientific curiosity, for their practical knowledge. But the so-called "sciences" then were theology, philosophy, and law. The educated class belonged to one or both regiments: that of the clergy, that of the lawyers. The pure Spaniards, being fond of lawsuits, had a great respect for the lawyer, the attorney; it was when the Neo-Spaniard, the native of New Spain, became a lawyer that they respected him. They were awed by courts and profoundly afraid of the already complicated legislation of that day, a labyrinth in which anyone could lose his liberty and, even more easily, his property, unless he had an Ariadne at his side to pick out the guiding thread for him.

Theology, philosophy, even jurisprudence were taught in the medieval spirit, by a method rigidly scholastic, the purely deductive method. Because theology and philosophy were derived from religious dogma

[15] This holds true until the last years of the eighteenth century, when there was a surge of official hostility toward native languages.

[16] Concerning this famous Mexican sage, see Leonard, *Don Carlos de Sigüenza y Góngora.*

and jurisprudence was derived from the premises of Roman, Spanish, and canonical law and the Laws of the Indies and because the student was not permitted the slightest analysis or criticism, the whole study was a matter of inferring chains of syllogisms from those premises and dogmas. The most exciting class exercises consisted in hiding sophisms within the dialectic fastness in order to have later the fun of rooting them out—or else in the infinite tedium of collating texts and digests. Thus intellectual vices occupied the minds which Spain was unconsciously, perhaps, preparing for future leadership.

There was no real philosophy, no contact with the ideas which illuminated the intellectual sky in the century of Descartes, of Newton, of Leibnitz, no real knowledge. This lack was not merely the consequence of summary refutations of scholarly treatises and of the great philosophical systems of antiquity. There were no wings to thought, which thus could not live outside its chrysalis. The soul of this new people would be abortive. The intellectual incarceration of that society, the unscalable high wall guarded by a black dragon, the Holy Inquisition, which never permitted a book or an idea to enter that did not bear its sinister seal,[17] produced not atrophy—for there was in fact no organ, since there was no function—but sterility, making it impossible for the scientific spirit ever to be born.

If philosophy was lacking, there was, instead, a surfeit of literature. It rained poets; literary festivals were commonplace events in colleges and churches, and in them the audience was lavishly treated to poems in Latin, in Spanish, in Nahuatl. There is nothing of genius in the works of Juana Inés de la Cruz, but her ingenuity and feeling evoke the esthetic emotion.[18] The man of genius, perhaps the only one produced by the Mexican Spain, was Don Juan Ruiz de Alarcón, a truly creative writer, but he did his work in Spain. Drama, both in the Church and out, resembled the productions of the great Spanish theater in its rude beginnings. Our remote ancestors enjoyed it; they had poor taste. A

[17] This opinion, general in Sierra's time, is no longer tenable, being exaggerated. We know now that, despite prohibitions, every kind of book got into the colony sooner or later.

[18] Opinion has changed: this poet is universally recognized today as one of the geniuses of the Spanish tongue.

young people like the Mexicans, whose intellect is formed by the conjoining of two dissimilar souls, can only succeed in imitating the weaknesses, the vicious exaggerations of the stronger parent. While the new soul was being formed—and it can not be said to be formed even yet—its diffuse and profuse literature could hardly be more than the dimmest reflection of the light that was shining overseas. There was no serious literature save such historical chronicles as Torquemada's great work, *La Monarquía Indiana*, and certain descriptions and travels.

CHAPTER SIX

SOCIAL GROWTH (EIGHTEENTH CENTURY)

The House of Bourbon: the immutable regime. Reign of Charles III. The Jesuits. The spirit of innovation, efforts to change the regime. The last viceroys of the century. The Spanish revolution and its repercussions in the colonies. New Spain at the end of the old regime.

THE CLASSIC DIVISION of colonial history between the House of Hapsburg and the House of Bourbon is factitious: the regime did not change in any respect, neitheir politically, economically, nor socially. Mexican society, with all its defects (its meannesses), so acutely observed by the Duke of Linares,[1] and with its heterogeneous composition, kept on growing in the same direction as in the beginning. But the growth was real and strong: the organism had now become conscious of its personality and from the seventeenth century on through the eighteenth acquired a definite shape. It was governed socially by an apathetic and profoundly corrupt clergy. There was now no difference between the Catholicism of the Indian and that of the Creole: an endless routine of devotional practices, without any spark of light; neither the Creole nor the Indian had a glimmering of religion. The mestizo, so long as he was dissident, did have glimpses of enlightened ideas, thanks to his essentially curious,

[1] Don Fernando de Alencastre, Duke of Linares, became viceroy in 1711.

restless, and discontented mind, and these were the yeast of the future Mexican society.

Two observations by the wise Duke of Linares deserve our attention.

1. The teachings of the clergy, plus the innate feeling of the Creole and the Indian (overt in the former, covert in the latter) that everything enjoyed by the Spaniards here was usurped—"robbed," they said—from those born here, gave to any attempt against property the aspect of a venial sin and made it everyone's duty, in charity, to protect the thief—even made it astonishingly easy to imitate him. This habit of taking what belongs to others must have been a common failing, since Mexicans were so widely criticized for it—and still are censured for it—by their own countrymen as well as by foreigners. The evil had its origin in disdain for personal property, preached by the mendicant orders through example and through word.

2. A passion for equality, an absolute refusal to acknowledge that there could be any basis for the distinction between the ruled and the ruling other than force and injustice, was characteristic of the new society's personality. Thus, the psychological mold of the Neo-Mexican, which gave his mind its fundamental shape, made him reject all authority as openly as he dared. Since he seldom dared, he acquired the habit of dissembling and the habit of flattery. There is no flattery that does not conceal contempt. The expression of obsequiousness is exaggerated with the object of hiding the inner protest. Unfortunately, these congenital habits of the Mexican will prove to be a thousand times harder to eradicate than Spanish rule or the privileged classes that it built up. Only a complete change in conditions of work and of thought in Mexico could bring about such a reform.[2]

But society grew on its lower—that is, its least conspicuous—levels through the mixture of the mestizo with the Indian, on its upper levels through the mixture of the Spaniard with the mestizo. The Spaniard who mixed thus was not the bureaucrat from Spain: he was the merchant, either the grand monopolist of trade who belonged to the aristocracy of the rich, a member of the ruling Consulado (the tribunal of commerce), or else the "vendor of oil and vinegar," as the Duke of

[2] Analysis of the Mexican character is a constant preoccupation with Sierra. Faults can be corrected only if they are brought out into the open.

Linares put it. This grocery-storekeeper, on the coasts and the central plateau, was the core of the mixture. A rude, pitiless exploiter of the buying public, he was faithful to his commitments and, once rich, spotlessly honorable, devoted to his Mexican family; with his habits, customs, routine religiously fixed, he was still extremely anxious to give his children the social superiority that he had not been able to achieve. The grocer, not the conquistador, is the real Spanish father of Mexican society, with his laughable faults and his solid virtues; his Mexican wife, infinitely gentle and docile, weak through the very strength of love, admirably chaste and good, dominated that rude male and wakened in him the nobility of character that lies dormant in the depths of the ruthless fighter for survival during his struggle to rise.

Linares (Don Fernando de Alencastre), Casafuerte (Don Juan de Acuña), and Amarillas (Don Agustín de Ahumada)[3] were viceroys whose genius, character, and capacity for rendering service had not been surpassed by the best who were sent here by the Austrian dynasty. So there had been no perceptible change. The bad governments of Spain, including that of the feeble-minded Charles II in the latter part of the seventeenth century, had not sufficed to paralyze the governmental machinery of New Spain; it was too well mounted to suffer serious damage. There was enormous decline in moral fiber among the agents of the royal power, there were worse abuses, more scandals, more fortunes made overnight—and that was all. The spontaneous decay in the body of Spanish royalty contaminated everything, and the men whose names we have just mentioned are the more remarkable because of this fact. The House of Bourbon, when it crossed the Pyrenees, brought in its baggage the habits of minute administration and of rigorous centralization that had long been established in France and the intention of implanting them in Spain and its colonial empire.[4] But incessant wars interfered with normal administration. Everything was allowed to

[3] The Duke of Linares became viceroy in 1711, the Marqués de Casafuerte in 1722, and the Marqués de las Amarillas in 1755.

[4] Hence the introduction of the administrative system of *intendencias,* French in origin, as Alexander von Humboldt has observed in *Essai politique sur le royaume de la Nouvelle-Espagne* [Paris: F. Schoell, 1811], II, 92. English translation: *Political Essay on the Kingdom of New Spain*, trans. John Black (New York: AMS Press, 1966).

follow the same course as before. There was an effort to find honest men for the highest posts in the colonies, but some mistakes were made.

And thus the first half of the century elapsed. The viceroys in the period were builders of notable edifices and of good roads. They played a fatherly role by taking charge of the public welfare when famines and epidemics, some of them terrible, struck the country. They pacified and definitively subdued such regions as Nayarit, within the jurisdiction of the Audiencia of Guadalajara, and a section between the eastern sierra and the Gulf coast, which was given the name of Nuevo Santander (now Tamaulipas). New towns, such as Linares (in Nuevo León), were founded; expeditions were sent to Texas; defense of the coasts was a constant, and expensive, care. As much money as possible was shipped to Spain, and as much of it arrived there as could be got past the pirates and corsairs that swarmed in the two oceans.

Everything, then, remained the same. In the intervals of peace with England (during the reign of Ferdinand VI) it was necessary to apply as much money as possible to the liquidation of the war debts. Taxes increased and were levied in an arbitrary manner; such governors as the first Conde de Revillagigedo [5] augmented the royal income and their own at the same time. Alberoni's great attempt to rebuild Spain's naval power, the first requisite for the security of its colonial empire, had failed miserably in the early years of the century, and the absence of a guardian navy and the formidable growth of the English navy forecast, in perfectly legible letters across the sky of the future, the fate of colonial Spain.

If the innovating reign of Charles III had also been a reign of peace, like that of his predecessor, perhaps Spain would not have lost its continental American empire in such a catastrophic way. But the King, determined to keep his onerous alliance with France and moved by a sort of personal hatred for England, subordinated all policy to the famous Family Pact, and at the end of his long reign the balance was completely unfavorable to him and the dismemberment of Spanish colonial power clearly inevitable. After Henry IV there was probably no better monarch in the family than Charles III, though he was

[5] Don Juan F. de Guëmes y Horcasitas, Conde de Revillagigedo, became viceroy in 1746.

great, not in the sense that he had a superior intelligence as a statesman or administrator, but only in his perception, through sheer honesty and good intention, of some of Spain's pressing needs and in his unfaltering support of men with the capacity to remedy certain evils. The despotism of the monarchy was not basically altered but became, to the contrary, more absolute. For power became more centralized, after the French fashion, losing the patriarchal character that it had under the Austrians and turning coldly administrative. The tyrant was no longer a father: he was an omnipotent manager, but one bound by his own regulations.

The first absorbing problem, posed by natural instinct for self-preservation, was how to effect a series of reforms in the Treasury which would augment the royal income. Unfortunately, the supreme fiscal reform is peace, and that existed only at rare intervals. Nonetheless, much was accomplished and more was planned. The King's advisers, influenced by the spirit of the times—a cyclone of negativistic and destructive philosophy, based on the French Encyclopedia, was sweeping Europe then—were enemies of the Catholic Church's authority because they were extreme royalists and also because they had but little religion. The King was not perspicacious enough to grasp the second motive, which would have hurt his Christian conscience, but did have sufficient faith in his divine right to approve emphatically of the first. If they had been able to strip the Church of its temporal possessions in those years, they would have done so, forcing it to sell its landed properties or expropriating them in the name of the State, with payment of indemnity. But that could not have been done anywhere then, least of all in European or colonial Spain. And yet, one of the Church's instruments of power, the Company of Jesus, had grown so wealthy, even setting aside exaggerations, and its power among broad social groups had grown so deep, the politicians believed it would be suicide for the State to tolerate this mighty force within its bosom, a force that could not and would not become national and was essentially antisecular. And the financiers believed it would be a drastic remedy for the precarious condition of the Royal Treasury to confiscate and sell the colossal properties of the Company, which, with its amazing commercial activity, resembled in some ways the medieval order of the Templars. The examples set by Portugal and France, which had struck mortal blows at the Jesuits, encouraged their Spanish enemies.

The story is a familiar one: the Company's imprudence in claiming its privileges in the matter of collection of tithes, which had been conceded by the Pope to the Crown in America, thereby encroaching on the Royal Patronate; the famous "riot of the capes and hats" in Madrid, which deeply wounded the King's susceptibilities and which was used as a pretext, because the Jesuits were alleged to have been involved; and, finally, orders for the expulsion of the fathers and their servants from all the Spanish dominions at the same time, carried out with staggering precision everywhere, and in New Spain by that honest soldier the Marqués de Croix,[6] with whom blind obedience to the king and to discipline was a religion.

In this country there were protests, murmurations, bloody tumults, but at last all was quiet, and when the Pope suppressed the Company of Jesus there was nothing to do but bow the head. What the Marqués de Croix put, soldier-like, in his celebrated circular announcing the expulsion was true: "Once and for all time, the vassals of the Great Monarch who occupies the throne of Spain must know that they were born to be silent and obey, and not to discuss or express opinions on the high affairs of government." Those who were capable of measuring the formidable dose of despotism contained in this formula were silent in the Viceroy's presence, but they discussed and expressed opinions as freely as they liked in the parish sacristy, in the barracks room, in the lay-brother's cell, in the convent refectory, in the seminary hall, in the residence of the hacienda, in the Marquesa's living room, and in the bishop's chamber. The expulsion caused astonishment, anguish, and indignation in the majority; only a few foresaw its consequences. Most of the educated Mexicans were pupils or admirers of the Jesuits. The fathers of the Company, while they were molding the classes in which a new national personality was becoming aware of itself, still kept this personality loyal to Spain. As we have said before, the clergy was the bond of moral union between the

[6] Don Carlos Francisco de Croix, Marqués de Croix, became viceroy in 1766.

motherland and the colony, and for those who were able to discuss and express opinions, the Jesuits were that bond. Their immense services to the Crown—they had conquered for it, with a legion of preachers and martyrs, the entire northern zone of New Spain—and the learned men who at the very moment of the expulsion were shining lights in its colleges (Fathers Alegre, Clavijero, and Abad) made their banishment harder to excuse.

The spirit of innovation not only swept aside obstacles, but succeeded in planning and carrying out a new political and economic program which, to be sure, did not allow for the least spark of liberty. Since the exigencies of the almost constant state of war in which the Spanish empire lived during the reign of Charles III grew more pressing day by day, the Court decided on a step whose consequences, if they could not then be foreseen, could from that time on be conjectured. This step was the organization of a permanent colonial army to take the place of the voluntary militias, which were raised locally in time of danger and dissolved when the danger was past. Officers were sent from Spain: an inspector general, who at once came into conflict with the viceroy Cruillas (Don Joaquín de Montserrat),[7] and instructors. They soon produced the desired result: an army, recruited by means of advances on salary or by that form of criminal abduction known as the levy, composed at first of two or three regiments (infantry and cavalry), and costing in 1765 more than 600,000 pesos. So the Mexicans took up arms, nevermore to lay them down.

On the administrative side, the advent of Don José de Gálvez,[8] future Marqués de Sonora and Minister of Indies, who came with the title of visitor but actually with omnipotent authority, was of prime importance. His activity inspired awe in Mexico. Dry, severe, but indefatigable, he soon reduced the Viceroy to little more than a nullity. Indeed, his secret instructions were to find out the facts concerning the charge of appalling peculation brought against Cruillas by his enemies. Gálvez attended to everything: he improved the military condition of the country, he established an honest financial regime, which, though based on ideas that nowadays would be

[7] The Marqués de Cruillas became viceroy in 1760.

[8] Arrived in the City of Mexico, August 25, 1765.

considered bad economics (monopolies, lotteries), resulted in a steady increase in the royal income; he pacified and organized the northern provinces of California and Sonora, a task personally supervised by the Visitor, who put the missions of the banished Jesuits into Franciscan hands; he took care to mitigate the effects of such novel and unpopular royal dispositions as those relating to the Jesuits and the sale of their confiscated properties and to the establishment of the tobacco monopoly, from which Gálvez expected to get a juicy increment for the Crown. And yet there was a noticeable restlessness in the land, a desire to protest, to shake off a burden, and it was summed up in this phrase: "The Spaniards let us take no part in the government of our country and they carry off all our money to Spain." The administrative projects of Gálvez, especially the one establishing *intendencias*, were not put into effect until, on his return from Mexico, he was made Minister of Indies. His intent was to create a sound administration in America, something that had hardly existed before, in order to strengthen the ties between the motherland and its colonies. These men around Charles III formulated vast plans, which, had the King lived fifty years longer and had these been years of uninterrupted peace, might have been carried out and might have brought about the emancipation of the colonies. We must remember the famous project of the Conde de Aranda, submitted to the King some years after the Marqués de Sonora started his broad program of administrative reforms: in this document, after prophesying with astonishing clairvoyance the rise to greatness of the United States, which had just been born (1783), he said, "Your Majesty should get rid of all the possessions that you have on the two continental Americas, keeping only the islands of Cuba and Puerto Rico in the north and some other suitable one in the south, to serve as way-stations for Spanish commerce."

Unfortunately, Charles' foreign policy revolved around the Family Pact, which committed him to endless wars at sea. For this he deserves no serious blame: the growth of England's maritime power consisted largely in the ingestion of Spain's colonial empire; Spain by itself could not hold this growth within bounds; France seemed to offer the balance that was required, hence the Spanish King's policy.

But the results were disastrous. Spain was obliged to take two steps that had the gravest consequences: (1) create a colonial army and (2) help the American colonies of England win their freedom. The first step was unfortunate because it sapped the colonial budget, which had been admirably strengthened by Gálvez' reforms; because it awakened the dormant military spirit of Spanish America, latent in the Mexican blood, which combined two warlike and adventurous bloods; because any army that is far from the center of authority and obedience is likely to turn rebel or oppressor; and because it gave Mexicans the idea that the military force which was needed to realize their longings for liberty could be raised by their own society. The second step, aid to the English colonies, was an example that could not fail to draw the attention of Mexicans: whatever was right against England must also be right against Spain. Independence as theory in the minds of thinkers—that is, the awareness of full manhood, which means a social group is ready to pass from paternal dominion to autonomous rule—was a phenomenon that had evolved completely within the last third of the eighteenth century.

Fortunately for Spanish rule, the last viceroys of the century were, with one exception, good men, and two of them were of the highest caliber: I refer to Bucareli and the second Revillagigedo.[9] Croix was very hard, but honest and fair. Mayorga,[10] was viceroy pro tem during the war between England and Spain, whose allies were France and the United States; he sent aid to the governors of Louisiana and Yucatán when they attacked, not without success, the English in Pensacola and Belize. The first of the two Gálvezes,[11] an old man of integrity, protector of the arts, was followed by his son, an officer ambitious for glory and popularity, who would have been a great viceroy if he had not died so young; together they represented the nepotism of the famous Minister of Indies. The rapid succession of viceroys and temporary governments headed by Audiencias and archbishops caused

[9] Don Antonio María Bucareli became viceroy in 1771. Don Juan Vicente Guëmes Pacheco, Conde de Revillagigedo, in 1789.

[10] Don Martín de Mayorga became viceroy in 1779.

[11] Don Matías de Gálvez became viceroy in 1783; Don Bernardo de Gálvez, Conde de Gálvez, in 1785.

no little confusion; Flores [12] tried to correct this but could not accomplish much: the deficit was over a million, debts twenty millions, and necessary military expenses were mounting. New Spain now had its *intendente general* of the army and navy, a sort of secretary of war and navy who shared the government with the viceroy. The country was divided up into *intendencias*, which were being implanted despite difficulties and resistance. [13] We have now reached the year 1788. The year before the pertinacious reorganizer of colonial administration, Don José de Gálvez, had died, and this year Charles III died, leaving a great record without having been a great king; with him died the House of Bourbon's capacity to produce men fit to rule over their subject peoples. At the same time that the inept Charles IV ascended the throne, the second Conde de Revillagigedo arrived in Mexico.

As we have said before, Bucareli and Revillagigedo came near reconciling Mexican society to the supremacy of the Spaniards, who were resented by a good part of the new Creole and mestizo generaation and passively loathed by the Indians, as every master is loathed, on principle, by his servant. Bucareli was one of those men who, through the power of benevolence and zeal, can make a bad regime appear to be good. And it was bad. The colony was sealed off tighter than ever in isolation from the rest of the world. For the rulers, unwilling to attempt a total reform of the colonial system, which would have required another such reform in Spain itself, grew ever more afraid, and with reason, that contact between the colonies and civilization would induce the colonists to throw off the yoke. And they knew, besides, that the longer this fatal moment was put off, the greater the danger of an explosion—so they took care of the evils at hand and hoped time would take care of those remote. They miscalculated badly. At any rate, in spite of the soaring cost of the efforts to pacify the vague frontier areas of Texas, Chihuahua, and Sonora, where hordes of nomads, clandestinely armed by the English, kept everything in turmoil, as similar hordes had done in central Mexico

[12] Don Manuel Antonio Flores became viceroy in 1787.

[13] The system of *intendencias* was implanted in New Spain by royal decree dated December 4, 1786.

immediately after the Conquest, the Treasury prospered and gave wings to commerce, which expanded during this period as never before, while credit rose amazingly. This was a happy period in the colony's history, one that muted its aspirations. It was the period when Archbishop Lorenzana,[14] an angel of charity, founded asylums to succor the most distressing cases of need; and in the Fourth Mexican Council, which he called, he manifested the same evangelical zeal and love for the conquered race that had burned in the apostles' hearts in the seventeenth century.

Ten years after the illustrious Bucareli came Revillagigedo, whose energy and good judgment were stupendous. México was a great city, and its inhabitants were fond of luxury; but as proper sons of Spaniards and pupils of friars they had only the vaguest notion of public order and cleanliness, of hygiene, of real comfort—in short, of culture. All this the Viceroy tried to change, and he succeeded so well that some of his dispositions would improve the capital of the Republic if they were put into effect today.

He was not merely the best officer the City of Mexico has ever had, he was a great governor. The overhauled Treasury, the *intendencias,* the courts—he had a hand in everything, and always for the good. Determined that the Mexican people should acquire self-knowledge, he founded elementary schools and fomented the higher ones. He sponsored the study of history and of the arts, protected agriculture, mining, and commerce, but always with practical measures, with apt political judgment. Why are there no statues to Bucareli and Revillagigedo in the City of Mexico, which owes so much to those two? The cry of independence, "Down with bad government," would have been unimaginable in their time.

The transition from the government of Charles III to that of his son was a downfall, a leap into the abyss. There ceased to be any slow and normal solution of the pressing problem of internal reform. Indeed, external forces imposed themselves with tremendous energy on a people who, while being cut loose from the past, had no clear

[14] Dr. Francisco Antonio Lorenzana y Butrón became archbishop of Mexico in 1766. He was later archbishop of Toledo and was made cardinal in 1789. He died in 1804. He was founder of the Casa de Cuña, or "Cradle Home" for orphans.

view of the future. The Spanish government's orientation was anything but national. The foreign dilemma can be summed up thus: a choice of war with England and loss of the colonial empire, or war with France—the France of the Revolution and of the Napoleonic Empire—and the shipwreck of the dynasty and of national independence. Not even the talent and experience of the men of Charles III would have managed to find a safe passage between the two terrible extremes. And those men had been shunted aside. Charles IV was a good man but a feeble and inept prince, absolutely incapable of shaking off domination by his wife; he was a watered-down Louis XVI. The Queen (Goya's realistic brush dared not palliate her ugliness, which grew more pronounced with the years and accouchements) combined a remarkable intelligence with surprising aptitude for intrigue and a fierce sensuality (for it is always fierce in ugly women). Between the King and Queen stands the figure of Don Manuel Godoy, favorite of both. Shameless exploiter of the passion that María Luisa had conceived for him, this supreme mountebank tried to drape his cynical bedroom prowess from history's eyes by window dressing, by a few noble projects that disguised him as an enlightened and patriotic statesman. This knave, climbing to high commands in the army, contrived to get rid of the Conde de Floridablanca, to whom we owe Revillagigedo's superb regime, and to put the feckless Conde de Aranda, subservient to French policy, in his place. Finally, the favorite made himself minister at the age of twenty-five. His portrait, painted by Goya, shows him decked out in military trappings, the utter moral vacuity of the courtesan plain to see beneath the pleasant sensual features. At the feet of this regal trinity a poisonous plant born of all that muck began to unfold and grew into one of the most spontaneously vile souls known to history: the young Prince of Asturias, the future Ferdinand VII.

Godoy, as soon as he felt sure of his official power, began doing openly what he had already been doing from his hideout in Her Majesty's chamber: distributing offices, honors, and the public money among his kinfolk and cronies. That Court, corrupt to the marrow of its bones, squabbled over the favorite's smiles and good graces. To this sort of politics we Mexicans owe the administration of the Italian

Branciforte[15] (Don Miguel de la Grua Talamanca), a venal man, who came to the viceroyalty determined to feather his nest. To his extraordinary gift for flattery the City of Mexico owes the fine equestrian statue of Charles IV, by the Spanish sculptor Manuel Tolsá, in which the misshapen figure of Don Miguel Godoy's king is so artfully sheathed that it disappears within a sovereignly majestic and noble mask of bronze. The imprisonment and trial of Louis XVI caused horror and indignation in Spain; his death, which Charles IV strove to prevent up to the last instant, bringing on himself the curses of the Convention in Paris, caused general stupefaction at first, then rage and the desire for vengeance. The enthusiasm was immense, and Godoy found himself the leader of a heroic people. The war, fought by the Spanish armies with all possible dignity, ended in 1795 with the peace of Basle, which was followed by a treaty of alliance between Spain and the French Republic against England (1796). Godoy, throughout all this, gave himself the airs of a great general and a consummate diplomat and was honored with the title of "Prince of the Peace." It was then that the war began in earnest.

England began by striking a nearly mortal blow at the Spanish navy (San Vicente), bombarded Cádiz, seized the important island of Trinidad near the mouth of the Orinoco, made some unsuccessful attacks on American ports, and commenced to sow ideas of insurrection against Spain in South America, even organizing efforts like that of General Miranda[16] in Venezuela, which failed. Branciforte prepared for the struggle with England. The governor of Yucatán, O'Neill,[17] attempted, without success, the reconquest of Belize, and in the midst of a tremendous financial crisis brought on by the favorite's extravagance and the war at sea, which was getting colonies accustomed to living in isolation from Spain, the King was forced by universal indignation and the insistence of the French to part with Godoy. An honest ministry, headed by Saavedra and Jovellanos, took office. Branciforte was immediately re-

[15] The Marqués de Branciforte became viceroy in 1794.

[16] Sebastián Francisco de Miranda was born in Caracas March 28, 1750; died July 14, 1816. His attempt to liberate Venezuela was made between September 1805 and January 1807.

[17] Arturo O'Neill y O'Kelly became governor of Yucatán in 1793.

placed by the enlightened Azanza,[18] who was Spanish Minister of War; this indicates the great importance attached by Spain to the security of the colonies, whose insurrection was planned overtly by England and covertly by the United States. If it had not been for the Spanish Rebellion in 1808, Mexico and the whole of Spanish America would have become, not a colony, as that was impossible, but an English dominion, to be divided up later with the Anglo-Americans. Soon Jovellanos, who had tried to make the Inquisition adopt the rules of the ordinary penal code, resigned, and a mob of adventurers and charlatans swept back into public office. Azanza, who could do little besides fortify the coasts and keep an eye on certain alarming internal movements (such as the "machetes plot" [November, 1799]), which were symptoms rather than dangers, for they indicated how easily thoughts of independence could be planted in Mexican brains, left the viceroyalty in the last year of the century. His successor, Marquina,[19] likewise was kept busy looking out for conspiracies and putting down some strange Indian uprisings. Godoy returned, not as mere confidant, for the relationship, though still persisting, had cooled, but to the throne, as regent, and he sent Don José Iturrigaray[20] to the vice royalty. The year before (1802) the peace of Amiens had been signed by France, Spain, and England. It was an ephemeral peace, a truce, for there was no possible conciliation of interests between these three. As soon as Bonaparte, dictator of France (who became emperor in 1804), realized this, he decided to stab England in the heart with an invasion. But, to carry it through, he needed all the equipment of the Spanish navy. Spain, when the Peace of Amiens was broken, had proclaimed its neutrality, but the demands of France and the aggressions of England forced it to declare war on the latter. While Napoleon, putting off the attempt against England, was facing and defeating the coalition of Austria and Russia, Nelson and the British fleet were dealing death wounds to the naval power of France and Spain at Trafalgar (1805). Here Spain made a supreme effort, and never again could win back a place among the prime naval powers; its colonial empire was at the mercy of the sea-lords.

[18] Don Miguel José de Azanza became viceroy in 1798.

[19] Don Félix Berenguer de Marquina became viceroy in 1800.

[20] Don José de Iturrigaray became viceroy in 1803.

Napoleon, forced by the disaster at Trafalgar to call off the invasion of England, conceived the vast project of stopping the English from entering European ports, thus reducing that nation of tradesmen to beggary, the project known as the continental blockade. He did with Spain as he pleased, believing that Spain was helpless—with its thoroughly corrupt Court; with its royal family split between the favorite Godoy and the Prince of Asturias, who was practically in rebellion; with its widespread ignorance, fostered by the Inquisition, which fought all ideas of reform; with its shocking poverty; with its perennial bankruptcy and a deficit mounting by hundreds of millions each year. First he catapulted Spain against the kingdom of Portugal, to all purposes an English dependency, which he divided up (on paper) between some of the Italian Bourbons, France, and a dummy monarch who was intended to be Don Manuel Godoy. But the Spanish people's hatred for Godoy grew day by day, as did their sympathy for Prince Ferdinand and their admiration for Napoleon—which was so great that, when French armies entered Spain on the pretext of invading Portugal, the people applauded, believing Godoy was about to be overthrown. But soon things took on a different aspect. The Emperor, who had accomplished the military occupation of Portugal, broke his promises to Spain, brazenly seized some fortresses in the northern part of the Peninsula, and in the early months of 1808 marched his armies to Madrid. Then the royal family made plans to flee to America and establish itself in New Spain, just as the Braganzas of Portugal had already done in Brazil.

The populace of Aranjuéz, determined to prevent the flight, egged on by Ferdinand's partisans, and finally aided by the troops, succeeded in overthrowing Godoy. And the rebellion ended in the abdication of Charles IV in favor of the Prince of Asturias, who was proclaimed king and made his solemn entrance into Madrid amid delirium, in the presence of French troops under Murat. Napoleon, when he heard the news, called them, every one—the King and Queen, the Prince, the favorite—to Bayonne, where he, as arbiter, would hand down his decision. They all went, and there he revoked the abdication of Charles IV, who repeated it in favor of the Emperor of the French, who then ceded the crown of Spain to his brother Joseph. The people of Madrid reacted to this outrage with the insurrection of the Second of May. The insurrection was drowned in blood at its focus, but spread country-wide. Men of all opinions formed committees to organize the uprising, men who hailed from the past and men who were headed toward the future. These committees proliferated cores of resistance and established contact with England's agents, who were watching events with profound attention. Naval preparations had just been completed for an attack on the undefended colonies, to be led by the future hero of the wars in Spain and of Napoleon's final defeat, the future Duke of Wellington. The Spanish revolution changed the course of English policy, and the British forces now took aim at Portugal.

The Spanish revolution—for that is what it was, since it would bring about, however slowly and painfully, the destruction of the old regime—met with formidable stumbling blocks in Mexico. But while it was easy to suppress the manifestation of ideas, it was impossible to prevent them from making headway in the dark. The creaking and discredited Inquisition tried frantically to stop up the cracks and to seal hermetically the closed doors. Impossible! Rays of the new light filtered in between their very fingers. Their refutations of the abominable errors, both political and religious, that had been the cause and the consequence of the French Revolution served to advertise the most alluring of these abominations, which were summed up in two divine sophisms: the individual is free; the people—that is, the majority of society—is sovereign. And then, some strange things had been noticed: the Spanish government's coziness, under Aranda, with the accursed French Revolution; Urquijo's impious doctrines, as minister of the Crown; scandals, which Godoy had built into a system of government. And then there was Napoleon's popularity: as the supreme gambler, he stirred all the adventurous yeasts in the Mexican's blood and infected him with an insatiable longing to conquer a new world in the unknown realm of the future.

Iturrigaray armed the Mexicans, as his predecessors had done, in order to prepare them for war with the English, whereupon a military class, something that had not existed for two centuries, came permanently into being and began to demand rights and privileges. Iturrigaray sought popularity among this class: he put on royal airs in the Jalapa barracks. Meanwhile he was getting rich in every way possible, holding out his hand for gifts and encouraging every sort of graft. He was another Godoy. And since communication with Spain was desultory and precarious, and since he gratified the Madrid government by sending it as much money as he could whenever he could, he felt secure and calmly watched events from a distance, confiding in his master's favor and lucky star.

In Mexico, nonetheless, opinion was coming out into the open and forming different camps. The conflict between Creoles and Spaniards became ever more bitter; more than ever the former insisted on their right to be agents of the king of Spain in the government of their country. A temperate petition to Charles III had got them little or nothing, but they instinctively felt their opportunity would emerge from the tremendous convulsion that was shaking Europe. The pure Spaniards, who were not one-tenth as numerous as the Creole Spaniards, claimed half the wealth and virtually monopolized the Audiencias and other high offices; they controlled some city councils (as in Zacatecas and Vera Cruz); the top clergy were theirs, and also the Consulado, a chamber of commerce which served as their core of resistance. They were determined to let nothing be taken from them. How would these two incompatible parties go into action against each other?

News reached Mexico of the uprising at Aranjuéz, the abdication of Charles IV, and the elevation to the throne of Ferdinand VII, who was proclaimed king of Spain and of the Indies by the fearfully nervous Iturrigaray. When Godoy was cast out the Viceroy trembled, tried to save himself, and waited; he had not long to wait. The events at Bayonne and the rebellion against French rule at Madrid struck Mexico like lightning: there was, in fact, no government in Spain. The colony, out of loyalty to the dethroned monarchs, unanimously rejected the government of Joseph Bonaparte. In the circumstances, power had to be assumed by the Viceroy and the Audiencia. But who was going to share it with them? The Creoles? That would amount to independence. The Spaniards? That would be a declaration of war against the Mexicans. It soon became patent that Iturrigaray leaned toward the Mexicans, while the Audiencia backed the uncompromising Spaniards. The Viceroy called together the Audiencia and the City of Mexico's council, organ of the Creole party. In September of 1808 representatives of the Spanish committees arrived, claiming sovereignty; they added to the confusion and gave the Spaniards heart because they brought proof of organized resistance on the Peninsula. The Mexican party insisted that none of the committees should be recognized, that a congress should be convoked in Mexico, to govern with the Viceroy until Ferdinand could regain his freedom. The solemn session held in the Palace revealed how much headway the new ideas had made, how widely the Mexicans had read, and how impotent the Inquisition had been to prevent the transformation of a people's mind. The program of the Spaniards was to recognize the committee of Seville and to block or throttle every move toward liberty in Mexico. "This word 'liberty'," said the men of the Consulado, "has the ring of independence here." In order to gain their ends, the rich Spaniards and their high officers conspired, and one night their paid henchmen invaded the Palace, seized the Viceroy, deposed him, and put an aged Spanish soldier in his place.[21] The leaders of the movement for provisional emancipation were arrested, and the Audiencia usurped the governing power. The Mexicans did not forget this lesson. They learned that he who has the might will rule. One must have the might.

There arrived in Mexico, at the same time as Iturrigaray, the illustrious writer on many subjects Alexander von Humboldt, who had been making an extended scientific study of the Americas, with the permission of the Spanish government. His impression on becoming acquainted with New Spain after visiting South America was that he had passed from semisavagery to civilization. He described the marvelous physical aspect of the country, the immense wealth of its mines, which produced more metal than all the rest of the world. And, although he sagely pointed out how the economic value of this wealth was diminished by scarcity of population and paucity of communications, especially of navigable rivers, he also described Mexico as the richest country in the world, thereby contributing to a fallacy with which the Mexicans have excused their indolent beggary ever since they felt themselves free. He defined, with admirable accuracy (in view of

[21] Don Pedro Garibay, field marshal, became viceroy in 1808.

the scanty statistics available in that day), the social divisions of Mexico, on the basis of information supplied by members of the privileged classes, mainly clergymen. He divided the population into about three million Indians, above two million mestizos, and fewer than one and a half million whites, one hundred thousand of whom were natives of Spain. He showed how, despite the efforts made by the ministers of Charles III to emancipate the Indian from the tyranny of petty officials and despite the nearly total extinction of the encomienda, the Indian continued to be shut off to himself with hardly any chance to strengthen his personality by acquiring his own land and so remained the serf of the Church, of the Spaniard, and of the Creole. He showed how the mestizo—there were comparatively few Negroes in New Spain, thus the mixture was mostly between whites and Indians—intermingled on farm and ranch with the Indian but attained a somewhat higher social level in the towns, where he received some education. A hard worker, at times highly honest (the tradesmen bought everything on credit and never failed to pay their debts), he was yet often ruled by the vices that the stagnation of society held in suspension, like pathogenic germs; he was remarkable for his ability to assimilate whatever came from outside, good or bad, and for his hatred of the white. At the top was the Creole, landowner, frequently addicted to vice, abhorring the pure Spaniard, who he felt had usurped such things as offices, grocery stores, silk and textile shops, and plantations. Humboldt discussed recent efforts to raise the level of education in New Spain. The seminaries and former Jesuit colleges, now run by the secular clergy, continued to manufacture priests and lawyers by means of the most routine and vapid instruction, with only a sorry smattering of courses in science—which was to bring upon the country the immense misfortune of being governed later by men with a purely literary education (lawyers). On the other hand, in the splendid palace called the Colegio de Minas, designed by Tolsá, and in similar institutes in the provinces, scientific teaching was notably advanced. He had high praise for artistic training and for the Academy of Fine Arts.

The famous traveler described also the political divisions of the country. There were two groups of internal provinces in the north, where the white population predominated, though the entire region was raided incessantly by the nomad tribes: (1) the western provinces (Sonora, Durango or Nueva Viscaya, New Mexico, and California) and (2) the eastern provinces (Coahuila, Texas, Nuevo Santander, and Nuevo Leon). These two groups of provinces had separate military governments, overlapped in part by *intendencias*. Then there were the *intendencias* of the City of Mexico (1,511,900 inhabitants), Puebla (813,300), Vera Cruz (156,000), Oaxaca (534,800), Yucatán (465,800), Valladolid (476,400), Guadalajara (630,500), Zacatecas (153,300), Guanajuato (517,300), and San Luis Potosí (230,000). All was peace, tranquility, and prosperity on the surface; all febrile ideas, longings, aspirations beneath.

Iturrigaray was succeeded, after a brief interval, by Archbishop Lizana,[22] a good man, whose main concern was to assuage Mexican discontent with lenience and indulgence—conspiracies were commonplace—and to send money to Spain, torn by the ceaseless struggle of its revolution.

[22] Don Francisco Javier de Lizana, archbishop of Mexico, became viceroy in 1809.

CHAPTER SEVEN

INDEPENDENCE, I

Antecedents; the parish priest of Dolores; general insurrection; triumphs. Calleja; war to the death; repression and conquest. Morelos; the war in the south; legal organization of the insurrection. Calleja's viceroyalty.

HEN THE STRUGGLE against French intervention started in Spain, Iturrigaray proclaimed, after a fashion, Mexico's provisional independence. "Left, as we are, to our own recourses," he declared, "we shall obey the King alone, and we shall not obey any committees unless they have been created by the King, and these alone we shall obey in accordance with the provisions of law." (But it was quite impossible for Ferdinand, in his situation, to create any committees.) The Spaniards, as we have seen, deposed Iturrigaray and placed New Spain under the control of Spain's Central Committee. This the Mexicans could not forgive: they almost unanimously agreed that they were subject to the king of Spain and not to the people of Spain, a new entity, alien to the Conquest and to the colonial regimes. They waited and plotted. Feeling that they had attained their majority (I refer to the group with superior education and social position), they were convinced they could free themselves; and, in view of Spain's situation, they were convinced they ought to do so.

There was plotting in Morelia, in Querétaro. The Querétaro plot, whose heart and soul was Don Ignacio Allende, a young officer who had known Iturrigaray in the Jalapa barracks, was painstakingly organized, on so broad a scale that the parish priest of the wine-growing town of Dolores, in the Intendencia of Guanajuato, played a part in it. The priest Don Miguel Hidalgo y Castillo was nearly sixty. The son of a Spaniard living near Pénjamo, he had received a thorough literary and theological education and, despite grave reprimands provoked by the dubious orthodoxy of some of his doctrines, he had been made rector of one of the best seminaries in the country (San Nicolás, in Valladolid, now Morelia), and then had obtained the choice curate of Dolores. There, no doubt, he continued to read forbidden French and Spanish books and to meditate. He was not, however, a contemplative man, but a man of ideas and action. He had tried to better the lot of his Indian parishioners by creating and fomenting new industries—wine-growing, silk-culture, ceramics—enterprises which did not endear him to the authorities of New Spain. He pondered events in Spain and their possible consequences in Mexico with rising but restrained excitement, and no sooner had he joined the group organized by Allende than he began to manufacture arms. The certitude that the Spaniards, for all their heroism, would not be able to turn back the Napoleonic invasion, the exasperation aroused by the constant siphoning off of the country's money for a lost cause (eleven millions in 1809 and 1810), the niggardly decree of the Central Committee granting each of the American viceroys the right to be represented in it by a single deputy, produced unbearable emotional tension. The first part of the struggle, ending in the withdrawal from Madrid of the puppet king, Joseph Bonaparte, had been followed by the period of French triumphs, inaugurated by Napoleon in person. There was now no hope; the cause of Ferdinand VII was a desperate one. The Mexicans were aware of this when they invoked it in their declaration of independence. The Regency organized in Cádiz, seemingly the last precarious redoubt of the Spanish nation, rushed emissaries to the colonials, who were now beginning to revolt in South America, with a proclamation which fully recognized their right to have a part in their own government and called upon them to send delegates to the Cortes. In the words of this proclamation, which could well serve as preamble and justification for any movement whatsoever aiming at emancipation:

Spanish-Americans: from this moment you see yourselves raised to the dignity of free men; you are no longer bowed under a yoke which has weighed the heavier the farther removed you have been from the center of power; no longer looked upon with indifference, exploited by greed, ruined by ignorance.

New Spain elected its deputies to the Cortes, thereby putting the municipal power into motion and arousing hitherto silent ambitions for liberty and autonomy.

The anti-Mexicans were the Gachupines, as the Creoles had called them from time immemorial, the tradesmen, who made up the Consulado, the mercantile senate of New Spain, which was able to influence the ministers of the Regency through its partners, the merchants of Seville. These detested Gachupines succeeded in having the Archbishop removed as viceroy and the government put temporarily in charge of the Audiencia, in which the anti-Mexican spirit prevailed. With this strongly reactionary Audiencia, the same party that had overthrown Iturrigaray returned to power. Its program could be summed up in the slogan "New Spain for the Spaniards." The plotters got ready to go into action.

The idea of insurrection was conceived in the barracks at Perote and Jalapa when Iturrigaray commanded them. Many brilliant Mexican officers met and came to an understanding there. The first form that the patriotic idea took for them—it was a nebulous obsession by this time, in many different sorts of minds—was the one outlined in the proposals made by the City of Mexico's council to the sympathetic Iturrigaray, who had acquired great popularity among the Creole officers in the military barracks. All their dreams of autonomy were shattered with the brutal overthrow of the Viceroy, and anyone who is familiar with the blunt and deeply humiliating and exasperating form that Spanish despotism habitually takes, even though it may be basically more generous than other despotisms, will understand the state of mind of these Mexican officers. Some, like the young Agustín de Iturbide, remained faithful to the Spanish cause; others plotted at Valladolid (Morelia) but were discovered and mildly punished. Yet the plot that aborted at Valladolid was reborn at Querétaro, where the conspirators included people of different classes, from the corregidor Miguel Domínguez, chief justice of the city, on down. The conspiracy had branched out to various cities, towns, and haciendas of the region by September 1810. The organizer was a captain of dragoons of the Queen's Regiment, Don Ignacio Allende, who had contrived to evade the persecution that overtook the plotters at Valladolid, whose active agent he had been. Patriotic sentiment was summed up in the slogan "New Spain for the Mexicans" (or the "Americans," as our ancestors called themselves). But in order to put this into effect, the country would have to be snatched from the Spaniards' grasp. There would have to be a struggle, and most likely a desperate struggle. This view, quite correct, was fully accepted by Allende and his collaborators. The soldier wanted to give the leading role in the revolution to Hidalgo because of the lofty prestige his priestly character gave him with the masses. In Hidalgo the idea of independence had a high social intent: he hoped to emancipate the Indian by declaring him to be of age and by opening for him a road to liberty through employment in industry (Hidalgo was the most enthusiastic and outstanding industrialist in the country). Foreseeing that he would pay for his effort with his life, Hidalgo gave his superb moral courage to the common task; he set the example. From the moment he joined the Querétaro plot his mighty will and conscience dominated the movement. His conduct as chief of the insurrection, at times deserving the severest censure from a humane point of view, was dictated by circumstances. His purpose was dictated by his love for a country that did not exist outside this love; thus it was he who engendered it: he is the father of his country, our father.

The revolution was supposed to start in December 1810, during a big fair in one of the cities of the region. Grave suspicions that the Spanish authorities had got wind of something caused the leaders to move the date up to early in October. But suspicion turned into certainty: the conspiracy, which, in branching out, had become known to a great many people, had been denounced in the capital, in Guanajuato, in Querétaro. The military plotters gathered instinctively around Hidalgo; while with him they received the news, sent by the heroic wife of the corregidor Domínguez, first among Mexican women, that all was discovered and that the plotters were being hauled off to jail. Hidalgo did not hesitate. He called together as many people as he could, gave them what arms he had, stirred them to enthusiasm with his word and his example on the morning of September 16, in the atrium of the parish church. Then he set out for San Miguel (Allende now). On the way he picked up a painting of the Virgin of Guadalupe, the Indians' Mother of God, and declared it the holy standard of his tremendous undertaking. The rural masses, abandoning their plows and hovels, followed him as a Messiah. To the cry of "Long live Our Lady of Guadalupe and down with bad government!"—"Down with the Gachupines," the mobs put it—the Querétaro plot had turned into a mighty popular uprising: this was insurrection.

Hidalgo strove to keep those unmanageable mobs under control. But, as always happens when masses of humanity, repressed for generations, are suddenly released, they burst forth in wild frenzies. Liberty for those people was not a right, it was an intoxication; it was not a normal attitude but an explosion of hate and joy. That horde could not be disciplined, could not be held back; it had the aspect of a force of nature in all its violence: lightning, hurricane, flood. Allende tried to create a military nucleus within that horde and then withdraw it, an impossible feat. The priest could keep some control by indulging the mob's whims, with dreadful results on occasion, like the massacres of Spaniards at Guanajuato, at Morelia, at Guadalajara, atrocities that distress us, for we would like to see the figure of the greatest Mexican in history immaculate. The consequence was an impassable sea of blood between the insurgents and the ruling class; compromise was no longer possible.

The insurgent chieftains triumphed all over the central plateau region known as the Bajío. They captured Guanajuato, where the *intendente,* a man of honor, improvised a doughty defense in the massive structure called "Alhóndiga de Granaditas," and died at its door. The frenzied horde committed crimes and every sort of excess, and then took the road to the capital by way of Valladolid (Morelia). In that city they met with no resistance except the edicts of excommunication hurled at them by Bishop Manuel Abad y Queipo, a man of eminent learning and just perception and friend of the insurgent chief. The edicts, refuted by Hidalgo in an unanswerable argument—it is not true, said the priest, that in order to be a good Catholic one must first be a good Spaniard—reveal the stupefaction and ire that Hidalgo's audacity had provoked, even among Spaniards of high intellectual quality. The insurgents ignored the excommunications, and the noble priest decreed the abolition of slavery and the suppression of the tribute paid by the Indians. The mob, which Allende was powerless to discipline, headed for the City of Mexico by way of Toluca, defeated the capital's scanty garrison nearly at its gates, and turned back without even trying to take the City.

Hidalgo never had time to form plans; his dispositions had to do with the business at hand, and the general ideas that they contained could be summed up as follows: Get rid of the Spanish ruling class in New Spain, so that the country, as its own master, can offer itself intact to the rightful king, Ferdinand VII (who, it was hoped, would never emerge from captivity). What kind of government would the new nation have? Hidalgo had given this some thought: a congress, with municipal suffrage, was basic. In any case, the movement had caught on. Armed bands rose in revolt everywhere. A great many men with faith in the new ideas bravely accepted posts of danger in the forefront of these scattered uprisings—some were soldiers, more were lawyers, many were priests. The priests were the ones who most bitterly resented the top clergy and were most familiar with the new theories, which they had learned from reading the orthodox refutations of them. They felt more keenly than others the social evil in the stagnation of the Indian masses and in Spanish supremacy and were dismayed by the fact that the always moderate and humanitarian authority of the monarch was no longer present as a counterbalance; they were therefore the most ardent patriots.

While the Bishop of Michoacán's edict was awakening echoes in each of the country's episcopal seats and the excommunication of Hidalgo and his followers was repeated again and again, the new viceroy, Venegas,[1] was taking over the government. He reorganized the capital's small garrison, which had been defeated not so much by Hidalgo's reckless horde as by Allende's valiant soldiers, and he called for aid from the brigadier Félix María Calleja, who, coming from San Luis Potosí and acquiring reinforcements at Querétaro, caught up with the

[1] Don Francisco Javier Venegas became viceroy in 1810.

insurgent army, straggling in aimless withdrawal, scattered it, and very nearly disarmed it. At the same time, however, the insurrection was winning smashing victories in the interior, capturing the cities of Guadalajara, Zacatecas and Tepic.

The two leaders, who viewed the struggle from different standpoints—Hidalgo seeing it as a people's uprising, Allende, as a military problem—separated in discord. Hidalgo went to Guadalajara, after permitting horrible murders in Valladolid, and Allende marched to Guanajuato. From the moment of Hidalgo's arrival in Guadalajara, where he was acclaimed by delirious crowds, he began to formalize the unprecedented powers that circumstances had conferred upon him, and reiterated [December 6, 1810] the decrees that he had pronounced at Valladolid abolishing tributes and slavery. Calleja, with terrifying swiftness, had wrested from Allende the city of Guanajuato, bathed in blood by the savagery of insurgents and royalists in turn, and was advancing on Guadalajara. After the desperate Battle of Puente de Calderón [January 17, 1811], in which forty thousand insurgents, many of them armed with pikes, slings, and arrows, were thoroughly routed, Hidalgo, a fugitive, took the road to Zacatecas in company with Allende, who, as the leaders of the insurrection were now agreed, was to resume full military command of the movement. The fugitives' plan, it appears, was to go by way of Texas to the United States, where they hoped to raise sufficient funds to arm the insurrection. Between Saltillo and Monclova they were trapped by a turncoat officer (it would be pointless to besmirch these summary pages with his name), and the clergy were taken first to Monclova and then to Durango, with the exception of Hidalgo, who was taken with all the rest to Chihuahua. From their capture to their death these men traveled a veritable *via crucis*. The frenzied imprecations of the crowds, who had been told that the captives were agents of Napoleon, and the inhuman cruelty of their guards made martyrs of them. They never complained. During the travesty of a trial which was held at Chihuahua—only the barest record exists of the proceedings, which the judges conducted to suit themselves—it appears that there were mutual and painful recriminations. Those men had lived in a state of feverish excitement consonant with the colossal boldness of their enterprise; it is not strange, but profoundly human that, in the period of depression brought on by the absolute certainty of imminent death, earlier beliefs and attitudes should reassert themselves and that there should be faltering and retractions—but none of these, absolutely none, was made with the hope of escaping death. On the contrary, they—especially Hidalgo—accepted responsibility of the most damning kind. The fatherland, born of their heroic blood, reconciles them in gratitude and absolves them in glory. Hidalgo and his companions were executed at Chihuahua, others at Monclova, the rest at Durango, in midyear of 1811.

Meanwhile, Morelos and Ignacio López Rayón were setting afire the southern mountains between the central plateau and the Pacific Ocean. Rayón had organized a governing committee at Zitácuaro. Thus, while the fathers of Independence were captured in full rout, the insurrection was still going full blast. Rayón and José Antonio Torres, insurgent hero of Jalisco, marched from Saltillo to Michoacán by way of Zacatecas, fighting one battle after another and proving that Spain's military power, in spite of its victories, was not what it used to be. The principal cities had been reconquered, but the countryside was ablaze with guerrilla warfare, and society smoldered with conspiracies. And, because the insurrection was being stamped out with heinous cruelty, the longing for liberty was whetted to a fierce desire for vengeance. It was a duel to the death.

The priest José María Morelos y Pavón, who had spent his entire youth as a donkey-driver, traveling back and forth over the southern sierras and acquiring great popularity among the mountain people, had resolved, no doubt, to attain a position that would serve as a shield against the contemptuous despotism of the Creole and the Spaniard. So he became a student at the College of San Nicolás in Valladolid, where he was guided by Hidalgo's counsel and remained from then on under the spell of his keen intelligence, of his dauntless determination to explore the ways to social reform. Morelos succeeded in entering holy orders and in securing a parish in Michoacán. This he abandoned as soon as Hidalgo, at the head of his insurgent army, passed that way and commissioned him to rouse the southern populace to revolt and to seize some port through which the insurgents could open up communication with the outside world. When the insurgent general Rayón, Hidalgo's former secretary, succeeded in setting up the nucleus of a political organization at Zitácuaro, Morelos had failed to capture Acapulco, but he had improvised, seasoned, and disciplined a rural army, with which he had been able to hold the royalists in check over an immense area. His staff, if we may call it that, was distinguished by the noble figures of the Galeanas, the Bravos, Vicente Guerrero, and, later, the dashing and indefatigable priest Mariano Matamoros.

The viceregal government made strenuous efforts to keep the new insurgent leader bottled up in the southern mountain region, where it expected to annihilate him. Meanwhile, Rayón's attempt to create a political and governmental center had brought down upon him the full might of the forces of repression. The campaign against him was conducted successfully by General Calleja; if Rayón had been able to hold out longer, the royalist victory would have been nullified by Morelos, who, taking advantage of the concentration of Spanish troops in Michoacán, was moving to occupy important points when he learned that Calleja had wiped out the insurgents at Zitácuaro and had returned to the City of Mexico in triumph. Morelos moved rapidly in the midst of royalist forces, often trouncing them and finally adopting the strategy of acting as lure for the main body of Calleja's army so as to give the insurrection growing-space throughout the southern region. The result of this strategy was the siege of Cuautla by the royalist army, the most carefully organized military operation of the entire insurrectionary war, and Calleja, who carried it out, did not overlook a single strategic or tactical recourse in his effort to force Morelos to surrender. When, after a series of heroic episodes, Morelos decided his position was untenable, he broke through the encirclement, skillfully frustrating the Spanish general's scheme, and turned up, livelier and more formidable than ever, in the state of Vera Cruz, south of Puebla, where he upset all the royalists' campaign plans by the celerity of his marches and the unexpectedness of his blows. After he had rescued the intrepid Valerio Trujano, about to succumb to a long siege at Huajuapan, and had taken Orizaba by surprise when nobody knew he was near, news reached the City of Mexico that he had captured Oaxaca. It was then that Morelos resolved to give his political program priority; it was time for the insurgent nation to show the subdued nation a united front, time to speak aloud to the world. With this in mind, as well as the need for a port which would afford communication with the outside world, in order to secure aid from those other independent Americans, the United States —for the insurgent armies suffered from a lack of firearms—Morelos undertook the campaign (for which he has often been criticized) which culminated in the capture of Acapulco.

With the remnants of the Governing Committee that had met at Zitácuaro, with representatives chosen in sporadic elections, and with appointees named by Morelos—all invested with supreme powers by the nearly unanimous sentiment of the Mexican people—an assembly was organized at Chilpancingo. This assembly gave the country a voice and was the vehicle of the leader's undeviating and perfectly sound ideas. Early in 1813 General Calleja, who had received the title of Conde de Calderón, was made viceroy—a sure sign that a war of extermination was to be efficiently carried on. Morelos perpetrated the most frightful reprisals; he had already shown himself capable of cruel extremes. But his program required that he be vested with legal authority, and this only the representatives of the insurrection could do. His main object, however, in organizing the Congress of Chilpancingo was to elicit from it a clear statement, without reservations or ambiguities, that the mind of the nation in rebellion against Spain was set on absolute independence.[2] The news from Spain convinced the perspicacious priest that the return of Ferdinand VII was imminent on the Peninsula, free of French occupation since near the middle of 1813. There would then be no further excuse for the insurrection, which had consistently proclaimed its loyalty to the captive King. Not without some trouble, Morelos got what he wanted, and the declaration of independence of November 1813 was so plain that no room for doubt was left. The enthronement of Ferdinand VII could not change it one whit.

Morelos, vested with full Executive Power, though hindered by the Congress' insistence on having a hand in everything, never attempted to bend it to his will, and thus set a superb example of civic duty. He started an ambitious new campaign, designed to make him master of

[2] In his speech read to the opening session, Morelos asked the Congress to "declare America free and independent of Spain or of any other nation, government, or monarchy."

Michoacán. But his attack on Valladolid failed, and its defenders, Llano and Iturbide, energetically took the offensive, winning a series of actions that culminated in the bloody Battle of Puruarán, which virtually dissolved the army of independence. Morelos never again succeeded in bringing it together for warfare in the grand manner, as he liked to wage it. His best lieutenants died or were hedged about with frustration. Oaxaca and Acapulco were reoccupied by the royalists, and the Mexican Congress and Executive roamed the bleak southern sierras, risking capture. In the war for independence the period of eclipse and depression, which always follows the initial period of expansion in great revolutions, began in 1814. It was to last six years.

These things happened in rapid succession: the final liberation of the Peninsula, the return of Ferdinand VII to the throne, the fall of Napoleon, and the derogation of the generous and idealistic Constitution of 1812, which was rather the formulation of the grand ideas of a few men who were the nucleus of a future Spain than a summation of the real hopes and needs of Spain in the century's early years. The noble Code of Cádiz was jettisoned, amid the multitude's imbecile cheers and the privileged classes' curses. In Mexico writers like Fernández de Lizardi (El Pensador Mexicano, "the Mexican Thinker," as he called himself), who tried to take advantage of the freedom of the press that it authorized, suffered persecution when it was done away with, amid the cynical rejoicing of the ruling class and the Spanish party, the indifference of the independence party, and the brutish apathy of the people, whose will and thought had been systematically paralyzed. The response of the Mexican Congress, deep in Michoacán, to the assassination of the Spanish Constitution by the king of perjuries and ignominies was to produce a constitution of its own, derived in part from the murdered one. The Constitution of Apatzingan, or, to give its exact title, *Constitutional Decree of Liberty for Mexican America* (October 1814), was not intended to be permanent, but merely provisional, "until such time as the nation, freed from the enemies that oppress it, shall dictate its Constitution." Like the Spanish Constitution, it comprised an electoral law and one for the administration of justice and the organization of courts, and it betrayed inexperience throughout, though ringing with the firm conviction that the old order must be made over. The Constitution of Apatzingan is distinguished from that of 1812 by its clear-cut republican character. It even made the error, incredible in that time of struggle for survival, of dividing up the Executive Power amongst a triumvirate, which could be indefinitely renewed. It is distinguished, furthermore, by greater emphasis on the exclusive authority of the Catholic Church. Congress had already decreed the reestablishment of the Jesuits, and the Constitution declared that no heretics, apostates, or non-Catholic foreigners could be citizens. Just as sailors on the verge of shipwreck cry to Heaven with all the strength of their dauntless souls, so did the first fathers of the Republic seize on their religious beliefs as on a lifesaver. When they said "God and Country" they put into the words all the faith of their conscience and all the love of their hearts. We who are sons of a century that goes to its death skeptical, disillusioned, and cold to the marrow of its bones should have the grace to respect and admire those whose faith and hope were identified with a single religion, even on the steps of the scaffold.

Some months later, in the fall of 1815, the Congress decided to move to a more central location, where it could exert its influence on the partisans of independence, though these had been defeated on all sides. It set out from the mountains of Michoacán for Tehuacán, a point between Puebla, Oaxaca, and Vera Cruz, and Morelos went along with an escort to protect his comrades, the deputies.

Attacked by royalists, the deputies were able to escape, thanks to the heroic defense put up by Morelos, who was taken prisoner, brought to the capital, degraded by the Church, and executed by Calleja. This was a fatal mistake. For in Morelos he executed the Insurrection in its most energetic, implacable, and fearless embodiment: the hero who was most self-possessed, the greatest of them all.

With the death of Morelos, the year 1815 ended and the disintegration of the insurgent nation began. The Congress was dissolved by an insurgent leader: the first coup d'etat in the history of a Republic as yet in gestation. Some thirty thousand men, scattered between the Isthmus of Tehuantepec and the central plateau, fought on in the cause of independence, but were unable to prevail, except for fleeting episodes in the strategic areas. In the autumn of 1819 Viceroy Calleja was called to Spain. He symbolized and personified the policy of ruthless repression. Like many an agent of Spanish rule in Europe and in America, he believed in triumph through terror, failing to perceive that the undying wrath which passes from the souls of the dead to those of the subjugated makes the success of most movements for liberation merely a matter of time. Calleja's policy turned the insurrection into a war without mercy, and independence, trampled, suffocated in blood, lived on in Mexican hearts. This became evident in 1821. Calleja himself pronounced judgment upon his policy in a document published later: "When six million inhabitants are determined on independence, there is no need for them to work in harmony or come to an agreement among themselves."

CHAPTER EIGHT

INDEPENDENCE, II

The new viceroy and the new policy. Heroic episode: Mina. Pacification. Guerrero in the south. Independence.

THE ARMY that Calleja left to his successor consisted of forty thousand men in a well-organized body and as many more in local corps about the country. Thus, there were eighty thousand men who unceasingly carried on the hard work of repression, which made steady progress. The Treasury was not lacking in funds, thanks to new taxes and in spite of the inroads of Calleja and his favorites. But, in any case, the cause of the insurgents, torn by dissension and without a central government or a plan of action was doomed to disaster by two circumstances. First, the new viceroy, Apodaca,[1] whose kindly nature contrasted with that of his predecessor, Calleja, was instructed to observe a policy of pardon and lenience. Second, troops could be sent from Spain with great facility, for those that had fought the war there now had little to do but were still under arms. The gravity of this last circumstance was alleviated, so far as the Mexicans were concerned, by Spain's having to spread its attention and resources over all Spanish America, which blazed with rebellion and conflict from Panama on southward.

It is really amazing how much the insurgents were able to accomplish, despite the royalists' superiority in discipline, arms, and resources. The rebels had built fortresses in well-nigh inaccessible spots,

[1] Don Juan Ruiz de Apodaca became viceroy in 1816.

where they deposited such arms and munitions as they could scrape together. The most celebrated examples of these fortified hills, some of them marvelous examples of military instinct, were Cóporo in Michoacán, El Sombrero and Los Remedios in the sierras overlooking the Bajío region of the central plateau, and Juajilla in the middle of swampy Lake Zacapu in Michoacán. The latter served as refuge for the last remnants of the Congress of Apatzingan, a governing committee whose radius of influence barely reached as far as the Bajío. Among the intransigent guerrilla leaders were Juan Terán and Guadalupe Victoria in the eastern sierras between Puebla and Vera Cruz; Guerrero, Pedro Ascencio, Nicolás Bravo, and Rayón in the massive southern mountains connecting the eastern and western chains; Torres, Pedro Moreno, and others where Jalisco borders the Bajío; on the eastern plains of the central plateau, Osorno and others. In Lake Chapala a handful of heroes, making themselves strong on the larger islands, defied the Spanish government's efforts to dislodge them, year after year.

The insurgents lived on the country. Their larders were the haciendas, almost invariably destroyed when they were the property of Spaniards. In addition to contributions and ransoms exacted from the towns, which often were burned by ferocious rebel chiefs, such as Osorno on the plains of Apam or the second Father Torres in the Bajío, they got supplies through levies on merchandise in transit, assaults on military convoys, and the like. All the patriots had recourse to these means, highly precarious because of the utter lack of organization. Furthermore, after five years of revolution the country was exhausted, thanks to the conduct of a majority of the royalist chiefs, though there were most honorable exceptions. We do not refer to their cruelties: in truth, there was competition in ruthlessness between the two sides, and Morelos was Calleja's equal, and Iturbide no more inhumane than Hidalgo, alas. For this very reason, Bravo's noble act in pardoning his Spanish prisoners and giving them their freedom when he learned of his aged father's death before a firing squad shines like a heavenly star in all that moral hell. We refer to the abuses committed by the royalist chiefs to enrich themselves. The brigadiers José de la Cruz and Joaquín de Arredondo had set up veritable satrapies for their personal profit, the first in Nueva Galicia, the second in the eastern internal provinces, in which the viceroy was actually powerless and commerce at the mercy of the rulers. José Gabriel de Armijo in the south, Iturbide in the Bajío, and a hundred others in as many places were intent on keeping alive a war that brought them a fat income and extracted sluices of blood and gold from exhausted New Spain.

Apodaca met with good fortune in his efforts to alleviate somewhat this state of things, endeavoring, at all costs, to bring the conflict to an end and alternating force with pardon, the regiments from Spain with amnesty, even for the most bloodthirsty of the insurgent leaders. In 1817, prior to Mina's expedition, Lake Chapala, after five years of unflagging resistance, was pacified by Cruz thanks to the honorable capitulation of a band of Indians on the island of Mexcala; this was the first official capitulation in that terrible war. The same thing happened at Cóporo, on whose slopes the royalists had so often been repulsed; it also capitulated. And the most brilliant of the Insurrection's military leaders, Manuel Mier y Terán, was obliged to surrender near Tehuacán. A great many insurgent chieftains, like Osorno, took advantage of the amnesties. Resisting still were Victoria, Bravo, Rayón, Guerrero, the Committee at Jaujilla, and the forts of Los Remedios and El Sombrero. But it was just a question of time: the insurrection seemed to be nearing its end.

Then there appeared on the Gulf coast a Spanish leader who came to renew the conflict: Francisco Javier Mina, not yet thirty. Leaving college at the outbreak of the national uprising against Napoleon in Spain, he had roused Navarre and upper Aragon to revolt. Captured by the French, he completed his education at the side of a tireless conspirator against Napoleon, General Lahorie, in the calabooses of Vincennes. With the Emperor's downfall, he returned to Spain, his heart full of yearning for freedom and his mind full of ideas for political and social reform. The actuation of Ferdinand VII on the throne that his abject cowardice had proved him unfit to occupy surprised and shocked Mina, and he protested by taking up arms. He was defeated and fled to England. There, Fray Servando Teresa de Mier, a Dominican who had been persecuted for his ideas by Church and State, convinced him that the best way to fight against Ferdinand, and for his ideals of liberty, was to serve the cause of independence in Mexico and that only in freedom and not through war would Spain and its colonies find a common bond again. Mina, whose influence in the Masonic lodges put him in contact with men prepared to sacrifice their lives on the altars of their vision of human emancipation, led a handful of cosmopolitan adventurers, eager and enthusiastic, from England to the United States and thence to Haiti and to the port of Galveston, where he completed the preparations for his expedition. Landing at Soto la Marina on the Mexican coast, he entered upon the heroic phase of his bold enterprise in April of 1817.

The march of the new chief from Soto la Marina to the fortress of El Sombrero, fighting, winning victories, and sowing dismay among the Spanish authorities, is an epic. His confrontation with Pascual Liñan, a brand-new officer imported from Spain with the auxiliary troops, his attempts to relieve El Sombrero—although the fortress fell at last to that officer, who seized the occasion to practice abominable cruelties on the prisoners—were amazing feats of energy and valor. Of the companions that set out with Mina, only a few choice spirits were left. In the hope of saving the fortress of Los Remedios, also besieged by Liñan, he tried to create a diversion by marching back and forth through the Bajío region, menacing various towns. He organized the bands of volunteers that joined him, invaded Michoacán, attempted to take Guanajuato by surprise. Finally, beaten and a fugitive, he was captured by the royalists and executed. In that dawn of new ideas and new nations, the holy cause which Mina fought for in Spain and in Mexico was a kind of loftier homeland for all men. Mina was looked upon by the Spaniards as a traitor. He was no such thing: he never felt that he was doing his country disservice by fighting against the abominable tyrant of Madrid. Today, as we view things calmly from a distance, we can say he was in the right, if not with regard to Spain, at any rate with regard to Mexico, who adopted him as a son and reveres his memory along with that of the heroic fathers of Independence.

The hill of Los Remedios did not fall when Mina died; it held on for a long time. The combats that took place there were exploits of a high order, in which Mina's foreign officers elicited prodigies of valor from their Mexican soldiers. But at last they surrendered. The enthusiasm that the revolution had recovered with the advent of Mina began to fade. The leaders were disappearing: some died bravely in battle; others received amnesty, as did most of Mina's officers; still others, like Rayón and Bravo, were captured, pardoned, and kept in prison. By 1820 the country was nearly pacified. The supreme effort made by 100,000 royalist soldiers, fighting scattered bands that had neither arms nor discipline, produced the expected results. Most of the insurgents not in prison begged for amnesty or joined the royalists. Only Guerrero and Ascensio refused amnesty and fought on doggedly in the south. Others, like Victoria, waited in hiding for the day of triumph that was sure to come. All of them were waiting for that day. The movement for independence was transmuted in the spirit into the flame of hope. For psychological forces are transmuted one into another, just as physical forces are. The country was an immense ruin. From the Isthmus on northward mountains and plains had been soaked in blood. And when world conditions would be favorable again, the outbreak of 1810 would be repeated, but this time with irresistible force. So it was.

The first outbreak of the Insurrection was due to Spain's peculiar circumstances between 1808 and 1810. The return of the absolute monarchy on Napoleon's fall made the temporary repression of the movement possible, but the idea had taken such hold on the country's mind that the Spanish party was confined to the higher officers, a part of the top clergy, a majority but not all of the Spaniards from Europe, a minority of the Creoles, a smattering of mestizos, and as many educated Indians. On the other hand, a good portion of the upper clergy and of the Audiencia, nearly the whole of the lower clergy, nearly all Mexicans employed in justice or administration, a majority of the Creoles, and the overwhelming majority of mestizos, who had borne the brunt of the struggle for independence since 1811, plus the Indian masses, controlled by their priests, belonged to the independence party and watched the dispatches from Spain for the propitious moment to go into action. The army, with some few exceptions, was infiltrated by Freemasonry, brought to Spain by the French near the century's end. All the Spanish Masons were enemies of absolutism and looked forward to the advent of constitutional government. The Mexican officers, even those who had fought the insurgents, were nearly all for independence; many were also Freemasons. Such was the psychological situation of the country in 1820. The news from Spain, which clearly showed the signs of an imminent revolution, alarmed the absolutists; not that they were against any constitutional government, but they were against the Constitution of 1812 because it seemed to them an open door to the destruction of Catholicism in Spain. Some of the clergy and prominent officials got together to decide what should be done in case the Constitution was proclaimed. And, feeling sure that the constitutional regime would entail the independence of Mexico, they preferred to promote independence themselves in order to exclude the Spanish Constitution, thus taking a step that was exactly the reverse of the one they took when they overthrew Iturrigaray.

When Mexico learned of the triumph in Spain of the constitutionalist revolution, partisan feeling ran high, and the anticonstitutionalist circle of Dr. Matías Monteagudo, perhaps the most influential of the clergy, prepared to take action. They sought and found their man: the Mexican royalist colonel Don Agustín de Iturbide.

Endowed with admirable valor, with the glamor that magnetizes crowds and soldiery, and with a vague but enormous ambition, which in those days, thanks to the dazzling reality of the Napoleonic legend, was bound to take on gigantic proportions, Iturbide had behind him a black history of bloody deeds, abuses, and extortions: it was the history of his ambition. Desiring independence, he fought against it because he believed the movement started by Hidalgo had no chance of success and thus no triumphant role for him to play. And in order to attain a high post among the royalists, he exaggerated his zeal, keeping it always at white heat, for the very reason that he was insincere. In his hands the sword of repression was red to the hilt with insurgent gore. When he felt that his merits were slighted, that the road was closed to him on the Spanish side, he used all his wiles to open a way for himself on the other side. The absolutists offered him an important military post, the one just left by Armijo, who had failed to crush Guerrero in the south. The Viceroy was glad to give the command to Iturbide: he had no idea that a revolution would be the result but felt sure that an army in Iturbide's hands could be used to put down the constitutionalists, in case the King, who was considered a prisoner of the liberals, should so order; the King might even conceivably appear in person in Mexico to give the order.

When in January of 1821 the intrepid and immaculate Guerrero, who had been Morelos' collaborator, gave Iturbide the famous embrace of reconciliation, he did not absolve him of the bloodshed, he pardoned him in the nation's name, in recognition of the supreme service that he was about to render it. And the nation has pardoned in the Iturbide of 1821 the Iturbide of 1813; it has confirmed the indulgence granted by Guerrero's great heart. As for the betrayal of Apodaca, Spaniards may condemn that, we do not. We believe that the Viceroy's insignificant personality was never taken into account by that ambitious spirit capable of rising above itself, impelled by the mighty urge to create a nation and by the opportunity to achieve, at the same time, a great benefit for Spain. The Viceroy really did not matter. The denouement of the drama was swift and almost bloodless; there was more blood spilled in a single engagement of the Insurrection's heroic phase than in the whole of the revolution that started at Iguala. There, in February of 1821, after Iturbide had made sure of his officers and had come to an agreement with the principal military chiefs of the central zone, both the Mexicans and the Spaniards, he divulged his idea by means of a manifesto and a plan,[2] which his army took an oath to support. There was a flutter of reaction when the Plan of Iguala became known: part of the army abandoned Iturbide; another part rallied round the Viceroy, but not for long, as the revolution spread rapidly, first on the Gulf coast and then in Michoacán and the Bajío region. General Cruz, who never seriously thought of resisting, turned over his sultanate in Nueva Galicia to a second and fled. Arredondo likewise turned over the eastern internal provinces and fled. All the provincial capitals were seized by the army called *trigarante,* because it sustained the Plan of Iguala, which was based on three guarantees: "religion, union, and independence." These were symbolized in the tricolor flag, adopted by the nation and hallowed by the river of heroic blood that has flowed for its sake.

[2] The Plan of Iguala is dated February 24, 1821.

At this juncture Apodaca was overthrown in Mexico by the Spanish soldiery, and a new viceroy, Don Juan O'Donojú, appointed by the constitutionalists in Spain, arrived in New Spain. This man understood, with great perspicacity, what was going on. With a Spanish patriotism that Spain has not been able to appreciate till after a full century of painful lessons, he recognized the irreparable fact, and signed with Iturbide at Córdoba the treaties that were to be the supreme law of the new empire.[3] Spain recognized and sanctioned the right of the Mexicans, who had attained their majority, as their vigor in war proved, to emancipation and approved these basic arrangements: the creation of a Mexican empire; the designation of Ferdinand VII or some prince of his house for the throne; the immediate appointment of a governing committee or of a legislative and administrative council to assist an executive or a regency composed of several members in running the country; the election of a Cortes or constituent congress which would give the country a new fundamental law, based on the three guarantees, and would reserve the right to designate the emperor.

On September 27, 1821, the Army of the Three Guarantees made its triumphal entry into the capital of the Mexican empire. New Spain had passed into history.

On September 27, 1821, the chapter of three hundred years of Spanish history came to a close. Then began the history of a people who were born of the blood and soul of Spain, but whose physical and social environment were *sui generis*. Both environments affected the evolution of this people: the physical, by forcing it to adapt itself to biological conditions that were markedly, though not entirely, different from those on the Peninsula; the social, by the native family's slow but sure ethnic fusion, which transformed it into the Mexican people. It is true that the Indian race was also changed. It had adapted itself admirably to its environment with a social organization that was highly vital at the time of the Conquest. But the Conquest, instead of enabling this society to expand indefinitely with the aid of new means of subsistence, of communication, with new moral and intellectual cul-

[3] O'Donojú landed August 3, 1821, entered into communication with Iturbide August 5, and signed the Treaties of Córdoba with him August 24.

ture, sunk it at once into absolute passiveness and kept it systematically sunk for three centuries in a passiveness that little by little pervaded the whole of the new society.

The Spanish evolution whose final product was the Spanish-American nationalities did not have as a conscious objective the creation of national personalities that would be self-sufficient (although this should be the objective of all well-planned colonization, the Spanish domination in America was anything but well-planned). On the contrary, by means of an interior isolation of the Spaniard from the Indian (abandoned to rural servitude and to a religion that soon became pure superstition in his atrophied mind) together with the exterior isolation of New Spain from the entire non-Spanish world, this evolution tended to prevent the groupings that took form in conquered America and grew strong, through immutable natural law, from ever achieving self-rule.

But the energy of the Hispanic race achieved that result just the same, thanks to a communication between the shut-in peoples and outside ideas that was a kind of osmosis. Spain discovered that, after three hundred years, it had engendered American Spains that could get along on their own, and waged an idiotic war to prevent them from doing so. This violence, which had such a damaging effect on the future of the new nationalities, could have been avoided if the Spanish statesmen in the aftermath of the French Revolution had possessed O'Donojú's profoundly patriotic foresight.

The new personalities, though they demonstrated their desire for emancipation and their power to achieve it, were lacking in training for self-government; they could not have received that training from a nation in which the absolutism of the Hapsburgs and the administrative despotism of the Bourbons had smothered all political germination. And they revealed the same handicaps as Spain in their attempts to adopt free institutions. Mexico wasted time and blood and came to the verge of losing its autonomy in the endless mire of civil strife, which was merely a new expression of the spirit of adventure so characteristic of the Spanish race and which can be explained psychologically by the belief that every individual and social problem finds its solution in the direct intervention of Heaven—that is, by a miracle. Another hereditary belief pervades our history since that day: just as the Spanish people had inherited from the Jews the belief that they were God's new chosen people, the Mexican also believed they were a chosen people, having received the seal of divine predilection in the mineral wealth of their soil. They were the richest people in the world.

Fortunately, the group that since colonial times had formed the intellectual nucleus of the country soon came to understand how vain this dogma was and how disastrous were those tendencies, and the economic problem that lies at the bottom of all evolution and of all social regression became plain to them. They understood that a way to solve it must be found, with these two axioms as a starting point: (1) Mexico, because of the lack of means to exploit its natural wealth, is one of the poorest countries on the globe; (2) the spirit of adventure is an energy, which must be channeled forcibly into the habit of work. Once the problem was stated thus, in order to solve it a policy directly contrary to that of domineering Spain had to be adopted: all inner and outer barriers had to be swept away. We are going to trace in broad strokes the painful yet virile history of this tremendous endeavor.

BOOK THREE
The Republic

PART I. Anarchy

CHAPTER ONE

THE EMPIRE

(1821–1823)

The government; man of Providence; financial difficulties; embryonic parties; Iturbide; the Congress; republican revolution. Iturbide's abdication and end.

PEOPLES WHO ARE ACCUSTOMED to praying for, and expecting, all benefits to come through the direct intervention of Providence—and what people does not show this inclination?—see their successful leaders as Messiahs, whether these be true geniuses or merely men with luck. This ingenuous belief, we find, was held by the governing committee that was installed in the City of Mexico pursuant to the Plan of Iguala and the Treaties of Córdoba (O'Donojú and other Spaniards were members of the committee), and is expressed in the following paragraph from the Empire's declaration of independence:

The Mexican Nation, which has not been permitted to make its will known or its voice heard for three hundred years, emerges today from the oppression under which it has lived. The heroic efforts of its sons have been crowned with success, and we see the consummation of the never-to-be-forgotten enterprise which a genius exalted above all the admiration, praise, love, and glory that his country can heap on him commenced at Iguala and, overcoming well-nigh insuperable obstacles, has carried forward to a triumphant conclusion.[1]

And yet, what the Mexican nation could look back upon was not three hundred years of life but three hundred years of slow and incomplete gestation. It was born during the eleven years of conflict in the same way that every nation is born: by becoming aware of itself.

Iturbide was no exalted genius: he was a lucky man who performed for his country an incomparable, a supreme service, and then was overtaken by the shadow of error and misfortune, which the ephemeral splendor of a crown could not dissipate; but his tomb is lighted by a nation's gratitude and compassion. The words of the committee expressed the sentiments of the country as a whole; only the party of the Spanish or Mexican constitutionalists kept ironically silent, laying plans to shatter the idol's feet of clay.

Since the form of government was an empire, and the throne was actually vacant, till such time as Ferdinand VII of Spain should make known his decision, a regency was named, with Iturbide as president. O'Donojú was also a member, but he died just then and was replaced by Bishop Pérez of Puebla, a reactionary who had been stripped of power in Spain, an enemy of liberals, and a man without moral dignity of any kind. So the government was organized, but the situation remained chaotic. It was impossible for the Empire to carry on anything like a normal administrative life because of the necessity of providing for both the Army of the Three Guarantees and the surrendered Spanish garrisons and of paying doubled costs of administration—when the country was absolutely exhausted and still being harvested methodically by the satraps who ruled the provinces; when, with the most generous lack of foresight, direct taxes on the Indians had been suppressed, together with other important levies; when the principal port for commerce, Vera Cruz, was dominated by the cannons of Juan Dávila, the Spanish commandant, who had his own customhouse on the island of San Juan de Ulúa.

But everything was going to be remedied by the elections for con-

[1] This declaration of independence was proclaimed at a meeting presided over by Iturbide at the National Palace, September 28, 1821.

stituents called for by the Plan of Iguala. The Congress met; the Regency paid it homage; the ministers adulated it as a divinity; it was addressed as Your Majesty.[2]

And the assembly declared all sovereignty to be invested in itself; a part of this was delegated to an Executive (the Regency), and a part to the Judicial Power, according to the ritual of the new political doctrine. Everything seemed to indicate, in those sanguine days, that the clouds would pass, that all would soon be well. The economic situation was black, but the political one seemed to be clearing up. Spanish bureaucrats and officials considered incapable of loyalty to the Empire were relieved of their posts and left the country, as many rich Spaniards had done already, as others were preparing to do.

The Empire rounded out its territory. The Yucatán Peninsula, which had taken no part in the struggle for national freedom but which had nevertheless been a focus for intellectual emancipation, spontaneously joined the Empire, even though its economic interests were opposed, and the move was facilitated by the Spanish authorities themselves. Chiapas, where the influence of the clergy was omnipotent, had been an extremely active center for anticonstitutional propaganda; here the Plan of Iguala was favored as a counterrevolutionary measure. For the same reason it found favor in some parts of Central America: hence a growing sentiment for union with the Empire. In Guatemala and El Salvador a strong party of patriots succeeded in obtaining a declaration of absolute independence (September 15, 1822). But Mexican troops began to occupy the country. Adhesions to Mexico were the order of the day, and calls for elections to the Congress of the Empire were published. These were held, and Central America came to form part of the "great new Hispano-American state of the south," in the language of the times.

A certain drift toward anarchy was to be expected in the Congress, in view of the nation's infancy and the novelty of parliamentary institutions in a land that had never even dreamed of them till lately. It was all a fascinating game, full of surprises, revealing inexperience and inspiring doubts. Those who had been members of the Spanish Cortes

[2] The first National Congress, with 102 deputies, was inaugurated February 24, 1822, and met May 19 in the church of San Pedro y San Pablo, City of Mexico.

those who had traveled abroad, those who had studied political treatises were the new assembly's guides and masters. Soon groups with sharply diverse tendencies began to form. One group could not forgive Iturbide for having declared independence (the very president of the Congress, José Hipólito Odoardo, was the leader of the group). Another could not forgive Iturbide for having frustrated at Iguala all hopes of grafting the Spanish Constitution onto the ancient viceroyalty. Allied to this group was the Bourbon faction, which wanted a prince of Spain's royal house on the Mexican throne. Then there were the republicans, who detested the Plan of Iguala as a shameful compromise with Spain—but what else could have been done?—and were anxiously awaiting the rejection of the Treaties of Córdoba by Spain in order that they might organize a government similar to those in the other American countries. They hated Iturbide because of his past hostility to the insurgents, to the fighters of the heroic epoch; one of the regents shared these views. The group adhering to Iturbide was in the minority, but the army and the masses adored him.

It was plain that Iturbide, strong in his popularity, in his army, in his consciousness of having rendered the nation a great service, was becoming more and more impatient with the Congress for its obdurate opposition. The press, the Masonic lodges, which had increased rapidly, the old patriots, who had retained their rank in the auxiliary corps, were preparing to attack the liberator. And he, taking advantage of an attempt at counterrevolution by the Spanish governor on San Juan de Ulúa, who was supported by forces which had not yet left the country, published a series of official accusations, remarkable for their incoherence, against his adversaries in the Congress and the Regency. The upshot of all this was, first, a skirmish between Spanish and Mexican troops, which was given exaggerated importance (General Anastasio Bustamante was honored with the title "Hero of Juchi," after the spot where the action took place; heroes like him we have had in Mexico by the thousands) and second, some deplorable scenes and personal wrangles between Iturbide and his opponents "in the very bosom of the Congress," as the saying went. Both the Congress and the Regency lost prestige. But Iturbide's adversaries succeeded in holding him to a minority in the Regency itself, and the conflict grew ever more acute.

Then the news arrived in Mexico that the Spanish Cortes had senselessly and insolently rejected the Treaties of Córdoba. The Bourbon faction, dismayed, sought alliance with the republicans and former insurgents, who, led and organized by the Masonic lodges, began to shower Congress with petitions in favor of a republic like those of Colombia, Peru, and Buenos Aires. But this was not the general sentiment, which was, rather, indignation with Spain and rejoicing because rejection of the Treaties by the Cortes had broken the last possible tie with the motherland and put the Empire on its own, as a truly national undertaking. A vehement desire to defy the power of Ferdinand VII, to confront him with a challenge born of Independence, prevailed among the people. To them, Iturbide appeared to be, more than ever before, a guiding light and a beacon: he was the national pride incarnate. This explains the stand taken for the Empire by such men as Valentín Gómez Farías and Lorenzo de Zavala, future leaders of the radical party: they were eager to root out of the land the very last trace of Spanish domination.

Urged on by Iturbide's enemies, who were under the sway of the Masonic lodges, which went so far as to debate his overthrow by assassination, Congress unwisely attempted to downgrade the Regency, forbidding its members to hold command in the army. This was a direct blow at the Commander in Chief.

Iturbide retaliated with a pronunciamento by the capital's garrison, declaring him emperor. Congress was assembled, under conditions that made all deliberation impossible because of the delirious excitement among the masses, the soldiery, and the friars, and sanctioned the move in an illegal act which was later made legal. And the Empire, created at Iguala, from this moment (May 21, 1822) was ruled by "Don Agustín de Iturbide, the first of his Name, Constitutional Emperor of the Mexican Empire," to quote the decree.[3]

There is no point in discussing the conduct that Iturbide ought to

[3] Decree of May 21, 1822. On July 21 Iturbide was consecrated emperor in the metropolitan cathedral of Guadalajara by Bishop Juan Ruiz de Cabañas.

have observed in order to prevent the collapse of a throne mounted on sand. It is easy to play the role of the prophet with hindsight when we know the disastrous consequences of his venture and to judge him harshly for not having torn up the agreements made at Iguala and organized an enlightened dictatorship, the natural pattern for governments in a state of transition, to rule until such time as Spain should cease to be a threat and the republic, sound and strong, should be utterly delivered from the colonial matrix. In the actual situation, an empire, because of its semidivine aura, seemed preferable to a dictatorship. It satisfied the ambition of the victorious soldier who believed, not without some reason, that the country owed its being to him. And the people, incapable of understanding the advantages of a republic, applauded his elevation to the throne with such demonstrations of solidarity among all classes as would have turned the head of a man superior to Iturbide in character and intelligence. The Indians and poorly educated masses who had grown up with a religious faith in a monarchy regarded a Mexican king as the living symbol of independence.

But if ideas, when they become emotions, can rule the world, it is only on the condition that they are identified with self-interest, which is a base emotion, but an overpowering one. The Empire, despite its popularity, was born dead because it was born a pauper. In no time it disappointed the hopes of those who regarded it as a magic formula which would convert into gold for its employes—and every Mexican aspired to a government position—the inexhaustible natural wealth of the world's richest country, a fact so self-evident that anyone who dared to doubt it was frowned upon as unpatriotic.

The coronation ceremonies, inevitably, had a ludicrous and ostentatious aspect and amounted to the apotheosis of the parvenu, the climber, and the bounder; this, to the cultured element of Mexican society, which had a taste for epigrams and could tolerate anything but pretense, was the unpardonable sin. But in his organization of the Imperial Court (which several nobles of the colonial aristocracy joined), and in his choices for the Cabinet, the Council of State, and the army staff, Iturbide was generous and wise, honoring even his enemies, and society as a whole was excited and enchanted by the pompous inauguration of the Imperial Order of Guadalupe, by the kissing of hands, by the religious and popular festivities and the oratory of the national dynasty's early days.

And yet the new regime was already being devoured from within by financial crisis, for the cost of its upkeep was extremely high. And the Emperor was scrupulous—for when was a Napoleon ever known to lay hands on his subjects' funds? (This name and this example were Iturbide's fatal obsession.) Rumors of conspiracies by the Bourbon faction or by the insurgent or the republican groups abounded. Whether the rumors were true or false, such conspiracies were not unlikely, and waves of anxiety and apprehension, starting from the capital, spread to the provinces. Iturbide, violating the deputies' constitutional immunity, had several of them arrested for no other reason than that they were his adversaries, as there was no evidence to substantiate his charges, and this was the start of his attempt to seize absolute power.[4]

The latent conflict between the Emperor and the Congress, muted and postponed by the frenzied enthusiasm of the coronation days, finally broke out in open hostility. Congress, concerned with politics, had acquired little experience in administrative matters; finances had been handled on a basis of expediency, from day to day. The deficit was appalling, and the cost of maintaining the pomp of Empire and a battle-ready army of thirty-five thousand, which the emperor had no intention of disarming, was out of all proportion to the available resources. Iturbide insisted on putting through an electoral reform which would reduce the number of deputies by one half, a sensible plan, but poor politics at this juncture. The scheme was proposed by Lorenzo de Zavala, a republican from Yucatán who had been cruelly punished for his advanced political ideas in his youth and who, after serving as one of New Spain's representatives in the Cortes at Madrid, had returned to his native land with extremely radical but clear and positive convictions about the art of government. To their promotion he dedicated an extraordinary and highly cultured intelligence and an

[4] The arrest of the deputies took place on August 26 and 27, 1822.

aggressive temperament which could become inflamed to a terrible vehemence. Zavala was a man of vast ambitions, a man of boundless daring. His political ideal was the parliamentary system of the Anglo-Saxons, and his aim was to implant it in Mexico. But, in order to clear the way, he judged it necessary to rid the new nation of Spanish influence and to destroy the privileges of the classes that had ruled until now. This was the program of the liberal party in Mexico, and Zavala was, therefore, one of its preeminent founders. He had in Iturbide an admirable instrument with which to accomplish his first design: national and social independence from Spain. Zavala's electoral scheme, endorsed by the Emperor, was ignored by the Congress; a plan to create new courts which would be empowered to try cases of conspiracy as well as of homicide and robbery was rightly rejected by the Congress. Iturbide then put several deputies under arrest, forcibly expelled the remainder from their official meeting place, and, declaring the constituent Congress to be dissolved, appointed a provisional committee to carry on the government and to convoke a new Congress after a change in the electoral system.

The committee was confronted with the financial problem from the first moment of its existence. A practical solution, however temporary, was a matter of life or death. But the question was: how to provide for the very next day? So critical had the situation become, it was decided to levy a forced loan, a form of excise very like official brigandage. The Emperor was authorized to seize a shipment of over a million pesos which was headed for Vera Cruz, and the execution of this order was very like a brigand's assault. Zavala, to repair a deficit of several million pesos, drew up a plan for the Treasury which provided for a head-tax, the coining of a certain quantity of copper, and the printing of paper money. This currency, despite the government's honest efforts to redeem it promptly, was received with such distrust that it depreciated at an appalling rate.

At Vera Cruz, the brigadier Antonio López de Santa Anna had made an unsuccessful attempt on San Juan de Ulúa, and as a result, his situation was anomalous. The Emperor was deeply perturbed. In order to relieve Santa Anna of command and to consolidate the forces in

Vera Cruz, he went down to Jalapa; there he thought he had put the quietus on the unruly brigadier. He was mistaken. Santa Anna roused the garrison at Vera Cruz to insurrection, under the complacent gaze of the Spanish governor on Ulúa, and proclaimed something—it was hard to tell just what. A manifesto and a plan calling for a republic[5] were composed for him by Miguel Santa María, the representative of Colombia in Mexico and one of the Mexican politicians persecuted by Iturbide.

Iturbide understood the gravity of these events and sent his best soldiers and the general in whom he placed the highest trust, José Antonio Echávarri, to take Vera Cruz. The General realized that it would be impossible to take Vera Cruz by assault and that his army would disintegrate through the mere action of the climate. Believing, no doubt, that he was doing Iturbide a great service, since his cause was hopeless anyhow, he signed a pact, known as the Plan of Casa Mata, with the rebel Santa Anna in Vera Cruz on February 1, 1823. The Plan of Vera Cruz had repudiated Iturbide and had called for the restoration of the Congress he had dissolved. The new Plan recognized the nominal authority of the Emperor but demanded the prompt election of a new assembly under the supervision of the "army of liberation." The army thus had embarked on a series of transmogrifications: once royalist, it had become the Army of the Three Guarantees, and now, the Army of Liberation.

So as not to leave the old insurgents without a candle at the funeral —and this is hardly a metaphor—Guerrero and Bravo stirred up rebellion in the south. Though they were defeated by Armijo, he finally joined forces with them, since the army throughout the country clamored for the new Plan. Iturbide's second in command, the Spanish general Pedro Celestino Negrete, placed himself at the head of the military insurrection. Iturbide reassembled the Congress he had dissolved and shortly thereafter, since he had no support for a civil war, he sent in his abdication. This the Congress refused to accept, declaring the Empire to have been illegal, null and void from its inception—

[5] The Plan of Vera Cruz, proclaimed December 6, 1822, by Santa Anna and Guadalupe Victoria, was endorsed by Bravo and Guerrero January 11, 1823.

which was untrue. Iturbide went into exile, and his public life came to an end in March, 1823.[6]

One year later, when there were manifestations of a reaction in Iturbide's favor, the exile took a ship for Mexico, in the belief that there was imminent danger of a Spanish invasion and in the hope that he once again would have a chance to play a role of the first magnitude. Just at this time Congress declared him an outlaw and sentenced him to death in case he should ever return to his native land. Unaware of this terrible decree, he landed in Tamaulipas. The legislature, carrying out the political sentence with ruthless haste, had him executed at Padilla July 19, 1824. This was a political move, not an act of justice. Iturbide had rendered his country a supreme service, which cannot be idly dismissed as a betrayal to Spain. He failed to measure up to his task, but never deserved the scaffold as his reward. If the nation could have spoken, it would have absolved him.

[6] The Emperor convoked the Congress March 5, 1823; it assembled March 7. Iturbide sent in his abdication March 19, and the decree declaring the Empire illegal was promulgated April 8.

CHAPTER TWO

FEDERATION AND MILITARISM

(1823–1835)

The Constitution of 1824: Victoria's Presidency. The federalist revolt: Guerrero. Militarism: Bustamante. The reform program: Gómez Farías. Reaction: Santa Anna. End of the federal regime.

THE REVOLUTIONARY Plan of Vera Cruz impugned the legality of the Empire; the Plan of Casa Mata subjected the Emperor to the judgment of the restored constituent Congress. When Iturbide, succumbing to the pressure, convoked the Congress, it not only spurned his abdication, declaring the Empire illegal, but in order to cheat the monarchists of their last hope declared the Plan of Iguala obsolete insofar as it implied an invitation to the House of Bourbon. Thus, at one stroke two parties were legally annihilated—the Mexican imperialists and the Bourbon faction—and a republic was made inevitable. But what kind of republic? The educated groups among the victorious oligarchy—the top clergy, the highest-ranking army officers, the richest landowners—preferred a republic of the French type, in which the provinces would be dominated by the capital, a system that would have grown naturally out of the systems of the viceroyalty and of the Empire. This probably would have been the most sensible solution, the most politic; moreover the Congress was inclined to go along with it. And the Bourbon faction, on dissolving, became fused with the party that advocated this solution and which now began to call itself the "centralist" party. Among its leaders were such prominent men as Lucas Alamán, Father Mier, and Santa María. While they drew up no definite program, their ideas could be inferred from their more or less frank hostility to the federalist party. They could count on the support of every conservative group in the country, including the Spaniards, who owned nearly the whole of commerce and most of the mines and haciendas. This alignment gave rise to a curious political phenomenon. The reform party, or the "Jacobins," as Father Mier called them, brought together by a common antipathy for the Spaniards and other privileged groups, were not centralists, like the Jacobins in France, but federalists, and their aim was to set up a republic modeled on the constitution of the United States, of which they had a strictly theoretical knowledge. The leaders of this party, Miguel Ramos Arizpe, Zavala, and Gómez Farías, among others, in their efforts to organize it found powerful allies in Iturbide's former followers, who had been the fomenters of regionalism in every corner of the land.

Local autonomy had become entrenched in the provincial committees created by the Spanish Constitution, veritable little Congresses, purporting to be elected by the people. These had flourished under the Empire and became the distributing centers for political jobs and for the funds of the small local treasuries. Thus, each important city had its political oligarchy, clinging with a death grip to newly-won power and determined to compromise with no system except the federalist one, which evinced a strong tendency to separatism. Leadership in the "states' rights" movement was assumed by the former province of Nueva Galicia, calling itself the Sovereign State of Jalisco, by the former Eastern Interior Provinces, and by Yucatán. Nueva Galicia in the last years of the colonial regime had constituted a kind of separate viceroyalty; the former Eastern Interior Provinces were presently in the process of being welded into a formidable new state in the north by Ramos Arizpe, the highly intelligent and liberal cleric and one-time deputy to the Spanish Cortes; and Yucatán, whose geographical position, history, and economic interests—even its ethnic and linguistic peculiarities—made it in fact a small separate nationality, hardly felt at home in the Mexican Republic and only gradually, and not until late in the nineteenth century, achieved real solidarity with the rest of Mexico. The leadership of these states was followed by all the other former provinces of New Spain.

In Guatemala the federalist movement took a clear-cut separatist and nationalist turn, as was natural in view of its remote position and historic autonomy. The Mexican Congress, wisely and honorably respecting the inhabitants' wishes, held a plebiscite throughout Central America, which voted for independence (with the exception of Chiapas, firm in its adhesion to the Mexican Republic). Mexican garrisons were withdrawn and the new nation was solemnly recognized.[1]

The Congress that had created the Empire knew when its day was done. After attending to urgent financial and military matters it convoked a new constituent congress and dissolved itself.[2] That assembly of intelligent and inexperienced men had created, then demolished, the Empire. Quick to destroy, they did not know how to build. Our first experiment in parliamentary government turned out badly; since then there have been others that turned out worse.

The preponderance of federalists in the new Congress was so great, they believed they held a mandate to convert the federation, which already existed in loose, anarchic form, into a legal union. Since the fall of Iturbide, the Executive Power had consisted of a triumvirate: Negrete, a Spaniard of high standing as a soldier, but loathed by the insurgents; General Bravo, of purest integrity, who leaned toward the moderate federalists; and José Mariano Michelena, an ambitious intriguer who owed his position to a plan for independence that he had authored previous to the famous conspiracy of Querétaro [1810]. This Executive Power was constantly reshuffled, the members being assigned to various commissions, but replacements were invariably chosen from among the old insurgents, such as Guerrero and Victoria. The soul of the government was Alamán, the foreign minister, who would later write the history of this confused epoch, not without political insight

[1] A congress known as the National Constituent Assembly, was installed in Guatemala June 24, 1823, and on July 1 declared the independence of the "United Provinces of Central America."

[2] On May 21, 1823, the first Congress promulgated the order convoking the second constituent Congress, which assembled November 7.

and always in noble style, though his opinions are naturally open to dispute.

Alamán, who had been outstanding among the advocates of independence at the Cortes of Madrid, had acquired, on returning to his country, the conviction that the colonial regime was still the one to be preferred. And while he had no illusions that the regime could ever be brought back, he dedicated his brilliant mind and vast store of knowledge to a proposition that may be formulated thus: What Mexico needs is to revert to the Spanish system, although not as a dependency of Spain, and to depart from it only when absolutely necessary, and even then with caution. This sophism proceeded from a comparison of the anguish and dark forebodings of the present with the peace, tranquility, and resignation of the times prior to Independence. Men with less prejudice and more historical perspective than Alamán and others who thought like him would have perceived that the dead calm and stagnation of colonial times was the very cause of the destructive tempests that came later. During his first ministry Alamán was a strictly moderate federalist, but the course of events impelled him to organize the conservative party, which as yet was lacking in cohesion.

The Congress, well aware of the country's anarchic trend, tried to expedite the promulgation of the articles of federation,[3] even ahead of the definitive Constitution, with the intention of appeasing the clamorous extremists of the triumphant party. The remedy proved merely a palliative; the trouble was deep-seated. One symptom was the military uprising in which the garrison of the capital took part and which was led by Colonel José María Lobato; he later denounced as his instigators Michelena himself (who, although a member of the Executive Power, never ceased to intrigue) and the brigadier Santa Anna, already under court martial for attempting a federalist revolt. The rebels' principal aim was to seize money and power; their slogan, "to run the Spaniards out of public office." This drastic step, a violation of the Plan of Iguala, was doubtless politic, in the circumstances, and inevitable. It was tirelessly demanded by the old insurgents. Some joined the army, which they, along with the Iturbidistas, inoculated

[3] The reference is to the "Act to Constitute the Federation," dated January 31, 1824; the oath was sworn February 3.

with their hate for the Spaniards, who, though they had been, as a rule, very cruel enemies during the war for independence, now enjoyed excellent positions. Others formed nests of anticentralist, anti-Spanish agitation in the provinces.

The agitation for the banishment of Spaniards was justified by the imbecile act of the commander on San Juan de Ulúa, who bombarded Vera Cruz when he learned that a French army had entered Madrid to overthrow the Spanish Constitution, and by the ominous warnings from Europe of an imminent invasion of Mexico by Spain, backed by the Holy Alliance. There was no justification for the revolt, however, which, thanks to the admirable civic valor of the Congress, quickly sputtered out. Most of the deputies, to be sure, shared the sentiments of the revolt's leaders.

The anti-Spanish feeling of the masses—resentment against a people they knew only as grocers, exploiting and fomenting with cynical disdain the poor man's drunkenness—was expressed by the war-cry repeated in every tumult: "Down with the Gachupines!" This resentment was turned to political advantage by the former followers of Iturbide, who were in control of Jalisco and the whole of the west. Their leaders, General Quintanar and the military commandant Bustamante, carried on an active correspondence with the proscribed Emperor, inviting him to return to Mexico and to arbitrate the dispute between parties; they induced him to commit this utter folly. Letters from Iturbide to the Congress revealed his intentions; the Congress issued the "atrocious order" (as Zavala calls it) which outlawed the liberator and which he did not hear of until too late, after he had landed on Mexican soil. The Congress sent the generals Negrete, Bravo, and José Joaquín de Herrera to clean the imperialists out of Jalisco. This was done; the principal leaders were sent into exile, their subalterns shot.

The Congress labored on the Constitution, which contains transcriptions from the Spanish Constitution and from that of the United States. But even more notable is the eminently French, and consequently quite nonfederal, point of view that prevailed among its authors. The debate over an outright federal system reached a climax with Father Mier's unanswerable argument in opposition:

Federation is a system for unifying what is asunder, and for that reason has been adopted by the United States. Their entire colonial history makes a federal pact imperative, as the only possible way to cement a new nationality. Here it would be tantamount to dividing what is already unified, at a time when our crying need is to make the new Mexican nation firmer and more compact. If our population, scattered over an immense territory, does require decentralization, to some extent, in the administration of government, it nevertheless needs to be bound together by political ties that will promote the work of unification and resist the centrifugal tendencies of the outlying regions. For the nation must prepare to meet two dangers: one that is imminent, coming from Spain, and another that will inexorably arise from the proximity of the United States, which is growing steadily stronger and more aggressive.

All this was true, and the Federation was built on bases that were factitious. But it was no less true that public opinion overwhelmingly clamored for a federation, and any Congress that refused to provide one would have been summarily ousted. The Constitution promulgated in October of 1824[4] could have been nothing other than what it was: the expression of the almost unanimous opinion of the politically-conscious segment of the nation. This is the only incontestable argument that Zavala puts forth in his manifesto preceding our first Constitution; his other arguments, based on the striking differences between the various regions comprised in New Spain, could just as well be reasons for dismemberment as for federation.

The Constitution simply and wisely distributes the powers of the Federation, setting out: (1) component members; (2) organization of the central government, called, in the American fashion, "federal"; (3) classic division of this government into three independent yet perfectly integrated Powers and the composition and functions of each; (4) limits to the sovereignty of the states; (5) conditions for reforming the federal pact. In this disposition of power, the Constitution of 1824 is a model of well-made laws. But there are other items that show the authors' good judgment: division of the Congress into two chambers (essential to the federal system); election of the senators by the

[4] *Federal Constitution of the United States of Mexico*, promulgated October 4, 1824.

legislatures, of the deputies by a two-step process; an Executive Power vested in one person (and not in a college, as it had been since Iturbide's fall, to the detriment of its authority), renewable every four years (a grave error); and creation of a sovereign Judicial Power, composed of magistrates with permanent tenure—the creation, that is, of a center of stability and a guarantee of social order for the democratic society about to emerge.

The electoral laws had barely been published when the presidential elections were held. The politicians distributed among themselves the votes of the mute and all-suffering people. With general approval, Victoria and Bravo were declared elected as President and Vice-President. The Congress was made up of the best men the parties had to offer. The Supreme Court was composed of highly honorable and respected judges, under the presidency of the famed, one-time corregidor of Querétaro, Domínguez. And the country began to live a normal life, made possible by two circumstances. After Iturbide was shot, amid public stupefaction, in July of that same year of 1824, the imperialist party disappeared, fusing with the conservative and military party that was then being organized, and with it there disappeared a virulent focus of agitation. The other circumstance was the alleviation of the financial problem. The army and the bureaucrats were paid. And, ever since, this maxim has been proverbial in politics: "When salaries are paid, revolutions fade." What could be more natural in a country where the upper classes, because of their habits and education, must get their living from the government, which was nothing else than a bank for its employes, a bank guarded by armed employes who were called the army? The financial respite was the result of loans obtained from English houses, operations which have been criticized as short-sighted, and, indeed, they were mainly responsible for originating Mexico's foreign debt. But it is hard to see how anything much better could have been done, considering the precarious infancy of our Republic. Because of the rate of exchange an obligation of more than thirty million pesos at five and six percent brought a net benefit to the government of a trifle over twenty million. Of these, eight were largely spent on bad ships, bad guns, and war supplies, for everything pointed to armed conflict with Spain, and it was imperative to take possession of Ulúa.

But there was another consequence of our dealings with the English money market, a portentous one. The announcement of the English cabinet, early in 1824, that it would recognize the independence of the Hispano-American republics completely paralyzed the efforts of the Holy Alliance to help Spain recover its colonies. Spain was not even able to prevent the capture of San Juan de Ulúa, which was to have served as our Gibraltar.

Victoria's first Cabinet of conservatives, presided over by Alamán, was replaced by one of ardent federalists like Ramos Arizpe and of moderate liberals like Manuel Gómez Pedraza, but the tenor of the government was strongly anti-Spanish. The radical party, exploiting the imminence of national peril, inflated the attempts at conspiracy of a few Spaniards into horrendous crimes, which were unjustly punished by death. The goal now was not merely the separation of the Spaniards from public jobs, on the grounds that they constituted the principal barrier to social reform, to the abolition of privileges (a view which was not far wrong); the goal now was their total expulsion from the country and the confiscation of their property, a program which put all the forces of greed on the side of the radical group.

The United States, at the same time as England and in a more forthright manner, had welcomed our plenipotentiaries and had recognized our Independence. What is more, in the face of the overt contriving of the Holy Alliance with Spain, in a scheme to reconquer us, President Monroe had set forth in December 1823 the famous declaration known as the Monroe Doctrine, which can be summed up as follows:

> The government of the United States holds it to be a principle consonant with its rights and interests that no part of continental America can be considered as a domain open to colonization by any European nation. Any attempt by any European nation to force the submission of any people of the Americas who have attained their independence, or any attempt to control the destinies of any such people, will be taken as a manifestation of hostility against the United States.

Spain's idiotic threats and the prevalence of federalist ideas impelled an influential group of Mexican politicians, led by Zavala, to seek closer ties with the United States in every way possible in the conviction that the Americans would never try to carry their expansionist movement so far as to use force against our territory. These politicians, however unrealistically, took American virtues and institutions as their models. Joel Poinsett, the American plenipotentiary, a man of the highest culture, but given to proselyting, was imbued with the anti-Spanish notions of the radicals. He persuaded them to form a political association, in which he naturally took no part but whose oracle he seems to have been, with the object of organizing the radical movement so adroitly as to drive all adversaries from power. With José Ignacio Estevá, Secretary of the Treasury, Ramos Arizpe, Minister of Justice and the fervid deputy José María Alpuche Infante, Zavala, and others as sponsors, they founded the Masonic lodge of the York rite, which aspired to become the "Jacobin Society" of the Mexican Revolution. Poinsett helped organize it. The lodges of the rival Scottish rite were almost emptied; branches of the new apostolate, which dealt with all political matters, whether local or federal, were established in all the states. Soon these lodges constituted a government in fact which purposed to pull the strings of Victoria's easy-going government. The President faced dark days, notwithstanding the respite which the loans had brought to the exchequer and the prestige which he had gained from the surrender of Ulúa. Nothing was done to organize the budget during the period of relief from financial stress. The few millions that the government had received were sadly misspent, and when the two London houses that had facilitated the Mexican loans declared themselves bankrupt a few months apart, the temporary fountain of fiscal recourse was cut off. On top of this catastrophe, an encyclical of the Pope, Leo XII, condemning the independence of the colonies gravely perturbed many consciences. In spite of Rome's attitude, the Mexican government considered itself the heir of the privileges which the Church had accorded to the kings of Spain when it granted them the Patronate, and the minister of ecclesiastical affairs interfered in the administration of the Church. Civil war was already in the air.

There was a surge of political excitement throughout the country. Following the example of the capital, where two newspapers, *El Sol,* organ of the Scottish rite, and *El Correo de la Federación,* of the York faction, engaged in a savage duel, newspapers sprang up in the states, and journalists burgeoned on all sides. The states were completing their own constitutions and the strife between the York and Scottish lodges had the effect of stirring up popular interest in politics, for both parties strove to secure the support of the masses in order to triumph. Here was a flowering of democratic activity which would atrophy later on. The Congress, abounding in clergymen, discussed a possible concordat with Rome; it suspended the constitutional guarantees in cases of highway robbery (bandits infested the roads) and even—and this was monstrous—in cases of subversion. But the burning question was: what to do with the Spaniards? Public opinion was inflamed by agitation. A number of the legislatures decreed their expulsion. At last the Congress, dominated by the York faction, decreed the expulsion of every Spanish military man in the country, of every Spaniard who had arrived since 1821, and of every Spaniard considered suspect by the government; all the rest had to renew their oaths of loyalty.[5] Generals Negrete and Echávarri were banished. Groups of missionary friars abandoned the country. The highest and lowest classes were filled with consternation, but the middle-class partisans of the York faction were unperturbed, convinced that, in the circumstances, there was no alternative.

An armed reaction against the dominant Yorkists, attempted by moderates and conservatives of the Scottish rite and led by General Nicolás Bravo, was put down by General Guerrero. The dissidents had clamored for the suppression of the Masons, for a new Cabinet, and for the expulsion of Poinsett.

This definitive triumph of the York faction split it in two. Those who wanted further reforms and measures against the Spaniards rallied around Guerrero; those who felt it was time to halt the revolution, lest it destroy itself, proclaimed the candidacy of Gómez Pedraza, Secretary of War, for President of the Republic. Once a royalist officer, then an adherent of Iturbide, whose fall inspired him with a terrible hatred for the Spaniards, he had a highly educated and emancipated mind and was gifted as a speaker. Because of his character and talents he was better fitted for the Presidency than General Guerrero, whose services

[5] Law of March 20, 1829.

to his country were immense but whose utter lack of education made him subject to the tutelage of his advisers, especially Zavala, the most active, intelligent, and feared of them all. Through pressure exerted by members of the Cabinet and by the President himself, Gómez Pedraza was elected by a majority of the legislatures. The result had scarcely become known when Santa Anna declared for Guerrero, thus setting the pattern whose endless repetitions made the bloodiest chapter in our history. Beaten and hemmed in at Oaxaca, Santa Anna found himself in an untenable position. But the revolution had gained support in several states, where the local militia had been created for the specific purpose of balking the military commandants appointed by the Federation. And, finally, the "revolution of La Acordada," as it is known, broke out in the City of Mexico, where it was organized by Zavala and led by Lobato and by Guerrero himself. Gómez Pedraza and the Cabinet fled. Victoria went before the rebels as a supplicant, hoping to prevent excesses. But the mob was unleashed, and not even the leaders of the revolution, not even Zavala, despite his energy, could keep it from sacking the National Palace and the cluster of Spanish-owned shops called El Parián, right on the Zócalo, the City of Mexico's principal square. Victoria named Guerrero Secretary of War; Congress, violating legal suffrage, declared him President and declared General Bustamante Vice-President. The federal system had fallen, alas, into dishonor.

General Guerrero's administration was born dead. Only great firmness of purpose could have redeemed his usurpation of power in the eyes of the country. But even if he had vigorously carried out the simplest and wisest of programs, not much could have been accomplished, for the transition between the colonial regime and self-government had been too abrupt, too poorly prepared for by social and political habits. Each step had stirred up such a tumult of discontent, had ignited such smoldering hate that years and years would have to pass before the earthquake could subside, before the Republic could acquire stability through the radical transformation of its economic structure. The disease was in the very nature of things, and was irremediable. In order to assess the relative virtues of the governments that followed one another in Mexico after the calamitous revolution of

La Acordada, we must ask ourselves this question: To what extent did they alleviate or aggravate the effects of an incurable disease?

The expulsion of the Spaniards by decree of Congress was not only unjust and unnecessary from the social point of view (for, whatever their defects—and these were absurdly exaggerated—the second generation of Spaniards always became Mexicans), it was political folly, for the last defense against the Spanish government's schemes of reconquest was thereby tossed away. After this measure was taken by the Guerrero government, in compliance, so it believed, with an imperative mandate, war with Spain, which did not exist as yet, became inevitable. And while any invasion was sure to fail, the financial situation, already disastrous, was bound to become incalculably worse through expenditures for defense. The government could, of course, have taken refuge in bankruptcy, but then the Republic's credit would have been permanently ruined.

Zavala, as President Guerrero's Secretary of the Treasury, drew up a remarkably sound plan for fiscal reorganization. Far from deceiving the country, as Victoria's Secretary of the Treasury had done, he courageously showed forth the problem with all its virtually insuperable difficulties. But the financial problem was not to be solved until the economic problem which stifled the society like a dense fog was well on the way to a solution. The expulsion of the Spaniards and the deplorable incidents that accompanied the triumph of Guerrero's revolution had killed whatever hope Europe's mercantile centers might have had that a fully responsible nation would be stabilized here. Our commerce began to wrest a precarious existence between the demands of the ravenous customs agent and contraband, which was being organized as a national institution. The exploiters of hunger and of the government's penury had a clear field, and they began their very simple system of sucking the blood of an anemic organism, thereby crippling the Republic for over half a century. The typical operation was this. The government was loaned a small sum, enough to defray expenses for one more day; this amount was delivered, the lesser part in cash, the greater part in paper of the public debt, which was acquired at extremely low cost and which the government accepted at par. Interest at a high rate was added, and repayment was made by means of drafts against the customs houses; these drafts were sold to importers. The resulting larceny and strangulation were an open scandal, but soon ceased to arouse protest because society and the government became inured to the system and submitted to it slavishly. This was the empire of usury, the actual form of government under which the new nation was forced to live, no matter whether it was called federalism, centralism, or dictatorship.

Zavala tried to cope with the system by resorting to measures which, though arbitrary, were essential. The result: all the money was hidden away. He tried, and failed, to restore foreign credit by assigning a percentage of the revenues to payment of the interest (which was not being paid) on the external debt. The only good he accomplished was the abolition of the government's monopoly of tobacco, a monopoly that was stifling one of the richest branches of our budding agriculture.

Then the war came. A small contingent of the Spanish army landed on the east coast, and the Republic, at the cost of a thousand sacrifices, was able to muster against it an army only slightly larger. But an exhausting effort was made to prepare a defense against the much more formidable invasion that was expected to follow the vanguard, led by Isidro Barradas. And the usurers, smiling ironically, once again took over the Department of the Treasury; one must live, even though it be with a dog collar around the neck. The invaders were forced to capitulate in Tampico—thanks to the intelligence, the skill, the serene and lofty valor of General Mier y Terán, plus General Santa Anna's temerity—after a series of hot battles during which Spanish officers were astonished to see that the Mexican soldier, whenever he acquires (through marvelous instinct) the conviction that his leaders are determined to fight to the death and will set him an example, is the peer of any soldier in the world.

But the government's position was still shaky. The Secretary of the Treasury inspired resentment because of his drastic measures and radical projects, and odium because of his friendship with the plenipotentiary Poinsett. Guerrero inspired the poorly disguised disdain of an upper crust that prided itself on a culture which, except for good manners, it did not possess. The President was irresolute; the Cabinet members were at odds. Not even the enthusiasm aroused by the victory at Tampico, which, as everybody understood, meant the end of Spanish attempts at reconquest, was sufficient to save the situation.

But the frustrated invasion had two consequences: the reorganizing of the army, in which the remainders of veterans corps were incorporated, and the forming of bodies of militia by the states, which thus acquired very nearly the footing of independent nations. Herewith began the rivalry between the national guard and the army, which led inevitably to the struggle between centralism and federalism. Guerrero's government realized that it had lost control of the armed forces and that two generals, Bustamante and Santa Anna, loomed larger in the country than the President. He, in an attempt to dispel the oncoming storm, dismissed Zavala as Secretary of the Treasury and asked that Poinsett be recalled. But the faction of the York party that the revolution of La Acordada had vanquished, in alliance with the Scottish party and all the conservative elements, was actively throttling the government, which had not a penny at its disposal and was doomed.

Toward the end of 1829 a military revolution breaking out in Campeche rapidly overwhelmed the entire Yucatán Peninsula. This rebellion proclaimed centralism, an odd thing in a state that clearly aspired to autonomy. But the Republic was federal, so the separatist movement had to be centralist.

At Jalapa, near the close of 1829, the reserve army declared against the government. Bustamante and Santa Anna were expected to head the movement, but the latter backed out in order to make himself available when the next revolution—as each barracks mutiny was called—came around. The Plan of Jalapa upheld the Federation but babbled of discontent, of violated laws, of a neglected—meaning an unpaid—army and demanded that the "august" Congress be assembled so that it could find a remedy for the country's ills. In short, the Plan was ridiculous, but Guerrero's administration had become so unpopular, everybody applauded. Guerrero marched off to combat the rebellion, taking his meager army south and then suddenly going his separate way. Bustamante occupied the capital, and the reserve army, descendant of the "Army of the Three Guarantees," named itself "Protector of the Constitution."

There was a pretext for the revolution in that Guerrero's authority was strictly unconstitutional. But so, for the same reason, was Bustamante's. Therefore the Congress, meeting in January of 1830, did not declare Guerrero's election null, but declared him morally unfit for the office. This legislative farce raised the curtain on the opening act of a tragedy for the deposed President.

General Bustamante, former royalist officer, dubious "Hero of Juchi," unyielding Iturbidist whose hate for Iturbide's enemies made him temporarily an ardent federalist, was prone to energetic and even bloody measures, being convinced that fearful, exemplary punishment should be inflicted as a deterrent to those who exploited anarchy (he excepted himself from this category, for he confused his ambition with the national interest). Earnest, brave, honest, he represented a general longing for stability (which is what the conservative classes that naturally supported him called stagnation).

His Cabinet, presided over by Alamán as Secretary of State, evinced a strongly reactionary trend. The privileged classes, frightened by the tendencies of the preceding government, felt their interests safeguarded by this one, in the belief that it would try to conserve and centralize, under a transparent mask of federalism, as much of colonial Mexico as could survive in the new nation.

The entire year of 1830 was devoted to pacifying the country. A number of states formed coalitions for defense against the central government. Others, such as Yucatán and Tabasco, remained outside the federal compact. Texas, now completely Americanized, gravitated more and more toward its natural magnet in Washington. In the southern reaches of the states of Michoacán, Puebla, and Mexico (the territory now covered by the state of Guerrero), the deposed President, though sick and inactive, was the focus of a flaming rebellion. The government deliberately adopted a system of military terrorism, and repression was bloody. Nearly all the leaders of the armed rebellion were executed. The press was silenced—only two periodicals were left in the City of Mexico—and some deputies were rabidly persecuted. The whole harsh and brutal system—we dare not add that it was unnecessary, for the civil war had to be ended at all costs—culminated in a great crime, the execution of Guerrero, one of the nation's founders, an honest, candid, zealous exemplar of rural patriotism, which was never bloodthirsty under his leadership. What horrified the conscience of the country was the vile treachery through which Guerrero was captured in Acapulco by the abominable Italian, Francisco Picaluga, and the astounding failure of the military judges to take into consideration the achievements of the unfortunate warrior. Ambitious partisans had tried to make a politician out of a man who was only a great Mexican.

The country, seething with revolt, was effectively subdued, and peace prevailed at last. This fact raised the national credit somewhat. The notion still persisted in foreign lands that Mexico possessed marvelous wealth, whose exploitation had been made impracticable by the insecurity born of civil strife. The mining enterprises that had been largely abandoned resumed operations, and English capital once again began to move toward the Republic. Foreign trade increased at the same rate as domestic business, and revenues rose. The government, which had found the exchequer wholly bankrupt and which had barely been able to subsist by resorting to the system of partial loans (usury), now enjoyed a breathing spell, could make a rudimentary beginning at shaking off the fetters of usury, and once again could pay the interest on the foreign debt.

Alamán, in keeping with his life-long principles, authored decrees prohibiting colonization by Americans along the northern frontiers (a most imprudent act of hostility, which our neighbors could not forgive) and organized a highly artificial system of protection for our domestic industry, which did not as yet exist. A bank was established, to be supported with part of the duties from imports, for the purpose of facilitating money and machinery to future manufacturers. Thus, he attempted to create, by fiscal legislation, a carefully protected industry in a country where the primary materials for it were not to be found. He tried to convert the Mexican Republic into a manufacturing country when there were no means of communication, no combustibles and no iron—not even any consumers.

Santa Anna started a strictly military revolution, inspired by the presence of cash in the customhouses of the gulf ports and the eagerness of speculators to acquire import permits at a low price (these had been brought nearly to par by Bustamante's administration). Moreover, he feared Bustamante less than he feared General Mier y Terán, a man of superior endowments, who had just been elected President by the legislatures and who a little later committed suicide.

The government forces dealt the insurrection a terrific blow at Vera Cruz. But the radical federalist party, at whose stronghold in Zacatecas the governor, Francisco García, had amassed large stores of military equipment, proceeded to set the hinterland ablaze. Bustamante went out to meet the advance of the federalist militia outfits and destroyed them. But the rebellion had already spread and had hoisted a legal banner: return to the state of things as they were in 1828 and, in consequence, the inauguration of Gómez Pedraza as constitutional President. When Bustamante became convinced that the civil war might drag on indefinitely, he made a pact with Santa Anna (December, 1832) and obliged his army to accept the new order of affairs. Although the Congress, with civic integrity, refused at first to rubber-stamp what the generals had illegally contrived, it had to back down, and Santa Anna, with his "Army of Liberation" (third transformation in ten years of the "Army of the Three Guarantees"), took possession of the capital.

The era of Mexican pronunciamentos may be said to have commenced in Spain, the classic land of military rebellions in our century. Only in the Hispanic countries has the army been regarded as having the right to speak for the nation, in spite of the fact that it nearly always speaks for the ambitions and the greeds of its chiefs and of the figures that control them. The example of the motherland has been most adeptly followed by Mexico in this particular. The revolution of La Acordada was hardly a military movement, nor yet a popular one, but a conspiracy of demagogues, who assaulted the exchequer in order to loot it, just as their followers assaulted the shops of El Parián in order to sack them. The army took revenge when Bustamante rebelled at Jalapa, and a thoroughly military regime was imposed for the first time. Militarism had not yet reached its apogee—Santa Anna would bring about its apogee—but it did prevail and, as is always the case, steeped the country in blood. Militarism is sometimes a remedy for countries sick with chronic anarchy, provided that the peace imposed by terror is followed by the peace that social welfare brings, by what we may call economic peace. Bustamante and his counselors had neither the time nor the foresight to turn their two years of political and financial order to good advantage. They had no interest in the social and economic problem, in the persistence of privileged classes, in the outrageous distribution of the public wealth. They sought to cure all ills by creating a factitious industry, thereby forcing the masses to support an ineffectual group of manufacturers and encouraging contraband, which leeched the main artery of revenue.

The reaction that overthrew Bustamante was led by men exasperated by endless political executions, by the torrents of blood that had flowed in the civil war. To them Bustamante's administration was like a black trinity, with the President and his ministers, Alamán and José Antonio Facio, in the background, with the satanic figure of the Judas Picaluga emerging from hell in the foreground, and, between this shadow and that sinister trio, the body of Guerrero, riddled by Mexican bullets.

The revolution had claimed to stand for resumption of the constitutional legality that had been interrupted. Hence, its titular chief was the President legally elected in 1828, Gómez Pedraza. He appeared with a coldly doctrinaire program, whose object was to make revolutions impossible by laying down rules of law. As if this were feasible so long as the evolution of the social state did not promote the instinct to preserve peace as the supreme guarantee for productive work, but, rather, encouraged the hope of obtaining, through sudden changes, indefinite and undefinable rewards!

The one thing about Pedraza's program that the nation could understand was his promise to turn the Presidency over to Santa Anna, who thus, after years and years of grasping for power, now had it handed to him on a platter. The populace paraded its idol's portrait on the garish floats of triumphal processions, while chanting in his praise hymns of puerile doggerel set to infantile tunes. The new radical party, having graduated from the Yorkist lodges to street-fighting and thence to barracks mutiny, to the civic militia, to prison, and to gory defeat, was driven now by passion for revenge. It raised Dr. Valentín Gómez Farías to the Vice-Presidency and filled the seats of Congress with inexperienced but irrepressible novices, who sought to salve their rankling grievances by pushing measures for reform.

The Spanish government, shortsighted as ever where America was concerned, failed to see that, despite the obvious futility of trying to regain the lost colonies, the situation of the Spaniards in Mexico could be saved only by recognition of Mexico's independence and that without such recognition a formidable party would feel constrained to proceed with the persecution of the Spaniards, who, without exception, had given either moral or material aid to the Bustamante regime, which had made no effort to enforce the harsh laws against them. Even Gómez Pedraza, a just and moderate man, was adamant on this point, and very nearly his first official act was to reactivate the order of expulsion.

General Santa Anna delegated his powers to his Vice-President, Gómez Farías—that is to say, to the extremists of the York party, the "pure ones," as they were called to distinguish them from those who favored reform by half-measures. This ruling party was clearly a small minority of the nation. The populace of Indian and mestizo farmers, who served under arms whatever force happened to be strong enough at the moment to rip the rural family asunder and snatch the father and sons away by the levy, had no light to guide them other than their priests and superstitions. The populace of urban workers obeyed their masters. The masses were a negative quantity: they did not count. The oligarchy, consisting of landowners, merchants, professional men, and more or less independent workers, as well as of bureaucrats, the army, and the clergy, was split into two factions. The larger faction was composed of the aristocratic and privileged classes, to wit:

1. The rich, through selfishness and cowardice, were almost wholly withdrawn from public affairs, endlessly parroting in the drawing-room, the manor, the sacristy, their favorite maxim: "Only those who have nothing to lose can afford to take part in politics." Had they been able to, they would have brought back the tranquil era of the viceroyalty.

2. The bureaucrats, almost unanimously conservative, resented any attempt to disturb their close ties with religion and the clergy. The rare emancipated individuals among them belonged to the expiring Masonic lodges. But the bureaucrats served those who paid them, and they plotted with deadly, unrelenting solidarity against those who failed to pay them.

3. The top clergy were now more than ever determined to defend

their rights and privileges, especially since the Pope had appointed as heads of the Mexican Church new prelates of outstanding virtues and attainments and had established that the Patronate was solely a prerogative of the king of Spain and did not pass to his forcible heirs, the American governments. The lower clergy, on the contrary, seethed with liberal and reformist ideas; not a few, in the legislatures or through the press, demanded the abolition of privileges, even the legalization of religious tolerance. They stemmed from Hidalgo and Morelos.

4. The army fluctuated between its sworn duty, obedience to the government, and personal loyalty to its chiefs, playing first one role and then the other. The cause of centralism brought about an alliance with the clergy.

The minority faction of the oligarchy, known as the reform party, consisted of the petty bourgeoisie or lower middle class, who hated Spaniards, and of young lawyers and others of the professional class, who turned out most of the eager and ambitious new politicians. At the forefront of a phalanx of intellectuals who were devoted to the ideal of equality and were recruited mostly in the state capitals stood a vanguard of highminded patriots who were perhaps ahead of their time and certainly ahead of their social environment. The reform party, always a minority, tended to increase through enlistments from the lower classes, recruited in the schools, in political societies and meetings, which were all forums for ceaseless propaganda. This faction, in 1833, was the instrument of democratic change and held the reins of power.

The program of this minority called for social and economic reform. The goal of the generation that now came to manhood, twenty years after the great insurgents of 1810, was to complete their work of emancipation, to extirpate the deepest root left imbedded in society by the colonial regime: the undisputed authority of the Church. The goal, in brief, was to make Mexican society over into a lay society. The first blows had been struck by the Spanish regime. The expulsion of the Jesuits and the confiscation of their wealth served as a precedent for the nationalization of Church property and exposed the incongruity of a state—officially recognized and with a foreigner, the Pope, for its prince—within a state. The reformist doctrines of Zavala and Gómez Farías were but the philosophic and economic amplification of the strictly royalist doctrines set forth by the ministers of Charles III. But the historic origins of the reform movement can be found in the petitions of the municipalities as far back as the first century of the colonial regime, when the king was asked to forbid the building of any more convents or churches and to put a limit on the number of religious allowed in the country. The immediate issue upon which the reform party seized was the question of the Patronate. The Pope had anathematized the Independence of Mexico, refusing to recognize the new nation, but then had carried on extraofficial negotiations and had filled the vacant bishoprics. The Mexican government claimed the prerogative, as successor to the kings of Spain, of nominating bishops and of taking a hand in Church affairs. But the Pope and the bishops contended, with irrefragable logic, that the Patronate had been granted specifically to the kings of Spain, was not transferable, and could be revoked by the Church at any time. This, indeed, was self-evident. Only a little less evident, however, was the new government's right to revoke the special privileges (exemption from taxes, immunity of the clergy from trial except by their own class) that had been conferred on the Church by the kings in return for the Patronate; likewise, the government's right to recover the immense territorial wealth that had been donated to the Church directly by the Crown. The blow might have been postponed indefinitely had the Pope been amenable to a concordat. But the Roman Curia was obdurate and resorted, as always when confronted by the irresistible tide of new ideas, to dilatory tactics. And the advocates of reform in 1833 were ardent apostles of new ideas. Though they were accused of being anti-Christian, they were not. Most of them were even good Catholics. But they burned with a passion for equality and, intent on their politico-economic goals, moved toward three objectives (which, however, were not attained for another generation): (1) to strip the Church of its privileges; (2) to bring Church property out of mortmain and into circulation as a part of the general wealth; and (3) to transform, by means of education, the minds of the young. Without education there could be no freedom of thought or of religion; this last objective, therefore, was the basic one. The Church, of course, could never consent to any such education, for the denial of liberty of conscience was the very foundation of its authority.

The Vice-President's first move, with the connivance of the vindictive and suspicious president, Santa Anna, was to stifle resistance by lopping off the leaders of the opposition. By an arbitrary and vengeful law many of the most prominent Mexicans were proscribed, after undergoing cruel harassment. The former President, Bustamante, was the first to be exiled. Some fled; others—statesmen, bishops, writers—went into hiding. Bustamante's ministers were indicted for the political assassination of Guerrero, even though not all of them were implicated, as the trial of Alamán established beyond any doubt.

Upper-class society was perturbed. The clergy denounced the government as a monstrous enemy of religion. Church services to implore divine protection, the lamentations of prophets, the wail of misereres were redoubled by the horrible calamity of a cholera epidemic. Official efforts to combat the epidemic by means of quarantine, isolation, and the suppression of public gatherings gave the cities the fearful appearance of deserted places by day, and by night the flare of fat-pine torches lighted biers on their way to graves and priests on their way to impart the last rites. The wrath of heaven was manifest in this calamity, brought down on the Republic by an impious government. So the Church declared. And upper-class society was perturbed.

But nothing could dismay those men with nerves of steel, who were like the Jacobins of the Great Revolution. The liberal press, unrestrained in its bitter attacks on the clergy, did not attack religion, but, on the contrary, rudely pointed out the contrast between the behavior of the clergy and the precepts of the Gospel. In several of the states the press stirred up a furor, and one legislature decreed the occupation of Church property and the suppression of convents. Extremely radical projects were debated in the Congress, in a kind of prelude to the definitive Reform that would come to fruition twenty years later. Important steps were taken, and even though a wave of reaction wiped them out immediately, these clearly indicated the goal toward which the liberals would continue to strive throughout the centralist dictatorships which were to augment their ranks, their experience, and their animosity.

The government pretended to believe that it was vested with the viceroys' right to the Patronate and proceeded to nominate curates, to exercise the veto over candidates for Church offices, to decide which of the Pope's bulls should be allowed to circulate, and to prohibit the collection of tithes and other ecclesiastical dues through civil action. In the states, priests were forbidden to exact personal service, and an attempt was made to extirpate the Indian custom of converting religious festivals into pagan orgies and farces, a custom which prevented the rural worker from accumulating anything and kept him in idolatry and which the Church ought to have suppressed in defense of its own decorum. These measures were all concerned with the present, however, and provision had to be made for the future. The University was abolished, with the aim of improving by destruction, instead of transforming by improvement. A wiser procedure would have been to replace the old University with a thoroughly national and secular one. In Europe the medieval centers of scholastic learning known as universities were constantly undergoing change, constantly adopting lay ideas of emancipation and of science, and today they are everywhere the sum of modern society's collective effort to free itself from antiquated modes of thought. Only in our country has "university" been mistaken as a synonym for "school of reaction"; this is an instance of the superstitious attitude toward words which has always been characteristic of the Mexican liberal party, wherein it has proved itself very Latin, indeed. With the University abolished, education was organized on a more rational plan. There was emphasis on the teaching of science, and a strenuous effort was made to propagate elementary schooling as the foundation for the gradual selection of teachers for the higher grades and the professions. This was a plan of education with a vision; the aim was to foster democracy, to make the Mexican people aware of their rights.[6]

The reactionary element, badly hurt, fought for its life. Salvation

[6] The University was abolished by decree of October 19, 1833. The plan for education summarized here was promulgated in a decree of October 23.

was at hand, however. The radical government depended, especially in the states, on the civic militia; therefore, it made an effort to eliminate the army, whose privileges were the subject of constant criticism. The army's interests thus became identified with those of the Church, for these were both privileged classes. Then the barracks revolts commenced, and the peculiar thing about them was that they all recognized the Presidency of Santa Anna and in several instances even proclaimed him dictator. The President would assume his powers from time to time, effectively suspending the work of reform, or would take the field to suppress revolt. And he was captured once by the very forces that had proclaimed him dictator, a contretemps that moved the Federal Congress to make highly ridiculous protestations of loyalty. But on the whole the astute general remained at his hacienda in Vera Cruz, holding himself aloof from the reform movement with the object of waiting to see whether or not it was going to prevail, so that he could either take the credit for it or else repudiate it and turn its failure to his personal advantage. Meanwhile, for suffering, afflicted upper-class society, he was a distant beacon of hope.

A barracks revolt in the capital itself was put down with admirable aplomb by the Vice-President, who declared a state of siege and called out the militia. Santa Anna, however, decided to take advantage of the situation, and, simulating flight from captors, who were in fact his own partisans, he showed up in the capital, where he made common cause with the reformers in order to secure their confidence and gain the time he needed to hatch his plans. He took the field against some rebel generals. By the beginning of 1834 the President had maneuvered so astutely, both parties in the conflict were assured he was on their side. In April of that year he suddenly took charge of the Presidency, dissolved the Congress, ran Vice-President Gómez Farías out of the country, and launched a persecution of the reform party. He abrogated all the reform laws and appointed a conservative Cabinet, to the tremendous applause of high society, rid at last of those wild radicals who, knowing themselves to be in the minority, still dared to take steps which pointed the way that Mexico must follow in later years or else renounce a place amongst the representatives of modern culture.[7]

[7] Santa Anna dissolved the Fifth Congress of the Union May 31, 1834. Elections for a new congress were convoked July 9.

General Santa Anna was a man with just enough intelligence to develop in himself to the highest degree the faculty called astuteness—an amalgam of crafty dissembling, perfidy, and perspicacity. His only religion was boundless ambition, swollen a hundredfold by his conviction that he was the Republic's founder and hence deserved the privileges of a conqueror, an ambition sustained, moreover, by figments of Catholic superstition, by his ingenuous faith in his role as an instrument of Providence. Vain as a mulatto, he was exceedingly susceptible to flattery, which intoxicated him and puffed him up to the pomposity of an African sultan. Without principles of any kind and without scruples, he was immensely popular with the troops, who felt he was one of them. Ignorant of military science, he would never hesitate to take command of any campaign, even though he had no qualifications except the ability to infuse the troops with his own ardor and so great a scorn for caution that he could look danger impavidly in the face. This idol of the permanent army never showed any more capacity as a soldier than a colonel of the national guard.

Santa Anna spent the year 1834 laying the foundation for a centralist reaction. The army disarmed the civic militia in many places, dissolved legislatures, besieged cities, and occupied a number of states. Several others, like Chiapas and Yucatán, were in chaos, and there were uprisings on all sides. The army's domination of the country insured the victory of the reactionary party in the elections for the new Congress, which assembled in January of 1835. Then, under the auspices of the Secretary of War, and while the President in the seclusion of his hacienda pretended to hold aloof, there was a spate of pronunciamentos in favor of changes in the Constitution of 1824. The Congress (with no legal justification whatsoever) decided it was empowered to declare itself a constituent body.[8]

The federal system had come to an end. The government of Zacatecas rebelled when an attempt was made to disarm it by decree. But Santa Anna conquered the state, forcing it to submit and dissolving the militia. Before the year 1835 had expired, the Congress had promulgated the bases of the centralist code.[9] Like nearly all the political

[8] By decree of May 5, 1835, the Congress declared itself invested with the power to reform the Constitution.

[9] "Law or Bases for the New Constitution," December 15, 1835.

vagaries that have made our history a gigantic tangle of difficulties, comparable only to the difficulties which nature herself has interposed in our path toward moral and material progress, the Federation was a phase which, in the transitory circumstances of that time, was brought about inevitably by resistance to social emancipation, a phase essential to the continuance of our political life.

CHAPTER THREE

CENTRALISM AND CONFLICT WITH THE UNITED STATES (1835–1848)

Texas; Santa Anna. The first centralist constitution; Bustamante; war with France. Civil war; second centralist Constitution; Bustamante; Yucatán. The United States; provocations and insults. The last of centralism; war with the United States. The federalists resurgent; Santa Anna; North Americans in the country's heart. End of the war; peace treaty of 1848.

HE FIRST THREE DECADES of our history as a nation were overcast by the menace and fear of a conflict with Spain. But, after the death of Ferdinand VII, the rise to power of the reform party in Spain and a terrible civil war changed entirely the situation which had produced the abortive attempts at reconquest. Assaults on the supremacy of the Church and clergy became progressively more drastic and were followed by frightful bloody riots. By comparison, the efforts of our York party to found a lay government in Mexico were mild and innocuous. Any further attempt at reconquest was out of the question. The next step, then, was recognition of the former colonies' independence, and this step was taken by the minister José María Calatrava toward the end of 1836 when solemn diplomatic sanction was accorded to relations between

Spain and Mexico. Had this been done ten years earlier, a great deal of grief and woe would have been avoided.

The truth is that federalism and sympathy with the United States to the point of seeking an alliance with them—notions cherished by the founders of our early liberalism—were natural consequences of Spain's attitude. When this began to change, our anxieties turned northward, where the Texas problem loomed on the horizon, scarcely eclipsing, however, the colossus of might and ambition that towered beyond. A war with Texas did not preoccupy the Mexicans; what did overcast the entire period of centralism was the fear of a war with the United States. The fear was well founded: the United States could easily cut off our meager revenues and our communication with the outside world by seizing our unfortified ports, so that we would have to devour ourselves in desperate civil strife. Fortunately for Mexico, the war came as a direct invasion which, while shamefully laying bare some of our intimate weaknesses, stirred our blood, arousing the valor of the most self-abnegating people in the world—for the masses had no positive blessings to defend, nothing but what was abstract or emotional—and the disorganized nation achieved a measure of cohesion at last.

The most redoubtable legacy left to us by Spain was the vast stretch of desert along our northern frontier, beyond the Rio Grande and the Gila, uninhabited and in the main uninhabitable, with extensive belts of fertile land and others hopelessly sterile. The distances separating these regions from our political center and the fact that most of our population was rooted to the soil and the rest sparsely scattered made it impracticable for us to exploit resources which, in any case, were still largely a matter for conjecture. What was certain was that the Anglo-Americans' formidable expansion would sooner or later engulf those regions. The easternmost, Texas, fell so naturally within the scope of that irresistible thrust that our statesmen should have considered only the best way to give away, literally, the land we could never occupy by inviting the whole world to colonize it—the Russians, the French, the English, the Spaniards, the Chinese—thereby erecting a Babel of peoples as a dike to stem the tide of American expansion. But it is easy to prescribe with hindsight; our fathers, prejudiced and necessarily ignorant as they were, could have taken no such step; our knowledge is the consequence of their mistakes.

A thousand little attempts at encroachment made it abundantly clear that the United States coveted Texas, fertile, well-watered, and teeming with cattle, from the day that the expanding nation reached the state's borders. The Spanish government stood staunchly on its rights and was very cautious and parsimonious in granting concessions. The concession that gave rise to the American colonization of Texas was granted to the father of Stephen F. Austin and permitted him to settle three hundred Catholic families in the province. The Mexican government, feeling the need of amity with the United States and lacking the power to assert its rights, confirmed the grant but failed to enforce the restrictions. Texas was soon dotted with small but growing American colonies. Grants made to Mexican citizens, such as those to Zavala and others, were sold to Americans, who promptly settled in the fecund region. The danger was patent and considered so imminent, a law passed in Bustamante's first administration prohibited the acquisition by foreigners of lands within the limits of the frontier states. This law was aimed at the Americans, who nevertheless continued to seep into Texas and to form colonies there, despite the military posts established by General Mier y Terán. The state, then conjoined with Coahuila, first took part in political affairs by siding enthusiastically with the revolution instigated by the smugglers of Vera Cruz against Bustamante's strict administration in 1832 and headed by the inevitable Santa Anna. The following year Texas declared itself, *motu proprio,* separate from Coahuila. Zavala, who owned land in Texas, moved by self-interest, by his Jacobin's venomous hatred for Catholicism (which in that day, to be sure, took on in Mexico the aspect of a vast superstition), and by his congenital affinity, as a Yucatecan, for loose federation, states' rights, and even for local autonomy and secession, carried the grim tidings of centralism's triumph to the Anglo-American colonists. Excited by his eloquence, and by Austin's, and counting on strong support from the United States, the Texans decided to secede from Mexico and declare themselves independent. This was a sad but unavoidable turn of events. Multiple ties bound the Texans to their blood brothers, but no ties at all to the Mexicans. What made our case worse was that the rupture of the federal pact gave a perfectly legal character to the separation—which was sure to occur sooner or later, anyhow. Even if the Constitution of 1824 had been legally reformed, the states of the Federation were clearly under no obligation to remain in the union unless they ratified a new agreement; as parties to a contract, they were at liberty to renew it or not, as they saw fit. Texas seceded without going through the formality of refusing to renew the contract because the Constitution was not reformed—it was abolished. Centralism was proclaimed, and an assembly convoked to stamp a seal of sanction on a *fait accompli.*

If our statesmen had been wise enough to see the matter in this light, if, accepting the secession as legal, they had set about extracting the best possible advantage from a settlement with Texas, the ensuing war, with its aftermath of shame and ruin, could have been averted, and also the conflict with the United States, which was the ineluctable consequence of that war.

The separatists seized San Antonio; receiving constant shipments of arms from the United States, they awaited the Mexican armies. The preparation of an army that was to fight a national war (for most Mexicans so considered the war with Texas) afforded Santa Anna and his cronies an opportunity for rich pickings. The country's fate was still in the hands of the moneylenders. The exchequer could not even take care of current expenses. Waste, disorder, and the tremendous deficit added by each triumphant revolution to the deficits incurred by previous revolutions made it necessary to resort to the implacable usurers of Venice, who built their fortunes out of our misfortunes. New taxes were levied, one on top of another, but the masses were unproductive. They produced solely for the landowner, who, by means of the rural system—the proprietor's store, his vouchers, his special currency for each type of transaction, and at times the practice of fostering alcoholism—kept the country laborer (and this means more than half the population) in bondage for debt and degraded. Thus, the peon paid indirectly the taxes assigned to his master. And the man who was free, who had his own little independent business, paid excises and tolls that devoured two-thirds of his profits and caused him to look on contraband as a deliverance. The head-tax in some states and the requisitions of the Church added the final cogs to the monstrous machine calculated to crush all liberty, just as it crushed every effort at economic independence, every attempt at saving. The Mexican has never known what it means to save, has never saved anything. The middle class, both rural and urban—the farmowner, the prosperous artisan, the storekeeper—was the perpetual victim of the tax system, the eternal plotter of new revolutions, always hoping that the triumph of a new order would bring him relief. This class, moreover, was the one that suffered perpetual exploitation at the hands of the guerilla chief, the general, the prefect, the governor. The merchant and the landowner were engaged in a desperate struggle with the government. They robbed their extortioners any way they could and cheated the law religiously. Abandoning their businesses, little by little, to the foreigner —the hacienda, the farm, the food store to the Spaniard (who had already returned), the clothing and jewelry shops to the Frenchman, the mines to the Englishman—they at last took refuge en masse in the bureaucracy, that superb normal school for idleness and graft which has educated our country's middle class. All this serves to explain why the Congresses would authorize the contracting of loans amounting to only a few hundred thousands of pesos, of which no more than forty-five percent was received in credit, with an interest not exceeding four percent per month and a term of six months until the entire sum must be repaid! Under this system, we were defeated before we ever started. Santa Anna, in San Luis Potosí, before taking the field managed to collect funds which were always exhausted, frittered away, in less than a month's time. He procured these funds from the clergy, from the concessionaires of the mints, and from private persons, who received, in return for a mess of pottage, national properties of the highest value (the salinas of Peñon Blanco, for example). Even so, the army was able to move from one place to another only with the most agonizing hardships. And nobody got paid.

The campaign in Texas made two things manifest: (1) the incapacity of the seceded state to defend itself alone, for the victorious Mexican army traversed a good part of the territory between the Rio Grande and the Sabine, and (2) the political and military ineptitude of that general who, though experienced only in civil war and barracks mutiny, was exalted by the Mexican masses as a military genius. His policy of shooting prisoners, laying waste the countryside and burning the towns roused the Texans to fury and added flaming indignation to the self-interest that had moved the Americans to sympathize with the Texans, who rightly appealed to the humanitarian sentiments of the civilized world for judgment against the savage invader. And the culmination of his strategy was a mad risk that turned a triumphal march into a shambles at San Jacinto, where the contingent that he led was annihilated and himself taken prisoner. Fear of losing his life impelled him to convert partial defeat into general catastrophe, and, in obedience to his order as President of the Republic and Commander in Chief, the army under General Vicente Filísola came back across the Rio Grande. Thus, the whole state of Texas was abandoned. In reality, the military problem was ended so far as this rebel state was concerned. Any further attempt to recover it would mean an encounter, face to face, with the United States.

The tidings of the disaster in Texas in the latter days of April (1836) were received in Mexico with stupefaction. Under the Provisional Presidency of a circumspect and well-intentioned lawyer, José Justo Corro, measures were taken to mitigate the effects of the blow. And Mexico raged at Santa Anna as a lover rages at an unfaithful mistress, with whom he is still in love. Meanwhile, a new political code was being composed by the deputies elected through governmental pressure at a time when the reform party languished in the lethargy that follows on defeat. This code embodied the program and sustained the power of the conservative oligarchy; but a majority of the deputies belonged to the moderate—we might even call them the liberal—wing of that oligarchy. Our republican statesmen, influenced by the doctrinaire politicians who governed Louis Phillipe's monarchy, clung to the belief that political systems, if they are minutely and ingeniously organized, can prevent the abuse of power and the turmoil of revolutions. They hated all tyranny, whether from above or from below, and believed devoutly in a parliamentary regime—that is, a regime of magistrates, of educated men, not a regime based on universal suffrage, which, in their well-considered opinion, in no way corresponded to the realities of our country. Thus they were so pleased with the balance they had achieved between authority and liberty, between political centralism and administrative decentralization (equally essential, they thought, to a nation threatened with immediate death), that they closed their session in the happy assurance of having done everything possible for the country's welfare, after invoking "Almighty God, who has destined men to form societies, and who preserves the societies which they have formed."[1]

We must not deny them, in all fairness, the respect that history owes them for their good intentions. Their creation was a failure, partly because it was too complicated and mainly because Mexico's problem was not of a political nature, but was social and economic. In order to solve it, Mexican society would have to be transformed and emancipated through the suppression of privileges, the diffusion of knowledge, the opening of all gateways to foreign currents, and the circulation of the immense wealth stagnant under mortmain. Obviously, this would mean a revolution; just as obviously, such a revolution was necessary. The reform party alone foresaw this, and was in the right.

The Constitution of the Seven Laws was, at any rate, quite liberal: generous in its bill of rights; hospitable to foreigners, who, as in the American system, were invited to become nationalized and to take up lands; intolerant on religious matters but retaining, in compensation, some of the Patronate's supervision of the Church. Continuing the classic distribution of Powers, it provided for a bicameral Legislature, with a House of Representatives based on a restricted electorate, in recognition of the country's narrowly limited suffrage; an Executive Power composed of a President, whose term was to be eight years, a Cabinet, and Council of Government; an irremovable Judiciary Power; and the division of the country into departments, each with an elected assembly that was to have broad administrative faculties. But the great novelty of the Seven Laws consisted in the compagination of a Conserving Power, intended as a balance wheel between the other Powers. It had the authority to annul the decisions of any one of them and to suspend and restore its functions, but never *motu proprio,* only when

[1] Preamble to the *Seven Constitutional Laws*, December 7, 1836.

instigated by another Power (the aim was to prevent tyranny), and it had the authority to declare, in emergencies, the nation's will—this was to prevent revolutions. The Conserving Power, an extra wheel in the machinery, acted merely as a clog and accomplished nothing. The Power that serves as moderator in a federal constitution is properly the Judiciary, and then only when instigated by private persons.

These good patriots, advocates of a strong but not despotic government, sincere but timid friends of progress, had for their leader General Bustamante, who again became President in April 1837. No one was better fitted to consolidate a centralist regime, as long as war with the United States, which now clearly loomed on the horizon, was not yet upon us. His ministers were patriotic and civilized; the country might have enjoyed a breathing spell.

But there was no time for a breathing spell. A humiliation inflicted on our navy, guarding the Texas coast, by the American navy, obliged the government to request authorization to demand satisfaction or to declare war on the United States. In this hour of approaching crisis, all our resources, all our sinews of union and of discipline should have been dedicated to upholding our honor in the world's eyes. At this very moment, however, a pronunciamento in favor of federalism launched a revolt at San Luis Potosí; the real object was to get hold of public funds and promote certain business deals. After a great waste of blood and money, the revolt was crushed, and its leader, the redoubtable General Esteban Moctezuma, killed. The bayonet that should have been pointed, with our ultimatum, at the United States, had been broken off in Mexican breasts.

The federalist revolt at San Luis had repercussions on all sides. Secession in Yucatán, uprising in Sonora, invasion in New Mexico, and insurrection in Michoacán proved the futility of any effort to pacify the country. No sooner would some measure of protection to industry galvanize the social body than the fear and anxiety induced by the desperate struggle for survival would prostrate it again. On top of everything else, we had to face an unjust and absurd war forced on us by the bourgeois government of Louis Philippe, a war which weakened us still further on the eve of the American conflict. This arrogant and short-sighted attempt on the part of the French King's ministers to make us subservient to their industry and trade, this grocer's diplomacy, turned away from France the soul of a new nation which had been powerfully attracted to her and did us even worse harm: it restored the prestige of General Santa Anna, who, since his return from Texas, had been living, unpunished but in disgrace, at his hacienda in Vera Cruz.

The diplomatic chapter is a dismal one, made up partly of preposterous claims filed by Frenchmen who, like the Mexicans, had suffered from excesses committed during our civil strife and partly of rational efforts to exempt Louis Philippe's subjects from forced loans and from laws that might exclude foreigners from retail storekeeping. The Mexican government essayed, with moratoriums, to gain time, but overbearing and insulting notes from the French minister, topped by an ultimatum that stirred the whole Republic to indignation, made war inevitable. There followed the bombardment and capitulation of San Juan de Ulúa, heroically defended with 40 superannuated cannon against the 140 in Baudin's fleet, and the attack on Vera Cruz, in which Santa Anna was badly wounded, fighting with his habitual dash and impelled by his instinctive love for his native soil and by his eagerness to wipe out dreadful memories of Texas (which he did with complete success). The port of Vera Cruz was occupied, and, more than two months later, through the mediation of England, an agreement with France was reached which required us to pay what we did not owe even when there was no one to receive it. Throughout the entire episode our honor stood intact. On the other hand, the nation's incapacity for achieving any kind of coherent life, even under centralism, was proved by the rebellion—a series of pronunciamentos from every port on the Gulf, deliberately provoked by the smuggling trade—which left us without resources and trafficked disgracefully with the French.

It is true that history, which in our day strives for scientific precision, should shun emotion and concentrate on establishing facts, analyzing them, and fitting their salient characteristics into a synthesis. But there are too many periods in our history when the repetition of the same errors, the same evils, over and over in dismal monotony, afflicts and oppresses our hearts with sorrow and shame. What a waste of energy, what a loss of vitality in the endless spilling of blood, the endless strife! How many humble homes darkened forever, how many, how incalculably many individual tragedies! And all to prepare the way for the ultimate humiliation of our country! The bandit who infested every road became indistinguishable from the guerrilla chief, who became a colonel, who between one tumult and another became a general, and between one revolution and the next, an aspirant to the Presidency. And each of them carried on the point of his bayonet a declaration, and in the wallet of his counselor—whether priest, lawyer, or merchant—a plan, and on his banner a constitution, all guaranteed to bring felicity to the Mexican people, who, trampled and macerated underfoot everywhere and by everyone, dragged themselves from the bloody mire to earn their daily morsel by drudging like beasts of burden or to earn oblivion by fighting like heroes. The period between the French and American wars was one of the darkest in our tragic history. There would be another one like it later, but then a ray of light would glimmer on the horizon. Now there was nothing but the black night.

Bustamante, a cold, skeptical man with no lust for power, became disheartened, called in Santa Anna, and offered him the command. Why not, since he was the idol, the tawdry, perennial seducer of the Republic? When French grapeshot had shattered his leg on the beach at Vera Cruz, he had sung his own glory, his martyrdom for his country, and with theatrically pathetic farewell had won back the heart of his Mexico. A romantic gesture, a heroic pose, and the nation swooned at the feet of this Don Juan of the pronunciamento, of the Te Deum, and of the forced loan.

This great comedian, whose soul was sheer vanity and ambition, could play marvelously well, when it suited his purpose, the role of the selfless, devoted subordinate. Although still ailing, he accepted the Presidency for the interim during which Bustamante, who led an army on Tampico, center of the self-styled federalist rebellion, was to be absent. Santa Anna, in an outburst of terrific energy, forestalled a revolt in Puebla by simply making his appearance there and, without waiting for the Congress' permission, sallied forth to meet the strong column, which, eluding Bustamante's generals near Tampico, was marching to capture Puebla. The force was commanded by two of the boldest and bravest military men on the federalist side, José Antonio Mejiá and José Urrea. Santa Anna defeated them and had Mejiá shot. Urrea escaped to Tampico, which finally surrendered, then to Tuxpan, which surrendered in turn, and was captured at last. Protected by a capitulation, he was taken to the City of Mexico, where he continued indefatigably to plot. Santa Anna had returned to his hacienda and Bustamante, once again in the presidential chair, was essaying, with a moderate Cabinet, a policy of appeasement when Urrea succeeded in hatching his plot. He incited a part of the garrison to mutiny, roused the rabble, gained possession of the National Palace, where the President was made a prisoner, and sent for Gómez Farías, who, since his return from exile, had divided his days between his residence and jail. Together they proclaimed a Federation. This coup of unexampled audacity was like a trumpet call without an echo. The government rapidly surrounded the rebels with a considerable force and after a few days of fighting in the streets was able to free the President and restore order.

This society mutilated without respite, without ever a ray of light to illumine its growth upward, without hope of reaching a solution to the problem that time not only failed to solve but rendered ever more complicated; this organism clotted with blood and ashes still wanted to live, still hungered for life, was conscious of its vital sap, conscious of its soul. At the first official contact with Spain—which sent us, as it should have done long before, a representative not merely of its government but of its literature, the closest tie that could ever bind us to the motherland once more—the tree of Mexican letters burst into leaf. All sorts of periodicals and essays appeared; in books, academies, theaters, festivals there seemed to be a dawn of the spirit, even though there was no light in the country's overcast skies. This renascence seemed to flower from a desire to spike the guns of the fraticidal wars with garlands of wit and poesy. But art—alas!—is not so mighty. And yet, one of the most illustrious promoters of this literary movement, José María Gutiérrez Estrada, a Yucatecan who headed the monarchist party in Mexico, as another Yucatecan, Zavala, had headed the radical party, set forth the argument at this time that rule by a foreign prince could be the remedy for our ills. No one has ever impugned this author's courageous honesty and sincerity, but nothing could be more artificial and impracticable in Mexico than a monarchy; nothing could be more galling to our national pride than rule by a monarch who is also a foreigner. But the error is easy to understand in view of our incurable dissensions and the lowering American menace. The pamphlet by Gutiérrez Estrada provoked the country's indignation. And the spokesman of this indignation was General Juan N. Almonte, son of the great Morelos and one of Bustamante's ministers at this time. Later on, Almonte would convey to the altar, arm in arm with Gutiérrez Estrada (banished from his country during the interim), the sacrificial victim, Maximilian, decked with flowers, in whom the author succeeded in personifying his impractical dreams and General Almonte, his rancors and ambitions.

It was plain by the middle of 1841 that the government was powerless to organize any effort, whether to force Yucatán to its knees, or to put an army on Texas soil and so persuade the United States to accept a definitive and mutually respectful agreement, or to exact obedience from its own agents in the provinces, who were veritable petty sultans of their departments. And yet, being determined to protect industry and needing funds with which to prolong its life a little, the government dared to decree a considerable increase in tariff rates on imports. There ensued a feverish dashing back and forth between Vera Cruz and Guadalajara of letter-bearers and of agents of the principal import businesses (smugglers, with a few honorable exceptions, all the more honorable because they were so few), intent on setting things right. The more cautious among them recommended protests to the government. The more aggressive advocated that grand national cure-all, the pronunciamento—revolution, as every tumult was called, though it is not as graphic a term as the common people's word for it: *la bola,* "the hullabaloo."

The leaders of the military action were to be Paredes in Guadalajara, Valencia in the City of Mexico, and the indispensable Santa Anna in Vera Cruz, where he had been allowed to restore his old satrapy by Bustamante, who, with all his defects, was a giant of honor and of selfless devotion to his country when compared to his rivals. The hullabaloo was agreed upon: Jalisco's government gave the signal by amending the decree of the National Congress; Paredes backed the challenge with his Guadalajara garrison and added demands of his own. Soon the Republic burst into flame. Valencia, with a good part of the troops in the City of Mexico, seconded the Guadalajara plan; Vera Cruz rebelled, and Santa Anna offered his services as mediator to Bustamante, and so stretched out his arms to strangle him.[2] The President refused the offer disdainfully but with deep misgivings. He wanted to resign but the Senate dissuaded him and backed him up. When the revolutionary forces were all gathered at Tacubaya, Almonte, who was Secretary of War, broached what he himself thought was a wonderful idea: let the Executive Power issue a pronunciamento of its own, let it declare for a federation. Bustamante adopted the idea in desperation. The masses in the City of Mexico rushed to his defense; chiefs of the civic militia improvised battalions of workers. And Santa Anna was beside himself. There were battles in the streets. And then, at the height of a formidable assault on the capital's gates, Bustamante laid down his sword and staff of office, turned his army over to Santa Anna, and for the second time went into exile. He would not return until the staggering disaster of 1847 would give him an opportunity for honorable service to his country in the endeavor to repair the damage. It was Mexico's misfortune that Bustamante could not be President during the American invasion; hardly a great general, he nonetheless would have organized the defense more efficiently; the victory would have been more costly and the peace less humiliating. We may regard him as politically dead from this instant; let the sentence we have just set down be his epitaph.

The Bases of the program announced at Tacubaya[3] constitute a most remarkable monument to the political hypocrisy of a military class obsequious to the orders of those exploiters of the public till—the generals, merchants, and usurers—and commanded by a power-mad man who thought of the nation not as his mother but as his concubine. This was a centralist revolution against centralism, with the pretext

[2] General Mariano Paredes y Arrillaga issued his pronunciamento August 8, 1841, was seconded August 31 by General Gabriel Valencia, and Santa Anna, then commander at Vera Cruz, offered his mediation September 2.

[3] Act of Tacubaya, September 28, 1841.

that the government was bad and that the Constitution needed reform. The Commander in Chief was to appoint a committee composed of two deputies from each department (because, so the plan read, no better way was known for the departments to make their views heard); this committee was to name a provisional chief of the Executive Power, who within a certain term must convoke a constituent Congress and who would be responsible to a constitutional Congress. Meanwhile, the Provisional President was vested with all the faculties necessary for the reorganization of the government, "with whatever powers may be necessary in order to do good and prevent evil." This was the famous Seventh Basis. This was dictatorship.

In protest against all this, Bravo in the south and the federals in Durango and Guadalajara rose in arms. Santa Anna was very clever, very astute. He appointed a Cabinet of federalists and reformers, who accepted with the vague hope of steering that government toward their goal: annihilation of the clergy's power. Among them were Gómez Pedraza and García, the incorruptible ex-governor of Zacatecas. Thus, partly by enticement, partly by mobilizing an army that for those days was formidable, Santa Anna succeeded in imposing peace. He was always successful in dominating new situations, but deprivation, the hardships of poverty soon made new situations old. Indeed, the hardships of the days when Santa Anna was ruler became legendary. How he squandered money on the army, on his favorites, on the regal pomp of his entourage! He exacted huge sums from the clergy, who paid him grudgingly, in driblets, and forgave him. Everybody forgave him. Moreover, Mexican arms won glory in the north, smashing the filibustering invasions of New Mexico. The dictator saw his star in the ascendency and hesitated at nothing. He dared to auction off property that the clergy claimed was theirs and to permit foreigners to acquire lands, a wise measure that had been viewed by the short-sighted with unjustified alarm. The construction of handsome theaters for opera and drama was begun at this time. The capital was embellished insofar as the prison-like and fortress-like convent walls permitted; these jutted into the principal avenues, cutting them short, impeding the growth of the city in every direction, and giving it in the murky shadows of dusk a sinister medieval aspect.

The dictatorship of a progressive man, provided he is an honorable and intelligent administrator of the public funds, is generally of great benefit to an immature country because it preserves peace; the people can work and store up strength. It may be abhorrent in theory, but theories belong to the history of political thought and not to political history, which can draw scientific conclusions only from facts. A dictatorship that obstructs justice and creates disorder and affords at best a precarious peace is a downright calamity, and that is what Santa Anna's dictatorship quickly became. The usurers kept on making fortunes; the favorites received splendid presents; to one of them, in the division of spoils, there fell a good part of the fortune confiscated years ago from the Jesuits. The clergy groaned, and the masses were moved by their affliction. The clergy, to cope with the incessant exactions of the government, had adopted the policy of outward compliance, dragging their feet, however, when it came to delivery and moaning and sobbing over the prospect of their ruination. By these tactics they were cleverly trying to avert the deadly blow that threatened them: loss of the privilege of mortmain. Taxes and loans steadily increased. The small part of the nation that was able to see anything—for the vast majority could only feel the pain of the lash and of the levy—was astounded to see that the budget reported an income of twenty-nine million pesos, of which not more than thirteen million came from normal sources, the remaining sixteen being produced by extraordinary and dubious means. And astonishment turned to dismay with the discovery that expenditures had exceeded income, leaving a deficit. True enough, the south was in rebellion; it had been necessary to send an army to Yucatán, which had seceded from the Mexican nation, and to prepare another for the reconquest of Texas; and at that very moment British and American envoys were clamoring for the payment of huge indemnities. But these troubles were all the fault of the selfsame bad leadership. This was no honest dictatorship; it was unendurable.

Elections were held for the new constituent Congress. The starving urban masses, who laid siege to the food stores and threatened to loot the grain deposits at any minute, as usual took no part in the contest. The vast rural populace remained mute as ever in their thinly veiled serfdom. But the electoral bodies of the towns voted for federalism and reform, always the slogan of those in favor of local autonomy, a cause still very much alive. Neither the conservatives, unwilling to risk their interests or their family's tranquility in political ructions, nor, to any effective degree, the bureaucrats of Santa Anna's indolent government, cared to bestir themselves in the campaign. The dictator, between fits of feverish activity, immersed himself in a life of pleasure: cockfights, luxury flaunted in the face of the people's appalling poverty, reviews of his new regiments in fancy uniforms. The election resulted (as always in our country when the people have the slightest choice) in a victory for the advanced parties. When the President realized what had happened, it was too late for legal remedies. But the cartridge belts of his henchmen were bulging with extralegal remedies. He contented himself, therefore, with advising against a federalist constitution and returned to his fighting cocks, his parades, his forced loans and assessments. He was gratified to see how his properties in Vera Cruz increased as if by magic. Adulation, the cancerous abcess of all tyranny, grew to such an extreme that ridiculous statues were erected in the President's honor, and an extravagantly sumptuous and dramatic funerary festival was dedicated to the interment of the mummified leg of the so-called "Hero of Vera Cruz."

The apogee of civil honor in our parliamentary history was attained by the Constituent Congress of 1842.[4] The representatives began at once their efforts to curb the dictatorship and to check its unrestrained financial folly. They demanded responsible stewardship and a strict accounting and joined bitter combat with the unyielding Executive Power. Two projects for a constitution were debated. One, put forth by the moderates, provided for a remarkably liberal centralism combined with administrative autonomy of the country's departments, and this was the most rational and patriotic scheme in view of the oncoming terrible war. The other, put forth by the liberals, was a return to federalism pure and simple. Both of them were repugnant to the government. In the debates, the reform party harped on its favorite ideas: abolition of privileges, nationalization of the Church's landed property, religious tolerance, freedom for slaves from the moment they set foot

[4] Convoked December 10, 1841, pursuant to Article Four of the Bases of Tacubaya, and installed June 10, 1842.

on Mexican soil (and this humanitarian proposal, in brave defiance of the brutal and menacing American agitation for the spread of slavery, instigated here in Mexico the solution of the great problem in the United States). The fervent speeches against the privileged classes, and then the adoption by the Congress of the project for a federalist constitution, determined Santa Anna to hatch his habitual plot. He claimed to be the defender of society's best interests against the "cruel and intolerant demagogues of 1828 and 1833," to quote his Secretary of War, José María Tornel, who had been one of those same demagogues, perhaps the only one of them who had been actually cruel. The dictator left for his hacienda; this was the signal that the governmental plot was ripe. General Bravo, with his noble and majestic figure, lent some dignity to the farce. Always wary of reforms, he felt that they were not desired by the people, which was true; what was equally true, however, was that they were desperately needed by the people. Tornel let the manifestation start just anywhere,[5] and the army all over the country protested against the constituent Congress. Bravo, as Acting President, bowed to the national will and dissolved the Congress, which responded, in the face of the capital's hostile garrison, with a wholly admirable protest. A little later, a committee of notables—that is, of conservative landowners, clergy, lawyers, and military—met to whip together some sort of constitution. They came up with one which was antireformist but not antiliberal, which expressly maintained the old privileges but also guaranteed individual rights, the independence of the Powers, and the responsibility of the Executive, setting forth a moderate centralism stripped of the encumbrances fastened upon the governmental machinery by the too-complicated Constitution of 1836. The new fundamental law, called "Organic Bases," was promulgated about midyear 1843.[6]

While the committee was at work on the new Constitution, the

[5] A pronunciamento against the Congress, December 11, 1842, at Huejotzingo, was seconded on the eighteenth by the capital's garrison; the next day the government dissolved the Congress and named the committee of thirty-seven notables, which was installed January 2, 1843, under the presidency of Archbishop Manuel Posada.

[6] *Bases of the Political Organization of the Mexican Republic.* Approved and published June 13, 1843.

President, who tirelessly flaunted his honorary title, *benemérito de la patria* ("National Benefactor"), returned from his hacienda to the seat of power, with no law to restrain him except the famous Seventh Basis of the Act of Tacubaya, which made him exempt from any law. On returning from his hacienda, he plunged into the three activities that engaged his entire political life: making war, raising money, and plotting. Santa Anna, when out of office, plotted against all three Powers; when in office, against the other two; always he plotted. He invariably returned from rural retirement with his energy for these three activities replenished a hundredfold. Purses quaked; the clergy uttered anticipatory sobs; the usurers rejoiced. The situation was indeed grave. Each new phase that the country passed through was more difficult than the one before. There was an accumulation of difficulties at a steadily accelerating pace. We were going downhill fast, headed for an abyss. The war went on along the Rio Grande, which the Texans had the temerity to cross, only to be soundly whipped by Pedro Ampudia. The war went on in the south, perennially torn by revolt, and in the seceded department of Yucatán.

Santa Anna had this critical military situation to cope with at the very moment when the United States was pressing him for settlement of the two million pesos award made to it by an international court of claims presided over by the Prussian ambassador in Washington. The order of the day was increased import duties, forced loans from the clergy and private citizens, and the whole of society at the mercy of assessors, who invaded all premises and attached everything in the process of their official pillage. These were the presents that the most ruthless of dictators made to his country. He paid a part of the debt to the United States and signed an armistice with Texas, which ought to have been followed at once by recognition of its independence, but the very idea was rejected furiously by Santa Anna, who still smarted with the humiliation of having been Sam Houston's prisoner.

Yucatán, remote from Mexico's center, hard to reach, and with divergent interests, easily became the satrapy of the commanders in charge of the dominating fortress of Campeche, who insisted on separation from Mexico under the absurd pretext of devotion to the cause of centralism, in spite of the fact that Yucatán was federalist by its very nature.

At any rate, the revolution that overthrew Bustamante and restored Gómez Pedraza to the Presidency (in 1833) had put an end to centralism in Yucatán, where the reform program was received with enthusiasm. When Santa Anna undermined and destroyed the Federation, his agents obliged Yucatán to remain in the fold.

But the calamitous war with Texas and later the war with France brought all sorts of vexations upon Yucatán: high tariffs, which raised the cost of bread; tolls, which hurt interior trade; impositions on maritime traffic, which spelled ruin to the Campeche fleet and, worst of all, the continual and furiously resented syphoning off of Yucatecan blood for the army. Rebellion, several times nipped in the bud, was finally successful, and Yucatán, exercising its rights, seceded from the centralist Republic.[7]

In 1841, Yucatán adopted an extremely liberal and reformist constitution and awaited the fall of Bustamante, with the expectation of receiving fair treatment and becoming once more part of the Mexican nation. Secession, as the Yucatecan leaders well knew, would leave the Peninsula, menaced always by its own restless, fierce, and cruel Indians, at the mercy of Spain, of the United States and even of Britain. They fixed their hopes on Santa Anna's ascendancy. But in vain. The dictator, after his first terms were repected, resorted to war, sending a fleet and a division of six thousand men to Yucatán in the latter half of 1842. A bitter struggle ensued, and the patriotism of the Yucatecans mounted to a feverish pitch that culminated in acts of heroism and in frightful crimes by mobs. The end came at the close of 1843 with the capitulation of a part of the army sent by Santa Anna and the withdrawal of the remainder. His military campaign had been a total failure. A pact between the national and local governments gave Yucatán a special status within the centralist framework.

Santa Anna failed, as usual, to keep his word. Nor did the merchants

[7] Santiago Imán proclaimed a federalist government in Yucatán February 8, 1840. The National Congress, by law of May 7, 1842, excluded Yucatecan deputies and declared the department an enemy of the nation.

whose demands ruled the precarious governments that came after his allow anything to be done for the relief of Yucatán, which seceded once again and did not return to the fold until 1846, when the Federation, the country's legal regime, was restored. But the worst was yet to come.

The United States had tried since the birth of the Mexican Republic to acquire the territory between Louisiana and the Rio Grande, from the river's source to its mouth. Poinsett had offered to buy Texas from the Mexican government; the leaders of the Democratic Party, which was strongest in the states of the South, never gave up the idea of acquiring it, either by agreement or by force. Soon they added to this ambition that of acquiring all the Mexican territory on the Pacific north of the tropic of Cancer, to forestall, they said, its acquisition by England or some other nation. In short, their doctrine was that all territory adjoining the United States which Mexico could not effectively govern should belong to the Americans.

Aggression was retarded by treaties and the practices of international equity, by the anxiety of England and France over the Union's expansion, and by the opposition of the Whig Party, led by Henry Clay, great conscience and great orator, to the pro-slavery, secessionist Democratic Party; but the trend of events made war inevitable.

If the opposing parties in Mexico had not used the Texas question as a political club, each accusing the other of traitorous intentions, catastrophe might have been avoided. The incontrovertible right of Texas to secede once the federal pact was broken should have been recognized to begin with, and the differences between the American political parties should have been exploited.

But no, the constant specter of war with Texas, which seemed certain, and with the United States, which seemed probable, served Santa Anna's purposes. It gave him an excuse to station the ghost of an army, starving and almost unarmed, on the Rio Grande, so that he could incessantly demand funds, which he incessantly frittered away.

In the field of international equity our diplomacy won consistent victories over the Americans. A series of impeccably reasonable notes remonstrated against the unceasing attacks on the dignity of the Mexican Republic which had been countenanced by the government in Washington. Open meetings in some cities of the Union urged war with Mexico and the annexation of Texas, and a sort of armed emigration toward the latter region was organized, a threat which not even Daniel Webster's talents could find excuses for.

But the course of events was inexorable. Over and beyond the issue of illicit aid to Texas (for whether Texas was regarded as a rebel state of Mexico or as an independent nation at war with a friendly nation, the aid was illicit) there arose the issue of annexation. And even if the Texans were within their rights in seeking to join the United States, the Americans had no right to proceed with annexation before arriving at an understanding with regard to mutual responsibilities. President Tyler's Secretary of War, John Calhoun, who would be the Moses of the secession movement, negotiated a treaty of annexation with Texas, which the Senate in Washington refused to approve and which shocked France and England—both had recognized the independence of Texas—into offering us their services as mediators in order to avert further insults. Meanwhile, Santa Anna made preparations to resume the war with Texas as soon as the armistice should expire, and thereby brought down the fulminations of the American plenipotentiary, who candidly bared his government's intentions by warning that any invasion of Texas would mean war with the United States. This was understood by the Mexican government, which had previously warned that the admission of Texas to the Union would be answered with a declaration of war. The whole question hung on the presidential election in the United States. If Polk, candidate of the Democrats and of the South and with a platform calling for annexation, should be elected, conflict was inevitable. If Clay should win, peace was assured. Polk won by fewer than 40,000 votes out of a total of 2,060,000. This spelled disaster for Mexico. One thing was clear, however: the cause of annexation and war in the United States was not a national but a Southern cause.

While the great electoral battle was being waged in the United States, a President was being chosen in Mexico, too. But here the campaign was strictly military: the guns of civil war took the place of ballot boxes. The President, who with all his multifarious powers was bound by law to render an accounting to the constitutional Congress, in which, to the government's chagrin, federalists and reformists predominated, refused to do so. Santa Anna declined to belittle himself by answering to the Congress. Like Scipio, who, when an accounting was demanded of him, invited the populace to a thanksgiving feast in the Capitol, the President, in the same situation, reminded the people that he had founded the Republic in Vera Cruz and had saved it at Tampico. There was unanimous protest against his conduct, immense disgust with the hero of usury, of the forced loan, of taxes and impositions without number. From Querétaro, from Guadalajara came the cry that he fulfill his obligation, under the Act of Tacubaya, to render a report to the Congress, which was sparing no effort to curb the dictatorship.

General Paredes y Arrillaga, a man of personal probity but of slippery political expediency and the incarnate hope of the party that wanted to anchor the country to centralism and to the old privileges until such time as an alliance with some European nation should make us more secure from the United States, even at the cost of raising here a throne for a foreign prince—this General Paredes, this always available card in the political deck that was constantly being reshuffled to see who would win honors and emoluments, backed the protest of the Jalisco assembly with a part of the army, while the National Chamber of Deputies openly supported the movement.[8]

Santa Anna, sensing danger, shifted suddenly, as was his wont, from sybaritic languor to feverish activity. He stationed a division or two in the center of the Republic. The task of keeping an eye on the Congress, which insisted that the government should conform to the law, he left to the Vice-President, Canalizo, in whose loyalty, like a faithful canine's, he had confidence. He hastened to the Bajío region, determined to put out the spreading fires of revolt by stratagem or by blood bath.

His outrageous acts at Querétaro[9] provoked indignation among the

[8] On October 29, 1844 the departmental committee of Jalisco petitioned the Congress to review Santa Anna's official acts, in accordance with the Sixth Basis of the Act of Tacubaya. On November 1, General Mariano Paredes y Arrillaga joined in the petition.

[9] He dissolved the departmental committee and imprisoned its members November 27, 1844.

national deputies, and the entire Chamber, led by the representative Llaca, took a firm stand, realizing that the time had come to bridle the runaway dictatorship. Llaca, in this moment of crisis, was the embodiment of civic honor, denouncing public shame, and the Chamber stood with him. Resorting to force, the government dissolved the assembly, which refused to adjourn.

All society seemed to hold its breath in the presence of this duel between the sword and the word; the outcome was soon decided: Valencia, in La Ciudadela, the capital's barracks, declared for the Paredes plan, and in an overwhelming outburst of enthusiasm the entire city, including every class, the magnate and the worker, the priest and the militiaman, joined in the most spontaneous ovation the capital had ever seen, in honor of the assembly, which serenely resumed the course of debate. The dictator, with an army still intact, headed for the capital, but fled to Puebla from Paredes' advancing column, while his own evaporated. He became a fugitive, then a prisoner, then an exile. The Presidency was assumed by General José J. Herrera, elected by the Chamber.[10] And thus ended the year 1844.

The Congress turned its attention to the American menace, ever more sinister—like a hand gloved in iron clutching the throat of a frail and bloodless nation, like a brutal knee in its belly, like a mouth avid with the desire to bite, to rip, to devour, while prating of humanity, of justice, of law. The government of the patriotic, honest, and prudent General Herrera did the best it could, and what it achieved was this: one army on the frontier, another on the way to the frontier, an appeal for unity in the cause of a country threatened with death, an admirable and circumspect dignity with regard to the Americans, but no refusal to compromise or to seek an agreement based on the independence of Texas. The underlying reality, however, was this: the minority that could think and read, anxious, febrile, critical, shaken incessantly by spasms of bellicose rage which made the government vaccilate, clamored for vengeance, yet balked at any self-sacrifice;

10 The capital's garrison ousted General Valentín Canalizo December 6, 1844, and General Herrera took charge of the Presidency. The Congress deposed Santa Anna and named Herrera President December 17.

money was being hidden away; the military were plotting new revolts; the rural masses were inert, ignorant, without affection for the masters who exploited them, without any common spirit, without feeling for their country.

The Herrera administration had barely commenced to function when the provocation of war which our government had warned against occurred: the Congress and President in Washington enacted and approved the annexation of Texas. Our minister asked for his passport: our relations with the United States were broken off. Since the appetite for territorial expansion, the primitive form of present-day imperialism, had come to be most voracious in the southern and western states, popular opinion there favored war with Mexico. The Mexican government maneuvered with skill, accepting the good offices of France as mediator with the Texans, who had not as yet taken all the steps required for annexation. But it was too late. A Texas convention ratified the act, United States forces entered Texas and, with flagrant contempt for international law, crossed the Nueces River, boundary of the Union's new state, and invaded the territory of a nation with which they were still at peace, on the pretext that Texas had always claimed the Rio Grande for its boundary. The moment our protests were dispatched to Washington our best troops set out for the frontier. If they could arrive before General Taylor received reinforcements, we might successfully take the offensive.

Our government, while refusing to deal with the American envoy in his official capacity, did not disdain to discuss with him ideas that might serve as a basis for future agreement. It was well understood by now that annexation must be accepted as a historical fact; the important thing was to save, if we could, the rest of our imperiled land. But the pressure of public opinion, violent in its unreasoning emotion, thwarted the delicate adjustments of diplomacy. What was needed in this emergency was not a people sick with distorted imaginings, with hatred and with poverty, but a robust, self-controlled people who would give our ministers leeway to dispel with artful correspondence the formidable danger that loomed over us. One point had already been won: the American plenipotentiary had agreed to have the naval squadron that was threatening Vera Cruz withdrawn; we conceded, in return, official status to our discussions with him.

At this crucial moment, the general[11] who had been sent with our best soldiers, with our supreme and ultimate recourse for repelling the invasion, made the excuse that Herrera's government was betraying the country, committed the infamy of pointing at the nation's heart the sword that it had confided to him, and with the complicity of Valencia, cleverest of Santa Anna's pupils, who supported the rebellion in the capital, overthrew Herrera in December, 1845. Herrera, that great citizen, departed from power, in defeat, exactly as he had come into it, with his heart full of patriotic concern and unspotted by the least shadow of guilt.

The Washington government, on receiving news of Herrera's fall, reinforced the fleet and ordered Taylor to advance on the Rio Grande, where our forces, looking in vain for assistance from Paredes, awaited him. And after one more effort to stave off war with diplomacy, words gave way to force. Meanwhile, the man who had committed the greatest political and military crime of that epoch was trying to organize an administration with a false front, behind which anyone could descry a plot to establish a monarchy. Instead of rushing his army to the Rio Grande, he kept it close at hand where he could rely on it for support.

Paredes had himself appointed President with discretionary powers by an assembly of persons appointed by himself.[12] He then convoked a "constituent" assembly because he found the centralist Constitution "of no use." What was actually of no use was the army, debased into an instrument of cynical ambitions; of no use was the middle class, cowardly, fawning and self-seeking; of no use was the clergy, who considered themselves more important than their country and spent their zeal safeguarding their riches, and, although they could boast men of exemplary Christian virtue, these only served as contrast to the mass of ignorant, superstitious, and corrupt monks. The only element that was

[11] General Mariano Paredes y Arrillaga. The army under his command revolted at San Luis Potosí December 14, 1845.

[12] The committee of representatives of the department named Paredes President January 3, 1846.

of any use was the people, who were ruthlessly exploited by all the others.

A group ostensibly in sympathy with the new President was formed by Alamán and led by him with his habitual skill. These men manifested the tendency of the more aggressive members of the conservative party to take their stand, not around the centralist banner, but around the monarchist one, which they themselves had helped to haul down when Iturbide was killed, which fluttered again in Gutiérrez Estrada's daring pamphlet, and which would prove, fifteen years later, how hopelessly unsuited it was to our country, when the world's first military power would try to impose it.

The menace of the United States sparked the plan for a monarchy with a foreign prince. But if the prince came unprotected, what would happen to the monarchy? If he came with a foreign army, what would happen to our independence? This was, as yet, no more than a dream. One day, translated into action, it would turn into a hideous nightmare.

The order [January 27, 1846] convoking the constituent Congress, a singular document composed by Alamán, divided the voting public, extremely restricted, into classes and allowed each class a fixed proportion of representatives. This was the second time the oligarchy had tried to entrench itself through a constitution. To a majority of the politically conscious part of the nation, whose purely verbal love for democratic ideas revealed the Latin origin of their thought, this was an intolerable outrage: a constitution establishing an aristocracy in anticipation of a monarchy. And that is exactly what it was. The storm of protest was terrific; the press was promptly persecuted, and most of the leading liberals were promptly muzzled, imprisoned, or exiled. But their voices already had been heard, with repercussions echoing in every town of the Republic. The government felt it necessary to reaffirm its allegiance to the republican creed.

Meanwhile, the war had become a fact, although hostilities had not yet commenced. Paredes, anxious to repair his irreparable guilt, was accumulating supplies and slowly sending reinforcements to the frontier. But the Mexican generals were never able to muster a numerical superiority in troops that was sufficient to overbalance the American superiority in armament. At the beginning of May, the Mexican

Commander in Chief, General Mariano Arista, resolved to chase the invader from the soil of Tamaulipas, pushing him back across the Nueces River into Texas. He crossed the Rio Grande with an army the same size as the enemy's and was defeated in hot battles on two consecutive days. Forced to retire to Matamoros, he fell back on Linares. This disaster was owing to the incompetence of Arista and his staff and the superiority of the American artillery.

The outcome of these battles inspired President Polk to declare, with a cynicism unexampled in history, that a state of war existed because the Mexicans had invaded Texas and that it must be prosecuted until peace was secured. The Mexican government declared war formally in June, adducing such moderate and sensible reasons, founded on justice, that not a single honest conscience in the United States or Europe could fail to admit that we were in the right.

The country, horrified by our defeats, now burst into flame. Revolution, breaking out at Guadalajara,[13] clamored for Santa Anna, of all men. The minute he got out of sight, the country became obsessed by a vague belief that he could work miracles. He was our man for emergencies, our *deus ex machina,* our savior who never saved anything.[14] What to do? Paredes needed near him a force strong enough to cope with the rebellion, and yet he needed all available forces in the north. He sent some, badly armed, badly supplied, in the direction of San Luis Potosí. One of these brigades, when it was about to march, declared for the Federation and for Santa Anna. The government of Paredes, his Congress, his monarchists, disappeared as if by magic; they never should have appeared in the first place.

The new military revolution took the form of a reaction against monarchism, and while Santa Anna, who had been advised beforehand, was on his way home in the company of General Almonte, for the time being an ardent republican, his allies in the capital convoked a Congress

[13] The garrison at Guadalajara declared against the government of Paredes May 20, 1846.

[14] The sixth article of the pronunciamento reads as follows: "Whereas, the glory of having founded the Republic belongs to His Excellency, Antonio López de Santa Anna, and whereas he has always been its strongest support, . . . the Jalisco garrison recognizes that distinguished general as its leader in the great enterprise to which this plan is dedicated."

and declared the Constitution of 1824 to be in effect.[15] The departmental committees were accordingly suppressed, and, as a manifestation of the return to pure federalism, Valentín Gómez Farías, leader of the reformist party, was brought in to head the Cabinet.

Santa Anna arrived; the Americans, with the most cunning Machiavellianism, had let him through, as if they were tossing an incendiary bomb into the enemy's camp. The month of August 1846 was coming to an end. What did this man bring to us, he who had so often been vilified by the common people, he whose statues they had dragged in the dust and who was, for all that, persistently regarded by them as a Messiah? What did he bring us, this betrayer of hopes, this champion of any cause that might serve his greed or his ambition, what did he bring to the desperate situation, to that army vanquished before any battle by nakedness and hunger, without confidence in its officers and without faith in victory? He brought but a single purpose: to be, redeeming his sins, a soldier for his country. Alas, this soldier who was not good enough to be a general was going to be Commander in Chief.

Paredes had left more than half a million pesos in the exchequer, and by the time Santa Anna arrived it had all been spent. But he set about concentrating troops in San Luis Potosí for a march on Monterrey. With three thousand men and provisions for eight days he finally started out, he who had been up to now nothing more than a revolutionary chieftain. Meanwhile, Mexico was in the throes of an electoral campaign. The radical element, it appears, with the protection of the authorities, prevented the moderates from voting and *ad terrorem* triumphed at the polls. Even the liberal journals protested. But the hour for men of action had come, and the reform party got set to give the clergy the deathblow.

When Santa Anna had barely started his march he learned that Monterrey had capitulated and that Ampudia's division, with the honors of war, was falling back on Saltillo. In this new and bloody episode of the war our eternal improvidence undid us. The soldiers fought bravely, some of the officers on both sides performed deeds of heroism, but the enemy's superior staff and his superior artillery were

[15] Decree of August 22, 1846.

effective again and again. And the story would be the same, over and over, to the end.

Santa Anna was a whirlwind of energy at San Luis Potosí. He begged incessantly for money or took it where he found it. His army grew to fifteen or twenty thousand men, what with merciless levies in the surrounding regions and the addition of some state troops and the remnant of the Division of the North. And as the army grew, his demands took on colossal proportions. The situation of the country was this: our ports were blockaded, most of the states paralyzed, the northern ones lost; Yucatán, seceding again, declared itself neutral so as not to fall into the Americans' power; the deficit soared to seven to eight millions; the press clamored against the government; the people of the capital formed battalions of militia, some to support the dominant reformists, others, of the middle class, to prevent any sacrilege against the clergy, who, less from patriotism, perhaps, than from fear, parted, sobbing bitterly, with tiny fractions of their fortune.

The Congress met [December 6, 1846]. The reformists were in majority, and even the opponents of reform were liberals. In the closing days of the year Santa Anna was named President and Gómez Farías Vice-President. Things looked ominous to the clergy and to the great mass of the people who, whether liberal or conservative, regarded the economic power of the Church as an inviolable institution.

Gómez Farías and his advanced thinkers arrived at an agreement with Santa Anna: the property held in mortmain by the clergy was to be taken over and either sold directly until fifteen million pesos had been obtained or sequestered until a loan was elicited. This was a drastic measure, but nobody denied the government's right to decree it. Let us recapitulate briefly. The clergy's possessions were not private, but corporative property; they were, therefore, subject to special restrictions which the State had the right to impose. The clergy's possessions could not, under mortmain, be sold, and so added nothing directly to the circulation of wealth. The government, then, for the common good could change or modify this condition. The clergy's possessions had been acquired through donations, either from the king or with his consent. And these were all definitely revocable. The Spanish kings stood firmly on their prerogatives in this matter. When His Most

Catholic Majesty Charles III confiscated the entire property of the Jesuits in his dominions, nobody denied his right to do so. What was criticized was the way he used this right.

The reform party's aims were threefold: political, social, and patriotic. The party considered the clergy's influence to be pernicious, since it was to the Church's advantage to keep the classes in the *status quo,* which meant keeping the lower classes immersed in religious superstition and the upper classes innoculated with the fear of new ideas. The party considered the Church's privileges to be the principal barrier against the advent of a democracy, in which all would be equal, and felt that so long as the clergy remained the dominant financial power in the country they could never be stripped of these special privileges. And the political aim was to do just that. As for the social aim, the same economic problem was involved. Until the vast mass of landed wealth under mortmain could be brought into circulation there could be no general prosperity; governments and private persons alike acted as parasites on the Church. Nor could there be any betterment of class conditions or any social progress. The patriotic aim was to save the very life of the country by securing the financial resources needed to organize an army for defense and to maintain it and move it about. The usurers would lend no money, preferring to wait till the famished Treasury got desperate enough to borrow one peso and pay back one hundred. The clergy would lend scarcely enough to suffice for a day. The recently enacted tax on incomes and rents brought in nothing. It was impossible to collect taxes systematically in the country's disrupted condition. There was but one thing to do: secure enough money to defray expenses for a year. And the only rich treasure belonged to the Church.

The opposition in the Congress consisted of moderate liberals. The majority consisted of radicals known as "reds"—"pure ones," they were called by the people. Both factions agreed on the necessity of stripping the Church of its privileges and landed wealth. But some of the moderates insisted that an indemnity must be paid, and this would mean a compromise with the Church. The pure ones countered that the Church would never consent to anything but an accomplished fact; this had been its invariable policy. The moderates, even those who held no brief for indemnity, were unanimously in favor of postponing the measure. Such a step, they predicted, would be futile or even disastrous at this juncture; there would be no buyers; the reform party was not strong enough to enforce its will, and the consequence would be civil war. But the reform party was confident of its strength because Santa Anna was on its side, confident that buyers would appear because the sequestered properties would be offered at prices so low that the clergy themselves would buy them back. So the law was passed[16] (January 1847). The ministers of the government girded themselves for the struggle with the clergy; protests in the form of pronunciamentos began to erupt here and there; some legislatures approved, and some refused to promulgate the law; the rabble, egged on by monks of the lowest type, swarmed through the streets of the principal cities, crying, "Long live religion, and death to the pure ones!" The whole country was in tumult.

What the government offered was too precarious to provoke any demand; nobody wanted to buy. And Santa Anna never ceased to ask for money. Finally, exasperated by the attacks of the press, which furiously criticized the new law and berated the Commander in Chief for his inactivity, he decided to go out and meet the American army, to cross a fearful desert without tents or adequate supplies, without having given his troops the rudiments of military training. With eighteen thousand men he marched across that interminable stretch of desolation, dust, and thirst, toward Saltillo (February 1847), and by the time he made contact with the enemy he was already beaten. He had lost four thousand men in his battle with the desert. The enemy had chosen an admirable position for defense (La Angostura), and there sustained two tremendous assaults. If the Mexican army had been led by a real general instead of by an officer who, though extremely brave, was vain, unstable, and ignorant, the assault would have been concerted instead of planless and chaotic, and Taylor would have retreated to Saltillo. The Mexican soldier proved his good qualities in this frightful carnage. He is a soldier who, when hungry and weary, still fights on with courage and ardor. But, subject to sudden fits of despondency, like all the undernourished, and to panic, like all the high-strung, when he

[16] Law of January 11, 1847: "The government is hereby authorized to raise fifteen million pesos by mortgaging or selling the properties under mortmain."

loses confidence in his officer or his leader he deserts; remembering that he was carried off by the levy and educated by the rod, he runs away.

Santa Anna was like him; Santa Anna embodied all the defects of the Mexican and one good quality: intrepid disdain for death. A fit of despondency when the battle was at its height moved him to beat a retreat. And he turned back across the desert, where sickness, nakedness, hunger, and desertion made a last assault on that bloodstained, gaunt column straggling under a pitiless sun, in a perpetual cloud of dust that tormented and very nearly devoured it. Santa Anna was fleeing from probable victory, on his way to certain defeat. He was fleeing toward the City of Mexico, where his power was threatened and where he had addressed a bulletin announcing his victory—cream of the jest! True, he had not been vanquished by the enemy: he had been vanquished by himself.

Mexico, at the same time, was likewise vanquishing itself. In the last days of February, while the national army was meeting disaster at La Angostura, a new American army occupied Tampico, previously abandoned, and disembarked on the coast near Vera Cruz. Thus the invasion took a new direction, from the east instead of the north. Vera Cruz was defended by a mere handful of men. It was imperative to contain the enemy till a new army could come to the rescue. The government, still trying to put the law disposing of Church property into effect, lived in a state of constant alarm. Battalions in which men of the upper class predominated were hostile to reform; these, petted by the clergy and promised backing, refused to obey orders to move on Vera Cruz. The mutiny declared itself to be a protest against the continuance in power of Gómez Farías, against the January law, against the Congress. There were incessant skirmishes in the capital, very little bloodshed. The youths from wealthy families who made up these battalions were popularly known as *polkos,* and with this name they pitted themselves against the pure ones. Santa Anna, chosen by the two factions as arbiter, arrived in the City of Mexico, took over the Presidency, and, furious at learning that Vera Cruz had surrendered, left the Presidency *ad interim* in the hands of General Pedro María Anaya, and went forth to cut short the American advance on the capital, beyond

Jalapa (his home ground), after abrogating the law which had caused so much unrest.[17]

With his usual access of energy, he soon managed to assemble an army on the rim of the Hot Country. He, and he alone, was in a position to choose the field of battle, among any number of strategic sites along the rugged staircase that climbs to the plateau. He chose the worst and was utterly routed. The same vain pretense, the same petulance, so characteristic of the Veracruzan, that had often defeated him before defeated him again. And still his ardor and activity succeeded in producing a new army out of the very fragments of the old, a feat that amazed General Scott, who advanced on the capital, scattering conciliatory and soothing proclamations to the four winds. He said that he came as a republican, to make war on the monarchist faction, and that no one could have more respect than he for religion and for the Catholic Church. And yet, the monarchist faction, headed by Paredes, had done nothing but sabotage the defense of the frontier. It was the liberal party, aided by some of the military, that was conducting and organizing the defense of the country; many leading reactionaries cooperated, but not as a party. Scott pretended to be unaware of these facts; in truth, the invaders were disappointed to find themselves face to face with the federalist reformers who shared so many ideas with the people of the United States and who took them for a model.

When the invaders occupied Puebla, the decision was made to defend the capital, and the Federal District was marshaled for the struggle. Among the intellectuals there was little or no faith: "The result is foregone," so their minds ran.

> [It is] impossible to vanquish an army that can be reinforced endlessly from the north and from the east. And what if we do lose lands that never belonged to us except in name: Texas, California? Perhaps that would be an advantage; a reduction in size might make for cohesion, concentration, strength.

But the people felt they must beat the Yankees. The people were not afraid; the vague terror that a series of defeats inspires in the masses was not present here.

[17] The law of January 11, 1847, was abrogated by decree of March 29, 1847.

"The Americans are not really winning; rather the Mexicans are defeating themselves with disunity, disobedience, and mistakes; all that is needed is a unified effort and that handful of intruders will disappear." So thought the people in their hate and contempt for a race incompatible in customs, language, and religion. They failed to recognize what was admirable in that valiant and level-headed handful of intruders who, taking advantage of the superiority of their armament and their cohesion and of the inefficiency of Mexican generals and the damaging dissensions of civil war, had penetrated to the heart of the country, sweeping all before them.

When Scott reached the Valley of Mexico popular excitement rose high. Why should we not be victorious? Here was a veteran's division containing the survivors of La Angostura, commanded by General Valencia, who now tried to outrival Santa Anna, and the President made moving speeches to them. Here were the civic militia, the *polkos,* in a picturesque camp, which the flower of high society turned into a continuous gaudy picnic, with the boys receiving, in the presence of their sweethearts and mothers, the eucharistic communion as the supreme viaticum for country and for glory.

The stolid invaders took a position on the lowest spurs of the mountains rimming the Valley on the south, where they could safely pick a time and a route to their liking. The core of the defense was Valencia's division, which took a bad position (Padierna) vulnerable to the invaders. The Commander in Chief ordered him to abandon it; the ambitious subaltern balked. Santa Anna, who probably did not care much what happened to Valencia, failed to enforce his order and watched the first day's battle, but not the second day's disaster. The defeat at Padierna entirely disrupted the defense, and the invaders would have entered the city in pursuit of the fugitives if they had not been exhausted by the heroic stand made against them at the convent and bridge of Churubusco. They were turned back at the southern fortifications. The invading army consisted of fewer than ten thousand combatants, and the same number, more or less, were pitted against them during those two terrible August days, when the Mexican army lost five to six thousand men—the best, no doubt. The American officers' superior tactics were demonstrated throughout the Valley campaign, in which they defeated our army piecemeal, always with stronger forces. Curious facts: Scott said in his reports he had captured two ex-Presidents of Mexico (Anaya and Salas); how surprised he would have been if he could have known he had two future Presidents among his officers—Franklin Pierce and Ulysses S. Grant.

Scott asked for an armistice, which was easily arranged. The object was a meeting of an envoy of the United States with Mexican commissioners in order to bring to an end what the American general justly termed "an unnatural war." The envoy, Mr. Trist, demanded a strip of our northern frontier which included New Mexico and the Californias. Our commissioners refused to concede anything except Texas, bounded by the Nueces, and a part of Upper California. The negotiations ended; the armistice expired, and Mexico's fate was decided in the first half of September. Santa Anna's eternal incapacity to concentrate his defense caused him to leave Casa Mata and Molino del Rey weakly guarded; a triumphant defensive fight could not be sustained on the offensive and was turned into rout. The same thing happened a few days later when Chapultepec was taken. The salient episode of these bloody battles was the defense of Chapultepec's summit by the cadets of the Military College; some of them died there. This simple and sublime act was the most glorious of all the brave acts in the entire war, on either side.

On September 15 of this same year of 1847, the victorious army occupied the capital. Scattered attempts at popular resistance were quickly quelled. Santa Anna, in disgrace, resigned as President of the Republic and headed east. A few days later, Manuel Peña y Peña, the Chief Justice, got himself recognized as President by most of the country, assembled some troops, called the governors together, arranged for the Congress to meet, and organized a government that could enter into negotiations with the commander of the invading army. There was a group in the Congress that passionately opposed the idea of peace, the idea that was incarnate in Peña y Peña and in his minister Luis de la Rosa and later in the Provisional President, General Herrera. They and nearly the whole moderate party had desired this peace from the first, foreseeing what was bound to happen. Now they were determined to secure peace in spite of the fulminations of the military and the theatrical eloquence of some deputies. Even before the annexation of Texas, peace was urgent; after that, imperative; after the war, our only salvation. The war had left us without soldiers (9,000 men dispersed about the country), without artillery, without rifles (less than 150 in the armories).

The principle that a country must never cede territory is absurd, and no country, once invaded and conquered, has been able to sustain it. The true principle is quite different: a country in the grip of dire necessity can and should cede a part of its territory in order to conserve the rest.

With these convictions the eminent jurists representing us entered into negotiations with the American envoy Trist, a highly deferent man, and were surprised to learn that the victors had not increased their demands to any extent since their decisive triumphs in the Valley. The discussions produced, one month later, the Treaty of Guadalupe Hidalgo. The Mexicans disputed each demand, yielding only to compulsion. Meanwhile, the national government was in Querétaro, struggling to stay on its feet amidst anarchy and the hostility of the principal states and latent insurrection in others, amidst penury and prostration. If it should fall, the Republic would fall with it. On February 2 the Treaty was signed. We lost what we had already lost in fact: California, New Mexico, Texas, the portion of Tamaulipas beyond the Rio Grande. The rest of the occupied territory was to be delivered to us shortly, together with an indemnification amounting to fifteen million pesos. This was not a price paid for one ceded territory which was already in the Americans' possession (and they delivered to us much that we had thought lost forever)—this was payment for damages caused by the war, and so vital that the government could not have survived without it and the consequences would have been chaos, dismemberment, and annexation. This was a painful treaty but not an ignominious one. A comparison with the treaty between France and Germany at Frankfurt, and with that between the United States and Spain at Paris, will enable us to judge our forefathers with more fairness. They did what they should have done, and did it well.

Mexico, a weak country because of its scant and sparse population, still partly ignorant of cultured life and of patriotism in its fullest meaning, has been vanquished in all its international wars, though never really conquered. But there is a fatality about the country, a sort of malign influence on its invaders which would seem to have some mysterious relation to justice. French intervention in Mexico led to the Franco-Prussian war; American invasion led to the War Between the States. From the disruption of political parties in the United States there arose the resolutely antislavery Republican Party, which opposed the spread of the black social plague to the newly acquired territories, and against this group the South, feeling itself strong (for to make itself strong it had insisted on the War with Mexico) resorted to arms. The Mexican War was the school for the future generals of the American Civil War.

PART II. The Reform

CHAPTER ONE

REORGANIZATION AND REACTION

(1848–1857)

Pacification; Yucatán; administrative honesty. Arista's Presidency; liberal government. Mercantilism and militarism. Santa Anna; personal government. Ayutla; end of dictatorship; the reformists. Comonfort's Presidency; failure of a constitutional President.

EXICO HAS HAD only two revolutions, that is, two violent accelerations of its evolution. They were results of that forward drive, propelled by the interaction of environment, race, and history, which continually moves a human society to realize an ideal, to improve its condition. This drive, when it collides with external forces, nearly always speeds up, at the risk of provoking formidable reactions; this, then, is a revolution. The first was Independence, emancipation from the motherland, which grew out of the Creoles' conviction that Spain was not able to govern them and that they were well able to govern themselves. This first revolution was triggered by Napoleon's attempt to conquer the Iberian Peninsula. The second revolution was the Reform, which sprang from the profound need for a stable political constitution —that is, a guarantee of liberty, which would be based on a transformation of the social order, on the suppression of the privileged classes, on the equitable distribution of the public wealth (stagnant, for the most part), on the regeneration of labor, and on the creation of a national conscience by means of popular education. This second revolution was triggered by the American invasion, which exposed the impotence of the privileged classes to save the country and the amorphousness of an organism that could hardly be called a nation. In the perspective of history, the two revolutions are successive phases of a single social movement: the first being emancipation from Spain, the second, emancipation from the colonial system. They were two stages in the creation of a national personality fully aware of itself.

The government scarcely wielded any authority anywhere. Each entity of the Federation did as it pleased, and a loose confederacy of insolvent republics had taken the place of the federal pact. The problems that confronted the President, the progressive, honest, energetic, almost too benevolent General Herrera, were these: (1) to build a central government that could unify the country—the war, by lopping off more than one third of our territory, had strengthened the center by shortening the radius to each frontier—and (2) to use the money of the American indemnity to the best advantage, not merely for current expenses but for the reorganization of the Treasury system, which was the key to political stability.

On June 12, 1848, the capital of the Republic was evacuated by the invaders and occupied by the national government, headed by members of the liberal party who believed that reform should be gradual and should consist of compromises, with a view to averting civil war. But stubborn resistance to any reform whatever was to prove this policy impractical. The government, having been authorized to spend the first three millions of the indemnity (its sole resource, for the scant revenue from customs was earmarked for the payment of creditors, and the states failed to send in their quotas), made every effort to spend the money to the best advantage. The cartridge rifle had defeated us, so the government provided the army with this weapon, bought from the invaders. Mexicans who did not want to remain in the ceded territories were repatriated. The Treasury was rescued from a ruinous contract. The northern states and Yucatán were assisted in their wars with savage tribes.

Yucatán, to escape invasion and possible annexation by the United States, had seceded once more at the very moment when a foreign army was knifing to the heart of the Republic. This crime against patriotism was expiated in a frightful way during the uprising of the Indians who made up more than half the population of the Peninsula. Sweeping away resistance, they took possession of nearly all the principal cities, burning, torturing, sacking, and looting endlessly, without mercy. The Yucatecans who survived fled to the coasts or from the Peninsula, and after the worst was over the population, which had consisted of nearly 600,000 inhabitants, numbered less than half that many. The Indians, implacable assassins armed by the merchants of the British colony of Belize, inspired such terror that the Yucatecans sought help from foreign nations, were even willing to sacrifice their precarious independence in the hope of gaining security for their lives and homes. But Mexico, at the close of the war with the United States, embraced its prodigal son and sent troops and money. Since that day Yucatán, previously bound to Mexico only by loose ties of expediency, has been united to the rest of the country by bonds of eternal gratitude. Meanwhile, in a war that went on year after year and was notable for heroic deeds, every able-bodied man on the Peninsula carried arms. Inch by inch, the Yucatecans won back their native soil. A zone of desolation and death, frequently crossed by bloody trails, separated the civilized people, living in ruined towns, from the kraals of the fierce and indomitable Maya.

This was not, however, the most distressing chapter in the work of pacification. The savages of Yucatán were eventually brought under control. As for the nomads of the north, the United States, according to Article 11 of the Treaty of Guadalupe Hidalgo, had contracted the "sacred" duty to prevent or chastise their incursions. But the government was threatened near to home by other savages: the perennial spawners of pronunciamentos and civil strife. And first in one band of rebels, now in another, appear the names of the future champions of reaction, the noble and intrepid Tomás Mejía, the terribly sinister Leonardo Marquéz. Throughout the revolt, General Bustamante, dead soon after, performed for the government services of the highest order.

There is no room for details here. The almost absolute autonomy of the states, the impossibility, due to lack of funds, of supplying the army adequately, made the task of pacification extremely arduous. On the administrative side, nothing could be accomplished. The crying need was reduction of the army, but this meant creating another army of discharged soldiers hostile to the government, the very same army which Santa Anna (who was no sooner lost from sight over the horizon toward the Gulf than he shone forth once again in the nimbus of a savior) could always find ready to hand when he needed it. At the end of Herrera's administration the country had been pacified, as far as possible, and there were promising signs of material progress. Literature and art made their divine voices heard, and there were tokens of an ineffable longing to go forward, to embrace the future. But alas for our country! The shore was still distant: an entire generation was destined to be shipwrecked in a shattering storm.

The exhausted Treasury, with no resource but the indemnity, was nevertheless brought out of chaos and into order, a giant step forward, by classification of the public debt, most of it being converted into bonds held by the British, the amount being definitely fixed and the payment of interest stipulated. A commission of public credit, consisting of highly reputable men, was set up; economies were made in the budget, and the impossible was achieved by General Arista, Minister of War, who managed to reduce, improve, and consolidate the army, with an eye to the abolition of all but strictly military privileges.

The conservative party was dispersed in factions, some supporting one government, some another. The army followed Santa Anna, who at times was a federalist and a pure one, at other times a centralist and proclerical. The clergy, unwisely led by their bishops, took their stand beside those who, strongly opposed to new ideas, insisted that the Church should rule society, even rule the government, who were determined to scotch the introduction of religious tolerance, which had been proposed by some politicians, and to halt the circulation of forbidden books.

A man of great intelligence, but whose political ideas were based on a fundamental error, of which they were the logical consequence, Lucas Alamán, strove with youthful enthusiasm to put his theories into practice, and now began to build the conservative party into a solid organization. His unpopularity, intense among the liberal middle class, filtered down to the masses. His *Historia de México* was consecrated religiously to the aim of destroying respect for the fathers of Independence. This book, together with the newspapers that he controlled, made him a veritable battleflag in the fight to the death against the reformist creed. The fundamental error of Alamán and of the party that he organized during the moderate administrations consisted in a belief in the goodness of the colonial regime, which had given the country peace, order, and prosperity. He drew the inference that what the country needed was to restore the old regime, and even to bring back monarchy, under the protectorate or tutelage of a European throne, preferably the Spanish one. To this inflexible doctrinaire, the terrible denouement of the colonial regime, dramatized by the struggle for Independence itself, meant nothing; he failed to understand that the purely mechanical peace and order of Spanish times ineluctably brought on the agitation and anarchy of Mexican times, precisely because the kind of education that we had received from the Spaniards was worthless as a preparation for a responsible life. To him, the changes in the times, the impossibility of restoring the mental and physical isolation which was the essential condition for the success of the colonial regime meant nothing. And he went imperturbably about his self-appointed task of bringing all the conservative classes and all the important men who shared his views into contact with one another. The Church, under new leaders, the Archbishops Garza in Mexico, Munguía in Michoacán, and, later, Labastida in Puebla,[1] now boldly entered the political fray; so did the army, eager for the rebellion which Alamán plotted assiduously in correspondence with the exiled Santa Anna; so did the wealthy (nearly all Spaniards) and the industrialists, frightened by the liberal doctrines of the reformists. Seldom has this country seen so much

[1] Dr. Lázaro de la Garza y Ballesteros was archbishop of Mexico from February 11, 1851, to January 17, 1860, when the government expelled him from the country. Dr. Clemente de Jesús Munguía, appointed first archbishop of Michoacán March 16, 1863, had been expelled from the country January 18, 1861. Pelagio Antonio de Labastida y Dávalos, transferred from Puebla to Mexico March 19, 1863, was bishop of Puebla from July 8, 1855, until May 12, 1856, when he was banished from the country.

energy, so much will power, so much talent placed at the service of an impossible cause. Alamán's assaults on the liberal administration were pernicious and senseless, hurting the moderates and causing them to fail, marshaling the reactionaries against them, making inevitable the rise of the radical reformists, the pure ones.

When that hero out of Plutarch, modest, honorable, selfless, serene, José Joaquín Herrera, turned the Presidency over to his Minister of War, Mariano Arista, elected by a majority of the legislatures, he could well say, "He who does what he can, does what he should." But not much could be done with the chaos resulting from the American war and from unbridled federalism, from the anarchism among the radical groups and the resistance to all change among the conservative ones. In spite of their sacred duty to prevent the incursions of savages in the north, the Americans failed to prevent them, and even perhaps encouraged the tragic raids of the Apache and their kind from Sonora to Tamaulipas, raids which paralyzed trade and agriculture in the zone between the new boundaries and the tropics. And in Yucatán the war went on, monotonous, merciless, endless, devouring the living flesh of the Yucatecan people, thanks to the government of Belize, which, counting on our impotence to follow protests with action, gave constant assistance to the Maya in return for their help in getting precious woods out of Mexican territory.

Thus, in January 1851, when General Arista entered upon the presidential term which would in fact end before the close of the next year, the situation was worse than ever. Many worthy projects had been started. But how to carry them out? The financial problem could no longer be put off with stopgaps. The funds of the American indemnity were nearly exhausted; revenue from customs was reduced to a dribble by smugglers, who maintained a warehouse in Monterrey and plied openly back and forth through all the ports of all the frontiers. The economies in the budget had filled the cities with soldiers out of work, eager to procure a salary and a rise in rank from the next revolt, as they had always done. And the public offices swarmed with bureaucratic traitors and conspirators, obstinate and ruthless, who watched everything and undermined everything. This was the terrible conspiracy, impalpable, irrepressible, of the unpaid or badly paid bureaucrats, an eternal conspiracy in Mexico, and one that has nearly always proved successful.

The government made an effort to assist the frontier states, to stop contraband in the north, to suppress rebellions, especially a most serious one in Guanajuato, and, above all, to find new resources. In spite of cuts in the salaries of the bureaucrats, in spite of the almost total abandonment of the northern frontier (Sonora, Durango, Chihuahua), the deficit amounted to more than thirteen million pesos. There were no funds with which to pay the interest on the so-called English debt, and the recent attempt to put our credit on a sound basis came ignominiously to nothing. When the government succeeded in halting the contraband that was sapping our one reliable source of revenue, Mexican filibusters (José María Carbajal and Antonio Canales), joined by the filibusters of Texas and financed by the businessmen of Matamoros, organized openly across the Rio Grande and began to invade our national territory in small armies that threatened Matamoros and Camargo, inciting those regions to secede and form a separate republic. The exhausted government managed somehow to repulse the invaders, but once back across the Rio Grande, they set about reorganizing their forces, with the knowledge and consent of the authorities, who gave them arms, just as they gave arms to the savages on the northwest frontier and to the piratic expeditions of William Walker and of Gaston de Raousset-Boulbon. The latter, intent on making himself the Hernán Cortés of Sonora, succeeded in taking possession of Hermosillo for a short spell in 1852 and then went back to his preparations for conquest, his poet-adventurer's dreams, his insatiable ambitions, so like those of his feudal ancestors in the days of the Crusades.

What brought on the first rumblings of disaster was a deed whose consequences could not have been foreseen. The commanding officer at Matamoros, in order to procure funds with which to beat off the filibusters, had altered, *motu proprio,* the tariff rates, lowering the prescribed duties on imported goods. The uproar was tremendous: appeals to the government, desparate protests from importers, especially in Tampico and Vera Cruz. But the harm, once done, was not easily undone. The Congress paid little attention to the government's financial projects, leaving it barely able to cope with the incessant pronunciamentos—in Vera Cruz, Sinaloa, Michoacán. The country, said the Secretary of War, Manuel Robles Pezuela, was disintegrating.

The year 1852 opened with a new Congress, but the situation was worse than ever, and the President painted it in somber colors in a discourse which seemed the *De profundis* of the Federation and of the Republic. He asked for revenues to apply against the appalling deficit, for measures that would compel the states to fulfill their obligations, which they completely neglected, for troops to consolidate the pacification of the country, still precarious, and he recommended that the interests of commerce and industry be attended to. The Congress was either not willing or not able to do anything. New and frightful raids by the savages down into Durango moved the inhabitants of the frontier to cry, "This is the end! We are doomed to disappear from Mexican society!" And neither the Congress nor the government could do anything.

The picture, during the months that followed, was always the same: savages, filibusters, pronunciamentos, infinite want. A Federation that had degenerated into a loose confederacy because the states took too much license. An Executive Power that asked for authority to do something because the Congress did nothing, only to be denied. The enlightened part of the public applauding the first telegraph, supporting literary publications. The conservatives, in their press, attacking the members of the government, even besmirching their private lives, and pouring sarcasm on the Federation, on representative government, on the republican system. And everything that happened seemed to put them in the right. The reform program scarcely showed signs of life, except in Michoacán, where Melchor Ocampo pushed it energetically, calling for religious liberty and preparing a bold plan for the nationalization of the Church property under mortmain. And this activity, says Alamán, was a prime factor in Arista's fall: because of this, the clergy decided to back a revolution. But the President, despite obstacles, followed the straight road of his constitutional duty.

In midyear of 1852 a rebellion broke out in Guadalajara against the high-minded and progressive governor, Diego López Portillo; the rebels, after taking the capital of Jalisco, invaded the whole state. While the federal Executive was readying forces to combat them, his enemies hastened to Guadalajara and succeeded in turning a revolt against a governor into one against the President. Santa Anna's partisans were the most active among these agents of evil, playing upon the army's greed and rancor, so that in September the local rebellion had become national. Finally, in October, the entire heterogeneous aggregation of appetites, of avid and rabid desires and reactionary instincts, all who feared reform (the clergy being mobilized by Alamán's agent, Antonio Haro), plus those who wanted to avenge something, those who wanted to rob something, those who wanted to eat something, and those who had become addicted to the hullabaloo, reached an agreement with that indispensable miracle-worker, Santa Anna. Hence the Hospicio Plan,[2] which upheld the federal system, impeached Arista, demanded a new Congress, which should reform the Constitution and save the country, and called Santa Anna, with fulsome praise, to the helm. The rebellion spread in all directions. General José López Uraga, who was chosen to lead an army against it, instead made himself the leader of the latest "army of liberation." Tampico, meanwhile, had published a declaration lowering tariffs, which put Vera Cruz in a predicament until that city likewise published a declaration adopting the same tariffs.

This was a mortal blow to Arista's government, for the Congress refused to grant him special powers. Many of his friends, in the army and in political life, urged him to dissolve the Congress. This he would not do. In January 1853 he made one more attempt to gain those essential powers and was denied them. Then he nobly and stoically presented his resignation. Thus, the man who had sneaked into history by the dark and tricky back door of barracks revolts walked out proud and erect and spotless beneath the triumphal arch of duty well done.

The Interim Presidency, according to law, devolved upon the Chief Justice of the Supreme Court, Juan Bautista Ceballos, who was confirmed in that capacity by the Congress.[3] The situation that he faced

[2] On September 13, 1852, the Jalisco garrison demanded the resignation of General Arista. On October 20 the Hospicio Plan was proclaimed in Guadalajara. In Article 11 of that Plan is the call to Santa Anna, "in view of the eminent services which he has rendered the country at all times" and which "have won him the nation's gratitude."

[3] On January 6, 1853, Arista resigned, turning the Presidency over to Ceballos;

was grave. The revolution had already taken over most of the country, and Arista's resignation gave it still more impetus; nothing could stop the tide. The problem, then, was how to work out a compromise in order, first, to prevent further bloodshed, and, second, to prevent Santa Anna, toward whom the whole movement was gravitating, from becoming President. At the mere thought of Santa Anna, Ceballos, like the other liberals in the government, felt something akin to horror, which was certainly justified.

If Ceballos could hardly count on the fragment of an army at his command—the only bargaining power that he had with which to contrive a respectable compromise—the unpopularity of the Congress was to blame. This body, behaving like Santa Anna's accomplice, had idiotically precipitated Arista's fall and was loathed by the liberals for that reason, and because it had proved inept in the financial crisis and, by bringing obloquy on the parliamentary system, had given the conservatives the pretext for an attack on the institution.

Ceballos, determined to get rid of this obstacle, invited the Congress to commit suicide, proposing to call a convention which would serve as a means of compromise with the triumphant revolution and which, whatever else it might do, certainly would not turn the Presidency over to Santa Anna. An army might do that—a Congress, never.

The Congress, indignant at the President's proposal, ordered him to appear before the National Grand Jury. Ceballos then dissolved the Chambers.[4] The senators and deputies defiantly persisted in meeting till the police dispersed them amid the jeers or indifference of the public. But Ceballos, by his illegal act, had destroyed his own title. He was no longer a constitutional President, and when the capital's garrison declared for him he became just one more revolutionary. He soon realized that he had lost his moral force. The commander of the government's troops, Robles Pezuela, met with Uraga, commander of the revolution, and together they invited Ceballos to sanction with his interim authority an agreement whereby Santa Anna was to wield dictatorial

on the next day the Chamber of Deputies accepted the resignation and named Ceballos Interim President.

[4] On January 19, 1853, President Ceballos dissolved the Congress and announced his adherence to the Hospicio Plan.

powers for a year; then a convention would be called.[5] Ceballos returned to the Supreme Court, leaving the government in charge of the general nearest at hand.[6] He had failed; only with the wholehearted cooperation of the Congress could his plan have succeeded, but that was not forthcoming and moderate government was wrecked, leaving the field for the extremists to fight over. The crisis could end only in civil war.

The United States, encouraging the savages and filibusters along the entire northwestern frontier and arming, or permitting to be armed, bands of smugglers on the Rio Grande, had been the primordial cause of federalism's downfall, so weakening the government that it could not exercise its constitutional powers with regard to the states. As a result there was a plethora of customs tariffs in the ports of entry; merchants became the instigators of revolt and took the situation in hand. They not only sent swarms of agents back and forth from Tampico to the frontier and from Vera Cruz to Mexico City and Guadalajara, to feed fuel to the conflagration in Jalisco, but also envoys with blandishing appeals to the exiled Santa Anna.

The exile arrived. He had forgotten nothing. He had learned nothing. What he brought back with him from banishment was the old ineptitude, the old boastful patrioteering, the old vanity, the old instinctive pattern for governing, which consisted in turning the Republic into a barracks and the Mexicans into a regiment and in looting the cashbox of the corps. On the premise that he could govern only without a constitution, he chose for his Cabinet men who renounced their constitutional allegiance and consented to act as spokesmen for the dictatorship, thereby ceasing to be conservatives and becoming revolutionary reactionaries. Alamán had set forth the creed of the new party allying the wealthy class, the clergy, and the military. In a straightforward letter without any trace of flattery he dictated (rather than submitted) to Santa Anna the conditions laid down by the reactionary party before it

[5] The agreement between General José López Uraga and Lieutenant Colonel Manuel Robles Pezuela was signed at the hacienda of Arroyozarco, February 4, 1853. On February 6, in the capital, the agreement referred to above was reached between Uraga and Robles Pezuela and the spokesman for the City of Mexico's garrison.

[6] On February 7 General Manuel María Lombardini took charge of the government as trustee of the Executive.

would consent to take part in his government. The Jalisco revolution became nation-wide, says Alamán, thanks to the clergy, who were frightened by Melchor Ocampo's approach to reform.

> We are thus in a position to propose an agreement on these points: (1) absolute religious intolerance, because religion is the one bond that unites Mexicans; no Inquisition, no persecutions, but war on impious works; (2) a strong government, but one bound by certain principles and by certain responsibilities; (3) complete abolition of the federal system and of elections by popular vote; (4) organization of an army capable of coping with the country's needs; (5) no Congresses; Santa Anna well counseled—that will be the whole Constitution.[7]

Alamán headed the cabinet; his companions were Teodosio Lares, Antonio Haro y Tamariz, Antonio Diéz de Bonilla, and Tornel—the outstanding enemies of reform. Alamán had not put all his intentions into writing for Santa Anna, but the dictator was aware of them and agreeable to them. This is what they boiled down to: in order to ward off the American peril, which loomed larger day by day, it was imperative to establish a Spanish protectorate and a monarchy with a Bourbon on the throne (the surest way, of course, to bring the American peril down upon us). The Mexican envoy, José Manuel Hidalgo, started to activate these intentions, through a series of conferences with the Spanish prime minister, but the latter lost his office and Alamán died, so the plan had to be postponed, much to Santa Anna's relief.

The reactionary cabinet, sharing the government with Santa Anna's exclusively military palace guard, promulgated but a single statute, a kind of laconic code for administration,[8] before getting down to work. Away with enemies, beginning with Arista, who was banished; so were all the important liberal leaders. Away with censors: the Lares law[9] made impossible not only liberty, but the very existence, of the press. Away with obstacles: the departments were put under military charge,

[7] On March 17, 1853, General Santa Anna was declared President-elect; on April 20 he took office.

[8] "Bases for the Administration of the Republic, Pending the Promulgation of a Constitution."

[9] Decree of April 25, 1853, "On License and Liberty of the Press." The author was Teodosio Lares, Secretary of the Interior.

the territorial divisions changed, and each governor, each prefect, each town council was constituted the direct agent of the central power, the only elector, the only distributor of offices, the only depositary of funds. This was not a central power but an autocratic power, in the strictest sense.

But, as always, the government, which steadily enlarged the army (the cancer of centralist governments) and spent the greater part of the public income on parades, processions, and military celebrations (the dictator's folly), found itself backed into the corner of financial impasse (the familiar blind alley of all Mexican governments). Haro, a very honest, very fanatical, very eccentric man, who had run off the usurers, had introduced bold economies, and was carrying on a fearless campaign against the dictator's extravagance, finally proposed floating a loan by mortgaging the clergy's entire propery. Santa Anna, who could not abide him, then forced him to resign. With Alamán's death and Haro's dismissal, government by the reactionary party came to an end. Many reactionaries remained in the administration on account of their loathing for federalism, but they were only second-string, well to the rear of the military, the real lords of the land.

Like most Latin politicians, Alamán was admirably apt in his criticisms of a regime he disliked, but hopelessly theoretical and impractical when it came to putting his precepts into practice. He organized the conservative party into a combat corps, aggressively hostile to the reform program and to the influence of the United States in Mexico, and he coaxed the Church into his camp. His antireform policy was a capital error. Instead of assaulting the moderate liberals, he should have given them firm support. And he committed a catastrophic blunder by entangling the Church with Santa Anna and dictatorship. By so doing, he in no way strengthened the Church, but made it subject to all the vicissitudes of politics and vulnerable to the ultimate reprisal, the lifting of mortmain. In addition, he bequeathed to his party the hope of foreign intervention and of a monarchy—which is to say, eternal death.

The reactionary program went aimlessly adrift. The great reactionary's notion that good advice could keep the dictator from becoming a tyrant proved to be an idle dream. One-man government prevailed, and the army heaped Santa Anna with titles, including even that of emperor. He was satisfied, however, with the title of "Most Serene Highness." And everything—the pomp and splendor, the resurrection of monarchic frills, such as the Order of Guadalupe, and of all the panoply and protocol of royalty—betrayed the dictator's mania for aping the second Napoleon (Napoleon III), just as Iturbide had parodied the first. The crown was not far off; the way to it was through the pettiest despotism, the most cynical extravagance, the most barefaced favoritism, hand-kissing, orgies, balls. Never had the soldiers been decked out in more costly and picturesque uniforms, the churches in more tempting ornaments, the ladies in more dazzling jewels; never had the Republic been mired any deeper in the muck of ignorance, want and vice; never had the Republic sported such gorgeous plumes.

The old Creole oligarchy, dreading reform, was content to give the despot a free hand, as long as the roads were comparatively safe and there was hope of a rich return from usury. The man who was soon to be the spokesman for reformist thought was now, ignoring the political situation, occupied with certain material improvements: building telegraph lines, projecting railways, compiling statistics and publishing useful information. His name was Miguel Lerdo de Tejada.

In March of 1854, an obscure army officer proclaimed at Ayutla, in the Department of Guerrero, where for months the generals Juan Alvarez and Tomás Moreno and the then Colonel Ignacio Comonfort had given the government cause for uneasiness, a plan supported by these men, who succeeded in taking possession of Acapulco.[10] The Plan called for ridding the government of Santa Anna and demanded respect for individual liberty, for the army, for commerce. Not a word about federalism or reform, but, on the contrary, a tendency toward centralism: a Commander in Chief would call together a small group of representatives of the departments, to be named by himself, who would elect an Interim President with broad powers and would convoke a Congress instructed to draw up for the nation a republican, representative, and popular form of government. That was the whole Plan.

The government had occupied beforehand strategic points in the south and on news of the rebellion launched an invasion which the

[10] The Plan of Ayutla was proclaimed by Colonel Florencio Villareal March 1, 1854. It was seconded in Acapulco and modified, March 11, by the Plan of Acapulco.

President himself headed. His campaign was a colossal failure. First-line troops broke through Alvarez's undisciplined bands to Acapulco, but, once there, could not overcome General Comonfort's indomitable defense of the port and returned to their point of departure. But the revolution was confined to the south (Michoacán and Guerrero) for a long time. Comonfort went to the United States to procure arms, which the revolutionists desperately needed, and the dictator tried to prevent the fire from spreading by resorting to a reign of terror. The terrible law condemning conspirators to death was frequently enforced: imprisonment, banishment were the order of the day. Arrogance, pomp, and extravagance were the only principles of government. And it seemed there could be no deliverance from the insane flattery, from the deification of His Highness, from the absurd apotheosis of the Hero of Tampico. Processions in honor of his saint's day rivaled the popular festivals in honor of the Corpus of Christ. Everything seemed to indicate that the Man of Providence, "first in war, first in peace," as the lickspittle newspapers that bought their right to survive with the most abject adulation were accustomed to calling him, would stay in power forever.

About the middle of the year 1854, Gaston de Raousset-Boulbon, feeling that the hour had struck for his dream of conquest and riches, since Sonora was believed to be an unexplored California, a hundred times richer than that region, led a group of Frenchmen and Germans who had previously been accepted as colonists in a bloody fight to capture Guaymas. He was taken prisoner, along with those of his comrades who survived. General José María Yáñez, after defending the city with consummate skill, pardoned the adventurers, with the exception of their leader, whose execution he felt duty-bound to order. This leader, with his arrogant and chivalrous manners, won everybody's sympathy and pity and died with the serenity of a paladin. A man of extraordinary imagination and energy, he yearned to make a novel of his life, and succeeded, even unto the final chapter, at once tragic and heroic.

While the whole country was applauding Yáñez, Santa Anna, with a sort of senile, brainless envy, subjected him, by way of reward, to a court martial. Santa Anna would have nothing to do with anybody but his cronies of the palace guard, whom he surfeited with gifts and favors.

Two upstanding judges of the Supreme Court, Justices Ceballos and Castañeda, were ousted for refusing to accept the ribbon of the Order of Guadalupe; the former chose to leave the country, never to return. Thus the principle of permanent tenure for the Judicial Power was destroyed, the only safeguard of the courts' independence, which was the only possible curb to despotism.

Comonfort's return to the country gave the revolution new impetus, and his victories, frequently followed by acts of clemency, contrasted sharply with those of the government, with their obligatory sequel of military executions. His efforts to soften civil war with humane practices and to build the chaotic revolutionary bands into a disciplined army aroused the country's sympathy, which on his triumph would swell into a tremendous popularity.

Santa Anna, to raise funds, agreed to sell a slice of the national territory, amending the Treaty of Guadalupe Hidalgo with the cession of the tract known as La Mesilla, which the Americans in fact already occupied, and cancelling their obligation (which they had contracted but had never fulfilled) to prevent the savage Indians from raiding below our border.[11] To carry the abuse of power to the point of bartering away a piece of the national territory seemed to the people an unparalleled outrage, especially since the only reason was to get hold of seven million pesos, which civil war and usury swallowed up in no time. What made it worse, the government tried to demonstrate popular support for despotism by holding a plebiscite (aping what Napoleon III had recently done in France) and grossly stacking the votes in the dictator's favor.

But Santa Anna was nervous: his old revolutionary's instinct told him that the rebellion was winning the country's good will, for the people were terribly tired of war and anxious for assurances of peace. The revolution spread from Michoacán to Jalisco; Colima, with one of the army's best brigades, surrendered to Comonfort, and Santiago Vidaurri took Monterrey and proclaimed the autonomy of an important section of the frontier.

[11] The Treaty of La Mesilla was signed in the City of Mexico, December 30, 1853, and ratified by decree of July 20, 1854.

Realizing that something should be done to mollify the general unrest, the dictator came up with the idea of consulting several eminently learned conservatives as to the manner in which the government might be transformed from a personal into a national one. The celebrated jurist Bernard Couto drew up their answer, which condemned, with devastating reasons, any attempt at a monarchy and set forth, as the salient goal of a new constitution, the real and effective exercise of individual rights. These men thus drew the line behind which both liberals and conservatives could rally in a common antipathy for tyranny and for anarchy. They were entirely separate from the group that Alamán had led, who were uncompromising reactionaries; these were true conservatives, as essential as the reformer to the normal progress of free institutions.

Santa Anna ignored the project. When the news came, in midyear of 1855, of revolts in the state of Vera Cruz which might cut off his escape, he fled the capital, abandoning his ministers, who hid themselves as best they could. After publishing a manifesto which lauded his own conduct and poured vituperation on the authors of the "infamous revolution of Ayutla," he boarded ship for foreign lands.[12]

A whole epoch of our history closes with his exit, even though he left gaping bloody wounds behind him. The history of domination by the military, beginning with the struggle for Independence and continuing with the ineluctable anarchy to which our education had condemned us, an anarchy whose most morbid manifestations were personified in Santa Anna, was now coming to an end. The tragedy was losing its protagonist.

Another epoch of history, another generation, another Republic would gradually but definitely take possession of the stage.

The situation threatened to become still worse. In the City of Mexico, the garrison, to the tune of wild mob scenes, declared for the Plan of Ayutla,[13] and its commander convoked an assembly, to his taste, which appointed an Interim President. The adherents of the established order,

[12] Santa Anna abandoned the Presidency August 8, 1855; he embarked from Vera Cruz August 16.

[13] The capital's garrison adopted the Plan of Ayutla August 13; on the fifteenth General Martín Carrera took provisional charge of the government.

frightened by the triumph of the revolution, and the heroes of the main chance, expert at the game of turning political crises to their personal advantage, tried by such methods to trick a revolution into a game of dice. Meanwhile the generals, each with his own army, stood by: Haro in San Luis Potosí, Manuel Doblado in Guanajuato, Vidaurri in Monterrey. His Serene Highness' army, still unbeaten, was still headed by officers of steel. But Comonfort's great sincerity won them all over. The army put itself in his hands; General Martín Carrera, who had been named Interim President at the capital, honorably resigned; Haro and Doblado chimed in. An assembly, meeting at Cuernavaca, chose as the new Interim President General Alvarez,[14] the old soldier who had served under Morelos and Guerrero (and whose craftiness and prestige had created a vast personal empire in the bleak mountain areas of the south which nobody dared to meddle with).

Alvarez gave Comonfort control over all that concerned the army, making him Secretary of War and Commander in Chief, and turned the rest of the government over to the reformists, with Melchor Ocampo as Secretary of State, Benito Juárez as Attorney General, and Guillermo Prieto as Secretary of the Treasury. Comonfort wanted to conserve the army by reorganizing it; most of the reform party wanted to do away with it and replace it by the civil militia. But the Secretary of War managed to get his way, with the result that the army, which had reached the apogee of its power under the dictatorship, became violently hostile to the reformists and looked upon Comonfort as a savior.

The Reform took its first steps gradually. The reformists went about their task with good sense and determination. They abolished the immunity of the clergy under civil law and barred them from voting in elections. The bishops protested, but too late. They themselves were responsible for their plight. They had not only stood adamantly against all attempts at reform, resisting even the timid efforts of the moderates; they had openly made themselves parcel of a political party and had used every weapon at hand, including money, to serve that party. During the dictatorship, which the more thoughtful of the clergy did not applaud, the most arrogant of the Church's heads had done everything

[14] General Juan Alvarez was chosen Interim President October 4, 1855.

possible to bring back the supremacy of their class in colonial times, setting themselves athwart the path of intellectual progress, a path whose signposts are freedom of belief and of thought. The liberties that are essential to civilization—and these are the very same ideals that the finest human minds strive eternally to achieve—cannot exist without freedom of conscience, any more than the planetary system can exist without the sun.

There could, therefore, be no truce. The battle was on. The reactionaries put their final trust in civil war, preparing for it openly. If only they could contrive to involve some great Latin nation in their crusade! Spain? A hope. France? A dream.

Comonfort was a man of great heart and unswerving purpose. He foresaw a sea of blood, and he wanted to save his country from this crushing calamity. His whole intent was to avert civil war, without betraying the revolution. With this in mind he accepted the Presidency of the Republic from General Alvarez in December 1855.

Comonfort's Presidency was the first gloomy act in a drama whose prelude began, long before the rebellion at Ayutla, with the beginnings of our national history. Every prospect was dreary, but especially that of our foreign relations—with Europe, that is, for the United States had learned to respect us a little. But England, to whom we owed the most money, and to whom we paid the least—because we could barely pay half the salaries of the army and the bureaucracy, when we could pay anything at all—treated us with disdain, showing her fangs from time to time and compelling us to obey her demands without regard for the justice of the case. France treated us suavely, sympathetically, despite a certain ineptitude on the part of her diplomatic ministers, who seemed incapable of clear vision; assuming a protective air, she appeared to be engaged in watchful waiting. Spain, like a possessive mother, tried to bring us under her diplomatic tutelage, and while her envoys, who quickly joined our high society, were always extremely deferent, their government was imperious, patronizing, severe in her exactions and often unjust, demanding exceptional procedures in the punishment of crimes against Spaniards. These, then, were our diplomatic guardians, who assumed an authority over us which had for pretext the state of perpetual anarchy in which we lived. These were three boots heavily planted, not on our neck but on our belly.

The interior was in turmoil. After the reformists began to carry out their program, not a day passed without a pronunciamento, without a revolt somewhere in the Republic. There was mounting unrest, as if the eruption of a volcano was building up underneath. When Comonfort became President, real heroism was required for him to face the complicated task of pacifying the country. Doblado and Uraga kept the Bajío region in uproar; Manuel Lozada, in the pay of topflight smugglers, ruled Nayarit, with Tepic and San Blas destined to become his tributaries; Vidaurri was lord of a vast sector of the northeastern frontier. But Doblado agreed to terms; Uraga was forced to terms; Vidaurri, supposed to be the sword of the radical faction, conveniently came to an understanding with the government and placed himself at its orders.

In Puebla, however, the army, feeling its privileges endangered, set up a formidable center of counterrevolutionary activity, headed by a bellicose priest at Zacapoaxtla and joined by Santa Anna's officers. There Antonio Haro, perennial presidential candidate of the conservatives, found asylum. The forces sent by the government went over to the rebels; Comonfort's best available general, Severo del Castillo, betrayed him and joined them with all his troops. The rebels were strong enough, then, to take possession of Puebla. There they waited for the rest of the old army to unite with them—the army that started out as the Army of the Three Guarantees, the privileged army that had gone on propagating itself, so to speak, through pronunciamentos and revolts, from 1821 to 1847, when the first generation disappeared and the second one replaced it, until finally, in 1869, the national army took over. But they waited in vain. The constituent Congress,[15] meanwhile, had met, giving legal sanction to the revolution, and at Comonfort's call resources had been improvised and civic legions had sprung up. To the brilliant corps of the permanent army that remained personally loyal to Comonfort there was added a well-trained national guard, which acquitted itself faultlessly. The President sent nearly

[15] The constituent Congress, convoked by decree of August 20, 1855, was inaugurated February 17, 1856.

fifteen thousand men against the scant four thousand of the reaction, who were forced, on the bloody field of Ocotlán, to shut themselves up in Puebla, where, after a rigorous siege, they surrendered and were chastised by loss of military rank—a humiliation which left them free to do mischief and burning with a desire for revenge.

Although Comonfort's program was most conciliatory, and he did his best to make the country swallow the Reform little by little, the reactionaries were able to frustrate his efforts. To do them justice, the secular clergy (but not the regular) tried to stay neutral and the bishops tried not to feed the flames of war. Among them, the Bishop of Puebla, whose diocese was the center of all the attempts at revolt, was especially distinguished by his fine personal qualities and talents. When the rebel soldiers, hoisting the banner of religion, took possession of Puebla, the Bishop declared himself neutral and yielded to their demands for money only because they organized a military government *de facto*. Ardent and aggressive in temperament, but sound in judgment, Bishop Labastida realized that it would be madness to tie the fate of the Church to the success of a barracks mutiny and that it was in the clergy's interest to support the cautious and well-meaning statesman in the Presidency. But after the military outbreak which had cost so much blood, Comonfort felt obliged to take the reformists' side, though he tried to mitigate his blows. The property of the bishopric of Puebla was confiscated in order to pay the debts incurred in quelling the outbreak, and the Bishop hurled one protest after another.

Comonfort's ministers wasted time trying to defend the legality of their act by citing ecclesiastical authorities. The Bishop triumphantly refuted their thesis. We look at the matter from a different viewpoint. The government's act was justified by purely political considerations, not by anything to be found in secular codes or sacred canons. It was justified by the nation's right to self-preservation. The Bishop of Puebla, who probably spoke the truth, denied any complicity in the mutiny and insisted that he had had no choice: the rebels had set up a government *de facto* in Puebla, and he could not have done otherwise than comply with their demands. In other words, the Church in Puebla declared itself neutral between two belligerents because it considered itself an institution beyond the reach of the State's authority, even where its temporal possessions were concerned—and what can be more temporal than landed property? If the State was going to meddle with these possessions, it would have to come to an agreement with the king of the ecclesiastical body, the theocrat in Rome. The Bishop's doctrine accorded perfectly with the teachings of the Church, and the controversy boiled down to the question of whether an ecclesiastical State with a foreign head could exist inside of a political State with a vital need for unity. On this need for unity the whole work of the Reform was based, and this was the basis for the right to confiscate the property of the diocese of Puebla. And because the Bishop (as was his right and duty) defended the Church's immunity with burning passion, and because it was imperative to countervail the clergy's massive resistance to the work of the Reform, the government forced the Bishop to leave the country. The exiled Bishop felt justified, thenceforth, in seeking to remedy the Church's Mexican troubles through a drastic change in the form of our government.

The festivals in celebration of Comonfort's triumphal return to the capital had barely subsided when he was confronted with new problems. The Congress, dominated by radicals of the reformist faction, balked at the President's conciliatory policy, which, like the fabulous lance, healed wounds even as it made them, for punishment on a large scale was followed by pardons and amnesties. Comonfort, despite his recent searing experience with mutiny, kept on trying to seduce the old reactionary army with leniency, tolerance, and promotions—blandishments almost invariably repaid with treachery, contumely, and rebellion. The widening rift between the Executive Power and the Constituent Congress tended, fortunately, to close whenever the government needed help to overcome a crisis or a rebellion.

But the government felt it should disassociate itself in a dramatic move from the so-called "demagogic" majority in Congress, and, *motu proprio,* decreed a kind of provisional constitution, which was called a statute[16] and which put into effect the limited dictatorship allowed by the Plan of Ayutla. By this statute, liberties were guaranteed, the President's discretionary powers were restricted—under no circumstances

[16] "Provisional Organic Statute of the Mexican Republic," May 23, 1856.

could he sentence anyone to death—and the clergy (who were not to vote or to stand for office) were relegated to a special class of citizenship. Thus, the moderates indicated how far they thought the country was ready to go on the road to reform.

And yet, the Executive Power wanted to make an unequivocal stand in favor of the Reform (but not the antireligious) program of the pure ones. The progressive Secretary of the Treasury, Miguel Lerdo de Tejada, soundest of economists, sponsored the law that delivered corporate property from mortmain.[17] Most of the landed wealth in the Republic was the property of the ecclesiastical corporations or of their affiliates, and the protest of the Church was deafening and long-drawn-out. The law, however, contained no political animus as drafted by Lerdo and approved by the Congress. The aims were all economic and financial: to put landed wealth into circulation and to fatten the Treasury with the incidental proceeds. But the effects amounted to a tremendous social upheaval, even though they were much longer in making themselves felt than the authors had expected. The value of the Church's property was not diminished. The property passed, it is true, into the hands of adjudicators, sometimes but not always the tenants. These, however, continued to credit all income to the Church. If the Mexican Church had been headed by a great statesman at this time instead of by an honorable but timid and unimaginative priest (Archbishop Garza), and if St. Peter's chair had been occupied by a political genius like Leo XIII instead of by a righteous, inflexible apostle [Pius IX], the Church would have accepted Lerdo's law, and, with its coffers stuffed with easily negotiable mortgages, whose value could have been tripled by investment in material improvements, such as the construction of railways (as the Bishop of Puebla once proposed), civil war could have been averted, and the country's progress and the Church's prosperity could have joined hands.

But the bishops blindly protested, and war was declared between the lay and the ecclesiastical states. This was the inevitable consequence of all our history. In colonial days the clergy, rich and privileged though they were, did not constitute a threat to the unity of the State,

[17] June 25, 1856. "Decree Delivering from Mortmain Urban or Rural Properties of Civil or Ecclesiastical Corporations in the Republic."

for, thanks to the Patronate, the State was still their overlord. When a parcel of the clergy, the Company of Jesus, was suspected of attempting to encroach on the authority of the State, the king ruthlessly cast that parcel out. But with Independence the Patronate was practically annulled, and the clergy felt free to undermine the unity, or rather the very existence, of the State, which fought back for its life. Hence the Reform, which meant a religious war, another epoch of blood and tears. The nature of the crisis was clear to all.

The Congress, considering that the battle was on, and scorning compromise, kept raining heavy blows on the clergy. In the process of revising Santa Anna's decrees, the deputies ran onto one that reestablished the Jesuits. This they abrogated, obliging those pedagogues so adept at crushing character, at making a religion of discipline, at eliciting an impressive mass of literary erudition from mediocre minds, to leave the country.[18] The fathers of the Company, who were the educators least in tune with the true precepts of teaching, which consist in freeing the mind and inculcating a sense of responsibility, were very few and inoffensive in the Mexico of those days; the radical party attacked, rather, their more or less legendary role as opponents of modern social doctrines and as proponents of a theocracy.

The terrific reaction to these measures became still more furious when the plan for the new constitution was divulged. The Executive Power publicly assailed this plan as unacceptable because of the innovations concerning religious liberty and those restricting the Executive and abolishing the independence of the Judicial Power, taking away its permanent tenure and making it subject to election.

There was a brief period of calm, during the second third of the year 1856, after Mexican society, egged on by the clergy, had succeeded in persuading the Congress to suppress the article establishing religious liberty, and a majority of the reformists had avowed their ardent Catholicism on the floor of the Chamber. But the Congress, shortly after making peace with the President, began to find him incompatible, as a leader, with their aims. After each decisive step he would resort to a series of measures designed to minimize its effect; Comonfort's vacillat-

[18] In a decree of June 7, 1856, the constituent Congress declared inoperative Santa Anna's decree of September 19, 1853.

ing and benevolent and short-sighted mind could not have done otherwise.

By the end of 1856 plots were simmering on all sides. The religious war, though still latent, was already dividing homes and consciences. Rebellion again broke out in Puebla, led by the same officers who had led the one early in the year; again Comonfort displayed extraordinary vigor; again the battalions marched to Puebla, taking the city, drowning it in blood. Of the two rebel chiefs, one was shot; the other, who would disappear for a time, was Miguel Miramón. Another rebellion broke out in San Luis Potosí and then another, long-drawn-out, costly and bloody, in the Bajío. Fresh troubles with England—caused by the British consul in Tepic, notorious organizer of a band of smugglers on the Pacific coast—were settled on humiliating terms. Some murders of Spaniards by those bands which always flourish in countries in a state of anarchy gave the reactionary, antireformist Spanish government an excuse to make extravagant demands, which were rejected. The ambassador broke off relations with our government, and preparations for war were ostentatiously started at Havana. But France and England offered their services as mediators.

A little later the Empress Eugénie said to the Mexican envoy, the extremely reactionary José Manuel Hidalgo, at Biarritz, "It would be a good thing to set up a throne in Mexico." These words of a silly woman contained the germ of the French intervention in Mexico, of Maximilian's death on the Hill of the Bells, of the disaster at Sedan. But to those who heard her they were the lovely voice of Spain, a voice from Heaven.

The debate on the new constitution had barely ended before the infallible voice of the Pope thundered in the ears of Mexican Catholicism, denouncing the entire Reform program and the constitution about to be promulgated. Raising his pontifical voice with apostolic license in the open Consistory, he condemned as an insult to religion and declared null and void the laws and the constitution and hurled anathemas at those who had obeyed their government. Not a glimmer of hope, not a word of peace, not a hint of compromise with the inevitable. Only the Church's inalienable right to its property and its privileges. And what of God's right to harmony, to love? Never, not even when the

Church denied us the right to be independent, had its voice been heard in such harsh accents, so pregnant with death and disaster.

The Constitution was promulgated in the midst of political uproar[19] and was solemnly sworn to by Goméz Farías, patriarch of the Reform, and by all the deputies, and by the President of the Republic, and by the administrative and political chiefs. The bishops, faithful to the commands of Pius IX, lashed out right and left with excommunications, demanding that the oaths be retracted. The result was complete anarchy in the public conscience. The new Constitution was furiously assailed from all sides. As everybody knew, the President himself was averse to it. The Reform party was painfully aware of impending civil war and terrified at the prospect that the President himself might start the conflict. To prevent such a misfortune, it invited the reactionary party to participate in the elections and to organize a majority in the first Congress under the new Constitution. Proffered, no doubt, with Comonfort's connivance, this invitation should have given the reactionaries every hope of victory. But they scorned it. What they wanted was war. The constitutionalists, making one more effort at conciliation, then chose Comonfort as President. This gained them nothing.

Comonfort ceased to be the dictatorial President prescribed by the Plan of Ayutla and became, with the opening of the new Congress in September, 1857, a constitutional President. The situation of the country was simply frightful. Everything was in turmoil: consciences and homes, the countryside, the towns, the cities. As when the violent dust storms announce, in Mexico, the oncoming downpour, there was neither village, ranch, nor city that escaped agitation from guerrillas, pronunciamentos, highwaymen, or Indian hordes bearing the red banner of commuism. "Religion and Rights," "Constitution and Reform," were the watchwords that added up to the word "death." The government was represented by the tax-collector, and by a swarm of adjudicators (those who took advantage of the lifting of mortmain were mostly foreigners and the clergy). It was also represented by the levy, which extinguished hearths, annihilated families, crushed labor, and withered future generations of Mexicans in the bud, deliver-

[19] The *Political Constitution of the Mexican Republic*, dated February 5, 1857, was promulgated February 12.

ing them over to marijuana, alcohol, and death. Our poor country! Mexico, which has suffered so much, deserves a far better fate!

The President, unable to operate with a Constitution that consisted mainly of curbs on the Executive Power, without faith in the law he had sworn to, anxious to calm the social tumult by compromising on the Reform, without confidence in the army, without a cent in the Treasury, felt obliged to cut matters short, and, giving up all that had been gained, to turn the clock of the Republic back to the hour that had struck right after the revolution of Ayutla. This staggering error was the preface to what appears to be the clearest case of political suicide in Mexican annals.

The Congress that proceeded from the revolution of Ayutla was legally the voice of the land. Actually, it was no such thing. The rural masses never voted, neither did the urban and industrial voters, except at their bosses' behest; the conservative party also abstained. The new assembly represented not even that minority of the citizens who took an interest in politics, but only a minority of the educated minority, which was made up, for the most part, of moderates and of the military and the clergy. But the new generation was, on the whole, devoted to the Reform; together with the veteran devotees of federalism, they were the most active group in the country, and they organized the Congress. This very youthful assembly included, besides the radical reformists and survivors of the federalist shipwrecks of 1834 and of 1853, a few moderates in favor of restoring the Constitution of 1824 and an oscillating majority which generally voted with the radicals, but remained loyal to the government in a crisis. Like all the great revolutionary assemblies, it was made up of diverse elements; like all the reformist assemblies, it constituted a minority. These men in no way represented the mind of the people. On the contrary, the mind of the people had gradually come to accept their ideas, to adopt their point of view.

Their design was not wholly impracticable, not mere theory. Their premise, true enough, was the metaphysical concept of absolute rights. "Man by his very nature is free; nature created all men equal." These were the dogmas of a social religion, the articles of faith formulated by the eminent philosophers of the century that preceded the French Revolution and most eloquently stated by Jean Jacques Rousseau, author of the revolutionary gospel. They are not true: man in a state of nature is not free but subject to an infinity of inescapable laws; nature knows no equality; inequality is her eternal way, diversity her norm. The supreme force which gives unity to all things does exist, but is unknowable. The Congress, beginning its work, invoked the name of God.

Liberty and democracy and equality—the abolition of privileges and the establishment of equal suffrage in elections—have nothing to do with nature but are conquests of mankind, of human civilization. They are not natural rights but ideals which the noblest of men strive to attain by changing the structure of the social body, which is the joint creation of nature and of history. No people, however high their culture, have fully succeeded in attaining them. But all peoples, though on different levels of development, are gradually moving upward in the direction of these ideals. An ideal is a force which can change and shape reality. There is an art in making a people aware of the necessity for a change, an art which consists in recognizing the ideal that their progress has made them readiest for and in holding it constantly before their eyes.

Now, a new religion, new dogmas, a new faith confronted the old. To the soul's yearning for Heaven, with the Church as guiding light, there was opposed man's longing to conquer the future. Never before, as in this Constitution, had the rights of man been defined so precisely or with such breadth, even though it was taken from other constitutions, including the American (which was poorly understood) and from our own, which, whether federalist or centralist, invariably tried to avert despotism by erecting a fragile barrier of constitutional guarantees. Here, however, each right had its condition, which was tantamount to a guarantee: that is, to the equation between social duty and individual right. The right to life was conditioned by the social duty of justice (for the Constitution recognized that society is a living being capable of rights and duties); and the rights of the accused and of the convicted were minutely defined, man being essentially free, according to theory.

Declared unconditionally free was the slave who took refuge in our territory,[20] and this declaration, in the purest tradition of our history, stemming from our own emancipation, amounted to a serenely heroic defiance of the slave-holding United States and Cuba. "All men are free"—this was the theme. Nobody may force a man to do anything without his consent; his liberty is so absolute, he may not even sell himself into slavery; only society itself may oblige him to respect the individual or social rights of others. The Construction set out, after this general thesis, a bill of rights: freedom to teach, to work, to express opinions and to publish them, to petition, to hold meetings, and so on, together with society's limitations on these rights.

But there were two things that gave the fundamental law, which otherwise might well be criticized as a tissue of theories, an eminently practical value. One was the organization of the federal Supreme Court of Justice, whose responsibility (among others) was to see that the Constitution was respected, and especially the guarantees of individual rights; but, unfortunately, the principle of permanent tenure was abandoned. The other was a new procedure known as the *amparo* (or "protection"), which permitted any person whose rights were invaded or threatened by any authority to appeal directly to the Supreme Court, whose duty it was to issue an injuction for his protection. This institution gives our basic code the distinction of profound originality. Even though the authors were inspired by certain procedures in the Anglo-Saxon courts and by some of our own constitutions, they went far beyond these recourses in the logical precision and liberal breadth with which they invested the *amparo* in the Code of 1857.

"Equality," so the authors of the Constitution solemnly proclaimed, "is the prevailing law in the Republic." Whereupon all social classes in the Republic became legally extinct. And yet, the exigencies of a revolution required that one class be made—legally—political pariahs: the clergy, who were not allowed to vote. The same exigencies obliged the Congress to forbid the acquisition of landed properties by religious corporations. And these contradictions between stated principles and

[20] Article 2 of the Constitution: "In the Republic all are born free. Slaves who set foot on national territory recover their liberty by that very act and are entitled to the protection of our laws."

the ineluctable ends of the revolution afforded the enemies of the Constitution a vantage point from which to attack its works. But the very dispositions that were most severely censured, those relating to the clergy, turned out to be, because of their vital place in the country's evolution, the most significant, the most lasting of all.

Comonfort's government, while accepting the social provisions of the Constitution, objected to the political part. The President was no federalist, save insofar as expediency required him to be one, in order to hold the support of liberals in the provinces. Actually, no central government had ever been able to prevent the states from nullifying its authority except by setting up a partial and temporary dictatorship: that is, by assuming "extraordinary powers." When we contemplate our history, our geography, and the realities of our social order, we must admit that the natural tendency of our political life has been toward dictatorship, as the only alternative to anarchy. But dictatorship has, nevertheless, proved loathesome. Far from acting as a mobilizing force to propel the creative energies of the country forward along the road of evolution, it has nearly always degenerated into despotism, into the exploitation of the country for the benefit of one man. A loathing for despotism is inherent in the whole plan of government as laid down by the Constitution.

This Constitution, in truth, made the Executive a mere agent of the Legislative Power. All of the President's acts, apart from the appointment and removal of ministers and certain other government employes, the command of armed forces on land and on sea, and a measure of control over ports and customhouses, had to be submitted to the Congress for approval. The Congress, on the other hand, reserved to itself a great variety of faculties; those not specifically mentioned were reserved to the states. In the foregoing provisions, the Constitution of the United States was copied (though poorly understood); what could be more surprising, then, than the provision for a unicameral Congress, without a Senate, in the style of the French Revolution.

In spite of the subordination of the Executive to the Legislative Power, this was no parliamentary government in the true sense because the Congress could not legally impose a Cabinet or a single minister on the President, nor require him to dismiss anyone. Rather, it was a representative government, in which the President and the Congress, both chosen by a majority of the nation, were theoretically on an equal footing. But the Constitution, after creating a Caesar, elected by popular vote, whittled him down till there was hardly any authority left to him except physical force: that is to say, the army.

When the Constitution was promulgated, there was not the slightest chance of enforcing it. The tremendous reaction stirred up against it by the enemies of the Reform made free elections or individual freedom impossible, even to the meager extent that the social conditions of the time might have permitted. For neither the press, nor the schools, nor the rural serf, nor the man kidnapped by the levy could be free in 1857. Nor could the death penalty for political offenses be done away with. Little or nothing could be accomplished. The law turned out to be scarcely more than a glimmering ideal. And so it remains, for the most part, to this day. What was indispensable in it was the Reform—that much, at least, had to be saved, or else there could be no social change, no advance in the national evolution, and the giant forward stride of the new law would come to nothing.

The President of the Republic, on the day after his legal election and solemn oath of office, had this dilemma to resolve: whether to govern with the Constitution and provoke civil war or to ignore it as impracticable and, by making this concession to public opinion, whose indignation at the new law had reached full tide, avert the dreaded conflict. The Constitution could easily have been modified, but Comonfort, badly counseled, opted for a dictatorship of the middle ground, of conciliation, being determined to realize his supreme ambition—to carry out two incompatible programs by putting the Reform into effect and at the same time averting civil war. But he allowed himself to be surrounded by a coterie which consisted, not of conservatives, but of moderates and some leading reformists. From quips and epigrams at the Constitution's expense, these courtiers, vowing to relieve the President of the straitjacket which the new code had imposed upon him, passed to plans and stratagems, and thus came to form a full-fledged conspiracy.

One of the conspirators, Juan José Baz, was also a pure one, a leader of the radical party, who believed that it was necessary to sacrifice a great deal of the Reform program temporarily in order to salvage some part. The President, while fully aware that a decision must be made, was loath to depart from the path of strict legality and vacillated, as always.

By December of 1857 the plot was ready to spring. The military force in the capital was prepared to second the President; the governors of the states, including the highly important state of Vera Cruz, had been likewise alerted; the truth is, they nearly all held the conviction that the new basic law was, in the circumstances, unworkable, and they had boundless confidence in Comonfort's integrity and prestige. The coup was triggered thus: an accusation based on authentic correspondence was brought before the Congress by a deputy [Juan José Baz] and led to the trial for conspiracy of the justice Manuel Payno, who serenely assumed all responsibility for the political crime. Then the brigade commanded by General Felíx M. Zuloaga, the close friend of Comonfort, "pronounced" in Tacubaya and quietly occupied the capital. The Chief Justice of the Supreme Court, Benito Juárez, was sent to prison, along with other reformist leaders, and the president declared his adherence to the Plan of Tacubaya,[21] "swapping his constitutional title of office for that of a beggarly rebel," to quote his own words. A majority of the Congress protested vehemently against this betrayal of the law by the chief magistrate, and dissolved.

The Plan of Tacubaya was short and clear.

> The Constitution is hereby annulled, because it does not correspond to the nation's sentiments. Respecting the unanimous will of the people, we declare Comonfort to be President with unlimited powers. A Congress shall be convoked to draw up a Constitution. A Council shall govern in the interim.

The loud jubilation of the clergy and other reactionaries disconcerted Comonfort, whose resolve had been to set himself above the parties in order to control them and who had never imagined he could find himself at the head of the party that he utterly despised, at war with the party that he had fought for all his life. He then made overtures to the moderates of both parties and awaited the results. He had not long to

[21] Plan of Tacubaya, December 17, 1857. The author sums up the six articles of the Plan in the passage below; this is not an actual quotation.

wait. From Vera Cruz, Puebla, San Luis Potosí, Tampico came assurances of allegiance. But a few days later, everything had changed. The reactionary officers, with General Zuloaga as their leader, tried to exact from Comonfort a promise to abandon any attempt to carry out the Reform, and the conservative politicians, heartened by this backing from the military, redoubled their efforts to bind the President to their cause. Meanwhile, however, in the heart of the country, the governors of Querétaro, Michoacán, Jalisco, and Guanajuato formed a coalition which rejected the Plan of Tacubaya, and the reformists converged on that region, rallying around the flag of the Constitution. This challenge was too much for Comonfort, who, visibly repentant, vacillated more than ever. When Vera Cruz reneged on its support for the Plan, he decided to make common cause with the coalition in the heartland, believing that he still could command the army in the capital. He was mistaken: before January (1858) was half over, the garrison pronounced again, but this time flatly against Comonfort. He nevertheless tried to make a stand, convinced that the "Plan of Tacubaya offers no hope of liberty, while with the Constitution, supposing that it could be sensibly modified, there would be a chance of maintaining order." He freed the Chief Justice from prison. Juárez made his way to the hinterland, where he became the standard-bearer of the Constitution. Comonfort, unable to persuade or to conquer his adversaries, abandoned the capital at the end of January and the country a few days later. In this fearful crisis, not a great heart, but a strong character, was needed: not a Comonfort, but a Juárez.

It was the nation's good fortune that Comonfort's enormous error had eliminated him, for he would have ended by thwarting, from sheer good intention, the whole work of the Reform. Certainly the Republic has pardoned, in the patriot, the weaknesses of the statesman. But history, if it has a right to judge and not merely the duty to analyze and synthesize, must take the same position as the Mexican people, who applauded Comonfort enthusiastically when he made his entrance under the banner of the Constitution, and saw him depart, defeated and alone, in sad, unbroken silence.

CHAPTER TWO

THE THREE-YEARS WAR

(1858–1860)

1858: triumph of reaction. A constitutional government. 1859: military dictatorship in Mexico. The Reform laws. The opposing parties in stalemate. Aid from abroad. 1860: desperate efforts of the reaction. The end of resistance. Triumph of constitutional government.

ANTA ANNA'S DICTATORSHIP, with unflagging zeal, had set about restoring the vigor and refurbishing the splendor of the Army. And a group of young, ambitious officers, trained in the Military College or in the practical school of civil strife, had begun, in the dictator's flamboyant new regiments, to push aside such veterans of his revolts and of the war with the United States as Félix M. Zuloaga, Manuel Robles Pezuela, Miguel Echeagaray, and Adrián Woll. Between these and the youngest of the new generals, Luis G. Osollo and Miguel Miramón, leaders of the forces that overthrew Comonfort, the transition was represented by a number of terribly fanatical warriors whose archetypes were Leonardo Márquez, Tomás Mejía, and the two Cobos, José María and Marcelino R. Nearly all of these men, forming a narrow circle in the capital of the Republic, were devout believers in military privilege, contemptuous of those governments that tried to lean on the national guard, and, from professional pride, lovers of war for war's sake. They could count on the applause of high society, of the rich, whose hatred for reformist ideas had become a religion; they could count on the coffers of the clergy, and, confident of their military prowess, they resolved to conquer the Republic at sword's point and then see who could stay on top. This was to be, for them, an exciting adventure, which they undertook without compunction and with boundless valor.

First, they had to have a President. So they called together, in the capital, the most prominent politicians, lawyers, clergymen, journalists, generals, and landowners of the reactionary party, who then picked General Zuloaga, author of the Plan of Tacubaya, as being the candidate least apt to collide with the highly explosive ambitions of the rest. Then the old army was set in march for the interior, the heartland. With what objective?

In the center of the Bajío, between Querétaro, Guanajuato, and Jalisco, a nucleus of resistance to the anticonstitutionalist coup had been organized. This became a vital nucleus when Juárez arrived, seeking the protection of the tri-state coalition, which forthwith proclaimed him legitimate head of the nation. In the face of such catastrophes as Comonfort's flight and the apparent triumph of the reaction, he raised the banner of legality. He himself, in truth, was all that remained of legality, for no other officers or organ of the constitutional government was in a position to function: he exercised every Power—the Executive, the Legislative, and the Judicial—all at the same time and represented the whole people. Nothing of the sort was provided for by the Constitution, but, in the circumstances, nothing else could be done. The rights of individuals had to be suspended, and the grim specters of execution for political offenses, of confiscation, of banishment, sat on the closed book of a Constitution that survived only in the person of one man.

Juárez was indeed a man. As an intellectual, he was far inferior to his two principal collaborators, Ocampo and Lerdo de Tejada. Ocampo, his thought pervaded by a passion for liberty and a love of nature, was a true pagan, like the authors of the French Encyclopedia, and the strength of his basic optimism inspired him to prophetic heights. Although less of a philosopher, Lerdo de Tejada had an acute understanding of the economic problem intrinsic in the social and political structure; a Mexican Turgot, he devoted his entire thought to the diagnosis of the malady, and his entire energy to its cure. Juárez possessed the great virtue of the indigenous race, to which, without a single drop of admixture, he belonged, and this virtue is perseverance. His fellow believers in Reform had faith in its inevitable triumph. So did he, but success, to him, was a secondary matter. What came first was the performance of his duty, even if the consequence was to be disaster and death. What he sought, far beyond the Constitution and the Reform, was the redemption of the indigenous people. In his pursuit of this ideal he never faltered: to free his people from clerical domination, from serfdom, from ignorance, from mute withdrawal—this was his secret, religious longing, the reason why he was a liberal and a reformist, the reason why he was great. It is not true that he was stolid. Deeply emotional, he suffered much, but nothing could move him from his path. He towers, morally, above any other figure of our civil wars. Beside him, the reactionary leaders, with all their words and deeds, seem as shadows fading into the past, while he stands, immutable, for the future, for the conscience of a nation.

When the crusaders of the reaction, heaped with blessings by Archbishop Garza as God's instruments to remedy the Church's ills, marched out to win laurels and Te Deums, the coalition had an army waiting for them, under the command of the honorable and experienced General Anastasio Parrodi. Meanwhile, Juárez and his ministers made their headquarters in Guadalajara. But not for long. By the middle of March the coalition had been completely shattered by Osollo, and Manuel Doblado, governor of Guanajuato, capitulated without a fight. In a mutiny of soldiers at Guadalajara the President was captured and about to be executed when the eloquence of Guillermo Prieto persuaded the firing squad to raise their rifles first and then to release him. The history of our country came near taking an utterly different turn.

The young generals of the reaction swept everything before them. The President fled to the United States by way of the Isthmus of Panama, thence to Vera Cruz, where, with the cooperation of Governor Manuel Gutiérrez Zamora, he established a formal government. The simple fact that a constitutional government whose authority was based not on proclamations but on law was functioning in the principal port of the Republic made the outcome of the struggle merely a question of time, no matter how many victories the reactionaries might score. And they scored a great many. A constitutionalist army, organized by Santiago Vidaurri and led by an able and valiant officer, Juan Zuazua, opposed Miramón on his march from Guadalajara to San Luis Potosí, and while forced to give away, succeeded in occupying Zacatecas. And after the death of Osollo, rightly mourned by the reaction as the most ardent and brilliant warrior for a cause already lost, Zuazua reoccupied San Luis. Miramón, after Osollo's death, took his place as ranking general, a place which he consolidated by a series of smashing victories. It was amazing how Miramón, only twenty-five years old, could make the veteran army respond to his will, how aptly he made use of that excellent weapon, organizing his campaigns with almost infallible skill and executing them with almost incredible audacity.

Faced with the prospect of having to shuttle indefinitely back and forth between San Luis, dominated by Vidaurri, and Guadalajara, threatened by Santos Degollado, Miramón opted to finish off the latter first, but did not succeed: Degollado, though defeated, continued to hold sway in southern Jalisco. Shortly after, with a greatly strengthened army, Miramón turned on Vidaurri and Zuazua, once again in possession of San Luis, and at Ahualulco crushed them with a terrible blow, which put an end to the constitutionalist army of the north as a first-line force. But in the weeks following Ahualulco (October 1858) Zuloaga's government began to appreciate the vitality of the reformist cause, for General Miguel Blanco, in a daring thrust, came near seizing the capital of the Republic, and the indefatigable Degollado took Guadalajara. Degollado's advantage, to be sure, was momentary, for in December he was pushed back south of Jalisco and utterly routed by Miramón in a decisive battle near Colima.

The year 1858 was ushered out in Mexico with a significant political comedy. Two leading generals of the reactionary camp (Echeagaray and Robles Pezuela) concerted a military movement and, with the pretext of forming a third party which would reconcile the other two, seized the capital, overthrew Zuloaga, and named Miramón President; he, however, disowned the coup and restored Zuloaga, who, naturally, appointed Miramón as his substitute and left him in power.

The first year of the war could hardly have gone worse for the reformists, could hardly have been more distressful to the country.

Families were torn apart by the religious nature of the struggle. The clergy, though not officially involved, gave their sympathies and ressources, as was humanly natural, to the reactionary side and made it possible to outfit the armies which had destroyed the best forces that the constitutionalists could muster. What was most appalling, the strife and the incessant executions which stained the banners of both parties had brought a country already anemic to the verge of exhaustion. This was quite evident to foreign powers, who would frequently send squadrons to visit our ports, always with some peremptory demand which, thanks to the diplomacy and the concessions of the government, never went beyond words. Now a schism began to part our international friends: while the countries with envoys in Mexico had all, more or less perfunctorily, recognized the Zuloaga government, in the course of the year Washington thought better of the move and laid plans to recognize the government of the Constitution. Spain, on the contrary, offered all her sympathy to the reaction. France and England, while endorsing this choice, observed events with a colder eye.

The year 1859 opened with the setting up of a dictatorship. While General Miramón was nominally the President's substitute, actually his powers were autocratic. And he minced no words: any meeting between the two parties was impossible, he said, and there could be no Congress until the states had ratified the Plan of Tacubaya—which was to say, never. Miramón appeared to assume modestly that his office was temporary and amounted to nothing more than an assignment to weld together the forces required for the capture of Vera Cruz, the bulwark of the Constitution. But his orders and proclamations were all pervaded by his youthful petulance, his consciousness of high personal mission, his "I." He was an autocrat. And no wonder, for the clergy had designated him as the Man of Providence, and thenceforth both parties, though in different tones, called him the "young Maccabeus."

The campaign to take Vera Cruz was launched with great fanfare: banquets, parades, Masses; contributions poured in. Miramón's advance, pulverizing the resistance offered by government troops in one of the ruggedest passes of the giant stairsteps by which the mountains descend to the coast, was steady all the way to Vera Cruz. Moving his army into position around the city's forts, he waited day after day for the convoy which was to bring the indispensable funds and ammunition for the assault. The convoy never set out from the City of Mexico, and Miramón withdrew his army, bringing it in good order back up the steps to the central plateau. This staggering military failure was soon to be followed by a resounding moral disaster for the reaction, the consequences of the barbarous executions of April 11.

Meanwhile, General Degollado, in whom defeat renewed the strength for battle, having gathered his scattered forces in southern Jalisco, no sooner learned that the flower of the reaction's army was on the road to Vera Cruz than he suddenly appeared in the Bajío, leaving Márquez, who was supposed to guard the west at Guadalajara, in his rear, and advanced on the capital, hoping to take it by surprise or else to draw down upon himself the lightning that was aimed at Vera Cruz. But General Degollado, model of republican virtues and tireless improvisor of armies, was no military man: he allowed the best contingents of reactionary troops in the hinterland to effect a juncture in the capital, and, on April 11, suffered a frightful rout.

Once again the constitutionalist army was dispersed, once again Degollado labored to rebuild it. Needless to say, he succeeded; that army was a phoenix. General Miramón, who returned to the City of Mexico just as the battle ended, ordered the execution of the officers taken prisoner. General Márquez, the victor, who had been decorated on the battlefield with the ribbon of a general in command of a division, had the order carried out and included, for good measure, the doctors of the vanquished army and a number of peasants, who were ruthlessly shot.

The abominable custom of shooting captive officers had prevailed since the struggle began. It was started by the constitutionalists (Zuazua in Zacatecas), who thought it was the way to stop the contagion of taking up arms against legal government. In reprisal, the reactionaries killed, rather than officers, all persons known to be reformists who fell into their hands, showing an especially fierce aversion for lawyers, many of whom took part in the strife, wielding, besides the sword, the pen and the word. They were looked upon, not without reason, as the soul of the reformist movement, and the war seemed to be a fight to the death between the clergy and the army, on one side, and the lawyers on the other. Márquez, in his venemous hatred, brought the tide of blood higher than anyone had ever thought it could reach: the shooting of the doctors reverberated throughout the country and even beyond. The reaction, which had taken a stand outside the pale of progress, now put itself outside the pale of human civilization. On April 11, the anti-reformists revealed their true nature before the whole world: the defenders of rights and religion dropped their mask and wallowed in a pool of blood.

Miramón's failure at Vera Cruz and Degollado's disaster at Tacubaya, the ceaseless bloodletting that disrupted all productive work in the land, forcing the rural populace to abandon the fields and become professional bandits or guerrillas (which amounted to the same thing) made the viciousness of the strife clear to minds that retained a spark of patriotism and inspired them with an infinite and dolorous longing for peace. Only the clergy and the professional soldiers, in close alliance, opposed any compromise which did not annul the Reform. Only the group whose ideas were personified by Juárez opposed any compromise which did not entail acceptance of the Constitution of 1857. There was no possible conciliation, and the people in general began to feel indifferent as to the triumph of either party. Self-interest spoke louder than religious sentiment, which the clergy had exploited to the utmost. The prospect of continued exactions, of the handout to the guerrilla in the hacienda, of pillage and kidnapping and the forced loan in the city, of confiscation and imprisonment everywhere, goaded to the limit of exasperation all thinking people who were not personally involved in the conflict.

While the hammer of civil war was heard beating the country to a pulp, both parties were seeking some way to solve the stalemate, some advantage that would give them final victory. Reactionary forces reconquered that eternal battlefield, the Bajío, but in Sonora and Sinaloa the reaction was definitively vanquished. New liberal champions entered the arena, like Jesús González Ortega, whose terroristic laws in the states that he temporarily dominated, such as Zacatecas and Durango, caused the clergy to seek refuge elsewhere. The reactionary army was sentenced to victory: the first important reverse would condemn it to death. The constitutionalist army, on the contrary, grew stronger with each defeat. Those campaigns were educational for the civic militias: learning the necessity for discipline and skill, they were becoming first-line troops. The old army was forging the new one by constantly fighting and beating it.

Normal sources of revenue had been exhausted, and even the tightest squeezing could barely provide enough to sustain life for one more day. The clergy's wealth had been vastly reduced because many properties were either at the mercy of liberal forces, or had already been sold in accordance with the Lerdo law, or had been occupied by the constitutionalist chiefs, who despoiled the cathedrals of their silver and jewels and the churches of whatever riches could be carried off. All this left both parties in a state of famine, and only the swarming gangs of highwaymen, captained by bandits carrying either the constitutionalist flag or the banner of the Cross, were able to find a living. Thus the leaders of both factions obviously had to resort to ruinous loans, ignominious treaties, the capture of trains bearing money or merchandise, and the like.

The very cordial and very explicit recognition of the Vera Cruz government by Washington was of crucial importance and, while not unexpected, cast the conservatives into a sort of stupor: American aid to Juárez in the form of arms and money (anything else was impossible) could well be fatal to them.

At midyear, General Miramón issued a manifesto in which his "I" predominated throughout a program that was administrative rather than political. In the crisis that was rending the Republic such a program was an absurdity. Political leaders were absolutely at the mercy of circumstances; they could lay down a general policy but not rules and regulations. The impetuous usurper gave the clergy reason for secret dismay by interpolating between protests of consagration to the "cause of religion," as the jargon of the times put it, the idea that it would be necessary to respect the interests created by the Lerdo law removing mortmain. But when the conquering champion of the Cross spoke, the response was always "Amen."

At the same time, President Juárez issued a manifesto of his own [July 12, 1859]. That of Miramón was probably intended as an answer. Juárez and his ministers decreed the separation of Church and

State, to take effect immediately. Basing their action on the fact that the clergy's conduct during the civil war had been absolutely hostile to the reformist cause, the Church was stripped of its property. This confiscation, an eminently revolutionary measure because it was prohibited by the Constitution, was called "nationalization of ecclesiastical property." In addition, and as a logical consequence, monastic orders were suppressed, a civil register was established, and various restrictions were imposed on the clergy. Miramón's manifesto, a mere response to the exigencies of the moment, had no relation to the future. The manifesto of the President and his Cabinet faced the future with serene confidence. When they described the country's transformation through material and intellectual progress—a transformation which should begin with the triumph of the reformist cause—those apostles climbed to the highest summit of their faith and saw the sun rise beyond the farthest mountaintops, while below, on the valleys of Anáhuac, there churned the dark storm clouds which were soon to blot the vision out. From where we stand, at the close of the century, the reactionary manifesto seems a farewell babbled in the night; that of the reformists is a welcome to a new day.

The Reform laws, though they were no surprise to anyone, had a tremendous effect: the number of those interested in the triumph of the reformist cause increased, and so did the fright of those who—religion having nothing to do with the question—stood to lose everything in the way of financial and material assets with the new legislation. The bishops spoke out in protest, as was their right and duty. The government at Vera Cruz, they said, was not the legitimate one, and so could decree nothing; the legitimate one emanated from the Plan of Tacubaya. This confession was sufficient to justify nationalization as a penalty. Even if the bishops' interpretation of the law had been correct—and it could not be—the constitutionalist government could not have conceded the point without committing suicide. Therefore the Church had to be declared a rebel; hence the penalty.

The head of the Mexican episcopate maintained that the Church had done nothing to foment civil war but had simply furnished the government established in the capital with the funds that it had requested, an ordinary procedure. Let us forget the many, and most natural, demonstrations of sympathy with reaction, the Te Deums and Alleluias that hailed every one of those reactionary victories which steeped the soil in Mexican blood and remember only that the Church, excommunicating those who obeyed the Constitution, authorized total resistance to the law, thereby giving the rebellion a deadly religious character.

But all these considerations are secondary. The evolution of the Republic toward full self-rule, toward the completely secular State, met with an insuperable obstacle: the Church, a power both spiritual and terrestrial. The State, though not concerned with the spiritual power, was greatly concerned with the material; it stripped its great adversary of landed wealth and passed on. This was inevitable, this was necessary. In politics what is necessary is lawful: necessity is the criterion of the just and the unjust. An individual may and sometimes should sacrifice himself; a people, never. And the same thing that impeded the evolution of the State was likewise a stumbling-block for the Church: in the time between the Reform and our day conscious Catholicism has gained more territory than it ever possessed when its temporal power was supreme.

The results of the constitutional government's new policy, which in the long run would attract, with the honey of the clergy's wealth, such a crowd of interests and appetites, were not immediately apparent. The country, completely exhausted, could not support, without the aid of a miracle, any prolongation of the crisis. The terrible year of 1859 was coming to an end. The reactionaries, convinced that no compromise was possible after the Reform laws, fixed their hopes on the military. The two poles that controlled strategic combinations continued to be Márquez in the west and Miramón in the east. The obvious plan was to annihilate Degollado's everlasting army, sweep the others into the Pacific, then turn on Vera Cruz and finish it off; this was Miramón's course. The risk he ran was not that he might incur defeat (and in his youthful arrogance he was sure of his ability to dominate fortune) but that Márquez, the real hero of the ultrareactionaries, might emerge from the smoke of some fresh victory and topple him from power. But the formidable proconsul chose this time to capture a packtrain of valuables about to be exported on the pretext that he needed to clothe and arm his ragged troops. Miramón ordered that the stolen treasure be returned and set march for Guadalajara. On his way he had to run over Degollado's army, which had been demoralized by the abrupt withdrawal of the Division of the North owing to the scandalous defection of Vidaurri, who once again had set himself up as lord of a sovereign section of the frontier.

Miramón's campaign in the Bajío was brilliant. He routed Degollado, continued his triumphal march to the capital of Jalisco, and in Colima inflicted another crushing defeat on the constitutionalists. Then, strong with the prestige of his victories, he divested Márquez of his post and brought him to the capital to answer for his conduct. Thus the chief returned, bold, confident, unrivaled, and visibly protected by Providence, as his admirers remarked. And he prepared his second expedition, the decisive one, to take Vera Cruz.

The appalling panorama that the Republic presented at the end of 1859 impressed upon the leaders of both sides the urgency of bringing the struggle to an end: otherwise, they believed, there was bound to be foreign intervention. What each thought was needed to bring it to an end was a large sum of money, sufficient to assure the superiority of their army over the enemy. The instinct for self-preservation had come to obliterate every other idea, for the dissolution of moral sentiments is the inevitable consequence of political crises that are indefinitely drawn out. Both sides allowed themselves to be carried away by this animal instinct and both succumed to this dissolution of principle. Miramón signed with the Swiss banking house of Jecker a contract for a loan toward the payment of the interest on which the government pledged a fifth of all revenues. These were the famous Jecker bonds, which for a benefit of less than one million pesos saddled the treasury with a debt of fifteen millions. The constitutional government signed another disgraceful contract: the MacLane Treaty.

The United States was preparing to intervene in Mexico. Because of the anarchy on our frontier, President Buchanan, in a message to the Congress, had recommended armed intervention in behalf of the constitutional government. That government, for some time past, had been receiving pecuniary aid from the United States, but in order to forestall intervention it negotiated a treaty which, in exchange for four million pesos (in cash, only two millions), granted to the American Union concessions in Tehuantepec and in a zone along the northern frontier. These concessions were equivalent to condominion, to the surrender of the Republic's sovereignty over national territory. That such a pact should have appeared feasible to men of such patriotic mettle as Juárez and Ocampo is shocking, and but for the attenuating circumstances, the delirium caused by political fever in crisis, no one would boggle at calling it a political crime. A little earlier [September 1859] Zuloaga's government, through its commissioner in Paris, had signed with Spain the most ignominious of treaties, known as the Mon-Almonte.[1] From Spain, no money was received, but an understanding was arrived at which was to have historic consequences.

For several months the hinterland was free of major military movements. Guerrillas continued to swarm everywhere and buzzed around the important towns like bees around the hive. In the Bajío, González Ortega was a cloud on the horizon, but he was even less of a general than the tireless fighter Degollado; he was a poet, a fanatic like those commissioners in the armies of the French Revolution.

The departure for Vera Cruz of the crusading army (February 1860) was saluted with chimes of church bells, sacred chants, the offerings of those who passed for an aristocracy, the cheers of the populace, prodded by the police. In Puebla the conquering usurper received a tremendous ovation. Early in March he had his army, perfectly aligned, facing the ramparts of Vera Cruz. The port was not impregnable so long as the seafront was open, and Miramón had prepared a surprise for the government. With the complicity of the Spanish authorities, a squadron had been outfitted in Havana, and the ships appeared before the harbor at Vera Cruz just when the siege began. The government, having been informed of the stratagem, and having rightfully forbidden the use of the national banner by the officers of the rebel squadron, declared them pirates and made their status known to foreign ship captains, who thus were in a position to take prizes. And that is what happened: the two pirate ships were attacked and captured the very day that they appeared by an American frigate-of-war. This

[1] The constitutional government protested against the Mon-Almonte Treaty January 30, 1860.

was a heavy blow to Miramón. He tried to reach an understanding, a compromise with the government, but it refused to negotiate, except on a constitutional basis. He thus had no alternative but to withdraw. The whole world could see that this was the beginning of the end for the reactionaries. Miramón himself was convinced of it, but pride obliged him to fight on.

For a moment fate seemed to smile on him again. In the hinterland the flag of the Constitution was raised by an old veteran of civil conflicts, General José López Uraga (without convictions but averse to the clergy), who won a victory with his first battle, a master stroke, and marched on Guadalajara. Miramón set out from the capital to head him off. Uraga, forcing his marches, managed to reach Guadalajara before Miramón could intercept him, but there he was routed by the able defender (also a veteran), the French officer Woll, who rendered him *hors de combat*.

Miramón had left the capital carrying amongst his baggage Zuloaga, still President, who had tried to resume his place and had been scorned with the phrase, "I am going to show you how one wins the right to be President." The captive made his escape, and thus gave a committee of dyed-in-the-wool reactionaries, a little later, an excuse to declare the young substitute President ad interim. Passing through Guadalajara, already saved by Woll, he followed to the south of Jalisco the trail of a young general from Nuevo León who had refused to second Vidaurri's defection and who now commanded the army that had been repulsed at Guadalajara. This general, whose name was Ignacio Zaragoza, handled his army with such skill, and placed it so artfully in Miramón's path, that he retreated to Guadalajara. By midyear of 1860 the military situation at last favored the reformists. Miramón, centrally stationed, tried to prevent their several forces from effecting a juncture, but in vain. Zaragoza, González Ortega, and others (Degollado was still commander in chief) shut him off from the capital. Miramón swiftly marched against them and was cut to pieces at Silao; he arrived at the capital almost alone. There he accepted his new investiture as President, receiving with this title the Spanish ambassador, who proffered the prestige and sympathies of Spain to the reaction at the moment when it was visibly sinking. The ambassador might well have heeded the petition in which nearly all the men whose financial position made them important in the country had voiced a supplication for peace.

> The dignity and independence of the nation, our property, our liberty, our life—everything is at the mercy of the assaults of blind force, everything is threatened or has perished already, everything becomes a victim of the fury of civil war, which is tearing society to pieces.

The dyed-in-the-wool reactionaries naturally rejected this appeal with disdain: "reaction or death" was their motto, and many of those who proclaimed it were brave enough to seal their noble and blind political faith with their blood.

The denouement was not far off. The victors of Silao, after making a stab at the capital, doubled back on Guadalajara, defended by the competent General Castillo. The property of the clergy would suffice to pay any debts that might be contracted in order to win the war, but as yet it did not yield the resources that were urgently needed for troop movements on a grand scale. Doblado therefore seized a packtrain of valuables, and the Commander in Chief, Degollado, who embodied the highest integrity of the revolution, took upon himself all responsibility for the deed: the government, without funds to reimburse those who had been despoiled, guaranteed them repayment in full out of the nationalized property of the clergy.

As the curtain rose on the gory and terrible final act of the drama, Degollado, whose conscience was perturbed by the painful duties he had performed, was moved to devise, in consultation with the English envoy, a way to bring the civil war immediately to an end; the plan was to convoke in the City of Mexico all the diplomatic representatives and state governors, who were to declare valid the principles of the Reform and to call a Congress which would give the country a new constitution. Degollado's project was spurned in the capital and vehemently disowned in Vera Cruz. Juárez, sorrowfully but justly, deprived the honored leader of his command. His place was taken by González Ortega, who commenced the siege of Guadalajara. Miramón sent Márquez to the assistance of the besieged, and the noose of fire around the unfortunate city, on which 125 cannon vomited death, had to be tightened. For days Guadalajara was a ghastly hell of extermination and valor until a series of assaults forced Castillo to surrender, just as Márquez was drawing near. In the hands of Zaragoza and Leandro Valle, two generals of thirty, the reformist army was a sword heated to the white with hope and passion. No sooner had Guadalajara surrendered than the liberal army put Márquez to flight, almost without combat, and in the early days of November slowly took up the march to the capital.

The reactionary chiefs had always protested that they could hardly be expected to lay down their arms when they held most of the cities and the country was on their side. But now, the entire Republic, except the City of Mexico and Puebla, was in constitutionalist hands. Duty required that they lay down their arms, but in a meeting of officers and bishops it was decided to continue the struggle at all costs. "If the revolution will not respect the Church, if it will not leave intact the eternal principles of our religion, if it will not hold inviolate the sanctum of the family, then let us fight on against the revolution, even if the social edifice should collapse on our heads." These were the words of the commander in chief of the reactionary army, and they signified nothing; they were theatrical phrases, striking a dramatic attitude of valor in the face of danger. The constitutionalists never meddled with dogmas of religion, and the Constitution was the shield of the family and of human rights.

Miramón needed a new army; the civil war had accustomed the immense majority of the Mexican people to compulsory military service, to being snatched from the sanctum of the family and marched to the battlefield; once again Miramón snatched what he needed. To maintain this newly armed multitude he seized the funds destined to pay the holders of the bonds for the English debt, funds that had been deposited in Her British Majesty's legation—an outrageous violation of international law which showed how desperate the reaction had become in its death throes. Miramón's new army was thoroughly routed at Calpulalpan in two hours of fierce combat, December 22. On Christmas Day the constitutionalist soldiers occupied the capital of the Republic. The reactionary party was finished forever. In an effort to resuscitate it, the mightiest military power in the world, hauling along in the baggage an Austrian prince and a fraction of Mexican society, would risk all its prestige and all its power, in vain. What was left of the reaction would play a part in our great national tragedy, but only as a specter, a haunt, already dead as an ideal or as a social or a military force. The foundation of the future Mexico was laid squarely on the Reform.

The Church, in order to defend its property, had converted the civil war into a holy war and had built of the whole ecclesiastical organization, from the hierarchy on down, a bulwark which was bolstered by all the dogmas, including the fundamental one of God's existence, and by all the fears, from fear of Hell to fear of the gallows. And yet, Providence, despite the prayers of the clergy, who constantly invoked divine protection for their reactionary champions, chose to ignore all that sanctified array and awarded the victory to a handful of makeshift generals thirty years old. The clergy's incredible blunder in binding together in a single package spiritual power and earthly wealth and so reaping a religious catastrophe from a political triumph gave impetus to the campaign of the younger reformists (who had their Rousseau in Ocampo, their Diderot in Ignacio Ramírez, their Danton in Ignacio M. Altamirano, and their Tirseus in Guillermo Prieto) to win the people away from Catholicism.

Three years of fearful strife had, in fact, brought about a transformation. The furious and fanatical but emancipating voice of the lawyer-turned-apostle and of the officer-turned-judge had been heard in every corner of the country. The spectacle of churches sacked, of friars shot or forced to join the naked battalions, of carved saints burned in public autos de fé by angry iconoclasts had terrified or amazed or excited every soul.

"And why did those saints fail to defend themselves with miracles?" asked the astounded Indians, as in the days of the Conquest when they saw their idols being rolled down the steps of the flaming temples. "And why did God give victory to the sacrilegious?" asked the artisans and servants in the cities. Furtively the ignorant masses began to lift their eyes to new ideals, and in many hearts the Equality, the Liberty, the Solidarity that permeated the Constitution struck the spark of a new religious spirit. But the Reform owed its triumph to the middle classes out in the states, to those who had studied in the schools, whose brains were full of dreams, whose hearts were full of ambitions and whose stomachs were full of appetites. The bourgeoisie furnished the cause with officers, generals, journalists, judges, and ministers, some of whom became martyrs and some conquering heroes, as the documents show. And, finally, the rich from love of peace, the foreign immigrant from love of the clergy's wealth, the educated classes from love of new ideas, and the lower classes from a vague hope of bettering themselves —and because they instinctively saw the sign of divine approval in success—together made up a majority which was either neutral or frankly reformist. What had been a minority on the day following the American invasion was a majority of the country on the eve of the French invasion.

CHAPTER THREE

THE FRENCH INTERVENTION

(1861–1867)

The interior: frustrated attempts at reorganization; bankruptcy. Exterior: American Civil War; the London Covenant. From European intervention to French intervention and war; the Fifth of May; organization of the invasion. The invasion triumphant: Puebla, the City of Mexico; the invaders establish a monarchy; the monarchy born dead; state capitals controlled by the invader; Prince Maximilian; imperial government and national government; fatal conflict between the Empire and the Intervention. The liberal Empire; last of the reactionary party. The United States. Final effort to consolidate the Empire. Juárez, legitimate dictator. The country liberated, 1866: end of the invasion; disintegration of the imperial government. Last act of the drama: Puebla, Querétaro, the City of Mexico. The Nation, the Republic, and the Reform become identical.

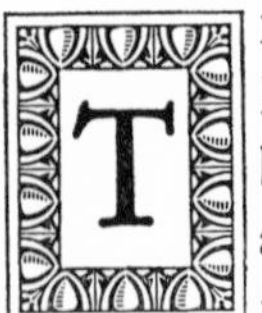

HE CITY OF MEXICO, clerical and reactionary city par excellence, where all the victories of Miramón and Márquez had been cheered from balconies and housetops, where the artisans and the "lepers" of the filthy stinking quarters of the poor, which lay in the colossal shadows of the convents, were sent into the streets to pull the carriages of the conquerors and to shout and whistle with enthusiasm while stealing watches and handkerchiefs and waving cornstalks and flags, this same city hailed the entrance of González Ortega's reformist army with a kind of delirium.

And the truth is, this was not a clerical but merely a Catholic city, and the civil war had finally made everybody indifferent to anything but peace. For the war had come to mean the literal theft by the fiscal agent of the meager earnings of labor and the blood-sucking levy which kidnapped the able-bodied man from the family and the workshop and tossed him onto the wooden barracks bench and into the carnage of the battlefield. The populace in the plaza, the bourgeois on the balconies and housetops all clamored for peace. And they seemed to find in the benevolent smile on the sensual lips of the Commander in Chief a sentiment of clemency and concord. His words, his manner, his enthusiasm electrified them all that warm winter morning and made the blue sky glow with the hope and glory of the brief interlude that was to link the two somber dramas of our nation's great tragedy.

Rich and poor joined in that ovation. The rich hoped to tempt the ambition of the victorious young general so that he would withhold the keys of the Republic from Juárez, because in their eyes Juárez personified the Reform; he was cold, implacable, repugnant; he was "that Indian, Juárez." The poor had been agitated by the young students and officers who had preached on the street corners the bold socialist doctrines of Proudhon and Lamennais and had pointed out the grotesque obscenity of the Franciscan friar conspiring and unsheathing his dagger, of the father of Mercy tucking up his white habit spotted with pulque and *mole* and dancing the *jarabe* in the fandangos of the squalid quarters, of the bishop plotting the destruction of independence. Rich and poor felt vaguely that a paradise of liberty, fraternity and prosperity was about to dawn.

But the curtain soon fell on that splendid act of heroic opera. Juárez arrived, and, however disagreeable and prosaic he might be, that Indian of porphyry and bronze carried reality in his hands; with him present dreams had to give way to truth. Ideas of pardon and harmony had to give way to practical exigencies of the Reform program. The civil war was not yet over. There were still reactionary generals in the land. Of the sixty or seventy thousand men under arms who dominated the country from one end to the other, those who had won the victory were too many for the government to support. They would either have to be furloughed or farmed out to the states, which would make use of their contingents to lay down the law to the Federation, as they had always done. The numerous scattered guerrilla bands would either continue to threaten life and property on all sides or else join the remnants of reactionary forces, which is what they did. The press, in the states as well as in the capital, echoing the hate and rancor of the victorious party, demanded justice and vengeance and seriously advocated building scaffolds on every plaza and converting the government into a revolutionary tribunal. But the government had other things to do. First, however, those men whose presence in the country provoked incessant demands for vengeance and kept the youth of the reformist party in a perpetual state of ebullition, had to be got out of the way so that the economic work of the Reform could go forward at once and be made solid and lasting. The first phase of the program was handled by Ocampo, while the Secretary of War, González Ortega, undertook to bring the civil war to a successful conclusion. Ocampo handed passports to the Spanish ambassador, the papal nuncio, and two other foreign envoys who had done their best to prevent the fall of the reactionary dictatorship. There was danger in the expulsion of the Spanish ambassador: after protesting the Mon-Almonte Treaty, the government, with this new act, seemed to offer a challenge. Spain considered this an affront, but not an act of war. At any rate, the expulsion was justified, for Pacheco was the declared enemy of the reformist—and of all democratic—government. He looked upon Mexico as having "lost the notion of right and the principle of decency" and requiring "the armed intervention of Europe to impose liberty and order, or else there will be no end to her shameful history, which is a scandal and a disgrace to civilized humanity." The expulsion of the bishops was prudent: while they deserved punishment from a political standpoint, for having explicitly and publicly denied the legality of the national government, it was urgent to get them out of the country at once. Otherwise justice was liable to turn into vengeance, with prison or worse as the consequence.

The men of Vera Cruz were not very fond of power. Ocampo resigned, leaving his task in new hands—Antonio Zarco, Ignacio Ramírez, Guillermo Prieto—and for a time the country suffered intensely. To the ministers, the Reform was a drastic operation on which the salvation of the sick country depended, and they were right, on the whole. But the performance of that vital operation was, of necessity, entrusted to the most fanatical, to the least humane, who wounded the secular Mexican in his habits, his venerations, his sentiments, in the sanctity of his traditions and memories and in his superstitions—which is to say, in the sensibilities that had been fostered by three centuries of unquestioning devotion. And the sorrowful beat of society's very heart was felt wherever the Mexican woman, all piety and compassion, with no interest other than love and no more reflection than her faith permitted her, presided over the normal pace of life in the family, even the reformist family. The bishops stoned in Vera Cruz by a mob led by a demagogue drunk on his own words, the walls of convents crashing to earth from the furious blows of the pickaxe, the denuded cloisters, the churches despoiled of their sacred jewels with brutal irreverence, the sacrosanct retreats of the nuns invaded while the poor women prayed for their tormentors, the archives, the libraries, the repositories of artworks ransacked—all this created an indefinable feeling of distress.

This distress had been anticipated by the men of the Reform, who for that very reason hastened to build between the triumphant revolution and any possible reaction a towering barrier of ruins and debris and to open by irreparable acts a yawning fosse between the past and the future. Thus, they did what had to be done. But the vital drama was played in dark offices behind the shocking public scenes of the Reform in action: the financial drama, the realization of the confiscation and sale of the clerical properties. These had depreciated sharply because of the insecurity of the sales, which a change in government could render invalid, and because the continuing civil war made the exploitation of rural property impossible and burdened urban property with endless exactions. Moreover, they had diminished through adjudications according to the Lerdo law and through others in Vera Cruz, which amounted to gifts as they could not be liquidated for years to come. Thus, the solution of the financial problem, the amortization of the European debt, the plan to subsidize railroads and colonies of immigrants, all turned out to be merely a dream. And since the civil war went on and on, with the military leaders of the reaction clearly rabid for revenge, and the army had to be paid or else disbanded and since taxes brought in next to nothing, the only recourse was to sell whatever could be sold, as quickly as possible, accepting five percent of the value. The reformists saw, with superb prevision, that the way to make their work of nationalization permanent was to surround it by an infrangible parapet of individual rights, rights which the new owners would defend furiously against any attempt at restitution. Because of this policy, the French intervention and its puppet monarchy would serve in the long run to consolidate the Reform. But, at the time, the policy seemed to be carried out blindly, with deliberate wastefulness. Perhaps the work could have been done in more orderly fashion, but the essential thing was to sacrifice the present to the future. What had been thought to be an immense fund of landed wealth brought in barely six millions, which had already been spent and hence availed nothing. This was a matter that the public never was able to understand, seeing only that the government, after making a lot of speculators rich, begged them for help, and was refused.

After the vortex had swallowed the piddling sum produced by adjudication of the clergy's property, there was no other road for the government to take except the one that led, by way of ruinous loans, to the abyss. The greater part of the revenue from customs was pledged to foreign debtors, the remainder to usurers. Internal revenue was nil because the states preempted all except that from the Federal District, which was what the government had to live on. In the repeated cabinet crises, which solved no problem, the dread word "bankruptcy" was heard again and again. The annual deficit approached five millions.

The Congress, very young and impassioned, with the illusion that society could be instantaneously transformed, was divided from the first into two equal parties, pro- and anti-Juárez. But the presidential election had already been held. With the reactionary party abstaining, as was natural, the part of the nation that could vote in the representative electoral colleges (the system wisely adopted by the Constitution and the only one possible in countries with an illiterate majority) had voted, first, for Miguel Lerdo de Tejada, next for Juárez, next for González Ortega. The country that had accepted the Reform saw in Lerdo the only man capable of finding a solution to the financial problem; in Juárez, a man of character, capable of riding out the storms that could be discerned on the horizon; in González Ortega, a generous idealist. But Lerdo's death gave Juárez a majority; he was declared constitutional President [by decree of Congress, June 11, 1861], and González Ortega, Chief Justice of the Supreme Court, became Vice-President. The opposition to Juárez could not prevent the Congress from granting powers of all kinds to the Executive, in the hope that he might save the situation. Finally, a decree was passed [July 17, 1861] which authorized the federal government to take all revenues for its own use and suspended payment on foreign debts for a term of two years. This step was inevitable in a state of bankruptcy and would have afforded leeway to reorganize the Treasury system and to pacify the country if the foreign creditors had been patient. But they refused to countenance a moratorium, and the financial problem became overcast by a grim international problem.

The civil war reached a climax of savage fury. Within a short period most of the reformist leaders vanished from the scene. After the death of Lerdo de Tejada and of Gutiérrez Zamora came the assassinations—accompanied by a vicious cruelty that bespoke the presence or proximity of the man [Márquez] who, more than any other figure of our civil strife, displayed the cold homicidal rage of the fanatic—of Ocampo, of Degollado, and of Leandro Valle, a young man full of hope, laughter, enthusiasm, and generous valor. Ocampo's serenity in the face of death, and Degollado's self-abnegation will always be for Mexicans lessons in high moral courage. The reformist party, deeply wounded, passed through the Congress drastic laws providing for death and banishment. Changes in the Cabinet were frequent, debates in the Congress tumultuous, like those of the French Revolution. The fiery and eloquent spokesman for the younger generation of reformists was Ignacio M. Altamirano, youthful poet and jurist from the south, and the irreverent thrusts of the parliamentary opposition seemed at times about to catapult Juárez from his presidential chair. Meanwhile, the military campaign to stamp out the reaction had been reorganized and was generally successful, though the rebel forces once came near attacking the capital and set up a fly-by-night government presided over by Félix Zuloaga, a government which nobody obeyed but which did summon the nerve to replace Márquez as commander with the Spaniard José María Cobos. More feared than Zuloaga's tattered armies were the numberless bands of highwaymen who robbed, killed, and kidnapped everywhere.

The fading of military threat enabled the government and the thinking part of the nation to fix their attention on the foreign horizon, where storm clouds had been gathering for some time. During the civil war the British, Spanish, and French cabinets had studied the possibility of intervening in our affairs in order to forcibly impose peace, impound our resources, and pay themselves what we owed them: a huge debt, which we acknowledged, in England's case; some dubious claims, in Spain's; and a few insignificant items in France's. But the attitude of the United States had prevented the Europeans from taking action. The protest of the Mon-Almonte Treaty recognizing Spain's tutelage over Mexico and the expulsion of the ambassador, the robbery of the funds destined to pay the bond-holders of the English debt, perpetrated by the reaction in agony, had exacerbated the impatience of the London and Madrid cabinets. But any concerted action by the two was unthinkable because of their opposed viewpoints: England was inclined to favor the reformists, Spain the clerical reaction. There was a potential intermediary, France, whose complaints against Mexico were nil. The French in Mexico had reaped huge profits from the Reform; debts to them were trifling; the Mexicans treated them with affection. Both parties in the civil struggle studied French books, but especially the reformists, who had acquired from them the passion for equality and the loathing of privilege. Educated Mexicans knew the history of France a hundred times better than they knew that of their own land.

But France was governed by a man who concealed, behind the gentle countenance of a dreamer, not the will power of a strong character, but the secret obstinacy of a fatalist. He was both talented and lucky. France, exercising a kind of continental hegemony in Europe, seemed to be his creation, and he passed for a politician of the first order. The French came to believe blindly in his genius and his star. This man, Napoleon III (nobody knows why he was the "Third," for the Second never reigned a single minute), cherished a grandiose and nebulous dream of binding the Latins of both hemispheres together in a solidarity that would not be of the blood but of the spirit and of making himself the arbiter of that amorphous confederation.

Mexico was the place to build a dike against the Anglo-Saxon tide in America. The Mexican emigrés in Europe (who represented Mexico in the same way that the stagnant pools at the river's edge represent the river) had for a leader one who, after insinuating himself into the family circle of the Empress Eugénie, was able to convince the moony Napoleon that such an enterprise would be feasible and that the Mexican people would thank him for it on their knees. The Empress, an ardent Catholic, anxious to redeem the Emperor's politics—for he had, willy-nilly, unchained the revolution that unified Italy—fell in with the reactionaries' project because of her hatred for the persecutors of the Church, because, claiming to be a descendant of Moctezuma, she was thrilled at the idea of establishing a throne in Mexico, and because only a monarchy could bring peace to the country. And the emigrés had gone so far as to settle on a candidate: the Archduke Maximilian of Austria. Who but a dreamer could make a dream come true? Napoleon had indolently given his assent, and the Austrian prince had not said no; it was well known that he burned with the desire to say yes.

The campaign acquired a recruit in a personage whose interest was strictly selfish. Not one of the Empress' circle of admirers, he was nevertheless influential with the Emperor, whose brother he was. The Duke of Morny, son of the Count of Flahaut and the adulterous Queen Hortense, was one of those great lords, at once statesman and libertine, so frequent in French history, and he concealed an insatiable appetite for money, pleasures, and honors beneath the exquisite manners of a punctilious, nonchalant, and very elegant prince. He had come to an understanding with Jecker, the banker, whose enormous claim against Mexico, however unsound and preposterous, seemed to the Duke a mine that a French intervention could turn into a bonanza.

Even the United States, during Buchanan's administration, had taken an attitude which, while friendly to the constitutional government, evinced an itch to meddle in our affairs. The offer to assume responsibility for our foreign debt in return for a mortgage on part of our territory, which was flatly rejected by the government, indicated the trend of world opinion, colored by our perennial civil war. But there could be no doubt, in the year 1861, that the United States would have to renounce, temporarily, any role in our domestic drama. Since its mere presence had kept the European nations at bay, the stage was now set for their intrusion.

The causes of the American Civil War, triggered by the secession of eleven states which decided to form a separate republic, were basically social and economic. From the Potomac to the Rio Grande the dogma (not merely the opinion) prevailed that without slavery there could be no profitable cultivation of the land. This dogma, which has since been proved to be fallacious, stemmed from a tradition originating with the founders of slavery in the South and respected by the authors of the Constitution, in spite of their humanitarian ideals, even by Washington himself. In the dissident states the firmly antislavery attitude of the North was attributed to purely economic motives, to a scheme that would bring about the complete subordination of the South by stripping it of slave labor while boosting the industrial development of the North with protective tariffs unfavorable to Southern agriculture. The slavery problem had become a political issue as a consequence of the Mexican War, when the question of whether to extend slavery to the new states was raised, a question which Henry Clay found a way to prorogue by means of clever compromises which actually were only truces. Buchanan's administration, prone to maintain the status quo and to exaggerate the importance of states' rights, saw the tempest approach with the growth of antislavery agitation in the North and of determination to resist in the South. The election of Lincoln was a triumph for the North, and his inauguration touched off the struggle. In this year of 1861 it was plain to European eyes that the War, in view of the mighty contending forces, would last for many years, unfitting the United States for any foreign enterprise. Here was an opportunity to paralyze forever the expansion of that nation in Latin America by making the split permanent: that is, by helping the South to win control of the seas, something it obviously could not do alone. This notion and that of Latin hegemony fitted together perfectly in Napoleon's brain, and the English, hoping to halt the industrial development of the Union for at least a century, acquiesced in the Emperor's grandiose projects.

The suspension of payments on foreign debts gave the initial impetus to Napoleon's plan. French diplomats persuaded those of Spain and England to sign a document called the Covenant of London (October 1861). The signatory nations, with the pretext of securing payment of the Republic's obligations to their subjects, agreed to send troops to Mexico in sufficient numbers to achieve that end. They added the solemn protestation that this use of force involved no scheme to acquire territory or to interfere with the Mexican people's right to govern themselves.

Here was a farce that would rapidly turn into tragedy, for the three signatories knew very well that Napoleon had already decided to go ahead with the establishment of a monarchy in Mexico; in doing so he betrayed an abysmal ignorance of the real situation. Spain was nervously aware of this, but acquiesced in the hope of gaining some advantage. England, though skeptical, was indifferent so long as her interests were respected. And shortly after signing the Covenant her minister signed an agreement with Mexico which, if our Congress had ratified it, would have obliged him to repudiate the London pact.

Nobody in Mexico believed the reports of an imminent intervention until, in December of 1861, a handful of Englishmen and Spaniards disembarked at Vera Cruz, which no effort was made to defend. They were the vanguard of a singular army of occupation consisting of a few English—and later some French—sailors and several battalions of Spaniards. President Juárez had entrusted the portfolio of foreign relations to the governor of Guanajuato, Manuel Doblado, a man with a talent for weaving or unraveling a political web, who set Mexican diplomacy on a plane that the Europeans were unable to reach, and this superiority was manifest throughout the war of the Intervention. Doblado, Antonio de la Fuente, and Sebastián Lerdo de Tejada kept the French invasion and the Empire encircled with an iron ring of legal right which was resilient and gave way but could never be broken.

The government stirred up against the intervention the deep hostility toward Spain which had been rife since colonial days and which the reformist party had tried to arouse throughout the struggle with the conservatives, who were actively supported by nearly all Spaniards. But propaganda had little effect on the masses, who indifferently let themselves be dragged from one party to the other, for both brought them only endless vexations—tolls, the levy, the lash and death—and resentment of anything like persecution of the Church acted as counterpoise to rancor against the Spaniards, which was social, not historical, in origin. The people failed to distinguish the benevolent and scupulously honest Spaniard from the immigrants motivated solely by greed. They saw only the hacienda-owner, who sometimes pitied but always despised them and knew how to keep them in peonage by fomenting their vices, and the storekeeper in the cities, who actually ran a pawnshop where the "leper" left his possessions in exchange for alcohol or, occasionally, food and seldom redeemed anything. Their impotence to shake off this exploitation (in spite of the eloquent articles in the Constitution that purposed to make an end of it) turned to wrath, and the terrifying yell of Hidalgo's mobs echoed in civic festivals half a century later.

While the government, seconded by the reformist press, was stirring up this old animosity, it succeeded in establishing contact with the commissioners of the three powers. Outstanding among them was the Spaniard, Juan Prim, Count of Reus. A hero of the African war and a kind of legendary demigod to his fellow countrymen in Catalonia, Prim was a political adventurer of extraordinary daring, with the unflagging heroic intensity that the conquistadors of the sixteenth century displayed. But his ambition, which, like theirs, expanded as he advanced, never obfuscated his clear view of reality or his amazing political insight, which bordered on the gift of prophecy.[1]

This latterday Cid Campeador, well acquainted with Mexican affairs, belonged to the progressive liberal party in Spain, had censured the conduct of the Spanish envoys who favored the reactionaries here, and was intimately linked, through his wife, with one of the few families of the upper bourgeoisie (here called, rather absurdly, the "aristocracy") that had not been hostile to the Reform movement. Despite the

[1] For example: Prim's letter to General Salamanca just before leaving Mexico. See Vicente Riva Palacio, *México a través de los siglos* (Mexico City and Barcelona: Ballescá-Espása, n.d.), Tomo V, p. 514 (Author's note).

stubborn opposition of the French ambassador, Dubois de Saligny (who was privy to France's secret object in joining in the intervention and to the Duke of Morny's machinations, and whose role in this sad drama was to be that of a brigand as barefaced as any known to diplomatic history), Prim reasoned with the English commissioners, well-intentioned men, and with the candid Frenchman Jurién, and persuaded them to cooperate with him in steps that should lead to the withdrawal of the intervention by means of a treaty with Juárez, whose government, he pointed out, was the only one functioning in Mexico, for the reactionary group that called itself a government flitted from village to village, and from murder to murder, escorted by a band of guerrillas. Prim's scornful rejection of this group was reiterated by Almonte, former leader of the Mexican emigrés in European courts, when he arrived and had himself proclaimed Supreme Chief of the nation by an obscure reactionary officer. But Zuloaga retorted that the Supreme Chief was himself. One claim was as valid as the other, and Marshal Forey would flick them both aside with the tip of his baton.

Within a short time the Count of Reus had got in touch with Juárez, had agreed with Doblado on the preliminary conditions for a future pact (the "preliminaries of Soledad"),[2] and had won first the good will and then the gratitude of all Mexicans by his concern for the nation's dignity. In Europe the direction taken by the commissioners was viewed with displeasure, but Prim and the Englishmen, who saw matters in the same light, firmly followed their judgment, aware of the need for haste, since the French had landed considerable forces and the emigrés had begun to arrive. Almonte brought with him Napoleon's authorization for the establishment of a monarchy—a project that seemed tragically insane to Prim, who insisted that the Reform should be fully recognized and hoped to settle all questions at the conferences which were to be held at Orizaba. But Almonte and Saligny proposed to see that they were never held. The Mexican government demanded the expulsion of Almonte, in view of the politically neutral character of the intervention, which the invaders had solemnly asserted, and the French seized on this demand as a pretext to break off relations. Prim

[2] Agreements between Prim, representing the three powers, and Doblado, as Secretary of War, February 19, 1862.

and the English commissioners then decided to withdraw, and the European intervention became exclusively French.

Prim showed Mexico an example of honest and chivalrous diplomacy such as the world seldom sees. The immediate effect in Mexico was that attacks on Spain in the press and elsewhere quieted down, and popular ire was appeased. Spain had approached us with a new face; we had glimpsed the Spain of the future. Why is there no statue of Juan Prim on our boulevards, when our gratitude is as enduring as bronze?[3]

It is never just to hold an entire people responsible for the faults of their rulers. There can be no doubt that the reign of Napoleon III was hardly an accident but the consequence of a deep-seated social malady. While he could count, to the very last, on the votes of a majority of the nation, because he had given the French two of the things that they love best—order, which permits work and saving, and military glory, which flatters vanity (the third is liberty, which permits expression of feeling)—the news that the intervention in Mexico had become the sole responsibility of France caused surprise and anxiety in that country. Obviously a rash adventure, it was unpopular from the start. The presentiments of the people are always well founded.

The "masterwork" of the reign of Napoleon III (as he himself called it) was entrusted to the ambassador Dubois de Saligny, whose counselor was Almonte and who had the commander of the French expedition, Lorencez, at his beck. The first of these was a scoundrel who smelled a fortune in that mess. Almonte, bastard son of the great Morelos, was an ambitious man who, aspiring to the pinnacle of power, had tried to attain it by switching from party to party, only to be convinced by his disappointments that the salvation of his country was to be found in its domination by some great military power, whose unconditional instrument he was willing to become. Conde de Lorencez was a run-of-the-mill dutiful officer. The three of them contrived to frustrate the La Soledad agreements (which Almonte asserted, with reason, would be rejected by the allied governments), and then, resort-

[3] An avenue in the City of Mexico with the name of Prim was inaugurated on July 28, 1904. On this occasion Sierra made a speech in his honor.

ing to a preposterous excuse, determined that the French troops (which the government had permitted to enter the temperate zone with the express understanding that they would return to the coast if no agreement was reached) should remain in Córdoba and Orizaba. The troops under Lorencez, therefore, did not descend to the coast; what did descend was the honor of his banner. Prim saw the Mexican soldiers as they concentrated in Orizaba, some nearly naked and many without arms, and he choked with emotion, comparing them to the soldiers who had fought against the other Napoleon in Spain. That chivalrous knight, astounded at Lorencez' decision, proceeded to Vera Cruz where he directed preparations for the departure of the Spanish expedition. The government of Spain approved his conduct; if it had been able to see into the future it would have given him the highest commendation.

Zaragoza, a young general formed in the civil war, strong and energetic like most natives of the northern frontier, was not a strategist of genius, nor familiar with the fine points of European warfare, but his tactics consisted in a thorough knowledge of the Mexican soldier and his terrific power of resistance, and his strategy consisted in a pure and simple faith in the triumph, not only of right, but of his country. From the moment that he took over the command from General Uraga (who had studied European armies at first hand and had no confidence in our own), he never doubted or hesitated: he never spoke, as desperate generals do, of victory or death but merely gave his cool, calculated word that he would triumph—and kept his word.

He retreated, in the latter days of April, stairstep by stairstep up to the central plateau, with a force slightly larger than that of the French, who followed on his heels and successfully stormed, in a bloody battle, the giddy heights of Acultzingo. He resolved to hold Puebla and improvised forts on the high places (the small hills of Guadalupe and Loreto) that overlooked the city and made it vulnerable. On May 5 the French attacked at the very places where the defense was strongest, and after repeated assaults in which reckless courage and the discipline of the drill ground availed nothing, the survivors of Lorencez' crack regiments fell back, bloodied, battered, stunned, to their camp and thence to Orizaba. There, seething in humiliation, they directed their wrath not against their Mexican foes but against Almonte, self-styled "Supreme Chief of the Nation."

The Fifth of May, when judged by the number of combatants or the strictly military result of the action (an orderly retreat to await reinforcements), was not a battle of the first, nor even of the second, rank. It was not Platea but Marathon: its moral and political results were immeasurable. The entire nation thrilled with enthusiasm. Surely, no Mexican, whatever his party, was downcast by the victory. The remotest Indian village felt the electric current of patriotism that sped like lightning through the land, awakening many a sleeping conscience. The people were inspired to make a supreme effort. At this lofty moment of our history, the Reform party, already a majority of the country, commenced its transformation into the political totality of the country: the Reform, the Republic, and the Nation set out together on the *via crucis* that would end with the resurrection of legal right when their identification would be complete. Apart from this, the country's new and definitive personality, there would be only errant fragments and tatters, relics of our formative period.

The Fifth of May blocked the French army for a year, giving the country a chance to organize resistance, which the invaders could overcome to some extent by their military superiority but never could overcome entirely except by a huge army of occupation, and even then only ephemerally. With the forces at the disposal of imperial France, not even a sketchy occupation was feasible. What was assured was a string of brilliant victories, at a moral and material cost that would reduce the invading nation to a second-rate military power in Europe.

The Fifth of May set back Napoleon's designs in regard to the United States a full year. At the very moment when Zaragoza was fighting the battle of Puebla, Robert E. Lee was winning battles for the South. It was a moment when the French Emperor, with an unarmed Republic virtually at his mercy, might have joined forces with the Southern rebels, and, being sure, in those days, of England's aid, might have freed the Southern ports of blockades and reestablished their traffic by sea. On the Fifth of May Zaragoza defended in Puebla not only the integrity of his country but also that of the United States—

an involuntary service, this last, but one of inestimable value, which may have been repaid, but could not be surpassed, by any of the services (none of them disinterested) rendered to us by the American Union.

After his victory, General Zaragoza, with his army considerably reinforced by the troops of the popular González Ortega, who was under his orders, tried to reap the fruits of the Fifth of May by chasing the French out of Orizaba, where they had made themselves strong, and out of the country before their reinforcements could arrive. His bold and ingenious plan for the siege of Orizaba was frustrated by the utter fatigue of González Ortega's troops and the incredible carelessness of certain officers who allowed the French, eager to recover their prestige, to surprise a whole wing of our army and dislodge it from an impregnable position, so that Zaragoza had to withdraw.

The country gave itself over feverishly to defense. But the masses who were the foundation of our nationality (Indians and mestizos), being apathetic, thanks to three and a half centuries of subjection as minors, passively let themselves be hauled off to the army and jammed into barracks. Not that they lacked the will to fight: what they lacked was initiative, and the traditional method of recruitment, the levy, was necessary.

Each state had to resolve its own economic and military problems in order to make work secure and productive, so that taxes (a portion of the revenues was earmarked for the federal Treasury) could amount to something. Bandits, proclaiming all sorts of plans and unfurling all sorts of banners, swarmed everywhere, ranging from bodies of considerable size, like that led by Manuel Lozada in Tepic, to gangs of highwaymen and kidnappers, who were commonplace in the Federal District itself. Those gangs recruited new members at the very foot of the gallows where their chieftains died. The middle classes resisted, as best they could, the payment of taxes, which were increased at a dizzying rate, from day to day, as the invasion grew more formidable. It is true that the taxes were arbitrary and unequal, being based on no fair scale, and that the methods of the collectors were brutal and vexatious. But it is hard to see how else money could have been obtained with which to fortify Puebla and the City of Mexico and bring the contingents from the states to these points.

In the midst of preparations for defense, Zaragoza died, passing, in the people's affection, from triumph to apotheosis; legend made the hero into a god. The Republic paid him the highest tribute: his funeral carriage, a pyramid of incense, flowers, and palm leaves, was surmounted by the bier wrapped in the nation's flag. And the laurel of his victory is still green.

The French invasion was organized in Orizaba under Forey and in Jalapa under Bazaine. They received a steady stream of reinforcements; convoys, frequently disrupted by guerrillas, climbed up the stairsteps to the central plateau in long files. French squadrons anchored in our ports on both seas. And it rained gold. The unemployed soldiers of the beaten reaction (such as Márquez, a tiny speck who cast an enormous shadow over that final period of our great struggle) attached themselves to the French and tried to form corps to fight their own country. Forey, a mediocre military leader, a fanatical imperialist, a solemn, candid, decorative imbecile, had been sent to take charge of the enterprize. He came armed with a letter written by Napoleon, who stressed the importance of stemming the tide of American expansion on our continent and communicated his decision (1) to respect the Mexican people's freedom to choose their own government and (2) to respect the rights of those who had legally acquired nationalized property which had belonged to the Church. This policy spelled the death sentence of the reaction and made the Intervention an absurdity. The contradiction between the decision to respect the Reform and the determination to destroy the government, whose reason for being was the Reform, sufficed to make the Napoleonic enterprise abortive from its inception.

After looking to the security of his lines of supply between the central plateau and Vera Cruz, entrusting the vigilance of the highways to a corps of Egyptians hired by Napoleon and to the foreign legion of outcasts commanded by the sinister Colonel Dupin, Forey advanced on Puebla with more than thirty thousand Frenchmen, plus a group of survivors from the reactionary shipwreck who, swallowing insults daily, had got themselves on the French payroll. Puebla was not a fortified city; what strong points it had were improvised, especially in the ancient, massive religious edifices so abundant there, but these, because of the range and power of the siege guns, became more dangerous to their defenders than to the enemy. The army defending Puebla was a sort of national assembly, composed mostly of contingents from the states, who vied with one another in enthusiasm and deeds of valor. The defense, sustained for two months, was heroic, according to the unanimous confession of the French officers who have testified before history, and rich in episodes that stir our emotions and make us proud.

The improvised, and improvising, General González Ortega, with his ardent lyricism, gave that defense, unique in the annals of our wars, a sublime air of poetry in action. Puebla was gradually surrounded by blood-soaked ruins, and the French, bruised and nerve-racked, for all their superb courage were thinking of lifting the siege. But the defenders were running out of ammunition. An army bringing provisions, under Comonfort, the ex-President, was slowly and cautiously formed on the French rear, but an attempt to force an entrance for the huge supply train resulted in defeat and dispersal. Puebla had to surrender, and this is how the thing was done: the army destroyed its arms, released its officers and arranged to meet with them elsewhere to resume the fight for the fatherland, and the officers threw themselves upon the mercy of the victors, without asking or accepting any terms, thus remaining free for future duty. This procedure has been analyzed and criticized, but the final judgment on it was pronounced by the French generals who, when Metz was surrendered, cried to Bazaine, "Why didn't you do as the Mexicans did at Puebla?"

No effort was spared to ready the City of Mexico for defense. The agents of the military authorities had mistreated the inhabitants outrageously in order to squeeze contributions from them; the Reform laws had been applied, not coolly and methodically, but with a senseless parading of vindictiveness that deeply offended the religious sentiments of the masses. All this notwithstanding, the heroic defense of Puebla so excited the people's patriotism that, faced with the prospect of having to defend their City, everybody begged for arms. Then came the staggering news that the Congress, the President and his Cabinet were abandoning the City, that San Luis Potosí had been declared the new capital of the Republic. This was an unfortunate error: the City of Mexico could have defended itself for a month, and it would have taken Forey the rest of the year to reorganize his army. Meanwhile, the defense could have been consolidated in the hinterland.

The massive resistance of the country, with conspiracy in the parlor and guerrillas everywhere, made it necessary to augment the army of occupation day by day. Plainly the people were aware that this was no intervention to arbitrate a dispute but an invasion to impose a protectorate according to a preconceived plan.

In Puebla and in the City of Mexico the clergy welcomed the invaders by donning their richest vestments and intoning, in the quavering voice of their decrepit dignitaries, impious Te Deums. The God invoked by the clergy was about to punish them by obliging them, at the height of the blessed and anointed Intervention, to sigh for Juárez. As the French approached the City there appeared on the streets, from heaven knows where, a group of specters in stiff frock coats smelling mustily of the sacristy and the archive; these were the former bureaucrats of the reactionary regime, who three years earlier had crowded the offices and churches. Now they seemed phantoms of yesteryear. They waited in the doorway of a public building to cast themselves upon the bosom of France.

Forey, with his gallant and picturesque army, heralded by Márquez' funeral cortege, entered the capital to the accompaniment of gay fanfares in June of 1863. Thousands of curious spectators, eager to miss no scene of this prelude to the tragedy that all divined, crowded the streets, surreptitiously whistling down and breaking up the squads of cheerleaders formed by the police in the poorer quarters with a few hundred sacristans and pickpockets. On the balconies, too, though these were decorated by official order, the witnesses were silent, except those occasional groups of *mochos,* as fanatical Catholics were called, who yelled and waved handkerchiefs in the houses of the rich. Old Forey, squat and pompous like some *imperator* of the Roman decadence, thought that the whole nation was kneeling before him in gratitude, tossing the wreaths prefabricated by the police and the ladies before the steed of the conqueror who had come, not to destroy, like Cortés, but to build (as he put it in his bombastic proclamations); he thought that dissension was a thing of the past, that the cry of *Vive l'Empereur!* which his army had heard as it filed by the national palace had united the country. And, carried away by enthusiasm, he assured the Mexicans that "the purchasers of nationalized property will be confirmed in the possession thereof . . . the Emperor would welcome freedom of religion." The hosannas in the sacristies were choked off by splutterings of shocked indignation. "And so the Intervention had come for no other purpose than that!" Precisely: it had come to make the Reform a permanent fixture.

The French ambassador, the egregious Saligny, appointed a governing committee[4] composed of rancid conservatives, who named an executive triumvirate composed of the Archbishop of Mexico and Almonte and Salas—that is, the head of the clergy and an emigré who had forgotten his country and a run-of-the-mill general who had been forgotten by his country.[5] After taking this action and issuing pro-Catholic proclamations that seemed to contradict everything said by Forey, the committee named an "assembly of notables," as Santa Anna and Paredes had done.[6] The two leading statesmen of the reactionary party, Lares and Ignacio Aguilar y Marocho, along with Almonte, were the wheels of this committee. Some favored annexation to France, but the idea of a monarchy prevailed. The word was passed that the Archduke Ferdinand Maximilian, whom scarcely anybody had heard of but who had been suggested by José Manuel Hidalgo, sponsored by Gutiérrez Estrada, and approved by Napoleon, was the one to elect, and this unfortunate prince was chosen. What if someone had told those two hundred bourgeois, representing nearly the entire reactionary party in Mexico, that they constituted in fact a terrible tribunal, that they had unwittingly condemned a man to death!

A monarchy in Mexico! The argument in favor of one, laid before the assembly of notables by the honest and intelligent but fanatical Aguilar y Marocho in a laborious treatise, seemed to advocate rather

[4] Appointed June 16, 1863, and composed of thirty-five persons, the committee was organized June 22 with Teodosio Lares as president.

[5] The Executive Power, consisting of Juan N. Almonte, Archbishop Pelagio Antonio de Labastida, and General Mariano Salas, with the bishop-elect of Tulancingo, Juan B. Ormachea, and Don Ignacio Pavón as substitutes, was inaugurated June 25 and became the Regency under the Empire, July 11.

[6] The committee of notables, inaugurated July 8, was charged with the duty of deciding on the form of government to be adopted.

the resuscitation of the colonial regime than the establishment of a new throne and had been annihilated years earlier. From the judgment delivered (in July 1855) to Santa Anna by the most responsible conservative leaders of that time and written by the eminent jurist Bernard Couto, we extract the following:

> It seems to us incontrovertible that Mexico can never be anything but a republic. Her present circumstances and those obtaining since the fall of the liberator Iturbide, the unanimous and unwavering consensus among us, now and in the past, the absolute lack of the elements essential to any other form of government, and finally, the kind of government that our neighbors have—all make it impossible for Mexico to be organized on any but republican lines.

This was common sense. But the notables fancied that, under the aegis of the French Emperor, by whom they seemed to be mesmerized, the whole social and political and idealogical state of things could be turned upside down. So they put their trust in an empire. Most of them, wounded in their religious feelings, believed that Forey, despite his proclamation, was a Godfrey of Bouillon and his invasion a crusade. This was arrant nonsense.

The assembly of notables had produced a monarchy and a regency (composed of Archbishop Labastida, Almonte, and Salas), and a committee was delegated to present Napoleon with a vote of thanks and Maximilian with the imperial crown. The grotesque farce was transparent: there was no disinterested French mediation between parties; there was only a brutal invasion, seconded by the remnants of a faction incapable of controlling the country and willing to become tools of the invaders, who spurned their aims and ideals from the first, leaving them no reason for existence. The object of this invasion was to convert Mexico's tiny debt to France into a huge sum by means of the Jecker commitment and the costs of the occupation—a sum that could never be paid and would keep the new empire under the thumb of France, who would then have the right to exploit the wealth of the invaded soil and to take over certain territory (Sonora). There had been no vote for the monarchy; the choice expressed by the assembly of notables (who were unknown to the nation and had no contact with it) was decided beforehand in the Tuileries. In order to placate the opposition in the French parliament, which cried out against the implantation of a government here without a vote of the Mexican people, Napoleon instructed the chief of the French expedition to require the councils set up by the invaders in the occupied towns to express their choice freely; this, of course, was a travesty. The fact was that the invaders proceeded to revive the dead reactionary regime, giving it power and arms so that it could again rule the country—a regime that was neither viable nor what Napoleon wanted. As for the American Civil War, the end was in sight: the triumph of the North was assured. The year lost after the Fifth of May, the formidable task of holding down a land defeated but not conquered, had prevented France from going to the aid of the South. Now it was too late, and the problem that Napoleon thought he had solved with an army and a letter had become terribly complicated, a dreadful mess.

The naked truth was this: the government engendered by the invading army after vanquishing the Republic was born dead, strangled in its own contradictions. It could not be national when it depended wholly on the support of a foreign army, nor a party government when the pious words of the reaction were denied by Forey's letter from the Emperor—which was the constitution of the new Mexican Empire—declaring that the Reform was sacred and freedom of worship a desideratum. What made everything still more confused and uncertain was that Napoleon, enlightened to some extent by letters from French officers and by the growing intensity of resistance during the first year, evinced a desire to compromise, to retreat, to withdraw from the venture. Forey, now a marshal, and Saligny, with his nose for money, who together had directed all French policy in Mexico, were suddenly called to France, to the dismay of the reactionaries, who understood, however, that France could not withdraw, that the initial error would force her, with inflexible logic, to attempt the conquest of the country, which Forey had declared beforehand would be impossible.

With Forey's retirement the grand operations of the French army under Bazaine commenced in the winter of 1863. So far the invaders had confined themselves to an important sector of the Gulf coast, plus the zone comprising the routes ascending to the central plateau from the hot region, including the road between Puebla and the City of Mexico and a slowly lengthened radius around the capital. Throughout this occupied territory the invasion demonstrated from the first the methods that it would employ to the last: disarming resistance by terror, pacifying by death, cleansing cities and highways with blood. Military courts carried out this program as if no Mexican government existed, and their justice was fearfully swift. Mere suspicion, the charge of having been a guerrilla or the friend of guerrillas, an expression on the face, a vague accusation, often poorly understood by men who could not speak a word of Spanish—any of these could bring death. This was the system of the Albigensian crusades: "Kill them all, God will take care of His own," said the capitains then. In Mexico they made sure that, out of every hundred shot, one third were bandits; this was sufficient justification for the courts martial. The whip, frequently used on dissidents in the cities, and forced lodging and other vexations, especially in the houses of liberals, were France's gifts to Mexican high society. And high society submitted to everything gladly, attending with thrills of pleasure mixed with fear the balls given by the French officers, who seemed elegant and charming to girls and old ladies alike, even when they were brutal. If not all dukes, nor even all gentlemen, they were Frenchmen, just the same!

The campaign of the winter of 1863–1864 left the legitimate government utterly crushed. The French army, with the help of well-paid bands of traitors, succeeded in dominating the entire central plateau and occupied all the principal cities of the hinterland. The republican army, cut to pieces, took refuge in the mountains of Michoacán, Jalisco, and Zacatecas or retreated in disorder over the vast northern plains. The generals in whom the highest hopes were placed failed dismally, and Juárez and his government, the very heart and soul of the nation's resistance, found themselves threatened morally by other republican leaders, who demanded that Juárez quit the Presidency because there was no other solution to the conflict with France. They were threatened physically, with death, by Vidaurri in Coahuila and Nuevo León. The only hope of the republican cause was Juárez' great soul, his stoical serenity, his immutable faith—not the blind faith of the submissive men of his race, but the clairvoyant faith of those men of his race who attain to civilization and emancipated thought. He weighed the difficulties of his task and foresaw future conditions with amazing political acumen, neither hesitating nor deceiving himself. Only Juárez remained firm, unshakable.

While the victorious French were overrunning the country, ruthlessly executing republicans, just as Santa Anna, Márquez, and Miramón had done before them, in the capital they were subduing the reactionary party, which had no other reason for existence than its adhesion to the Church and hence its opposition to Reform. The Regency of the Empire proceeded to carry out Forey's orders to respect the property nationalized by the Reform. But the bishops, led by their prelate, the intelligent and aggressive Labastida, protested. The Supreme Court refused to go along with the Regency, from which the archbishop resigned; the Court was thereupon dissolved. And the contendents in this battle royal made their confession before the bar of history. The episcopate said that the reactionary party existed solely to defend the interests of the clergy and had brought about the Intervention for that purpose; that the Church had been better off under the Republic. The Intervention replied that the clergy's aims were outdated and could never be realized; that their party was a tiny minority in the country. Thus, there was no need for the Republic to make its own defense.

Prince Maximilian, brother of the Austrian Emperor, possible heir to the Empire, sometime candidate to the throne of Greece, was married to the daughter of a Belgian king highly respected in Europe for his strength of character and firm adherence to constitutional rule; her mother, a princess of the House of Orleans, had bequeathed to her a secret loathing of Napoleon and a devotion to the French army. Maximilian accepted the Mexican throne the minute it was offered to him, at the outset of the Intervention, despite his pretense of accepting it only under certain conditions. To the committee that waited upon him in his castle of Miramar to offer him the crown of Mexico in the name of the nation, represented by the assembly of notables, he said that the notables represented the capital only, that he awaited a plebiscite which would clearly express the will of the nation. This, of course, was easy for the army of occupation to obtain. The sacrificial victim selected by the emigrés as being the least objectionable to any European court had been a fairly popular governor of Lombardy under Austrian rule. From pose rather than from principle, and to annoy his brother, he liked to flaunt liberal ideas. His brother was glad to get him out of Europe. Napoleon, aware of Maximilian's anticlerical bias (promoted by his wife, the princess Charlotte, who adored her protestant father) and knowing his weak character, supposed that the new Emperor would be a mere tool in his hands. But Charlotte, who undoubtedly persuaded him to accept the crown, was a proud woman impatient of any secondary role. Loving her husband, she had ambitions for the two of them. Her mind, quick and high-strung, became overexcited at the very start of the terrible Mexican tragedy, and her final dementia was the consequence of four years of psychoneurotic tension.

Maximilian was an adventurer, in the accepted meaning of the word: a man who boggled at no rash undertaking so long as he could envision some grandiose result in keeping with his ambition. Like most adventurers, he was a second-rater who dreamed of playing a principal role. Mexico seemed to him a slate, intact, though spotted by civil war, on which he could draw a nation made in his own image, and he felt endowed for that purpose with courage, with enthusiasm, with inspiration, with a divine gift for governing. He was indeed about to become the protagonist of a drama, but a drama ending in tragedy, for he was neither a politician nor an administrator nor a soldier: he was a dreamer, a poet. Charlotte had all the common sense in the family; he saw everything in a theatrical light, as a stage effect. Compassionate in the extreme, but (this is a documented truth) basically a double-dealer, he lied without compunction. When we attempt to sketch Maximilian's psyche, we are reminded of Macaulay's succinct analysis of Charles I, who, he said, had many of the qualities of a great prince, writing and speaking with the elegance of an intelligent and well-educated gentleman, with excellent taste in art and in literature; it was faithlessness that caused his downfall.

While the voluminous returns from the plebiscite in the towns under the thumb of the invasion were being delivered to him, Maximilian reached an agreement with his brother by which he irrevocably renounced his rights as heir to the imperial Austrian throne, for himself and for his descendants. He visited the courts of Europe and heard words of encouragement from Napoleon, who had already said, "The Mexican expedition is the most brilliant page of my reign," and who pledged the support of France so long as Maximilian should remain in Mexico. "I give you a throne on a heap of gold," he said.

After making a pact with Napoleon which included secret clauses and provided for a loan to the new Empire at a ruinous price, Maximilian received the benediction of Pius IX, who promised to send a plenipotentiary to Mexico at once to settle Church matters. The solemn ceremonies of the renunciation and the coronation were followed by a meditative spell, and for three days, seeing no one, he seemed to contemplate the abyss into which he was about to toss his youth and his life, and wrote the following lament:

Now I must leave my fatherland forever,
Leave the skies that smiled on my first tender joys,
Leave my gilded cradle; for the holy bonds
That bound me to all these are riven!
The land where childhood spent the laughing years,
Where I felt the infinite woe of the first love,
I must give up, moved by ambition which, thanks to you,
Fills my heart to the very brim.
You beckon to me, showing me a throne,
And bewitching visions that lure me on.
Should I listen to the sweet song of the sirens?
Unhapy is he who puts his faith in sirens.
You speak of golden scepters, castles, power;
A limitless vista opens before my eyes.
Now I must follow you beyond the sea,
To an unknown world on the farther shore!
You wish to adorn with diamonds and golden thread
The fragile texture of my quiet life.
But can you give me, in exchange, peace of mind?
Or is happiness, for you, only gold and power?
Let me go unnoticed down my obscure path;
Let me wander joyfully amid the myrtles:
Learning is sweeter to me, and the cult of the Muses,
Than the splendor of gold in the shining diadem.

The frigate *Novara* brought him to Vera Cruz; he busied himself aboard ship by drawing up economic regulations and arrived quite happy. The people were full of curiosity; the conservative, wildly excited, were viewed by them with ironic amusement; the French officers and the Empire's lieutenant, Juan N. Almonte, were on hand to pay homage. The Prince passed quickly through the crowd, saluting everybody with his tall gray hat, which became stylish, and smiling through his long blond beard, artistically curled and parted below his weak chin and neurotic mouth. With his slender figure, his benign and clear-eyed expression, he was quite attractive, and the populace felt his magnetism. Charlotte, very tall and straight, with her intelligent and penetrating gaze, seemed more masculine than her husband and less attractive: she was an intellectual, he a sentimental type. The journey to the capital was one unceasing ovation. Curiosity, the desire to applaud a good show, the compunction to behave well in the presence of a foreign prince, the reverence of the Indian masses, who had hardly made a century's progress since the Conquest, for any potentate—all gave these demonstrations, organized by the upper class of society, an extraordinary effervescence. And patriotism was forgotten in many minds, confident that this fair-haired man was going to work a miracle of harmony, forgiveness, and peace.

In the City of Mexico, the spectacle was superb. The municipality spent all its funds on decorations, and the entire city took part in the fiesta. The aristocracy, so-called, decked itself out sumptuously, in triumph, and picked a fine lady to read the Empress a lesson in politics, from the Church's point of view. The populace, into whom the police had poured a terrific dose of enthusiasm in the pulque shops, yelled deliriously. The middle classes, coldly watchful and anxious, did not believe that the opera would last long. A hundred or so of us students cried "Death to the *mochos*!" in the principal plaza, without anyone trying to stop us. Our voices were lost in the immense roar of shouts, bells, cannon shots, and music.

Months passed, and the Emporer accomplished little or nothing. He seemed to be studying, cogitating. He suspended the blockade of the Mexican coasts, thereby upsetting the plans of the French navy; he named a moderate liberal as foreign secretary. He courteously withheld political power from Almonte, the author of the French Intervention, and from Gutiérrez Estrada, chivalrous devoté of a decayed ideal and author of Maximilian's candidacy for the throne of Mexico. The rest of the Emperor's acts can be characterized as futile and wasteful: the ten million pesos of the French loan vanished in no time. What was Maximilian doing—studying, cogitating?

In any case, the imperial government was in far better condition than the national one. The former, at least, could count on the close, if desperate, adhesion of the wealthier classes (who put religious loyalties, material interest, and puerile vanity above patriotism), on the indifference of the masses, on the disintegration of the reformist party, which began to seek a new center of gravity now that Juárez' government could hardly be said to exist, and on the overwhelming superiority of the French army. The national government was fleeing ever farther northward, menaced by French columns, while the peripheral states of Yucatán, Campeche, Tabasco, and Chiapas were being overrun. Only in Oaxaca was there a solid core of resistance, slowly being firmed up by the most earnest of the young republican chiefs, General Porfirio Díaz, and preparing for the tempest that was sure to come. The principal republican army, in the west, demoralized by the defection of the Commander in Chief, Uraga, was saved from shame and dissolution by the simple, honest patriotism of José María Arteaga, who, on receiving the appointment as commander of the headless army from Juárez, replied with these words:

> In accepting this responsibility I have consulted not my vanity but my will to sacrifice my person on the altar of our common future. The times are unpropitious, and I pledge my honor not only to commit no depredations but to make no senseless sacrifices. If I could have my wish, the whole Republic would break out in armed protest at once. But I understand perfectly that the human spirit is subject to reverses which affect entire societies, and that a breathing time is needed. Silence does not mean acquiescence, for when the revulsion comes it is like a torrent of fire that sets everything ablaze. Therefore, I expect great things of you, and very soon. But, until your day dawns, you may be assured that this army, which is you vanguard, will maintain the sacred flame of our independence.

These words, uttered in the hour of the Republic's agony by a man at the head of a disorganized, naked, and hungry horde, when there was nothing on the horizon but a tornado bringing disaster and death, are among the noblest and most exalted in the history of mankind.

Three months after Maximilian's arrival, thanks to the fact that thirty thousand French soldiers and twenty thousand venal Mexicans had swept his path clean, he could make a triumphal tour of the hinterland. All those who were undecided or had lost hope turned to him, seduced by his liberalism, his smiling benevolence. He celebrated the Sixteenth of September in Dolores Hidalgo, rendering such heartfelt tribute to the fathers of our country that many good Mexicans were converted.

He returned to Mexico and faced the unsolvable problem brought up by his anti-French secretary, Félix Eloin: was he a puppet emperor? Was he or Marshal Bazaine the real ruler? Who was emperor, he or Napoleon? How long could the situation last unless it was clarified? Was the military supremacy of France compatible with a free government?

The solution of the imperial problem seemed to lie in building the Empire on the foundation of a new party strong enough to make the French occupation superfluous. The prince had observed and meditated, and he rightly failed to see any vital political group in the country except the reformists, and of these, both moderates and radicals, he composed his cabinet and council.

Why did these good republicans and honest reformists lend their talents to the Empire? Because they had been educated, as lawyers, engineers, or statesmen, in France or by French authors, and so were intellectually good Frenchmen. They believed in the infallibility of French thought and the immortality of French military power. They were also good contemporaneous Frenchmen and held a blind faith in the talent and authority of Napoleon, as did nearly all the European statesmen of that day. With such notions, and the conviction that Juárez' Republic was dead, or could be resuscitated only by the direct intervention of the United States—a prospect that horrified them—they decided to make the best of the situation and salvage the Reform from the shipwreck of the Republic. This was Maximilian's plan, and they must help him. Once the Reform was rescued, the French army could be dispensed with. But first (so Maximilian's eloquence persuaded them) the Empire had to be consolidated. Since none of them (all knew their Mexican history) believed the monarchy could last, they expected the Intervention to end with the restoration of a Republic, and Maximilian was in accord with this program; neither did he believe in the monarchy, except as a provisional regime. We might add to the reasons for the rallying of a good portion of the reformist party around the throne the prince's charm, his magnetism.

This writer, for highly personal reasons, is ashamed to confess that, when the conduct of those who let themselves be deceived is compared with that of those who resisted all blandishments and, facing every danger and undergoing every sacrifice, remained faithful to their banner and political religion, the latter proved themselves as patently superior to the former as truth is to error.

Everything that happened seemed to vindicate those who had given their support to the liberal Empire, the "democratic monarchy," as Maximilian liked to call it. Victory, with her wings soaked—alas!—in Mexican blood, rounded out the Empire's sphere of control. Tamaulipas, martyrized by Dupin's vandals, was overrun. So were Coahuila and Nuevo León, where the army that had served as a shield for Juárez and his associates was dispersed in a fearful battle, which made fugitives of the government. In Jalisco, Arteaga's forces were cut to pieces; there and in Michoacán resistance appeared to be at an end. In Oaxaca, last stronghold of the armed Republic, morale was at low ebb. The year of 1865, it seemed, would most likely see the consolidation of the Empire and the withdrawal of the French Intervention, which reformist officials, foolishly perhaps, tried to undermine. Meanwhile, Maximilian proceeded with his Reform program, thereby keeping his pact with Napoleon. (In any case, as a reputed liberal and a Freemason, he could hardly have desired the ascendancy of the Church.)

The reactionaries, nonetheless, expected him to come to terms with the Church: they expected him, indeed, to sign, and be guided by, a concordat with the Pope. But the inflexible Pius IX managed to put any sort of agreement out of the question. Following the stupid advice of the Mexican bishops, he sent a nuncio without authority to seek a compromise on the matter of the nationalized property of the Church but with a list of demands which would have placed the new Empire on a plane with respect to the Church vastly inferior to that of the old viceroyalty. Maximilian took a firm stand, applauded by the French as well as by the reformists, and, after a brief but hot battle with the nuncio, declared that the Empire had the same right as the kings of Spain to the Patronate, that the official religion was Catholic but that other cults would be freely tolerated. And he asked the Council of State to review all the transactions involving disamortization and nationalization since 1856, in order to invalidate the illegal ones. This was the definitive sanction of the Reform (though some of those who had profited by the transactions were deeply disturbed); this was also the death sentence of the reactionary party. Unable to prevent the Reform by its own exertions, it had appealed to France for help, had totally transformed the nation's institutions at the cost of a sea of Mexican blood. And France and her puppet Empire now declared the Reform a legal fact, fully recognizing its identification with the needs and interests of the Mexican people, as the logical corollary to Independence, as the final curtain falling on the society of the colonial regime. The party that had fought against the Revolution ever since the first stirrings of unrest in the Spain of 1813 fell dead at the feet of the man it had almost deified (while noting with surprise that his crown was surmounted, not by the cross, but by the pineapple, symbol of tropical abundance); the man from whom it expected miracles gave it the deathblow.

But the reactionaries dragged down to the tomb with them the man who was at once their executioner and their victim. For the staggering contradictions that the Intervention and the Empire had embraced were now all too patent. This regime, which had been contrived for the purpose of stopping civil war, had done more in the way of killing, burning, and piling up ruins than all the internecine wars of half a century put together. Contrived for the purpose of creating a national Treasury that would be able to pay off the European debts, it had raised those debts to a dizzying height, while permitting Napoleon to exact payment, not in cash, but in a monopoly on the exploitation of a national territory, Sonora. Contrived for the purpose of building up a truly national party—backed by a foreign army!—Maximilian now wanted to use the party to get rid of the army. The party consisted of a military group incapable of controlling the country once the French had left, of a majority of the landowners, of some reformists, and of many reactionaries who remained loyal to Maximilian or to the idea of a monarchy. The imperialist party had no roots in the masses, the source of armies and of triumphs; it could legislate but it could not fight.

When news came that the American Civil War, which had been expected to last a year or two longer, had ended with Lee's surrender, that Lincoln had been assassinated, but that his successor was as warm a friend of the republicans in Mexico as the great martyred President had been, or even warmer, it is said that Maximilian exclaimed, "This is the end of the Empire!"

And indeed it was. If the shattered Mexican resistance could still force the French to maintain an army of occupation, then where would they get the men and the matériel to cope with the hundreds of thousands of soldiers standing under arms in the United States? And now, France imperatively needed to concentrate her power in Europe, where the old German confederation, coming apart, threatened to bring on violent and earthshaking convulsions. But for this European crisis, France would not have feared a war with the United States so long as she could count on Britain as an ally. Now, of course, such a war was unthinkable.

The year of 1865 started out with the pacification of the hinterland and the adhesion of those who believed in the Empire's future and put their personal interests above their country's, of those who were blinded by France's military prestige and by fears of American aggression. This was the year that proved, while the Empire was reaching the zenith of its triumph, how hopeless the future of any Mexican empire must be. Executions by the thousands failed to stifle resistance, which again flared in Michoacán, in Sonora and Sinoloa, and in the northeast. The situation of the country halfway through the year was this: armed resistance had been fragmented, was reduced to bands of guerrillas, who swarmed in every corner of the country, while moral resistance in the minds of the people grew to giant stature; the reactionaries, though chained to the Empire, were unhappy; the new proprietors created by the Reform were angered by the revision of their transactions; the landowners, losing confidence in France, sought to escape from Maximilian's tottering palace. In the words of General Félix Douay, most respected of all the French officers who came to Mexico:

> The political organization set up by the imperial government has so far been ineffectual. The tranquility that prevails in certain parts is merely superficial and owing entirely to the French occupation. The sincere adherents of the government are very few. In the present state of the people's mind, it would be foolish to expect the cooperation of anyone, no matter what party he belongs to. (August 1865).

Maximilian, a decorative emperor who made laws and speeches and awarded medals and arranged festivals, also continued his reformist work, giving the committee charged with negotiating a concordat with the Pope instructions to demand pontifical sanction for the entire code of the Reform. The Emperor's gratitude to the Indians, whose passive loyalty to their priests and to anyone who offered them relief from the tribute and the levy he confused with loyalty to his person, led him to decree the emancipation of the serfs, the peons of the haciendas, in a law inspired by a splendid sense of justice, but unfortunately impossible to enforce. In every other respect he was simply Bazaine's pupil. The tutor was not only lord of the army but also of the Treasury, since the Empire, in order to live, had to beg the French incessantly for loans, which bore such onerous terms that they would have eventually killed the Empire with starvation if the Republic had not killed it first with the rifle. The tutor kept urging Maximilian to economize, to organize an army, because France was about to withdraw.

France was determined to secure recognition of the Empire by the United States before withdrawing, and a French column chased the national government from Chihuahua to El Paso del Norte [now Ciudad Juárez] in order to convince Washington that no republican government existed in fact within our territory. Bazaine obliged Maximilian to decree the famous draconian law of October 3, 1865, which was iniquitously applied in Michoacán to Arteaga and his heroic companions, its first victims. By such methods the incurable fantasist of Miramar hoped to arrive at the understanding with Juárez which was his obsession.

Juárez, who had managed, by surmounting vast obstacles, to keep in touch with all the republican leaders of the country, reached the end of his constitutional term of office in the last months of 1865. There was no legal way for him to prolong his term or to succeed himself; the Vice-President and Chief Justice of the Supreme Court (González Ortega) lived in the United States. The moment was critical, and the separation of Juárez from his post meant the end of resistance, the suicide of the Republic. The President then went beyond the law and sacrificed the Constitution to the good of the country. This act, which made the President a dictator, in the name of the Republic's highest interests, was applauded by a majority of the republicans.

Here was the situation at the beginning of 1866. (1) Moral resistance to the regime born of the French invasion, as well as armed resistance, was growing in spite of the appalling reign of terror; in the border states, especially, the insurrection was stronger than ever. (2) In the United States, the victorious army clamored for war against France in Mexico; General Grant declared it was necessary to go to the aid of the Republic; the men released from service wanted to invade our territory on their own account, thereby poising a more frightening danger than that of the French invasion. But the American government restrained these outbursts of Anglo-Saxon aggressiveness and took diplomatic measures to compel the French army to leave our territory in short order, and thus applied the Monroe Doctrine which forbade any European nation to entrench itself in the Americas, the object being to insure the Union's control of Latin-American markets. With this diplomatic offensive against the French Intervention, the United States repaid us for the immense service we had rendered in 1862 and 1863 by our resistance to the French, which prevented them (and probably the British) from becoming allies of the Confederates and indefinitely prolonging the Civil War. (3) Napoleon was deeply worried by the bitter opposition of a minority in his parliament to the Mexican venture. Not that a handful of eloquent liberals could make him change his policy. But the sentiment of the country was almost solidly on their side, and the deputies as a whole greeted promises to withdraw the army from Mexico with increasingly enthusiastic applause. Napoleon's hand was forced, finally, by the combination of Washington's impatience and the crisis in Europe. Washington had always recognized the Juárez government as the only legitimate one, and the impertinence of the Tuileries in trying to secure recognition of the Empire by the White House as the price of French withdrawal bordered on insanity. Johnson's government replied by permitting guns and munitions to be furnished to the Mexican republicans, immensely strengthening the national resistance, which had heretofore fought practically unarmed. And the diplomatic notes of Johnson's Secretary of State, from the last day of the Civil War to the day when the French took ship, ran such a gamut of hints, warnings, and threats—to elicit the promise that the army would be withdrawn, to set a deadline for the withdrawal, to make sure that no portion of the French army would be surreptitiously diverted to the service of the Empire—that Secretary Seward might be said to have directed the course of the Intervention during 1866. But his demands happened to coincide with the disturbing events in Europe. There Napoleon was determined to destroy the equilibrium contrived by the (odious, to him) anti-Napoleonic pacts of 1815. Believing that the new nations formed by the plebiscite system, with his help, would remain his allies, he ignored the prophetic warnings of Thiers, who predicted that the Italians and Germans, as soon as they achieved their unity, would naturally turn against France. Napoleon let himself be blinded by faith in his allies and seduced by Bismarck's projects (though he thought Bismarck was an impractical dreamer), and he allowed Prussia and Italy to join forces against Austria and to break up the old German confederation, expecting to rise above the chaos as the mediator of Europe. But to play this part he would have to brandish his military power. The decision to withdraw from Mexico was irrevocably made by October 1865. The Austro-Prussian War, which everybody expected to last much longer, ended in July 1866 with the staggering surprise at Sadowa. Napoleon, eager to assume his role of arbiter, was confronted by a statement of Randon, his minister of war, who said the war in Mexico had so disorganized the French army, "it would not be possible to mobilize even fifty thousand men on the Rhine." The prime result of the French Intervention in Mexico was the frustration of France.

Napoleon then began to harass Bazaine with pressing orders. "Wind up affairs in Mexico one way or another. I have told the Empress Charlotte that I cannot give Mexico another penny or another man." And what was to be done with Maximilian? Napoleon's idea was to have him abdicate, and with this in mind the politics of the invasion were wholly reversed. Maximilian was to be carried out amongst the baggage of the French army! As a matter of fact, he had been brought in that way.

The French Caesar, having made his decision, now began to make excuses for the Intervention: the French had never intended to impose a government on Mexico; the Mexicans had chosen a monarchy and Maximilian of their own free will. And so on. His mind teemed with projects: to cut the empire up into a federation of several entities, under Maximilian's hegemony; to have the Emperor abdicate and convoke an assembly, before whom, after expounding the purity of France' motives, he would offer to return absolute liberty to the nation. And so on. All this is to be found in Napoleon's letters to Bazaine.

While the diplomatic and political comedy was being played, events followed their ineluctable course.

In the first months of 1866, the north was ablaze. In Tamaulipas guerrilla bands joined to form a considerable force under the command of Mariano Escobedo, who, after an unsuccessful attack on Matamoros, scored a brilliant victory over the French at Santa Isabel. Though pushed to the Rio Grande, Escobedo's force returned, better armed, to shatter a column escorting a highly important convoy between Matamoros and Monterrey. Then Tomás Mejía, famous Indian general of the reaction, the bravest, most loyal, and most sincere of the Mexican Empire's soldiers, capitulated in Matamoros, and in July and August the republicans, treading on the invaders' heels, took Tampico, Monterrey, and Saltillo, and menaced San Luis Potosí. President Juárez was already securely installed in Chihuahua, valiantly reconquered by Luis Terrazas and Sóstenes Rocha. Soon thereafter the French were driven out of the city and state of Durango.

The campaign in Sonora and Sinaloa was ferocious from the start. Beginning with the intrepid repulse of the French attempt to take Mazatlán in May 1864, action was on a limited scale until after the rout of the French and the imperialists at the Battle of San Pedro in

December. But Lozada made his hordes available to the French, who were joined also by remnants of reactionary bands, and the campaign against the indefatigable republican chief, General Ramón Corona, became extremely lively. The French, unspeakably savage, massacred prisoners, burned entire towns, and committed all the crimes that marked their passage throughout the Republic.

Four names stand out in the French endeavor to civilize by means of extermination—Castagny in the north, Dupin in the east, Pottier in the south, and Berthelin in the west—but many others could be added to this list of hangmen; the African troops in particular delighted in murder. There was, in truth, a respectable element among the invaders who strove ineffectually to correct this wicked policy, which was based on the premise that, since there was a government in Mexico constituted by the will of the people, all dissidents were bandits, outlaws who should be shot. And so they were shot. At times the republican chiefs inflicted terrible reprisals; at times they showed a noble magnanimity.

In Sonora, the French occupied Guaymas and other important towns, defeating the guerrillas day after day but never destroying them. Guaymas was recaptured at midyear of 1866, and the entire state fell into republican hands, as did Sinaloa shortly, when the French were driven from the principal port. Soon that laboriously organized Army of the West, as it was officially called, under General Corona, entered Jalisco, and Guadalajara was occupied before the year's end. In Michoacán, the ruthless and tireless imperialist, Ramón Méndez, still held the advantage over the patriots, who battled unceasingly.

In Oaxaca, the national flag was raised by victorious hands. There, General Porfirio Díaz, who had escaped from captivity in Puebla, organized an army from the scattered bands of guerrillas. A man with a gift for order, for administration, for leadership, prudent in making plans and astoundingly bold in executing them, General Díaz felt confident enough of his strength in the last months of 1866 to undertake the siege of Oaxaca. First, the Battle of Miahuatlán enabled him to surround the city, then he destroyed, at La Carbonera, a column sent to its rescue. Oaxaca, at his mercy, surrendered, and he thus returned to the Republic all that had been lost there in men and supplies in 1865.

Now the Gulf coast rose in arms, and the mountains of Vera Cruz swarmed with bands that would be organized by the victor of Oaxaca. Only the central plateau was controlled by the invaders, who were surrounded by a growing and advancing wall of fire.

It must be admitted that the French troops, dominating the lines of retreat from the capital to the Gulf, showed astonishing energy, boldness, and elasticity. While they could not hold back the republican armies, which, like the giant in the myth, grew larger as they approached, neither could the Mexicans deal a telling blow to the invaders, so rapidly did the French retreat and contract. Wherefore the belligerents, arriving at a sort of silent pact, refrained from attacking each other.

Meanwhile, Maximilian, trusting in the word of honor, from one gentleman to another, that Napoleon had given him in Paris when he promised that his army would remain in Mexico for five years, interpreted all the announcements of imminent withdrawal as efforts to spur him to activity, as reactions to Bazaine's invariably hostile reports, or as diplomatic sops to the United States. But messengers and envoys went back and forth across the Atlantic, and finally the Marshal spoke out and delivered the ultimatum, which can be condensed as follows: no more intervention, no more Empire; withdrawal and abdication. Maximilian, against his will, began to see things clearly. Charlotte, with more virility, intelligence, and pride than her spouse, was terrified by the prospect, which her vanity could not bear, of playing the role of a queen without a crown, while living on an Austrian pension. She resolved to make a descent in person on Napoleon in order to hold him to his word and thus stave off the catastrophe that she foresaw as inevitable if the French troops were withdrawn. She set out in a state of high nervous excitement. The fever of insatiable and frustrated ambition which had ravaged her for five years was approaching a crisis. When, on horseback, through a torrential downpour, she threaded her way by the flare of torches down the trail along the dizzying fastnesses of Chiquihuite with her subdued and frightened retinue, she brought to mind the picture of her remote ancestor, Queen Juana the Mad, accompanying her husband's body through the Castilian nights. She reached Paris and talked with Napoleon, who flatly went back on his word. From the cold lips of that disillusioned dreamer she heard the death sentence of the Empire and went away mentally wounded to death. The curtain was raised on a tragedy that might have been created by an Aeschylus with the power to show portentous happenings and move whole nations on a vast stage.

Maximilian, between spells of indolence and diversion, succumbed to his old fatalism. Bazaine and Napoleon's emissaries, not wishing to be held responsible by history for a gory catastrophe, implored him unceasingly to give up the throne. The Treasury was bare. A good portion of the second loan from France had been earmarked to pay part of the debt to Jecker, that sinister vulture hovering over the ruins of empires, both in Mexico and in France, where it was finally shot down by the Commune and buried in debris. The French had taken over the custom houses, so revenue was nil.

Some caprice of the political actor moved Maximilian to make a pact with death, and he opened his arms to the reactionaries. A few undoubtedly sincere but desperate men accepted his invitation and entered that house without a foundation, without a roof, and in the throes of an earthquake. Maximilian knew very well that all was lost. What he sought was not to save the throne but to strike a heroic attitude. What he should have done was abdicate and explain to the world how he had been deceived by France, avoiding a drawn-out struggle by yielding the cities not yet liberated to the national government, thus bringing to a dignified if not brilliant close his fleeting dream of greatness. And, harkening to his best friends, he had decided to do just that. But suddenly, like the statue of the Comendador appearing to his murderer, the skeleton hands of the reaction, killed by Maximilian, clutched at his robes to drag him to his grave. What happened? Did Maximilian receive a letter from his mother, speaking of honor, which the princes of his line valued higher than life? Did Eloin actually write the famous letter entreating him not to abdicate till after the French had departed and the Mexican people had declared themselves in favor of a Republic, for otherwise he would return to Europe under a cloud, too discredited for the role awaiting him in defeated Austria, where Franz Joseph himself was about to abdicate? Who knows! The fact is that Maximilian, suddenly turned into the last leader of the military reaction, made an about-face at Orizaba, on the road to abdication, and, accompanied by Lares, by Miramón, and by Márquez, retraced his steps to the capital in the first days of 1867.

In March the last French battalion embarked at Vera Cruz. The banner of France, disgraced, was carried from the tragedy here to the tragedy over there.

The Republic, from the outset of the Intervention, armed itself with inflexible laws that obliged all citizens to rally round the flag of their violated land. There could be no neutrals, said the law, only Mexicans and traitors, and the traitor's life was forfeit to the gallows, his property to confiscation. And to prove that this was a law to be rigorously enforced and not just a means of intimidation, it had been sealed with the blood of General Robles Pezuela. The Republic, as its armies advanced, punished the unfaithful: fines, confiscations, executions marked the path of the implacable Nemesis. Those who had taken up arms against it, those who had usurped power, foreigners who served in the enemy army were sentenced to death.

The imperialist party was dissolved in Orizaba when its head took up the fratricidal sword of the reaction. Its members fled the country or, confident of the Republic's triumph but personally loyal to the Emperor, awaited their punishment with stoic resignation.

The ill-starred actor who by a tidal wave of fate had been deposited on a throne (a river skiff, of which he had nothing left but a single plank) could have refuted those who told him that his honor required him to stay and die with this simple truth: "Thousands of men would have to pay with their lives for my death; I cannot bequeath my honor to history as a chalice filled with blood." But the truth is, the young Emperor's flightly temperament took him from one extreme to another with amazing celerity. When he set out from the capital to direct the campaign in the hinterland, concentrating all the imperialist garrisons and retaining only Vera Cruz, Puebla, the City of Mexico, and Yucatán, places where a majority of the well-to-do accepted the Empire and remained chivalrously faithful to it, he seemed confident of victory. Miramón, striking out with dazzling boldness, set his march for Zacatecas with the intention of surprising Juárez and his government and bringing him as a hostage to Querétaro. He came near succeeding, but once having failed, his retreat was bound to be disastrous. A large wedge of the Army of the North cut into the daring General's column, shattered it, and applied the law requiring execution of foreign prisoners. The defeated officers joined Maximilian at Querétaro, where, with Márquez, Mejía, and Méndez as his first-line generals, he made his headquarters at exactly that vantage point from which the republican armies could be pounced upon as they converged—one from Michoacán on the west, another from San Luis on the north—and could be beaten one at a time by his warwise and desperate (and therefore all the more formidable) troops. But arguments and rivalries took the place of action, and the republican armies effected a juncture. Escobedo, noted for prudence, constancy, and devotion to the Republic, assumed the command and at once immobilized the Emperor in Querétaro. What was obviously needed was an auxiliary army to crack the steadily thickening circle of the besiegers from the outside, and Márquez left for the capital to organize one. The terrible battles around Querétaro in April revealed the courage and the impotence of the besieged. The blunders of the Republic's irregular forces, inferior in tactics, were counterbalanced by the successes of admirably trained and well-armed troops. By May it was clear that the siege could not be lifted.

Márquez could not come to the rescue. While the Republic's grand army was pinning Maximilian to Querétaro for all time, Díaz was besieging both Vera Cruz and Puebla. The garrison at Puebla put up a good defense, and the republican general, with undisciplined troops from all over, expected the siege to be a long one. Márquez decided that Puebla must be saved at all costs. He set out from the City of Mexico at the head of a splendid column perfectly equipped but closely followed by a cavalry division detached from Querétaro by General Escobedo. Seldom, perhaps never, in our military history has a besieging army found itself in such a critical position. Díaz saw clearly that not only the fate of Puebla but that of Querétaro as well depended on his resolution. With the relief column approaching his rear at an accelerated pace, he threw his entire force at the enemy's fortifications. The swift, terribly gory action, strewn with heroic episodes, ended with the surrender of Puebla, April 2. This, the most brilliant battle in the war against the Empire, was just the first act. Márquez' beaten, broken column had barely reached the capital when republican forces surrounded the City, pinning him there. He has mistakenly been accused of intent to betray Maximilian. Nothing of the sort: he failed to carry out the plan commended to him because he was overwhelmed by events. And this was the second act.

Meanwhile, with each new battle the defenders of Querétaro grew weaker. But the besiegers were constantly receiving reinforcements: if there had been enough arms to go around, 200,000 men might have joined the siege. Querétaro was doomed. The best plan the defenders could think of called for a desperate sally which would allow one-fifth of the army to escape for the time being while the rest was slaughtered. They were ready to add another river of blood to that already spilled. In any such idiotic venture, Maximilian would surely have been killed or captured.

The commander of the post on the Hill of the Cross, a very intimate friend of the Emperor, held a parley with General Escobedo and delivered up his post; the city, thus dominated, surrendered in a few hours, May 15, 1867. The Empire's main army, nearly all its important soldiers, and Maximilian himself fell into the hands of the republican army. This was merely precipitating the end which no human power could have averted.

Maximilian, tried under a law that antedated his acceptance of the throne, legally deserved death. His military judges, whose duty it was to apply a peremptory law to a clear case, could not have done other than what they did. The supreme political act of pardon was in the power of Juárez. He refused to grant it, and he was right. It is a sad thing to say of Maximilian, who believed himself destined to regenerate Mexico, or of the brave men who were the companions of his calvary. But the future peace of Mexico, her absolute freedom from foreign tutelage, her acceptance as an equal in the comity of nations required that Juárez be, not inhumane, but inflexible, just as Maximilian felt obliged to be inflexible with the victims of his decree of October 3, 1865. The solemn act of justice was consummated at Querétaro June 19, 1867. Maximilian, after writing a noble letter to Juárez, was executed together with his companions, Miramón and Mejía, on the Hill of the Bells. He gave his place of honor to the intrepid Miramón, and all three met death with equanimity. Morally, the Indian Tomás Mejía stands taller than the other two. Steadfastly faithful to his ideals, he founght and died for a cause which he identified with his immutable religious faith. When he battled for reaction and the Empire, he thought of himself as a servant of Christ. For him there could be no difference between patriotism and Catholicism. He was the stuff of which martyrs and crusaders are made: he could have saved his life, but would do so only if his companions were spared. Mexicans of all shades of thought should salute his tomb with pride and respect.

General Díaz, after his brilliant victory at Puebla, besieged Márquez in the City of Mexico with an army which, after the surrender of Querétaro, swelled till it was the largest, perhaps, in our history. Time and again he could have taken the capital by assault, but he never considered such a drastic and destructive measure: being sure of his prize, this great economizer averted an immense waste of blood. The Empire's lieutenant, behind an incredibly clever smoke screen of deception, prepared his getaway and hiding place; suddenly he vanished, and the City of Mexico surrendered to Díaz on June 21.

With the end of the Empire and of the Second War of Independence, as it was officially called, the grand period of the Mexican Revolution, which really started in 1810 but was definitely renewed in 1857, came to a close. In this last phase, Mexico lost on battlefields and in consequence of the war certainly more than 300,000 souls, but meanwhile acquired a soul of her own, a national unity. Destroying a throne, appealing constantly against force in behalf of law, mortally wounding the military power of France and the Empire of Napoleon III, incarnating in Juárez an adamant resistance against any foreign meddling in our sovereign affairs—neither European intervention nor American alliance—Mexico redeemed her independence, acquired thorough self-knowledge, and won for herself a secure place in history.

The republican government was profoundly aware, as was the whole thinking nation, of the permanence of these conquests. No matter how guilty many individuals might be of offenses against the Republic, all were now acquiescent and resigned, their parties dead beyond hope of revival, and the government was moved by the people's infinite longing for peace to equate justice with mercy, with clemency.

Then the Republic became the nation. All understood that irrevocable changes had been made, that the Reform, the Republic, and the country were thenceforth one and the same, that there was but a single banner, the Constitution of 1857, under which all would again be citizens, Mexicans and free. The Constitution, which had divided the country like a sword, now united it by pointing the way to an ideal: to make the Constitution serve the needs of society, safeguarding rights through education and labor—that is, through intellectual and material progress; and still the fundamental law could be changed whenever any part should prove to be incompatible with those supreme necessities, liberty and order. The process would take time, would be the work of generations. The revolutionary tremors, the earthquakes that mark the period of dying volcanoes, would not be lacking: the past is not done with in a century but lingers on, gradually fading, through the course of history. But a new era began on the day when Juárez, the greatest citizen the Republic has ever produced, uttered this sentence, engraved on the gate of the future: "Let the people and the government respect the rights of all. Among individuals as among nations, respect for the rights of others means peace."

PART III. The Present Era

E NOW APPROACH THE END of our long labor. We feared, on undertaking it, that it would prove to be beyond our capacity, and only the special sort of fascination that a difficult, almost insuperable intellectual task has for men of studious habit persuaded us to make the attempt. In the end, we must confess defeat. There could have been no other result in view of conditions in this country, where statistical data are just beginning to be available, where there has been no interest, except occasionally on the part of individuals, in collecting and classifying facts, where our archives, unorganized, uncatalogued, without facilities for research, are immense mounds of old papers turning to dust with time and indifference, where our historians have shaped their works as partisan weapons, interpreting events superficially to suit their theories and falsifying them to fit their prejudices. As for official documents, neither can these be trusted as evidence in the absence of other sources, for they are designed as propaganda.

In short, whether political or economic or juridical or moral, the sometimes tiny and always inconspicuous fact which, emanating from heredity and environment, really determines the visible structure of social history eludes us more often than not. Either it leaves no trace, or the trace has disappeared. And without this elusive fact any study must be sketchy, a mere makeshift.

What we have done is just that: a makeshift. Others who will have access to a greater store of data, scientifically classified, will do what we have attempted to do and succeed where we have failed. But our effort will not have been futile, for while we have tried to analyze the dynamics of our society without prejudice, we have nevertheless followed a system. We have taken as our premise the concept that society is a living being and consequently grows, develops, and undergoes transformations; these transformations are continuous, and their celerity is in ratio to the internal energy with which the social organism reacts to external elements, assimilating them and utilizing them in the course of its growth.

Science, converted into an amazingly complex and efficient tool, has accelerated a hundredfold the evolution of certain peoples. The other human groups either become subordinate and lose self-awareness and personality or else, finding strength in ideals, in moral forces (which are every bit as real as physical forces), tend to absorb every foreign element, in the process of rounding out their own personality, thus quickening the pace of their evolution, which, while still not equal to the pace of those who have been advanced by peculiar circumstances to the forefront of human progress, is still lively enough to insure self-preservation and well-being.

From this viewpoint we have analyzed the social phenomena of Mexico as revealed in books, documents, and the personal experience of the writer. And we have inferred that, since all the facts in our possession point to a recent forward movement impelled by a conjunction of internal and external factors, this movement is equivalent to Mexico's social evolution.

I[1]

Finally free of the foreign pressures which, exerted from the first day of Independence, culminated in an intervention proposing to change the manner and course of our internal life, the Republic, in 1867, had earned the incontestable right to call itself a nation. Respected by foreign powers, thanks to the prestige won by the vigorous struggle against France and the Empire, a prestige which grew with the growing obloquy fastened upon the government of Napoleon III by

[1] Here begins the text used as the penultimate chapter of Sierra's book, *Juárez: Su obra y su tiempo* (Vol. XIII of *Obras completas de Maestro Justo Sierra* [Mexico City: National University of Mexico, 1948]), pp. 514–524.

the triple error, diplomatic, political, and military, called "the Mexican question"; secure in the support of the United States, which, however self-interested, was firm and reliable, the country had only internal problems to worry about. Political conditions seemed perfect: the reformist (successor to the liberal) party, in unchallenged control of the country, had for its program the Constitution of 1857, to which the Reform Laws were soon to be added, and had for its chief the man who embodied the victorious cause, the President of the Republic, Juárez. His men held nearly all the federal offices and state governorships; the old reactionary party had died with the Empire and would never rise again. The national army, reduced to a select number after the war, ardently admiring the great citizen whose unshakeable faith brought victory out of disaster, rallied round the government and the law.

Thus, conditions augured well for an era of political discipline, peace, and order that would permit the Mexican people to approach the solution of their economic problems. And those problems had to be solved before there could be any realization of those supreme ideals: liberty, the country's welfare.

Immigration, workers, and capital to exploit our great wealth, a system of communication to make it circulate—such was the social desideratum. It was imperative that the Republic pass from the military to the industrial phase, and pass rapidly, for the giant that was growing ever larger beside us, and ever nearer, because of the agricultural and industrial development of the border states and the spreading network of its railways, would be apt to dissolve and absorb us if he found us helpless.

To make the desideratum a reality, Juárez and his ministers followed the only feasible plan, that of strengthening the power of the central government at all costs within the bounds of constitutional procedures, a plan to which Juárez was devoted, though not to the point of obsession. The central power must be strengthened because it was responsible for peace and order throughout the country and would have to furnish the leadership and the means to transform the country's economic life.

The task was a staggering one, like endeavoring to return a flooded river to its banks and to build dikes that would prevent any future inundation. Every active person in the country had taken part in the struggle, a few from patriotic motives, but most from a spirit of adventure, and a good many from self-interest—that is: to protect the abuses they had perpetrated on the people in order to exploit them.

This was not the work of a day. Juárez never expected to finish it but was determined to lay foundations of granite. The urgent need was for an army like a steel sword that would inspire respect and fear. The main obstacle to achieving firm control of the army was the victorious generals, the heroes of the late war. All aspired to positions of privilege and power, not only for themselves but also for their friends, who had fought at their side. The common soldiers, mustered out or furloughed to their homes, waited for another revolution or joined one of the bands of marauders that kept the countryside in a state of alarm and unrest and the whole Republic in a state of nerves, whose cure would obviously be a matter of the remote future.

Juárez' Minister of War was able to disarm hostile generals, when they were needed, by giving them honors and expectations. And if they were tough enough to resist flattery, then their subordinates, the second-line generals, the colonels—and there were magnificent soldiers among them—were solicited, given posts, and separated from their chiefs. Juárez' great prestige did the rest.

The army's outstanding general, popular with soldiers from every region but the especial favorite of the old Army of the East, was Porfirio Díaz. The government, regarding him as dangerous, passed over his merits and services, while the chief of the Second Division, unbending and aloof, disdaining flattery, retired tranquil, unappeased, and strong.

Without him, there was no iron shield of resistance to governmental pressure, and the transformation of the army was rapid: now was born the normal republican army, brave, disciplined, and loyal. There would be no more pronunciamentos. Some fragments might fall into the abyss of revolt, it might be broken up, in times of political confusion, into parts that would each passively follow a different banner, but never again would it take, as a whole, the initiative in bringing on civil war, as it had done under Echávarri, Bustamante, Santa Anna, Paredes, Zuloaga.

The government could not, however, carry out its program unless financing was available, and the tremendous difficulty of reconstructing the country and our absolute lack of foreign credit made the quest for adequate funds appear utterly hopeless. The foreign situation is explained by our attitude to European creditors; we rightly rejected some of their claims as invalid from the beginning and insisted on the revision and renegotiation of others. The considerable loss of national wealth owning to eleven years of uninterrupted war, the impossibility of defining, in the total absence of statistics, a sound basis for taxation, the failure of attempts by the Federation to recover any part of the revenues legally due it, which local governments had diverted to supply their own needs, all gave authority to the pessimists who prognosticated the final calamity that was to befall us: our people (who, as a famous Mexican poet of the time put it, "do not know how to command, and do not want to obey") were inevitably headed for collapse and absorption by the United States.

The ministers of Juárez formulated a financial program which did not include any effort to eradicate usury—that cancer of the budget, that invading parasite sapping our life's blood—but did set forth a rational scheme of reforms to our Treasury system, a scheme whose guidelines we still make use of today in fomenting and in reaping the benefits of our economic transformation. The scheme was as follows: (1) to concentrate and systematize tax-gathering under a single administration; (2) to adopt a policy of continual readjustment of tariff schedules; (3) to create a revenue stamp in order to transfer the basis of the government's income from external to internal sources; (4) to make every effort to balance the budget (without ever succeeding); (5) to keep an account of the Treasury and to prosecute fraud and peculation to the full extent of the law.

The statesmen of Juárez' cabinet, while determined to enforce the Constitution, realized that the country's welfare was of paramount importance and that the fundamental law needed to be modified in order to be made viable. They summoned the voters to the polls in an effort to reform the law by means of a plebiscite. The propositions to be voted on called for strengthening the Executive by giving him the right of veto, for diminishing the neurotic despotism of the Chamber of Deputies by obliging it to share its power with a Senate, and, finally, for providing the foundations of a new and law-abiding conservative party by returning the right of suffrage to the clergy, who were denied it by the Constitution.

The ideas embodied in these propositions were sound, except the one concerning the clergy, but the plebiscite was a sad mistake. All the discontented, the old enemies of Juárez and of his ministers, waved the flag of the Constitution, and the plebiscite failed dismally. As a result, a highly articulate opposition arose within the constitutional party, and even Juárez' candidacy, which was a matter of the national honor, was contested among all the groups that had marched in his triumphal parade.

The government held a majority in the Chamber, but an unruly one which would as soon as not applaud the opposition. It took all of Juárez' prestige, all of the influence commanded by Sebastián Lerdo de Tejada's talent (which was compared with that of the great chancellor Bismarck), all of the respect inspired by the brilliance and energy of the other Cabinet members to bring the majority into line.

Every progressive step taken by the government was stubbornly opposed by a good part of Mexican high society in the large cities, especially in the City of Mexico, Puebla, Guadalajara, San Luis, and Mérida, cities where the resistance to change was strongest among the uneasy rich, among those who had been hurt by the fall of the Empire and those who saw in the Reform, as incarnated in Juárez, an antireligious instead of an anticlerical movement. At any rate, the government proceeded with its program and the Republic gained confidence: the President's resolution to make his authority respected and to maintain order at all costs made the people feel secure in their work.

As if by magic, capital began to circulate, and the government's power was fortified by a solvent Treasury and the almost invariably punctual payment of salaries to the host of bureaucrats who made up a highly important social and economic class. This rosy state of things was reflected abroad, and the urgent problem of communications was started on the way to solution by the organization of the enterprise that was to link by rails of steel the political and commercial capital of the Republic with our principal port, Vera Cruz.

In other fields also the government was energetic. Juárez, because of his race and convictions, felt it his duty to raise the indigenous family from the moral prostration which is superstition, from the mental abjection which is ignorance, from the physical abjection which is alcoholism, to a better life, even though this must be done little by little. And he put his faith and hope in the main instrument of regeneration, the school. One day he said to this writer, a student with youth's impatience for the realization of dreams and ideals: "I would like to see the Indians converted to protestantism; they need a religion that will teach them to read and not to waste their pennies on candles for the saints." And aware that the middle classes, from among whom the country's leaders would necessarily be drawn, needed an education that would prepare them for the future, he entrusted the reformation of the higher schools to a pair of eminent savants; the "preparatory" [national junior college] is a creation inspired by the soul of Gabino Barreda.[2]

Flower of those days of hope and respite, literature attained a triumphant epiphany. The Republic listened to the voices of its beloved orators and poets, Ignacio Ramírez, Ignacio Manuel Altamirano,[3] Guillermo Prieto, Manuel María Zamacona, and Manuel Zarco, and in their fecund shadow was heard the sonorous hum of new voices, those that were twenty years old. The vanquished were appeased by the music of the lyre, and it seemed that a new era of love and harmony was about to dawn.

II

Unfortunately, storm clouds loomed on the horizon. Never had there been so many armed men in the country as on the day of victory. The states, when they tried to absorb those left over after the selection of the soldiers needed for the national army, discovered that men accustomed to adventure, pillage, and combat felt only disdain for work in the factories or fields, work, moreover, so poorly paid that the mere offer of it seemed an insult. They would prefer to fight as guerrillas under whatever political banner or to take up banditry on their own,

[2] Sierra's "Panegyric of Barreda" and "Funeral Oration" are published in *Obras completas*.

[3] Sierra delivered a funeral oration in honor of Altamirano (published in *Obras completas*).

and the shades of distinction between the one thing and the other were not easy to discern.

At the time of Juárez' election there were sporadic manifestations of latent anarchy, but these were subdued by the country's desire for peace and the government's will to maintain it. From this moment the national mind became obsessed with the idea that peace was an absolute necessity, that without it we would come to the dead end of our internal development and to a fatal international cataclysm.

And still the government had to spend its resources putting down disturbances, which broke out at a distance, in Sonora, Sinaloa, and Yucatán, and close by, at Puebla. These were symptoms of an acute disease which required a drastic cure. The measures designed to forward the mental evolution of the Mexican people by means of the school and their economic evolution by means of the railway were not neglected for a minute, but the good results of those measures would be long delayed, and meanwhile the malignancy was spreading.

Even the army, for a time, became a menace. But the government reacted by probing and reorganizing it and tightening discipline, and it crushed the rebels everywhere, even overcoming a formidable insurrection involving the most important states of the hinterland, Zacatecas, San Luis, and Jalisco. The suppression of these outbreaks was bloody, but the people began to feel confidence in the government's capacity to put down any revolt, and they dared to hope for peace.

Election time came around again just when the agonizing labor of reconstruction had reached a most critical stage. There was no leader in sight who could make a showing against Juárez. Without his support Lerdo, who for all his intellectual prestige was not popular, had no chance to become President. General Porfirio Díaz, having passed with unfaded laurels straight from victory to retirement, was the focus of the ambitions and rancors of the military men cut off the payroll or excluded from public office. He was to be reckoned with for he was popular (as men of the sword always are when they are believed to be capable of triumphing in any mighty undertaking), but there were grave doubts concerning his aptitude for statesmanship, and his popularity did not extend to his civilian friends, known to everybody, whose influence over him was thought to be absolute.

The short presidential term, copied from the Constitution of the United States (where stability is a potent factor in politics), forced us to choose between a series of disjointed administrations unable to conclude any program and the inevitable argument, in the case of reelection, as to whether there were violations of suffrage, a question that was rather absurd in a country where the immense majority never voted. And how can a President who has himself reelected prove that he did not surreptitiously violate the public choice? And since a disputed election, among Latin peoples, is not followed, as among the Anglo-Saxons, by a call for a new election, but by armed revolt, it was foregone that Juárez' decision to have himself reelected (and he made the right decision, for otherwise anarchy was unavoidable) would be the prologue to civil war.

The President, with iron resolution, was ready to face the storm. Motivated by a thoroughly human ambition to keep hold of power, which he felt he could put to good use, and believing that a civil war would give the central government an opportunity to show its strength, he scorned any suggestion that he withdraw his candidacy, for to do so, he considered, would be tantamount to retracting his views and betraying his duty. Once again he showed himself to be made of bronze, which the hurricanes could shake but could not move.

And the storm broke: on the eve of elections a military mutiny took possession of an important Gulf port. The government ignored the refusal of the Chamber to give it emergency powers and drowned the mutiny in blood. The elections were held. The public as a whole abstained from voting, as usual, or passively let itself be led to the polls like sheep by political committees. Threats of revolution were heard in the Chamber and even in the offices of some governors. The upper classes in the cities, loathing Juárez, who personified the Reform and the tragic end of the Empire, though they feared a civil war, were secretly disaffected. This dangerous animosity was offset to a degree by the faithful devotion of almost the entire mass of bureaucrats, from self-interest and from dread of the horde of ravenous job-seekers filling the ranks of the government's opposition, or perhaps from real loyalty to the President, despite lapses in payment of their salaries. Serving as a backdrop for the fratricidal drama about to begin were the traditional domains of the caciques in the sierras of Nayarit, Guerrero, Querétaro, Tamaulipas, and Puebla. Those baronies, safely beyond the government's reach, declared themselves neutral when they actually served as springboards for the revolt. Like huge granite monoliths varnished with blood, they were reminiscent of the sacrificial stones.

The results of the election, in which the official element took a shamelessly active part, were to be expected: President Juárez won by a clear majority; Díaz and Lerdo shared the rest of the vote. The results had not yet been announced when a riot broke out in the capital. It was poorly organized, hence swiftly crushed; otherwise it would have had terrible and decisive consequences.

After the election came the formidable rebellion of all the unhappy military men and politicians; from Oaxaca to the northern frontier the sierras rose in arms. After some hesitation, Oaxaca, the natal state of Juárez, took the lead in organizing a rebel force. Oaxaca was also the natal state of Díaz, and, after pondering the matter for some time, he laid on the side of the rebels his moral authority over his fellow citizens—only the authority of Juárez was greater. He decided, no doubt, that the country needed changes which could be achieved only by force. And his resentment of the jealous and suspicious attitude of Juárez' ministers, who had coldly shut the door to the advancement which was clearly the right of a man who had performed such eminent services, was probably the clinching reason for his decision, which, once made, was irrevocable. From that time on his conscience as a republican and as a ruler has been obsessed by a single idea, which might have seemed an aberration once, but which we can now see was nothing of the sort: "The only way I can make amends to my country for the great harm I do her by plunging her into civil war will be by one day putting her into such condition as will make civil war impossible forevermore."

The rebels waged a vigorous campaign; their marches around the military strongholds ably selected by the government, if marked on the map in red ink, would make a network of red. But they were dispersed, vanquished everywhere. By the middle of 1872, only wracks of the storm clung to the peaks of the most remote fastnesses; the rebellion, wounded and fugitive, sought hiding places, not springboards for new attacks.

The moral authority of the government, having acquired new strength in the struggle, was now applied to a program for peace, which had the following goals: to teach the politically active classes, brought up in a perpetual revolution, that the peace must be preserved at all costs; to drown banditry in blood; to foment the material progress on which everything else depended; to establish diplomatic relations with European countries in order to safeguard and increase foreign trade; to study the possible solutions of our economic problems (immigration, systematic irrigation of farming land, free trade in the interior, and the continuing improvement of the Treasury system); finally, to enlarge the educational system so as to transmute the Indian and lower-class mestizo into social assets. For all his attention to this program, Juárez did not neglect political reform. The two last projects of his iron will were the creation of a Senate to give balance to the legislative branch and the incorporation of the Reform Laws into the Constitution.

He had barely made a start on this ambitious program when death cut his labor short.

Much of his achievement has endured, but he wanted to see his ideas in action. He accomplished a great deal and would have accomplished more. When Juárez died, a breath of clemency and concord passed over the battlefields, the old, the recent: the breath of spring, of renascence, the beginning of a new era.[4]

In the whole perspective of our history the death of Juárez is in the nature of a national calamity, but at the moment it had one good effect, for it brought the civil war to an abrupt end.

In an atmosphere of perfect peace grateful to all the Chief Justice of the Supreme Court assumed the Presidency and a little later was elected constitutional President of the Republic without an opponent or any protest. The tranquil succession of governments, the end of the military drama, and the faith of the people in the ability of Lerdo de

[4] Here ends the text used for the penultimate chapter of Sierra's *Juárez.*

Tejada combined to cast roseate glow over the first cloudless inauguration since that of President Victoria half a century earlier.

The vote had been unanimous; hence the whole social organism experienced a sensation of respite and well-being. There was not only hope, which is a kind of passive desire, but aspiration, which is desire animated by effort—an immense aspiration for peace and for the insurance of that peace by means of profound changes in the economic structure of the country.

The new President had a clear understanding of his mission, and when he began his term by starting construction of the railway between the City of Mexico and Vera Cruz, one of Juárez' favorite projects, everybody thought that economic transformation had advanced from the long prologue to the first chapter. A few months later the outstanding points of the President's program were plain to see: incorporation of the Reform in the Constitution, which should be made more practical and viable; integration of the national territory, actually broken up by the caciques' domains, beyond the reach of the law; entrusting the building of railways in the hinterland to a combination of European and Mexican capital. Liberal and reformist opinion, eloquent with the appeal to reason, the emotional fervor, the idealistic ardor of the days of epic struggle, spoke up as one voice for the President's laws embodying the so-called "liberal dogmas": the separation of Church and State, the suppression of religious communities as illegal, and the ban against the acquisition of property by religious bodies. But the discussion of these laws and their promulgation came as a fearful shock to many a conscience. The Church, inspired by the narrow intransigency of Pius IX, loosed its thunderbolts. And the feminine part of society, who had applauded in Lerdo's advent the reign of a respectable gentleman, turned its back on the President and waged with implacable tenacity that insidious war of the salons and kitchens which attacks the most intimate inner springs of government. What was called, for some unknown reason, "the expulsion of the sisters of charity," plus the expulsion of a few Jesuits, brought this kitchen tempest to a boil, with tenderness and commiseration championing the victims of persecution.

An outburst of insurrection in Michoacán with a religious pretext, among the ignorant peasants, covered the state with blood and for a time appeared to be invincible, but the revolt was first isolated, then extinguished.

The real danger in the situation was psychological, within Lerdo himself; it was an intellectual blind spot often found in men of extraordinary talent. He thought he needed no one's advice and often took action based on inadequate information. The pride that isolated him from other men was not armed with one of those energetic wills that impose themselves on everything and everybody. He had a tendency to delay indefinitely his attention to the most important matters, preferring to discharge his duties in a kind of perpetual conversation, in which he dazzled his interlocutors with the brilliance of his insight and ingenuity and dismayed them by his fatalistic inaction and incurable skepticism. President Lerdo was by temperament lordly, conservative, and authoritarian, with no religion except faith in the greatness of his country—and much of that, he felt, was due to his own efforts. He was an autocrat who could accomplish admirable things. Incapable of compromising with fear when the honor of his country was at stake, he was capable of sacrificing liberty out of contempt for his fellow man. In two years, 1874 and 1875, he slipped from high prestige to none at all, from almost unanimous popularity to what became in the end virtually unanimous unpopularity. Isolated by pride, with more vanity than ambition, he felt no qualms about losing his old friends, in whose administrative talents he had no confidence and whose expectations of sharing his power seemed to him presumptuous. He filled his cabinet instead with the friends of Juárez, men who would never become attached to him save by the brittle ties of self-interest.

Following the great President's policy of strengthening the central power, he sponsored and obtained the amendment to the Constitution providing for a Senate, which body, it was hoped, would not only act as counterweight to the Chamber, but, in giving representation to the states, would prevent their local grievances from spreading. Already the crusade against the caciques of the sierras, indispensable to national dignity as well as to national unity, had achieved a brilliant success in Jalisco and Tepic with the extermination of the chieftain Lozada, a fierce patriarch of mountain tribes organized in a primitive satrapy.

Everything would have seemed to be turning out well for Lerdo if it had not been for his stubborn quirk of keeping unpopular governors in office or imposing them on the states with a blatant display of military force, which gave rise to a vague but growing uneasiness among the people. At the same time a violent antipathy, not for the man but for the ruler, was growing among certain groups which became steadily more numerous. This resentment found mordant expression in a popular weekly in which the gifted humorist General Vicente Riva Palacios, aided by the diabolically clever pencil of Villasana, made merciless fun of the men in the government.

Hostility to Lerdo, though widespread, remained diffuse till it was crystalized into blocks of adamant resistance by a decision of the Supreme Court. The most eminent of Juárez' ministers after Lerdo, José María Iglesias, a republican of stoic temperament whose religion was duty and whose vast intelligence was lighted by an amazing erudition, took his seat as Chief Justice and also Vice-President with the intention of facilitating (insofar as the granite wall of his conscience should permit) the faltering administrative labors of his good friend the President.

It so happened that the arbitrary acts of certain state governors caused the Court to intervene in local politics by means of the constitutional procedure known as the *amparo* [akin to *habeas corpus*]. And a majority of the supreme tribunal set forth the theory of original competence, which meant that the Court had the right to decide whether the title of any authority against whom the recourse of *amparo* was invoked was legitimate to begin with, for if it was not his acts never had been valid. By this theory, the justices made themselves arbiters of the country's politics, a court of no appeal. President Lerdo resisted without apparent success this arrogation of faculties, which really upset the balance of powers. But the Court, led by the Chief Justice, stood firm. When a rebellion broke out, because of purely local grievances, at Tuxtepec, in Oaxaca, the great majority of the country took the position that Lerdo must not continue in the Presidency.

From pride and from indignation at his unpopularity, which he felt was grossly unjust because it denied his right and his ability to govern a people to whom he had rendered outstanding service, the President announced his candidacy for a second term. And then the cry of "no reelection," heard in Oaxaca early in 1876, echoed throughout the Republic. The President's ostensible friends, secretly his enemies, were in sympathy with the revolution's motto.

The dissidents had been placated, for a time, by a vigorous program of material improvements. But the President's idea (which he sincerely believed to be patriotic) of entrusting those works to European capital, combined to the fullest possible extent with Mexican capital, turned out to be infeasible. And the thinking part of the nation began to suspect that, from fear of the Americans, the building of the railroads would be deferred indefinitely, and so would any hope of improving the economic conditions which had caused our civil wars—perhaps until too late to avoid the very danger that was feared.

The rebellion, called the "revolution of Tuxtepec," could not be extinguished, and the government was able to isolate it in Oaxaca only at the cost of terrific losses. But when General Díaz appeared on the scene and captured Matamoros, the conflagration became nationwide. Still, the now superb federal army defeated the rebels everywhere, driving them into the mountain regions of Puebla, Vera Cruz, Oaxaca. But the country waited uneasily for the subdued fires to burst forth at some other point. Something extraordinary and decisive was expected.

The Chief Justice of the Supreme Court, after long deliberation with his conscience, decided to void the election which had returned Lerdo to office because it had been held, with only bureaucrats voting, at a time when a considerable portion of the states, being officially under military rule, had been incapable of freely exercising the right of suffrage. The dictamen of Iglesias, though not within the scope of the Constitution, was by no means outside the law, for it proceeded from his double duty as Chief Justice and Vice-President. He thought it best, nonetheless, to accept the hospitality of the revolutionary forces rather than submit to the indignity of a dark prison cell. At the invitation of the governor of Guanajuato he took refuge in that state, and when the reelection of Lerdo was announced in the City of Mexico, he assumed the Executive Power, whose legal title the President and Chamber had abandoned when they infringed the Constitution.

The revolution owed its triumph to the consternation produced by the Chief Justice's action. He was well aware of this and certain that he stood to gain no personal advantage from his course, but persisted in it nevertheless. He vainly tried to steer the revolution into constitutional channels. But the leaders shunted him aside.

From the moment that Iglesias appeared in Guanajuato, events moved rapidly. The government's army of the interior, while marching to deal with the rebels in the sierra, was diverted to confront those of Guanajuato and lost its front-line troops, who dribbled away to join the forces of the state. And not this army alone but every other one wavered, and their officers as well.

The two armed hosts of the revolution made a juncture on the fields of Tecoac, trampling the bodies of the government's troops, and soon took possession of the capital, whence Lerdo departed for overseas. From then on there was no stopping the victorious march of the revolutionary army under General Díaz. For a moment he seemed to bow to the Vice-President's clear right, but insisted on conditions which the stoical integrity of Iglesias could not accept. Finally, sweeping every obstacle from his path, Díaz marched to the Pacific. By New Year's day of 1877 the revolution of Tuxtepec was in full control of the country.

III

The country was a wreck. Everywhere the civil war had left ruins and squalor amidst pools of blood. Everything had fallen to earth. Among the rural masses, the return of the levy, one of the endemic diseases of Mexican labor—the others are alcohol and ignorance—had scattered the people to the army camps as cannon fodder, or to the guerrillas, where they regressed to the life of the savage horde, and to banditry, nomadic school of all the antisocial vices. The urban masses, their factories and workshops shut down or idle from fear of the war or for lack of markets, lapsed into vagrancy or escaped by joining the hullabaloo or let themselves be dragged away in coffles to the barracks. The middle and upper classes, pitilessly squeezed by local tyrants and warring governments, hid their money and their sympathies. They were glad to see the fall of the central government (except in two or three states which Lerdo had emancipated from odious petty despots), but the action of Iglesias had seemed to them a bit of constitutional hankypanky with all the air of a pronunciamento by lawyers and professors. And they feared and distrusted the heterogeneous mob of appetites, resentments, and ambitions called the revolution of Tuxtepec which had taken possession of Mexico. They believed in the good faith of the revolution's leader and in his probity, but they supposed him to be, now as before, hopelessly subservient to the interests of his advisers; and if he was granted administrative gifts, he was denied any political talent. "This man," it was said, in our familiar way of condensing opinions, "this man will never get the ox out of the gulch."

The situation in the army was deplorable. The federal army, bewildered by events, had become divided between the two banners that called themselves constitutionalist, but the majority had remained faithful to duty, to the Lerdo government, and now, as they entered in mass the army of the victorious revolution, they felt humiliated, resentful. And the revolutionary mob was intent on despoiling the legitimate army of all rank and prerogative, on casting it out on the street, disarmed and naked, and on punishing it besides, and this they demanded of the revolution's leader as a booty of war.

As for the bureaucratic phalanx, poorly paid when it was paid at all, it barely performed its duties, spitefully criticizing the ignorance and manners of the conquerors, organizing the familiar conspiracy of unfaithful servants, or deserting.

Abroad, the circumstances and end of the civil war had caused a painful impression. Here was the proof that Mexico was an ungovernable country, and the United States should put a stop to such disorder now that Europe was powerless to make another attempt. The sociologists took us as an example of the organic incapacity of the nations that had been formed in the Americas out of the remnants of Spain's colonies. And the American ambassador assumed the attitude of a haughty and disapproving tutor in his interviews with the revolutionary Executive.

The Constitution had been buried in the ruins of legality. The reforms advocated by the revolution were altogether Jacobin: neither Senate nor reelection, which meant omnipotence of the popular Chamber and the debilitation of the Executive Power through the constant peremptory change of Presidents. There remained the Supreme Court as a safeguard of individual rights. But how can a tribunal act as a positive brake on political despotism when that tribunal is likewise subject to popular election, which has always been manipulated in Mexico by the prestidigitators in office?

What made things worse, the press clamored for strict compliance with the revolutionary promises, two of which, put forward as the supreme aspirations of the people, were respect for free suffrage, meaning that local and general elections should be abandoned to the governors and their agents, and the abolition of the internal revenue stamp, a very popular promise, whose fulfillment would mean the financial suicide of the administration.

The country's real desire, manifested everywhere, was peace. No one wanted a resumption of the war except those who thrived on anarchy, those who were misfits in any normal situation. Seldom in history has there been a people with a more unanimous, more anguished, more determined aspiration.

Having understood and analyzed this pervading sentiment, the revolution's leader decided to build his authority upon it, for it was in accord with his personal vow to make another revolt impossible.

In order to make this seemingly visionary ideal a reality, all interests, from the highest to the lowest must be involved, and the leader believed that, to accomplish this, all must have faith in him and fear him. Faith and fear, those two profoundly human emotions, have been the pillars of every religion and were to be the pillars of the new political regime. Without losing a day or wasting an opportunity, President Díaz has marched in this direction for twenty-five years: he has founded the political religion of peace.

The first political step was the return to constitutional order. It was necessary to reactivate the legal branches of the government. Only the Supreme Court had been halfway respected; the rest would have to be manned anew.

An election held under the revolutionary auspices, with most of the qualified voters abstaining, gave a legal title to the leader; as President his action was firmer and more direct. But at the same time there were clear indications of danger. The partisans of the exiled President ignited plots, for which there was plenty of combustible, all over the country, and when they were on the point of flaring out in a fearful conflagration, they were washed out in blood. There were shocked protests; it appeared that many of the innocent were sacrificed. But the President won the respect, the fear—not to be confounded with terror, the instrument of pure despotism—of the nation. Peace was a fact. Would it last?

There are no firm classes in Mexico, for the classes, so-called, are separated from one another only by the shifting differences of money and good manners. Only the middle class progresses, for it absorbs the active individuals from the lower levels. Among those lower levels we include what might be called intellectual plebeians. They consisted, after the definitive triumph of the Reform, of (1) a good many descendants of ancient Creole families who had never been mentally disamortized but lived in the past, creeping toward today's world with painful reluctance, and (2) the illiterate. Both groups were devotees of superstition, and the second was enslaved, besides, by alcohol. But the middle class made proselytes in both of them day by day, assimilating some by means of the bureaucratic budget and others by means of the school. The division by races, which might be expected to complicate this classification, has had a steadily diminishing influence as an obstacle to social evolution since the intermediate mestizo has grown steadily more numerous; in him the dominant middle class has its center and its roots. There is a constant infiltration between the social classes, an osmosis, a physicist would call it. Thus, the middle class has never been cured of either alcohol or superstition. Those are socio-pathogenic microbes which pullulate in colonies wherever the culture is propitious to them.

This middle class, having absorbed the old oligarchies, both reformist and reactionary, understood where it wanted to go and by what road the day it realized that it was ruled by a man who would let nothing come between him and his objective, peace. And the whole class formed a single party, taking a name and a personality for common denominator: Porfirio Díaz. The Mexican middle class, in its present aspect, is the work of this statesman because he furnished the condition essential to its organization, a government that would brook no opposition. General Díaz, in turn, is the creation of the Mexican middle class, which has given him the immense authority of an arbiter, not only a political but a social arbiter, thereby enabling him to carry out his program.

Never before had peace been so patently a matter of urgent national necessity. The industrial development of the United States, already colossal twenty-five years ago, required a concomitant development of the railroad system, for without this it ran the risk of paralysis, something American "go-ahead" could never permit. The builders of the great systems that approached our frontiers planned to complete them in Mexico, which was regarded by the communications experts as forming a single region with the southwestern United States. The financial object of the Americans in extending their railway network to Mexico was to dominate our markets to the profit of their industry. This American need could be satisfied by declaring the country to be in a state of anarchy and intervening to give the railroad builders protection, or it could be satisfied in a normal, pacific manner if they could be convinced that there was a stable and viable government in Mexico whose word in treaties and contracts could be trusted. From this moment, civil war could be considered not only as the gravest of the country's internal ills, but also as responsible for attracting the most imminent external danger. Lerdo had tried to forestall this danger by seeking the concurrence of European capital, but to no avail. European capital would come to Mexico only after long years, and then as backing for American enterprises. President Díaz had the perspicacity to understand the situation and, believing that our history and the state of our society put us in a position where we were liable to be hooked and carried off into the future by the formidable Yankee locomotive, he preferred to make the journey under the auspices and through the action of the Mexican government, as equal partners with the obligation to preserve peace and order, thereby maintaining our national integrity and achieving progress.

Many who have tried to analyze the psyche of President Díaz—who, without being either an archangel or a tyrant of melodrama, is in the true sense of the word an extraordinary man—find in his mental processes a noticeable inversion of logic: his decisions are quick, and deliberation follows the act of will, deliberation that is slow and laborious and modifies or even nullifies the original decision. This mental pattern, characteristic, perhaps, of the mixed family to which the majority of Mexicans belong, has given rise to imputations of political perfidy (deceiving in order to persuade, dividing in order to rule). These imputations, contradicted by the qualities that we all recognize in the private man, are mechanisms by which some individuals of Mexican society attain contact with power and identify with the powerful. This society has inherited from the idiosyncracies of the indigenous race, from colonial education, and from the perennial anarchy of the epochs of revolt an infinite distrust of rulers and all their acts; what we criticize, no doubt, is the reflection of ourselves in the other person.

In any case, Díaz' resolution in the matter of the international railways was prompt and never faltered: it is today what it was then. One of Lerdo's invincible fears was that perilous conflicts with the United States would arise if we should contract obligations which the condition of our Treasury would never allow us to meet. Díaz, counting on the economic, and therefore financial, transformation which the country would undergo with the building of the railroads, had the courage to contract national obligations amounting to millions of pesos at a moment when our Treasury was empty, when there was no money to buy supplies for the army.

In fact, the financial problem threatened to paralyze the President's efforts to promote material improvements. The northern frontier was completely disorganized by the connivance of local authorities with the kings of contraband—a business that had grown to colossal proportions. The markets of the Republic were flooded with merchandise illegally imported, and the slump in custom-house revenue induced a state of alarm, for it was thought to be irremediable.

Meanwhile the end of the presidential term approached. General Díaz broke with his intimate advisers, who wanted to impose their candidate, chose his own, and put him at the head of the army. He gave his office to one of the bravest and most loyal of his collaborators in the revolution. But the nation had its doubts about the new President.

General Manuel González was quite a soldier. Was he suitable to head a government?

The new Cabinet, composed of highly reputable citizens, including the ex-President, inspired confidence, however. And there were clear signs of rising prosperity. The big international railroad companies seemed to sow dollars in the furrows over which rails were stretched from the frontier to the heart of the country. While the Treasury's coffers were being repleted, the bureaucrats made happy, and the army surfeited, the Mexican workman was receiving a better wage than ever before. The spirit of enterprise, at white heat, fabricated fantastic schemes: colonies, irrigation projects, canals, chimerical interocean railroads on the Isthmus of Tehuantepec, construction of artificial ports where none existed on the Gulf of Mexico, plans for a national navy, to be created all at once, and banking institutions to receive the Mexican capital needed to finance industry and commerce in the bright new era that glowed on the horizon. But in order to operate profitably the lines already built, it was necessary to build others, and again others, till the country was covered by a network, and the cost of these absorbed the American money that had created the boom which some financiers thought would last forever. During the euphoria of the boom, administrative habits became careless. The nation's welfare, in the hands of speculators, was gambled for personal profit; more than one public official made a fat fortune overnight by lending his influence to businessmen.

None of this was a secret to the new President. A sensible man, incapable of fear or duplicity, he was ruled by a spirit of adventure and conquest innate in his Spanish blood and fomented by more than twenty years of violent and daring military life. General González, it seems to this writer, was an example of atavism: like the companions of Cortés and of Pizarro, heroic in temper and capable of mighty deeds and Gargantuan greed. The President felt that he had conquered the post that he now occupied at the price of his blood, spilled on the fields of Tecoac. It was his office, fairly won, and he exploited it as he pleased.

There came an end to the building of railroads and to the flow of American dollars. Once again the Treasury was bare, without money to pay the most essential administrative services. Again there was recourse to the most degrading expedients; and still the graft went on and on. The public protest, echoed in the press, sprang from the fundamental honesty and love of justice that make up the protoplasm of the Mexican social conscience. There was no denying that, as the electoral period opened, the government could hardly take any action whatsoever. A new coin, which may have had its merits, was rejected as false, refused, regurgitated in a public riot. Our acknowledgment of the English debt was a most urgent contract, and, though objectionable in some of its clauses, it was the prerequisite, *sine qua non,* to the restoration of our foreign credit. This was denounced as an infamous swindle. The news spread, with evident exaggeration, that fabulous fortunes had been made from the negotiation of this contract. Since González' term was running out and the President-elect was General Díaz and since everybody considered that the politicians about to retire would never return (and they never did), a parliamentary opposition arose and grew more and more obstreperous, like the sea lashed by a hurricane. And the people came to hear and applaud the oratory, as to a show.

While this lesson, proving how quickly power can lose touch with the public conscience and how little the public had learned in the way of political education, was being taught to the government that was going out and to the one that was coming in, General Díaz commenced his new administration, indefinitely reprised since then, not so much by the suffrage as by the will of the people.

Something like angry unanimity had returned the one-time leader of the revolution to office. Administrative anarchy and financial penury likened the situation to the last days of the legal government in 1876, and it seemed to everyone that eight years had been lost and there would have to be a fresh start. President Díaz had been put in office by public opinion, not as conferring an honor, but rather as demanding that he perform a duty.

In the appalling bankruptcy of 1884, the preponderance of the liabilities was overwhelming. We had no credit abroad, and there seemed to be no possibility of acquiring any in view of the popular hostility to acknowledgment of the English debt, key to that credit.

The Treasury, in chaos, must be put in order, and first a partial suspension of payments would be necessary. It was imperative to restore prestige to the courts, to enforce respect for law, to break up certain loose coalitions of local governments (a sure sign of morbid weakness in the central authority), and to provide constant and tangible safeguards for work, whether in factory, field, or elsewhere.

As assets, the new administration had the finished railways and General Díaz' reputation. But if the President was going to accomplish the heruclean task that he had set himself, he must hold in his hands the maximum weight of authority—not only legal but political authority, which would permit him to direct actively the political bodies of the country, including state legislatures and governors. He must have also social authority, which meant he would become, by general consent, supreme arbiter of the peace, adjudicating the conflicts of Mexican society. And, finally, he must have moral authority, that indefinable power deriving from personal character, manifest in Díaz' exemplary home life and his absolute freedom from pride or vanity, in spite of power, flattery, and good fortune.

With this leadership, the country made progress, though not without hitches. Both here and abroad, among the holders of Mexican bonds and among the investors in the railways, there was a demand—clear, insistent, and emphatic—for reliable assurance that General Díaz would continue his work until he had made it proof against unforeseen accidents. He gave this assurance, within the limits of human provision, by restoring the original text of the Constitution, which provided that the President of the Republic could be reelected indefinitely.

With this measure the program of the revolution of Tuxtepec had been utterly wiped out. Consisting of three abolitions—of the Senate, of the revenue stamp, of reelection—it had failed to abolish a single one. The only result of that gory convulsion had been a new situation—but this new situation was a transformation, rather, the bringing of foreign capital to exploit the amortized wealth of the land. This was the last of the three great disamortizations of our history: that of Independence, which gave life to the national personality; that of the Reform, which gave life to our social personality; and that of the Peace, which gave life to our international personality. These are the three phases of our evolution. In order to realize this last one, we needed a man, a conscience, a will to unify our moral forces and transmute them into normal progress; this man was President Díaz.

Is his an ambition capable of subordinating everything to the conservation of power? Posterity will be the judge. But this power, which always has been and always will be the irresistible magnet, not for supermen of thought, perhaps, but certainly for supermen of action, was a desideratum of the nation. And this nation that as one voice acclaims the man has composed his power with a series of delegations, of abdications, extra-legal if you like, since they are of a social nature, without his having solicited them, but without his having boggled at this formidable responsibility for even a minute. And is this dangerous? Terribly dangerous for the future, because it forms habits that are incongruous with self-government, without which there can be great men but no great peoples. But Mexico has confidence in that future, as the President has in his star, and believes that everything will come later, will come in its own time. Let us hope we are not wrong!

Thus, without breaking a single law, President Díaz has been invested by the will of his fellow citizens with the lifelong office of supreme arbiter. This investiture—the submission of the people in all their official manifestations, the submission of society in all its active elements, to the President's judgment—could be given the name of social dictatorship. The truth is, it has singular features which keep it from fitting any of the classic definitions of despotism. It is a personal government that defends and reinforces legality, springing as it does from the national resolution to banish anarchy once and for all. Hence, while our government is eminently authoritarian, it can never, at the risk of perishing, refuse to abide by the Constitution. It has been entrusted to one man, not only for the sake of peace and of economic progress, but also in the hope of neutralizing the despotisms of the other Powers and eradicating the caciques and disarming the local tyrannies.

In short, the political evolution of Mexico has been sacrificed to other phases of her social evolution. This is proved by the plain fact that not a single political party exists in Mexico, nor any group organized around a program rather than a man. Every move in this direction has been blocked by the government's distrust and the general apathy. The day that a party succeeds in maintaining an organization, political evolution will resume its progress, and the man, more essential in democracies than in aristocracies, will come later: the function will create an organ.

But if we compare Mexico's situation at the instant when the parenthesis in her political evolution was opened with the present moment, we must admit that the transformation has been amazing. Only we who were witnesses of preceding events can fully appreciate the change. A peace lasting from ten to twenty years was an idle dream, they said. But ours already has lasted a quarter of a century. It was mere dreaming, they said, to think of covering the country with a railway system that would unite the ports and the center with the hinterland and the outside world. Only in a dream would one see a national industry in rapid growth. But all these things have come true, and we still move forward.

The undeniable achievement of the present administration consists, not in having brought about this change, which an extraneous combination of factors would probably have brought about anyway, but in having done everything possible to facilitate the change and exploit it to the best advantage. In the course of this task, nothing has been more beneficial to the country than the intimate collaboration between the President's firm resolution and his Finance Minister's application of scientific procedures to financial problems. To this collaboration we owe the revival of our credit, the balancing of our budget, the freedom of internal trade, and the concomitant increase in public revenue. To this we may owe, if circumstances take a favorable turn, the stabilization of that alarming phenomenon, the drop in the price of silver, our most valuable product.

There exists, we repeat, such a thing as Mexican social evolution. Our progress, made up of foreign elements, reveals, on analysis, a reaction of our social body to those elements in order to assimilate and make use of them in developing and intensifying our life. Thus, our national personality has been enriched and made stronger by contact with the world. This evolution, no doubt, is just beginning. When we look back at our condition previous to the final third of the past century we see what a long way we have come, and even if we compare our progress with that made by our neighbors (and this should always be our frame of reference, without succumbing to pernicious illusions or to cowardly discouragement) it is not insignificant.

We still need to revitalize the earth by means of irrigation. We need to attract immigrants from Europe so as to obtain a cross with the indigenous race, for only European blood can keep the level of civilization that has produced our nationality from sinking, which would mean regression, not evolution. We need to bring about a complete change in the indigenous mentality through education in the school. This is our great, our urgent obligation, and we must comply with it promptly or we are lost.

To convert the native into a social asset (and it is the fault of our apathy that he is not one), to make him the principal colonist on intensively cultivated soil, to blend his spirit and ours in a unification of language, of aspirations, of loves and hates, of moral and mental criteria, to place before him the ideal of a strong and happy country belonging to all—to create, in sum, a national soul—is the goal assigned to the future, the program of our national education. Whosoever helps to attain this goal is a patriot; whosoever places obstacles in the path is an enemy.

The obstacles are familiar. There is the danger, along our frontiers, of shifting from an indigenous to a foreign tongue and rejecting the national language. There is superstition, which only the humanistic and scientific spirit, only the secular school can successfully combat. There is the civic sacrilege of the impious who, taking advantage of the Mexicans' ineradicable religious feeling, persist in setting the principles that are the basis of our modern life against the ones that have been the basis of our moral life. And then, there is the skepticism of those who, doubting that we are fit for liberty, condemn us to death.

Thus, our duty is plain: to educate, which means to make strong. Liberty, the marrow of lions, has always been, among nations as among individuals, the patrimony of the strong; the weak have never been free. Mexican social evolution will have been wholly abortive and futile unless it attains the final goal: liberty.

INDEX